# MARITIME CULTURE AND EVERYDAY LIFE IN NINETEENTH- AND TWENTIETH-CENTURY COASTAL GHANA

# MARITIME CULTURE AND EVERYDAY LIFE IN NINETEENTH- AND TWENTIETH-CENTURY COASTAL GHANA

## A Social History of Cape Coast

*Kwaku Nti*

INDIANA UNIVERSITY PRESS

This book is a publication of

Indiana University Press
Office of Scholarly Publishing
Herman B Wells Library 350
1320 East 10th Street
Bloomington, Indiana 47405 USA

iupress.org

© 2023 by Kwaku Nti

All rights reserved
No part of this book may be reproduced or utilized in any form or by any means, electronic or mechanical, including photocopying and recording, or by any information storage and retrieval system, without permission in writing from the publisher. The paper used in this publication meets the minimum requirements of the American National Standard for Information Sciences—Permanence of Paper for Printed Library Materials, ANSI Z39.48–1992.

Manufactured in the United States of America

Cataloging information is available from the Library of Congress.

ISBN 978-0-253-06791-3 (hardback)
ISBN 978-0-253-06792-0 (paperback)
ISBN 978-0-253-06793-7 (ebook)

First printing 2023

*To*
*Peniel*
*Generously Gracious and Grateful*

# CONTENTS

*Acknowledgments   ix*

*A Note on Orthography   xiii*

*Maps   xvii*

Introduction   *1*

1. Settlement and Nascent Society: From Earliest Times to the Nineteenth Century   *31*
2. *Ebusua* and *Asafo* Systems: Gender, Complementarity, and Conflict among the Fanti   *62*
3. Coastal Communities, Intergroup Wrangling, and Aspects of the Colonial Experience: Historical Undercurrents   *86*
4. Art, Symbol, and the Written Word: The Audacity, Dignity, and Sovereignty of Private Property Ownership   *117*
5. "Hɛn-ara Hɛn A-saa-se Nyi": Land in Everyday Life, Colonial Policy, and Indigenous Resistance   *134*
6. The Politics of Modernization and Clash of Official and Indigenous Interests: Judiciary, Military, and Urbanization   *158*
7. "We Won't Cooperate": Legislative Council Elections, 1932 Conflict, and Frustration of Colonial Authority   *197*

Conclusion   *238*

*Notes   245*

*Bibliography   293*

*Index   319*

# ACKNOWLEDGMENTS

I RECEIVED HELP FROM MANY people in writing this book, and it is impossible to thank them well enough for it. I am eternally obliged to them; recognition in the brief space of an acknowledgment is only one of several ways to express appreciation.

Accordingly, I salute all my teachers for their instruction. They nurtured me, often an unsure and faltering learner, with encouraging words and pure patience. I might have forgotten one or two, but I remember many of them. The *Asafo* History Program, a collaborative effort between the University of Ghana and the Norwegian University of Science and Technology, Trondheim, Norway, deserves great mention. I had the idea for this book during my time in that program. For this privilege, I thank Professors Irene Odotei and Per Hernaes, as well as my colleague Dr. Ebenezer Ayesu, who offered me sustained support. All my professors at Michigan State University encouraged me greatly, especially Professors Pero Dagbovie and Peter Limb, both of whom believed in me when I remained unsure of myself.

Many people readily helped me during field and archival research in Ghana. I appreciate their commitment in collaborating and spending time with me. They drew on their knowledge and memory to give me so much information that helped shape this book. I have made extensive individual acknowledgments elsewhere in these pages; however, I need to mention the following people for their sincere dedication and commitment: *Supi* Kobina Minnah, *Obaahinmaa* Nana Amba Ayiaba, *Odomankoma Kyirɛma* Kwamina Prah, Taufik Ebo Labaran, and Kobina Ebo Fynn. I equally received help on the field from the following people in various forms and at different times: Ebenezer Otu Walker, Kofi Atta, Joseph Nana Kofi Adomako Addae, Eric Kwaku Boakye Frimpong, Emmanuel Kofi Boadi, Anthony Kweku Arthur, Kingsley Obeng Amoako, and Felix Gyamfi. Dr. Ebenezer Krampah Aidoo, Dr. Paul Kafui Kosie Kekesie, Dr. Yaw Ayewubo, Dr. Michael Acquah, Dr. Daniel Nkrumah, Godfred Ahianyo, Nii Okyne Adjei, Pastor Joseph Gyebi, and Festus N. A. Owoson have all become representative of my days as a teacher at Mfantsipim School, Cape Coast. I equally thank the librarians at the University of Ghana, Legon, particularly in the Balme and Institute of African Studies Libraries. Additionally, I received considerable help from the librarians at the University of Cape Coast Library Complex. The archival staff at the National Archives, Kew-Richmond, Great Britain, as well as the Public Records and Archives Administration Department offices in Accra and Cape Coast, proved quite helpful. I particularly thank William Otoo for his time and services; as well as being full of great appreciation for the constancy with which Stephen Baidoo coordinated the initial efforts to have the maps drawn in Ghana and for Becky Smith (Becky Photos) for sizing the photographs according to IUP specifications. To Elvis Abokyi Arthur, Dr. Alfred Kuranchie, Samuel Kwadjei Danquah, and Ampah, I owe a debt of gratitude for their moral support. The old guards of St. Mary's Secondary School—Apowa, Takoradi, Victor Atsu Dzikunu, Ahmed Nunoo, Dr. James Allou, Christopher Allou, Kenneth Asare (who put up with me at St. John's School, Sekondi, as well), and Dr. Benedict Atta Baidoo (Owaski) (who has been a great example in many ways)—commended and encouraged me.

ACKNOWLEDGMENTS xi

I am greatly indebted to my colleagues in the Department of History at Armstrong Atlantic State University, now Georgia Southern University, Armstrong Campus, Savannah, for their strong collegiality, encouragement, and support, which helped me to settle into the job. Their professional excellence created conducive conditions for me to work hard. Professor Michael Price particularly sacrificed time and effort to help me hone my scholarship. He worked closely with me to get this book to acceptable standards. Professor Price read the entire manuscript in its raw state, and Professor Christopher Hendricks went through parts under different forms. Together, they helped make it crisp and clear. Professor June Hopkins and her husband, Christopher, graciously accepted to read other aspects of my work. I am grateful to Dr. Julie de Chantal and her husband, John Colbert, for their input on the maps and pictures. Dr. Bennett Parten took it quite well, the many times I barged into his office to seek his opinion on grounds of grammatical consultation. Colleagues, I thank all of you. Mrs. Machelle Moore gave me ample assistance here and there. Similarly, several of my students graciously read through some of my work, especially during the reviews, and often made comments that sharpened my writing. I can readily recall Kelly Westfield, Daylon Bonner, Bruce Harry Crosby, and James Landers engaging in intellectual discussions with me. Above all, Riley Merritt merits (no pun intended) meaningful mention for having read and edited the entire manuscript as part of his honors college volunteer work.

My siblings at home in Ghana encouraged and offered ready and warm help. I thank Frank, Elizabeth, Jemimah, Eric, and the rest sincerely for all they did. Maa (Gloria Eileen Gyepi Garbrah, daughter of the venerable Master George Ernest Gyepi Garbrah of Cape Coast) and Daa (Edward Kwaku Nti otherwise known as Nana Toku Dum IV of Assin Nkran) would be so proud of you for all the support. Finally, I must thank Bessie and the children, Peniel, Ed, and Nana, for their moral support. They remained with me through it all, in both challenging and happy times. I am grateful for their patience with me when I became testy and disagreeable under enormous pressure—and especially for Peniel for his charming personality and character.

Ultimately, I thank the anonymous reviewers for their great job in reading the content closely, immersing themselves in it, and coming up with insightful comments and recommendations that helped bring this book to the threshold of scholarship. They helped make the book crisp and better than I envisaged. Finally, I am sincerely grateful to the staff of IU Press, particularly Dr. Gary Dunham, the acquisitions editor who discerned promise in this project, as well as Ashante Thomas and Anna Francis, his two hardworking assistants, and Darja Malcolm-Clarke and Vickrutha Sudharsan, for all the meaningful work done right from the beginning of the publication process to the end.

To all whose help I have been able to acknowledge, as well as any whom I failed to mention, I thank you most sincerely, and may the Almighty God bless you.

# A NOTE ON ORTHOGRAPHY

AKAN, LINGUISTICALLY ONE OF THE *Kwa* branches of the Niger-Congo language family, is liberally used throughout this book. It is the main language of nearly 48 percent of the population that occupies the middle belt of Ghana, extending all the way to the coast in the south. Basically, Akan as a language consists of several dialects, the two major ones being Twi and Fanti, as evident in the *Asan-te, Akwa-pem, A-kyem, Akwa-mu, Kwa-hu* Twi variations and the *O-guaa* (Cape Coast), *Ano-ma-bu, A-kyem-fo, Man-ke-ssim, Apam, Go-moa, Ago-na* Fanti variations. Both major dialects are mutually intelligible (as are British, American, and Australian English, for example). The initial linguistic effort to reduce the various dialects of the Akan language into written forms started with *Akuapem* Twi, which experts adjudged as quite median given its seemingly commutative cadences that mimic aspects of the other variants. The dialect that recurs throughout these pages is Fanti, spoken extensively among the littoral Akan societies, because Cape Coast is the focal town in coastal Ghana within the context of this book.

Fanti, like all dialects of the Akan language, uses the standard alphabet for its consonants and vowels; although a few peculiarities bequeath its unique accent, accentuating the culture as well as identity of the people who speak this variant. The alphabet in this language includes "a," which has both the short sound, as in *A-ta*, and the long sound, as in "ate," *Kwa-ku* in Asante-Twi, or *Kwe-ku* in Fanti. "E" sometimes has the regular "e" in the English language or the long "a" sound as in *Ebu-sua*; "i" has the same sound as in "it." In some contexts, "e" and "i" have the same sound, depending on who is speaking: *Asante* (the preference of its speakers, because it defines their culture and identity as Twi speakers who refer to the coastal Akan speakers as *Fan-te*) or *Ashan-ti* (as in the colonial records and all official government documents thereafter), and Fanti or *Fante*. Coastal Akan speakers also choose designations such as *Fanti*, *Mfan-tsi*, and *Fan-tsi*. Hence, there is a consistent use in this book of the spellings *Fanti* and *Asante* because, predominantly, the speakers of both dialects prefer these renditions for their authentic cultural undertones. *Ashanti* in this work is used in contexts referring to its status as a historical entity, as in official records and documents. "U" has the double "oo" sound as in the word "coop." The few unique letters, with their peculiar sounds, include the backward "C"—ɔ—as the "o" sound in "or." The backward numeral 3—ɛ—sounds like the "a" in "air."

Vowel combinations, or dipthongs, such as *ao, eɛ, ei, ia, ie, ii, oo, oɔ, ue,* and *uo* occur in Fanti words (as well as suffixes) in stretched out or long sound forms as means of emphasis, provocation, teasing, joviality, jubilation, and other such tendencies. Fanti consonants in most cases have similar pronunciations as in the standard alphabet "b," "d," "f," "g," "h," "k," "l," "m," "n," "p," "r," "s," "t," and "w." However, there are a few consonant combinations unique to the Akan variants and, in this context, the Fanti dialect. The ones with equivalent sounds in English include *dw*, which has the "j" sound, and *gy*, as in the "g" of "Georgia." Difficult combinations, such as *tw* and *hw*, do not have any immediate sound equivalents in English. The sound closest to *tw* is the "ch" sound in "chop." Likewise, *ng* comes close to the "ing" sound in "singing." *Ny* is correctly pronounced when both consonants are sounded together. *Hy* is equivalent to the "sh" in "she"; *kw* may have the "q" sound; and *ky* is equivalent to "ch" in "church."

Of all the Akan dialects, Fanti alone has *dz*, in which the "d" is treated as silent, rendering a "z" sound. The eccentric nature of Fanti is seen in *ts*, which has no clear-cut English equivalent, except the "ts" sound in the word "tsunami."

Like most languages, the Akan language, and the Fanti dialect in this context, is quite tonal, with low, mid, and high variations to enhance meaning as well as emphasis; tangentially, the resulting accent is definitive of the culture, worldview, and identity of its respective speakers. Hopefully, the repetitive use of Fanti words, phrases, clauses, and short sentences in this book provides a measure of cultural immersion necessary for the appreciation of this historical account.

To help with pronunciation of Akan or Fanti words, expressions, and statements throughout the pages of this book, some have been hyphenated to demarcate their syllabic components, especially where they are used the first time. All Fanti words, phrases, and clauses (nearly all italicized) are translated in the same instance of their each statement.

# MAPS

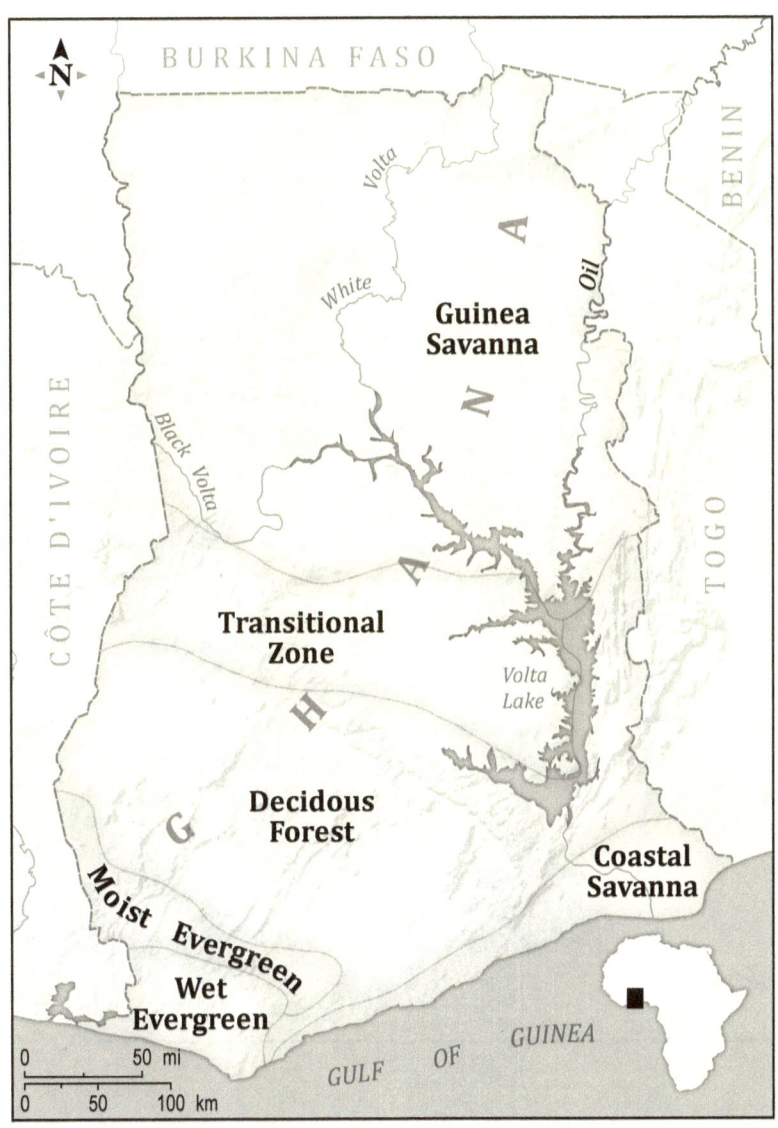

Map. 0.1 An environmental map of Ghana. Map by Johnson Cartographic LLC.

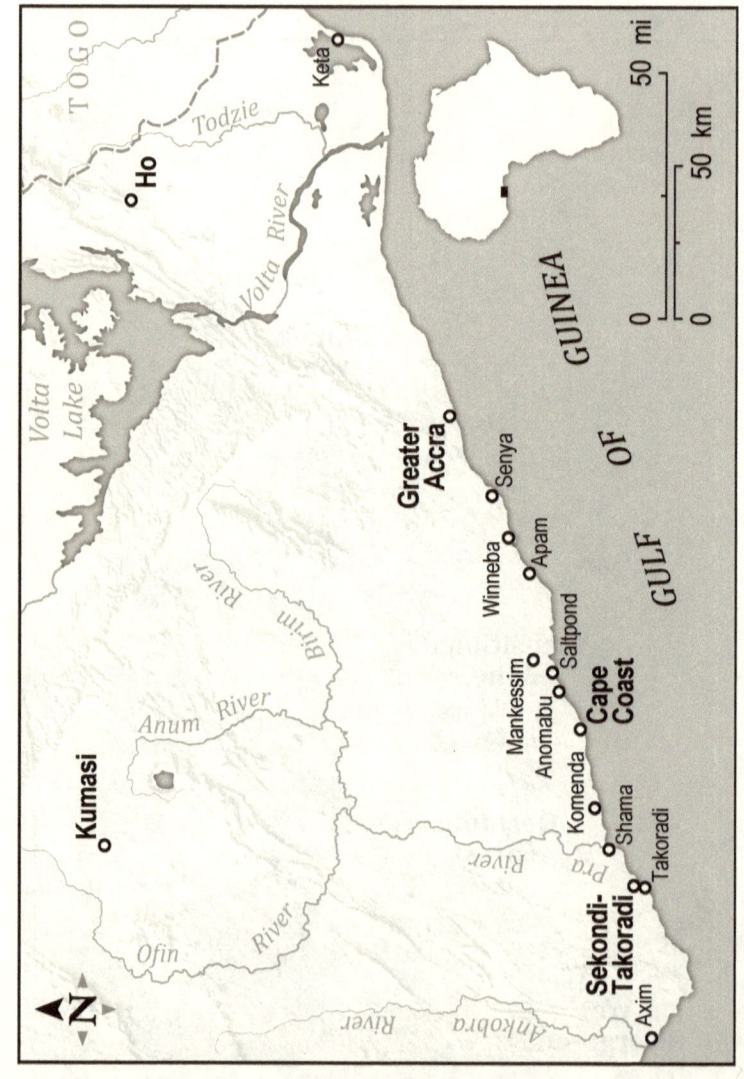

Map. 0.2 A map of southern Ghana showing the major coastal towns. Map by Johnson Cartographic LLC.

# MARITIME CULTURE AND EVERYDAY LIFE IN NINETEENTH- AND TWENTIETH-CENTURY COASTAL GHANA

# INTRODUCTION

THE 334-MILE COASTLINE OF GHANA, hardly the longest in West Africa, possesses a long history of vibrant maritime culture. The multifaceted nature of everyday life in these parts of Ghana has unfolded vividly and distinctly at different levels. Up to the nineteenth and twentieth centuries, everyday processes were based on both available natural resources and time-honored ideas, expressed in the formation of traditional institutions. Livelihood and socioeconomic developments on the coast of Ghana hinged on the manifold resources acquired from streams, ponds, rivers, lagoons, and, ultimately, the sea. In pursuit of increased skill capacity, creativity, discipline, and responsibility geared toward individual and collective well-being, indigenous organizations became indispensable. These organizations proved relevant both in facilitating varied life processes and in providing requisite defense mechanisms. Especially in the twentieth century, indigenous organizations actively demanded the benefits of colonial development plans for their respective communities and defended time-honored ways of life, aspects of which struck a note of disapproval among the colonial officials. The peoples of coastal Ghana found it necessary to defend and reinforce established dynamic patterns to ensure community survival as well as social cohesiveness in these crucial situations.

*Maritime Culture and Everyday Life*, therefore, examines how coastal communities, under the auspices of popular indigenous organizations, proactively sought to secure familiar ways of life and, correlatedly, demanded their share of emerging development dispensation under the colonial regime. The central argument of this book is that, almost invariably, aspects of daily life constituted matters of misunderstanding between coastal communities and colonial authorities. Likewise, everyday life served as a medium of contestation for the former against the latter. In expatiating this thesis, the book focuses on the impact of indigenous organizations; customary rite performances; fishing; concepts of ownership, land, urbanization, and infrastructural development in the history of coastal Ghana.

Ideas from the cultural repertoire of coastal communities came in handy as these communities endured the colonial experience, especially in dealing with officials of the British administration. Even so, reactions and strategies of local peoples in response to colonial government actions remained deeply diverse—organized groups of men and women sometimes acted in unison, separately, or across generational lines. These communities and their chiefs often collaborated with compatriot recipients of European education to make their grievances known to the colonial administration through picketing, delegations, protest letters, newspaper articles, and editorials. Occasionally, they took advantage of the momentary confusion, inaction, and indecision of colonial officers. Two major issues form the basis of this exposition: the cultural milieu, indispensable for understanding the social experience in coastal Ghana, and the fractious relations among indigenous organizations. The nuances of both issues proffer a broader and deeper appreciation of these parts of the country during the period under consideration.

*Maritime Culture and Everyday Life* explores social setting; operational dynamics; indigenous institutions and assaults on their power and authority; entrenched ideas of indigenous property ownership that influenced reactions to colonial land policy; and, ultimately, the politics of colonial urbanization, including infrastructural development. These interconnected and mutually dependent issues, in differing degrees, are relevant for appreciating the nuances of society, culture, and history of coastal Ghana.

In all these discussions, the emphasis remains on the role of everyday people, the most numerous and essential part of society, and how the dynamics of cultural practices informed their decisions as well as actions. The conclusive historiographical significance of this approach hinges on the shift in priority from prominent national leaders to everyday people, organized under indigenous institutions, within their familiar spaces.

The importance of social settings and structures for the comprehension of subtle variations in the history of Ghana is incontestable—as in its coastal communities, given their proximity to the sea. Under the auspices of indigenous organizations, these communities drew on cultures developed around maritime locations and consequent occupations. Familiar ways of life, ideas, and strategies developed from time immemorial became useful in shoring up confidence as these societies navigated new issues in challenging times.

The seriousness with which chiefs in coastal Ghana attempted to stave off the weakening of their power and authority in the early nineteenth century also manifested in strategies and processes of reaction. The establishment and operation of modern court systems was an enduring issue, revolving around who had the right of adjudication over everyday matters. This situation became overly contentious with the mushrooming of indigenous and English courts—as well as the unavoidable clashes between them. It undoubtedly gnawed at the core aspects of the coastal Ghana chieftaincy institution. Chiefs, aggrieved and concerned about the encroachment of colonial administration on their influence, collaborated with various peoples organized under indigenous sociopolitical institutions and with the few beneficiaries of European education. This considerable collaboration between ordinary people and elite, evidently, demonstrated that acquisition of formal European education meant neither a snub of local culture nor a lack of respect for those less privileged. The local beneficiaries of European-established schools worked with indigenous institutions for the achievement of community interests. They participated in activities of indigenous institutions based on patrilineal associations, a fundamental element of *Asafo* membership. Contrary to elsewhere in southern Ghana, collaboration in the coastal belt, particularly in Cape Coast, worked productively for the parties involved—albeit with unique challenges and manifold complications. That abiding cooperation further bequeathed this coastal town with remarkable agency in the history of the country.

Ostensibly for this activism, the fishing community in Cape Coast often used the expression *pun-tu-siee, pun-tu-siee, sɛ ehom hen-du oo, ann-hum hendu oo, yɛ tar nsu enyiwa oo!*—literally, "we possess the tenacity comparable to that of the cork or gourd! Whether you suppress us or not, we retain our capacity to float!" The ontological significance of these floating objects to the main occupation in this part of the town remains more obvious than imagined. Yet the folk praise poem of Cape Coast provides a smattering of self-redemption:

> Oguaa
> Oguaa Akɔ-tɔ
> Akɔ-tɔ dwir-dwirba a
> Wo-gu hɔn tu ano
> Edua-sa a wɔ nye apem koe a
> Apem enn-tum hɔn
> Yɛɛ Oguaa dɛn na
> Oguaa ann-yɛ wo bi?

This is translated as follows:

> Cape Coast
> Crabs of Cape Coast

> Tiny and nimble crabs that
> Stay within the immediate vicinity of their holes
> The seventy that fought a thousand
> And never suffered annihilation
> Let the world know what offense you
>     enacted against Cape Coast
> For which Cape Coast failed to retaliate?

This short stanza signifies a cryptic expression of the nature of the people of Cape Coast, imbued with resilient strength and character. They would react to the slightest provocation; and when overly vexed, they would not hesitate to retaliate. This popular poem amounts, in part, to a brief and powerful statement of origin, history, oath, and identity, with the crab designation underscoring the estuarial environment. Its recitation in critical contexts challenged both the individual and society to defend the beliefs expressed therein. The challenge became nonnegotiable, especially when the chief divine drummer expressed those same words in drum language, invoking concomitant spiritual elements. In a typical war situation, men and women acquitted themselves or, essentially, acted out the letter and spirit of that appellation. This expression was a call to meet confrontation with confrontation, aggression with aggression, and defiance with defiance. Such ideas underpinned social as well as political motivations and actions across coastal Ghana. Particularly in Cape Coast, the deployment of these ideas within *Asafo* units in their engagement with colonial authorities marked an evocation of this remarkable agency.

The enduring involvement of indigenous organizations in various issues reiterates their indispensability for understanding the history of coastal Ghana. As major social institutions, the *Asafo* (patrilineal) and the *Ebusua* (matrilineal) systems remained pivotal to coastal communities. Both systems, unsurprisingly, piqued the curiosity of the colonial authorities. Additionally, the *Asafo* and *Ebusua* systems had far-reaching implications for issues of gender complementarity, identity, belongingness, and inheritance. In the predominantly matrilineal Akan societies, avenues existed for the strong expression of patrilineal influences.[1] This feature proves quite significant, especially given the tendency of feminist scholars to emphasize predominantly patriarchal structures that relegated matrilineal matters to the background. The exemplification of predominantly matrilineal societies giving prominence to patrilineal systems remains intriguing and unique. Focus on the vibrant indigenous institutions of coastal Ghana adds to the growing research on salient aspects of societies and cultures, notable elements of microhistory.[2] Along these lines, the dynamics of indigenous values, concepts, and expectations become crucial in understanding why and how things happen.

The discussion of indigenous institutions proffers an opportunity to examine how their interrelations, especially long-standing *Asafo* conflicts, influenced their engagements with the colonial administration and vice versa. Relations among *Asafo* groups thrived on rivalry, which found new and most welcome venting during a disputed municipal council election, much to the chagrin of local colonial officers. As in other vexatious official measures, the election became a national issue that consequently aggravated relations between the people of Cape Coast and the colonial government. Against this background, old *Asafo* conflicts evolved into new strategies in response to measures and policies the administration introduced.

Hence, *Maritime Culture and Everyday Life* explores methods, resources, and values drawn from the wider cultural milieu within which indigenous organizations operated and were applied to navigate everyday life in coastal Ghana under colonial rule. To this end, the beliefs, origins, emblems, paraphernalia, nature, and function of these institutions become central. The *Asafo* system is, undoubtedly, an essential component of the various Akan indigenous political and military organizations necessary for

INTRODUCTION 7

understanding societies in this part of the country. Appreciation of the importance and indispensability of this institution among the Akan groups, especially the Fanti peoples, requires a melding of their social fabric, or nature, and roles relevant for the proper functioning of society. Despite close association with conflicts, the *Asafo* ranks highly in coastal Ghana along social, political, and economic lines. Indeed, Fanti customary law and practice underscore the legal role of the *Asafo* in the indigenous tribunal system, reiterating its deep-seated influence in all aspects of life; ultimately, the *Asafo* dynamic remains the axis around which society spins.

That institution had a powerful presence in the central and western coastal towns of southern Ghana in the nineteenth and twentieth centuries. Important occasions, such as festivities and other ceremonies, could hardly happen without the presence of men and women marching in powerful processions, singing, beating drums, and dressing in colorful uniforms. Some would fire obsolete guns, mainly flintlocks and matchlocks, as flag bearers acrobatically displayed a variety of motif-embroidered flags. In towns, especially coastal Fanti states, that had several *Asafo* companies, groups would differentiate themselves through the choice of colors of their varied uniforms, flags, and emblems. Intercompany taunts and occasional altercations remained some of the most salient, definitive characteristics of the institution, often stemming from persistent rivalry among competing companies of the same town or state. Although competitive coexistence of companies may, indeed, be considered a basic feature of the system, that element hardly ruled out cooperation among *Asafo* companies.

As indigenous institutions, these groups can generally be analyzed within the modes of locality, competition, display, innovation, prestige, status, and mutual aid. The internal vibrancy of the *Asafo* fostered various forms of competition and expressions of superiority through new styles of dress, dance, and song. Hence, innovation stands out as another essential feature of these organizations. Undoubtedly, the element of rivalry among the Cape Coast *Asafo* groups became the fulcrum around which opposition to the municipal council election for a representative on the Legislative Council found expression.

Everyday expressions of ownership reiterated the significance of individual acquisitions in these coastal societies where collective ownership remained paramount. These manifestations, originally artistic or symbolic, came full circle by melding with a wide variety of written statements after the establishment of European schools locally. In these instances of expression, the sovereignty and pride of ownership and dignity, as well as the sense of audacity that came with proprietary rights, are self-evident. These ideas and the various attitudes they engendered came into play in the country's response to the infamous Crown Lands Bill.

Admittedly, the vigor with which the inhabitants of Cape Coast contested the efforts of the colonial authorities to seize so-called vacant lands and arbitrarily introduce British land regulation standards in Ghana produced political problems for the town. In this context, the contention hinged on the indigenous meaning and significance of land not only as an economic or political capital but also, comparably, as a cultural and religious resource with great implication for everyday life. This time-honored conceptualization of land elucidates the crucial nature of various efforts to obstruct the passing of the bill with detrimental consequences particularly for Cape Coast, as the pivotal place in the squabble over land in southern Ghana.

*Maritime Culture and Everyday Life* highlights an intriguing aspect of colonial urbanization and infrastructural development. Urbanization in coastal Ghana transcended economic considerations and unleashed a period of decline for Cape Coast as an old port city, given the unflinching resoluteness with which people sought to obstruct the administration. When the British moved the nerve center of the administration from Cape Coast to Accra, they cited sanitation concerns as their main justification rather than political motivations, interests, and preferences. The loss of capital city status amplified the tensions between local colonial officers and the people of Cape Coast. Consequently, this deprivation caused an intensification of defiant acts toward governmental policies and actions. The reaction of the colonial authorities stood in sharp contrast to similar scenarios in other parts of Africa, especially in South Africa, where cases of disease and sanitation became an often-cited justification for excluding people from parts of the city. Rather than creating a cordon sanitaire or even excluding "undesirable people" from certain locations in Cape Coast, the colonial administration chose to move the central government machinery to a supposed haven not in any measure different from the original capital city. Expansion and improvement of the railroad infrastructure in southern Ghana, given the growing export-import sector of its booming economy (particularly increasing cocoa cultivation), equally exacerbated those rancorous relations. Despite expressly articulated promises, the extensive and elaborate railroad infrastructure materialized to the exclusion of Cape Coast; the consequential protest, hardly a small matter, sparked a variety of interpretations, including the emergence of conspiracy theories.

In all these engagements, notwithstanding its relative military might, the colonial administration encountered challenges and difficulties that often translated into overwhelming experiences for officers. Indecision and inaction on the part of local colonial officers as they vacillated on the implementation of policy at critical times woefully worsened the evolving conflict. Subsequently, colonial officers appeared partial in the eyes of disputing factions, some of which exploited perceived weaknesses to flout government orders. This testy relation between coastal communities and colonial administration complicates the simple resistor-collaborator binary in the interpretation of the history of Ghana. Although communities in coastal Ghana often come across as collaborators with the British colonial administration, *Maritime Culture and Everyday Life* in its entirety demonstrates that the supposed collaboration had its own challenges, complications, and complexities.

### HISTORIOGRAPHY

The effort to write the history of Ghana (formerly the British Gold Coast Colony), like that of Africa in general, has undoubtedly come a long way.[3] The first generation of Ghanaian academic historians followed W. W. Claridge, W. E. F. Ward, Thomas Edward Bowdich, Brodie Cruickshank, F. M. Bourret, John D. Fage, E. B. Ellis, R. S. Rattray, David Kimble, Dennis Austin, Eva L. R. Meyerowitz, and others in the second half of the twentieth century.[4] In addition to writing general histories of the country—from its peopling, state and kingdom formation, contact with Europeans, and colonization to the struggle for independence and the era after—that generation of academic historians ventured into local histories of various ethnic groups and encouraged their students to pursue similar research trends. From the 1970s to the contemporary era, historical writing on Ghana has acquired vibrance in theme, scope, and style. Five of the erstwhile ten regions, namely Ashanti, Central, Eastern, Greater Accra, and Volta, have become the focus of massive scholarly research.[5] For instance, historical research and writing on Asante has been the most prolific, dealing with subjects such as kinship, the kingdom, trade, cocoa farming, institutions, culture, and so on.[6] Asante equally dominates scholarly efforts to account for and give recognition to the role of women in the historiography of Ghana.[7] Scholarship on the greater Accra region focuses on the Ga and, quite recently, Ga women.[8] Where does *Maritime Culture and Everyday Life* fit in these scholarly developments?

In focusing on Cape Coast for its pivotal role in subsequent developments, and on coastal Ghana in general, this book seeks to etch a new historical constituency to extend and enhance the Fanti component in the historiography of the country. This effort is done within the context of the social history of a coastal town that experienced creeping imperialism and incorporation into the British Gold Coast during the nineteenth and twentieth centuries. Given this dynamic, indigenous institutions became useful in the contestation of, as well as efforts at influencing, the sociopolitical transformations of the era.

Social history as an emergent genre in the academic efforts to place the past of this country in proper perspective remains relevant. In this direction, Emmanuel Kwaku Akyeampong has made two relevant contributions to the field, aspects of which inform my work. In his social history of alcohol in Ghana, he considers how this "powerful fluid," functioning as a metaphor for power, informed intergenerational and gender-based conflict as well as the process of urban social formations and temperance movements in precolonial and early colonial Gold Coast.[9] The present work, along these lines, considers the use and abuse of alcohol in the resistance to colonial rule in coastal Ghana, especially in Cape Coast. I focus on not only how alcohol imbued *Asafo* operations, with immoderate consumption causing and/or facilitating conflict among various groups, but also how local colonial officers paradoxically used alcohol in conflict resolution efforts as *asom-dwee nsa*, or "peace drink." Again, in his insightful work on an environmental history of the Anlo, Akyeampong establishes the foundation for the field within the Ghanaian context.[10] He examines the dynamic relationship between the Anlo and the geographic space in which they lived and how this dynamism reflected through social structures, processes, economy, livelihood, accumulation, social differentiation, marriage, family, knowledge, belief, power, modernity, social change, and sustainable development. Both the Anlo and Fanti peoples, specifically in Keta and Cape Coast, respectively, possessed nuanced understandings of their environments in terms of opportunities and constraints, aiding to forge cultural tools, social structures, and relationships in their interaction with their locales. However, Akyeampong focuses these discussions on the twentieth-century coastal erosion experience of the people of Keta, which brought a collapse of the balance between nature and culture compounded by progressive marginalization in the late colonial and postcolonial political economy of Ghana. Spared the disastrous and demoralizing experience of coastal erosion, the people of Cape Coast could conveniently control the balance between nature and culture. And as some people of Keta, amid their disappointment and hopes for (colonial) government intervention in the battle with erosion, resorted to indigenous religious beliefs for relief, the people of Cape Coast equally deployed their belief systems and institutions to confront the colonial government and contest its policies, albeit partly in the interest of southern Ghana.

The environmental factor remains crucial for better understanding and appreciating the history of the people of Cape Coast, who, like the Anlo, lived on the Atlantic coast of West Africa, albeit a considerable distance apart. The relationship between Cape Coast and the sea has barely been explored in historical research. Accordingly, I invoke W. Jeffrey Bolster to engage the dynamic relationship between the fishing or coastal community of the town and the sea.[11] To what extent can it be said that living so close to the sea and making a livelihood from it (as they affirm, *Yɛ fow po da-biaa-ra!*—"we climb the sea every day!") shaped the nature and conduct of these people?[12] To what extent can these influences explain the frequency of conflict and ideas of resistance as expressed through indigenous organizations? How did these ideas influence wranglings with the colonial authorities?

Aspects of resistance have turned up in historiography of Ghana as well as Cape Coast, particularly on the *Asafo*.[13] However, nearly all these efforts could be described variously as footnotes, passing comments, slight references in chapters, or at best essays, dissertations, and articles. Resistance is barely discussed within the context of maritime culture and everyday life. To ground my discussion of indigenous social institutions, I discuss the beliefs, origins, emblems, and paraphernalia of the *Asafo*, as well as their nature, function, and how these groups became useful to coastal communities in contesting and influencing the sociopolitical transformations of the era.

J. A. Aggrey, for instance, sees the *Asafo* system as an essential component of Fanti and Akan culture, especially political and military aspects.[14] He describes the anatomy of the system and looks at its essence, including beliefs about origins of the institution among the Fanti peoples, as well as its emblems, paraphernalia, and songs. The depth of detail and breadth of discussion reflect his intimate understanding of the system. However, Aggrey hardly examines how the Fanti states, or Akan groups in general, used this institution in their experience of and response to colonial rule. Moreover, the wealth of information contained in Aggrey's work has a regrettable limited readership because Aggrey writes entirely in the Fanti dialect.[15]

I. B. Chukwukere, on the other hand, attempts an anthropological interpretation of the nature and function of the *Asafo* in some Fanti communities.[16] He unmistakably establishes the importance of the institution among the Fanti, indicating its deep roots in the social fabric and indispensability to the proper functioning of their respective societies. Despite his work's enlightening nature, Chukwukere only does a general study of the *Asafo*.

The work of J. C. DeGraft Johnson on the Fanti *Asafo* is widely referenced.[17] Writing against a backdrop of serious criticism from colonial political officers vis-à-vis rampant scuffles and disturbances in the nineteenth century, he presents the institution as germane to the sociopolitical fabric of the indigenous state.[18] To justify its place and relevance, Johnson attempts an analysis of the warrior organization, briefly discussing its origins, history, development, and scope, just as Aggrey does. He places emphasis on the *Asafo* as a dignified and formidable force despite its close association with conflict. Johnson opines that purging these group clashes and introducing some reforms would make its social, political, and economic relevance self-evident. His motive for writing the article makes him eschew any thorough analysis of *Asafo* conflicts and assessment of its modes of operation against colonialism.[19]

In his pioneering work on Fanti traditional law and national constitution, John Mensah Sarbah mentions the *Asafo* system.[20] He provides a broad overview of Akan-Fanti communities and explains the principles that underpin their governance. The *Asafo* system, despite being a vital component of the Akan-Fanti culture, only features intermittently.[21] Given his background as a lawyer—the first indigenous person in this profession—Sarbah elaborates on the basic forms of the constitution of Fanti societies as well as indigenous legal arrangements, hardly broaching the broad matter of their experiences under colonial rule.[22]

Ansu K. Datta and R. Porter in their work equally look at the special nature and origins of the Fanti *Asafo*.[23] The authors point out that anyone who visited a coastal town in central or western Gold Coast at an opportune time would have likely seen men and women dressed in colorful uniforms, marching in energetic processions, a few of them beating drums, and all of them singing.[24] Some of the participants would have been carrying, if not firing, obsolete muskets, with flag bearers displaying a variety of flags embroidered with different motifs. Diverse, colorful uniforms, flags, and emblems distinguished the various groups in towns with several *Asafo* companies.[25] Additionally, the authors discuss *Asafo* development over different periods and refer to the penchant for conflict, albeit briefly. Datta and Porter observe that intercompany fights and disputes persisted as a defining feature of the system given the rivalry between various companies in the same town or state. Therefore, competitive coexistence of companies might indeed be considered a basic feature of the system.

Again, this element of rivalry notwithstanding, the groups cooperated against common enemies.[26] The authors, however, scarcely explore their engagements with the British governing authorities.

In an article, Datta rues the inadequacies of DeGraft Johnson's and Christensen's work.[27] He posits that their silence on certain salient features of the Fanti *Asafo* system reflects a serious weakness.[28] Datta expresses the hope that his work, based on materials collected from field investigation over a period of several years in various Fanti towns, might complement that of these authors. In all his efforts to mitigate these weaknesses, however, Datta ignores the *Asafo*'s role in leading their various societies to contest and influence sociopolitical transformations.

John Argyle produces what appears to be the first scholarly effort at comparing indigenous social organizations across the continent from eastern, southern, all the way to western Africa.[29] He conducts his analysis using the modes of locality, competition, display, innovation, prestige, status, and mutual aid. Argyle cites the close connection between a particular dance association and the part of a town in which its members lived; he establishes the division of older Swahili towns into two distinct local sections, sometimes called "moieties" in the literature, as a fundamental feature of their political and military responsibilities.[30] Moreover, he observes that the internal vibrancy of these sections and of the wider society fostered the various forms of competition to achieve success through new styles of dress, dance, music, and song.[31] Such innovation, therefore, constituted an essential feature of these organizations. Referring to Terrence Ranger, Argyle argues that these organizations constituted a way of recasting the network of relationships within a moiety. Where is the locus of the *Asafo* system in these discussions? He reiterates the competitive spirit inherent in the Asafo system. It is this rivalry that provides the linkage to aspects of my work. To this end, my study suggests that the element of competition in inter-*Asafo* relations served as a key factor from which resistance to the Cape Coast

Municipal Council election for a representative to the Legislative Council evolved. The scholarly significance of Argyle's work cannot be denied. The detailed analysis of the eastern and southern Africa case studies, however, overshadows his discussion of the *Asafo* of West Africa, or in this context, coastal Ghana.

The work of Roger Gocking on Cape Coast suggests that the British policy of indirect rule caused beneficiaries of European-established schools in Cape Coast to exploit indigenous political institutions for personal gains.[32] He sets his study between 1843 and 1948, reexamining the British policy of indirect rule as well as its effects on the Gold Coast. Gocking demonstrates that the policy exhibited much more complex outcomes than have been ascribed to it, especially in the politics of the coastal polities.[33] He suggests that indirect rule fueled unprecedented competition for office in the "native" states among people who had little or no claim to legitimacy. To this end, indirect rule gave indigenous political institutions and their affairs a new air of importance, encouraging local recipients of European education to enter the indigenous political order and seek office.[34] Gocking mentions the *Asafo* system of Cape Coast as one institution that offered an opportunity to fulfill those political aspirations.[35]

In another work, Gocking focuses on what he calls the growth of coastal societies of Ghana through two major factors: "Akanization" and "Europeanization," specifically, "Anglicization."[36] He asserts that focus on cultural interaction moves his work beyond the form and force of protest to colonial rule. Consequently, Gocking concentrates on the extent to which nineteenth- and twentieth-century Gold Coast communities became Euro-African environments, linking people across putatively traditional and westernized boundaries through participation in common activities and affiliations to indigenous institutions.[37]

*Maritime Culture and Everyday Life* challenges aspects of Gocking's conclusions. The Africans—or in this case, the coastal Ghanaians—who accessed European education hardly took advantage of indigenous institutions such as the *Asafo*. Far from being guilty of such a charge, this educated class in Cape Coast participated in these institutions because of their patrilineal connections, the fundamental element of membership (men and women became automatic or natural members of *Asafo* through their fathers). Additionally, while Gocking focuses on early local recipients of European literacy and numeracy (to whom he specifically refers as "Creoles") in his analysis of the "Akanization" and "Europeanization/Anglicization" process in Cape Coast, I highlight the activities of ordinary men and women and their collaboration with those beneficiaries in consequential efforts at contesting and influencing aspects of the sociopolitical transformations of the era.

Other scholars have looked at varying aspects of inter-*Asafo* relations, and their conclusions have been relevant to my research.[38] Stanley Shaloff's article on the 1932 *Asafo* conflict falls, to some extent, within the purview of this book. He attributes the outbreak of the conflict to an incidence of opposing opinions in Cape Coast regarding the Gold Coast Colony Order-in-Council of 1925, with respect to the Legislative Council elections. Shaloff states that the conflict hardly manifested "traditional" violence among rival military formations in the frequently turbulent precincts of Cape Coast.[39] Although I agree with his argument regarding the Legislative Council elections, my work reiterates the presence of perennial inter-*Asafo* rivalry that underpinned the buildup and burst on the day of the incident. This act of drawing connections to, or dwelling on, linkages from precedent conflicts remained an invariable characteristic of the *Asafo* system in general, and of the *Asafo* in Cape Coast in particular. In drawing these connections to trends from earlier periods, my work provides necessary contextualization to political decisions and actions in the town.

The fact that none of the scholars on Cape Coast or the central part of coastal Ghana referenced here account for the overwhelming presence and impact of the sea in their work firms up the originality of *Maritime Culture and Everyday Life*. This book reckons the clearly visible and unmistakable maritime presence and its resulting way of life, influences on worldview, and ways of conduct, all of which remain indispensable in appreciating this history.

### THEORETICAL FRAMEWORK

James C. Scott proffers an instructive lead regarding the capacity of ordinary people to affect history by causing things to happen in their favor.[40] For him, it is important to understand everyday forms of peasant resistance—that is, the prosaic but constant struggle between the peasantry and those who seek to extract labor, food, taxes, rent, and interest from them.[41] He avers that "here I have in mind the ordinary weapons of relatively powerless groups: foot dragging, dissimulation, desertion, false compliance, pilfering, feigned ignorance, slander, arson, sabotage and so on."[42] Although many might see the people of Cape Coast and their *Asafo* as weak relative to the colonial authorities and the implicit power of the British Empire, it bears asking whether they considered themselves so severely disadvantaged given their indigenous ideas of resistance, as seen in the folk praise poem and other statements already discussed in this introduction. Far from the weapons Scott mentions, the tools people used included indigenous ideas, beliefs, as well as institutions—the same ones the colonial authorities sought to sanction and even suppress. This book's other departure from Scott's involves the modes of application of weapons of the weak. He writes that "these Brechtian or Schweikian forms of class struggle have certain features in common. They require little or no coordination or planning; they make use of implicit understandings and informal networks; they often represent a form of individual self-help; they typically avoid any direct symbolic confrontation with authority . . . just such kinds of resistance are often the most significant and the most effective over the long run."⁴³ Scott reiterates this view with the invocation of Marc Bloch, historian of feudalism, who notes that "great millennial movements [are] ... flashes in the pan compared to the patient silent struggles stubbornly carried on by rural communities."⁴⁴ On the contrary, the evidence from communities in coastal Ghana, especially in the case of the people of Cape Coast and their *Asafo*, is of anything but "patient silent struggle." These struggles were stubbornly carried out and quite well planned and coordinated yet equally "often the most significant and the most effective over the long run." Hence, Scott's discussion of the weapons of the weak scarcely captures the spirit of indigenous forms of social organizations, such as the *Asafo*—of their local effectiveness and strength in the face of colonial impositions. These dynamics are fully illustrated through specific cases of *Asafo*-driven social engagement and change in this book.

As the awareness for "putting the ocean" in history gains traction, it can be argued that W. Jeffrey Bolster makes the strongest case in that direction. He touts the possibility and necessity of systematically writing the living ocean into history.⁴⁵ Acknowledging the inclusion of other oceans, Bolster affirms the preeminence of the Atlantic and its history for "blurring historiographical and disciplinary boundaries, ignoring national boundaries, and probing novel social and cultural interactions. . . . [The Atlantic] has become a dominant organizing principle for the early modern era."⁴⁶ The increasing historicizations of oceans and seas, according to him, "are reorienting conventional geographies and emphasizing oceans as access points for innovative histories. For historians, the past has never looked so watery."⁴⁷ Admittedly, the proximity of coastal Ghana to the Atlantic Ocean makes the previous statement aptly applicable in this context. Any exclusion of the objective reality of the sea "as a set of linked ecosystems ... fluctuations of which impacted"⁴⁸ aspects of the culture and everyday life in coastal Ghana amounts to an abject abandonment of a great historical resource. Most significantly, the origins of colonial establishment that confronted the people of coastal Ghana issued from across the sea. Bolster divulges that "as nature becomes more central to the scholarly conception of the past, rigid disciplinary boundaries and ossified categories of analysis are crumbling and the ocean is appearing in new light in written histories."[49] Assuredly, the location of Ghana on the historic Gulf of Guinea, which bequeathed its coastal communities with a rich maritime culture, makes a compelling case for seeing its history in a new light.

Correlatedly, waterscape concepts add to the relevance and necessity of this approach to the history of coastal Ghana. Although its people hardly have legends of origination from the ocean, as Karin Amimoto Ingersoll claims for the Kanaka Maoli (native Hawaiians), the people of coastal Ghana certainly include it in facets of their essence and identity. These connections derive from their shared geographic spaces, albeit in different parts of the world. Ingersoll discusses seascape epistemology, among other things, as an approach to life and knowing—organizing events and thoughts according to how people move and interact, as well as emphasizing the importance of recognizing one's roots, one's center, and where one is located.[50] For coastal Ghana peoples, particularly the fishing community in Cape Coast, these views prove vital, as the sea remains pivotal to their world and everyday life. Indeed, the sea, in many ways, endures as a term of reference for their self-identification: *hɛn mpu-ano-fo*, "we the seashore people," which their hinterland Akan Twi-speaking neighbors use to refer to them as well (with the designation *ɛ-mpu-ano-foɔ*, or "those seashore peoples"). Relatedly, Kevin Dawson avers that waterways do not constitute empty, cultureless, historical voids.[51] His statements constitute a clear censure of overwhelming terrestrial perspectives that treat water as a border for land-bound events, implying that cultural creation remains restricted to land.[52] Quite within the perimeters of this book, he observes that some African societies maintain intimate interactions with water during work and leisure time, regarding it as a social and cultural space, not an interval between places. Again, many African societies weave terrestrial and aquatic experiences into amphibious lives, interlacing spiritual and secular beliefs, economies, social structures, and political institutions—ways of life—around relationships with water. Therefore, water pervades as a defining feature for African-descended peoples living along seas, rivers, lakes, and estuaries, as immersion traditions enable many to merge water and land into a unified cultural milieu.[53] In explaining his views on waterscapes, Dawson holds this approach as beneficial because it dramatically expands our historical perspective, adding tens of thousands of miles of cultural backdrop.[54] This view, without question, is appropriate and applicable in the case of coastal Ghana societies.

Everyday life in this book must be construed contextually. The application here hardly refers to vivid moment-by-moment, day-to-day accounts of life, although a few are highlighted. The trope of everyday life largely encapsulates varying lived ideas, and the expressions thereof, regarding worldview, beliefs, thoughts, and practices that enabled the peoples of coastal Ghana, as indigenous residents of their communities, to control their own fortunes appropriately. It includes how the people's perceptions of their world influenced the full range of social, cultural, and economic endeavors. Everyday life also extends to political relations (within communities and with neighboring societies), including arrangements and mechanisms available when dealing with consequent complications. With the empowerment of the values and vitality of everyday life, coastal communities navigated issues among themselves and responded accordingly to colonial rule, establishing their agency over time in the bid to live as they deemed culturally fitting and proper. Hence, the use of everyday life in this sense is an exercise in social history that captures the activities of a considerable number of ordinary people, organized under indigenous institutions, proving themselves willing and able to deal with shifting situations.

### PREPARATION, METHODOLOGY, AND EVALUATION OF SOURCES

I went to the field with the accumulated benefit of research seminars complemented by requisite readings and a wealth of advice rooted in the rich experiences of colleagues. On the field, practical issues and ideas in various methodology literature facilitated my research, in addition to oral history techniques such as the unscripted oral interview format.[55] Even though this work is scarcely entirely within the realm of feminist studies, I found feminist methodologies meaningful to the extent that they proved practical and results oriented.

Allowing interviewees to take control empowered them to provide information they deemed relevant, making them active participants in the statement and interpretation of their own history. This methodological model enabled me to practice history from a grassroot perspective. I read and interpreted notes taken during the interview process, as well as transcriptions, to those who could neither read nor write. This gesture allowed respondents to correct misunderstood or misinterpreted evidence. Literate participants had the opportunity to read the notes and some initial on-field writing.[56]

With funding from the Michigan State University Summer Support Fellowship and other sources, I spent seven months (May to November 2009) in Ghana. At the University of Ghana, Legon, and the University of Cape Coast, I spent two months consulting with faculty as well as reviewing BA, MA, and MPhil theses on Cape Coast, coastal Ghana, and related issues. These reviews provided interesting leads as well as useful bibliographic references. Consultations and discussions with faculty proffered significant ideas.

INTRODUCTION 23

The need for written records took me to the head office of the Public Record and Archives Administration Department (PRAAD) in Accra and its regional office in Cape Coast. Two months of extensive search in these offices produced crucial files relevant to my project. These included miscellaneous letters (concessions and confidential), memos, and civil record books. A search of the card index registers and guides turned up files on medical and sanitation issues such as infectious diseases. The harbors and waterways file had information on the Cape Coast port and other such infrastructure elsewhere in coastal Ghana. The municipality and township file had interesting information on the Cape Coast town council. Under the card index and register guide, the native affairs section yielded records of disturbances, clashes, chiefs, and agreement between chiefs and the *Asafo* companies.

The Civil Service Ordinance (CSO) turned up a wealth of information. These records included the J. C. DeGraft Johnson report on *Asafo* organizations, clashes, and disturbances; Cape Coast Native Affairs; the threats of company fight as well as clashes; representations of the chief of Cape Coast on the inquiry into the 1932 scuffle; and the breaching of bonds. Additionally, other papers and reports provided relevant information on the origins and power of indigenous institutions; notes on Cape Coast *Asafo* company emblems; rates of the Central Province Railway; treatment of the ports of Cape Coast and Saltpond on the opening of the Takoradi harbor; and reports on acting district commissioner G. E. Skene regarding his responsibility for the Cape Coast clash of 1932.

An intensive two-week search in December of 2009 at the National Archives, Kew, Richmond, Surrey, United Kingdom, was enormously productive. Documents found included confidential letters and reports on Cape Coast, the *Asafo*, local beneficiaries of European education, and colonial officers who became subject of investigation after the 1932 clash. The registers also helped with references to conflicts in other parts of coastal Ghana; they turned up photographs of the *Asafo* companies and parts of the Cape Coast township, all of which provided leads on its development and expansion.

Nevertheless, archival documents are rarely sacrosanct because of their subtle subjectivities and slants. One important category of documents that came up in the Cape Coast archives includes writings of local recipients of European education. Prolific writers in this category include John Mensah Sarbah, J. C. DeGraft Johnson, and Kwesi Johnston. Their documents provide insights into matters of custom and the nature of the *Asafo* companies, as well as other aspects of Cape Coast history and coastal Ghana history in general. The composers of these documents comprised local individuals well placed to record events. However, their accounts rarely go into any depth on the conflicts and clashes among companies. Most (if not all) of the documentation constitutes written responses to the hostile attitude of the colonial government toward indigenous institutions. Did the *Asafo* not have any flaws or excesses? This and other critical questions come to mind with the use of these sources.

Contrary to common suspicion regarding lack of understanding as well as questionable attitudes of colonial officers toward African customs, institutions, beliefs, values, and practices, at least a few British officers recognized and revered aspects of coastal Ghana culture. Letters and comments from British colonial commissioners such as Captain Lynch and James Crowther reflect the understanding of fair-minded and objective individuals who lived and worked in Cape Coast. They lived in the town long enough to speak Fanti, know the culture, and appreciate its indigenous institutions; certainly, they became critical when some of the town's activities called for censure. On the other hand, most colonial officers consistently saw nothing good and worthwhile in the *Asafo*.[57]

Most of the southern Ghana newspapers that, for a considerable period, operated in Cape Coast constitute another source of information and material for this book. Reports, comments, editorials, and articles shed light on coastal Ghana politics as well as politics of Cape Coast. These newspapers almost invariably represent the views of the few lucky locals with access to European education. The newspapers provide insight into their political aims and aspirations in wrangling with the colonial authorities, especially when the Aborigines' Rights Protection Society (ARPS) came into existence in 1897 in Cape Coast. The potential bias of the patrons of these newspapers raises questions about the extent to which they can be accepted as objective historical sources.[58] Equally, the Legislative Council Debate collection from 1925 to 1933 made for interesting reading, divulging vivid accounts of proceedings as members pressed home their points for and against issues on the floor of the house. Events in Cape Coast received prime attention, helping to gauge a nuanced perspective.

My quest to write popular history, or better still, social history, necessitated the tempering of written records with oral tradition. An Akan-Fanti proverb, *yɛ tua tua adwen an-saa-na yɛ abɔ pɔw*, reiterates the wisdom inherent in piecing bits of information together before coming to a conclusion. Consequently, I interviewed men and women of the Cape Coast *Asafo* for their perspectives on the history, *Asafo* system, and king list of the town. I recorded oral tradition about the origins of the Fanti peoples, Cape Coast, and indigenous institutions. These recordings constituted rich historical sources to complement written documents. The interviews equally revolved around indigenous perspectives on conflict, the place of men and women in the town's social institutions (particularly the *Asafo* and the *Ebusua* systems), and other sociocultural practices of various Akan groups.

I spent two months in the fishing community of Cape Coast interviewing men and women as well as youth. The most active members of the *Asafo* institution, who provided it with its vitality and spirit, comprised those who lived near the sea. We had interesting discussions about their acquisition of fishing skills, development of maritime culture, relationship with the sea, worldview, and so on.

Without a doubt, oral interviews have much to offer, particularly when one locates well-informed and enthusiastic collaborators in possession of memory and good judgment. My field research revealed, however, that such people are few and far between. Some earnest and enthusiastic informants reiterated the significance of cultural practices that colonial authorities sought to denigrate. They unanimously explained the value and virtues of these practices to everyday life, emphasizing the elements of continuity and change. Chronology remained a difficult exercise for most informants, as some referenced dates or years with common events in the community or in their respective families.[59] Their commitment and attachment to the traditional area and its institutions might have made them less candid in their responses to my follow-up questions, remarks, or comments. When observations tended to be quite critical of Cape Coast in general, or their respective *Asafo* in particular, they equivocated in their responses. These shortcomings notwithstanding, time spent with them proved productive and relevant.

## CHAPTER DESCRIPTIONS

Various stories of origin pertaining to the history of some coastal Ghana towns are discussed in chapter 1 to set the social, economic, and political milieu against which the main issues in *Maritime Culture and Everyday Life* unfold. The discussion gives an early hint of the nascent tension and the consequent struggle for political control between the emerging colonial rule and the indigenous establishment.

Social organizations, particularly the *Asafo* and the *Ebusua* systems as major aspects of maritime culture among Fanti societies, are explored in chapter 2. Issues of gender, identity, and their implications for inheritance, rights, and responsibilities of various groups provide an opportunity for understanding the nature and drive of the *Asafo* institution, with its penchant for conflict. The chapter facilitates a grasp of social and political institutions, including their requisite values, concepts, and expectations crucial to everyday life.

The pervasive influence of indigenous organizations, especially the *Asafo* system, in everyday life is further expatiated in chapter 3. The core of *Asafo* membership in the coastal region comprised men and women from the fishing communities. Therefore, the chapter is an account of their main means of livelihood, dispositions, as well as the sociocultural settings in which they lived and functioned. Essentially, the chapter details the worldview of these communities and how it ran through their life experiences. For an effective understanding of the system that influenced historical occurrences in coastal Ghana, a full grasp of that worldview remains relevant. For instance, the causal factors of inter-*Asafo* conflict in Cape Coast between 1860 and 1909 reveal a recurring trend that went a long way to impact relations among the locals and the colonial administration. To this end then, *Asafo* use of alcohol, provocative drum language, taunting songs, display of offensive emblems, vilification, and the active role of women in conflicts are thoroughly reviewed. Relatedly, this chapter discusses at great length two companies, *Bentsir* and *Ntsin*, the principal belligerents of the 1932 conflict that engulfed all other groups, subsequently roping in the colonial administration.

Chapter 4 discusses how time-honored expressions of dignity, sovereignty, pride, and audacity inhering property ownership underwent intriguing transformations, from the use of simple artistic features and symbols to hybrid forms, with the introduction of formal education. This chapter primarily expounds the fact that although the idea of collective ownership prevailed, it rarely ruled out the undercurrent sense of individual acquisitions as both dynamics gained elaborate expression in everyday thought and parlance. The reduction of indigenous languages into written forms, as well as the addition of English as a lingua franca in coastal Ghana through the initial facilitation of missionary and colonial authorities, proffered an unbridled freedom of style in the statement of ownership and the contentment thereof, with its attendant bragging rights. This unbending idea of property ownership underpins the land issue discussed in the subsequent chapter.

The sharp contention that arose from the introduction of the Crown Lands Bill claiming all "waste lands"—a designation the colonial government replaced after much critical challenge with "public lands"—particularly between 1894 and 1897 comes up in chapter 5. Again, the focus here is on Cape Coast, where the ARPS played a leading role. The chapter holds this land issue as one of several precedents that led to the aggravation of tension as well as deterioration of relations between the townspeople and the colonial administration. The crux of the matter hinged on the competing conceptualizations of land between the two contending parties. While the colonial government conceptualized land as part of the crucial economic and political trappings of power, the people of coastal Ghana considered land, among other things, as a cultural and religious resource that provided necessary connections with their ancestors. These considerations, in the estimation of the various societies, made land and landownership nonnegotiable issues pivotal to everyday life.

The next two chapters exhibit a thematic approach rather than a chronological contour for better understanding the issues discussed. Similar occurrences happened at different periods in the nineteenth century, and these are discussed in respective chapters. This approach helps to draw connections among underpinning factors in analogous issues across time.

The gradual and systematic assault on the chieftaincy institution and the corresponding effort to checkmate that tenacious encroachment both became factors in the intriguing issue of colonial urbanization and infrastructural development, as discussed in chapter 6. The determination of *Omanhin* Aggery to obstruct British efforts at entrenching their growing power took the uneasy relations between the people of Cape Coast, the colonial administration, and resident officers to a different level altogether.[60] Although the atrophy of chiefly power and authority started in southern Ghana well before his reign, Aggery's confrontation represented the culmination of that evolving tensity. In all these efforts, Aggery acted on his own convictions as an individual and preeminent indigenous ruler, yet in collaboration with local recipients of European education. The chapter additionally discusses the already rancorous relations between Cape Coast and the administration during the reign of *Omanhin* Mbra, as well as the politics of colonial urbanization and infrastructural development in southern Ghana, which went a long way to adversely affect Cape Coast's fortunes as a once brisk port city. The reaction and responses of the colonial administration irredeemably occasioned the emergence of conspiracy theories.

Immediate political developments in coastal Ghana preceding the 1932 clash in Cape Coast and the consequent challenges for the colonial administration are the focal issues of chapter 7. The municipal elections for representation on the new Legislative Council became the tipping point in these matters. The conflict is traced to issues arising from the implementation of colonial policies such as indirect rule, the Native Administrative Measure, and the Order-in-Council of 1925. This chapter highlights the main course of events in the conflict, placing extensive emphasis on the immediate cause of the ensuing clash. The chapter foregrounds the interface between "old" and "new" *Asafo* issues as precedent rivalries came into full display in a bid to settle scores contemporaneously. These events took place against a backdrop of perceived powerlessness, reluctance, indecision, inaction, and alleged bias on the part of local colonial officers in the face of mounting tension and pressure.

Marshaled with these chapters, *Maritime Culture and Everyday Life* establishes coastal Ghana as a relatively new historical constituency that reflects an equally unexplored historical narrative in which individuals, peoples, communities, and societies, organized under indigenous institutions, became active agents contesting and influencing the sociopolitical transformations of the era.

ONE

# SETTLEMENT AND NASCENT SOCIETY

*From Earliest Times to the Nineteenth Century*

DISTANCING THEMSELVES FROM THE RECURRING and intensive indications regarding the external origins of the Akan people, scholars such as Adu Boahen agree that the Akan bassinet remains within the confines of the area in West Africa that became modern Ghana. Boahen had this to say:

> Many hypotheses have been advanced in answer to the question of the present peoples of Ghana. Some scholars such as Eva Meyerowitz and the late J. B. Danquah think that the Akan migrated into their present area from the ancient empire of Ghana . . . Most of these hypotheses have been challenged in the light of recent historical and linguistic evidence. For instance, since the Twi . . . language . . . spoken here in Ghana is not found anywhere else in West Africa, or in the rest of the world, . . . [it] must have evolved in Ghana. And since it takes well over a thousand years for a language to develop into a complete entity of its own, its original speakers must have been in Ghana for at least a thousand years.[1]

As various Akan groups spread and settled throughout the Middlebelt and a larger part of the coastal stretch from their cradle near the confluence of the Pra and Ofin rivers, they came to constitute the largest ethnic group in the country long before the fifteenth century, when the Europeans arrived.[2] By the time of that arrival, the Akan had established a slew of hinterland as well as coastal polities, strengthened with requisite cultural and institutional traditions.

As a subsequent significant settlement in coastal Ghana, Cape Coast (similarly referred to as *Oguaa* or *Iguae*) shared, like most neighboring states, the Fanti strand of Akan identity and culture. Three popular traditions of origin—namely, the *Fetu* hunter story, the Kwamina Nimfa claim, and the *Yabiw* version—all endure as accounts of the town's beginnings. The second and third traditions scarcely come close to the popularity of the first, the uniqueness of which inheres in its possession of two variants.[3] Significantly, both renditions affirm the credibility of a Cape Coast–*Fetu* (*Effutu*) connection that remains undisputed. The original settlers of Cape Coast invariably traced their roots to the inland *Fetu* Kingdom.[4] Before the arrival of the Portuguese, the first Europeans on its shore, the town was a fishing settlement of the *Effutu* people. All Europeans who traded in the area recognized the authority of the *Fetu* king over Cape Coast. For instance, the king regularly received several pieces of cloth as payment for ships that landed at Cape Coast and would often let several months elapse for the sums of money to accumulate before collecting ground rent.[5] These allowances, more than anything else, affirmed the overlordship of the *Fetu* king.

On the coast, the larger Fanti groups encountered remnants of weaker groups, namely the *Etsii* and *Asebu*, originally part of the Guan ethnic group.[6] These assertions regarding the presences of earlier groups lend great credence to the view that the original group of people who started the Cape Coast settlement comprised an admixture of *Etsii* and Fanti. The latter eventually established hegemony over the former through sheer numbers and possession of relatively enhanced Akan social, political, religious, and military traditions and iron-working technology before the arrival of the Europeans.

The fifteenth-century Portuguese influence on this coast waned in the late sixteenth and seventeenth centuries after Dutch, French, English, and Danish challenges. When the dust of persistent inter-European rivalry settled, the English established exclusive trading rights in Cape Coast. Trade initially consisted of the exchange of linen cloth, small basins, brass pans, rum, assorted spirits, ammunition, and guns (specifically muskets) for gold, corn, fish, and other similar supplies. Most of the guns were old and unserviceable, with the remainder useful for firing salutes during indigenous military parades.[7] Before emergent commercial activities with the Europeans, transactions of sorts happened between Cape Coast and the *Fetu* Kingdom. Traders from the latter supplied corn, oil, and palm wine to the former in exchange for fish and salt.[8] However, the arrival of Europeans increased and diversified nascent economic activities.

The existence of a Fanti-established trading network with hinterland neighbors, evidently, was one of the factors that first attracted the English to that part of the southern Ghana coast.[9] Starting as a small settlement, Cape Coast increased in size to over twenty houses in the sixteenth century. Onward of the middle of the seventeenth century, the number of houses increased to about five hundred.[10] This gradual growth and expansion resulted from the eventual middleman role of Cape Coast in the trade between Europeans and the interior regions of southern Ghana. Given its emerging commercial fortunes and concomitant abounding opportunities, the town experienced an influx of people from the immediate vicinities and beyond. Moreover, with European activity (especially English) increasing in the mid-seventeenth century, Cape Coast, with its expanding layout and basic infrastructure, gradually became the most beautiful coastal town in that part of the country.[11] The town grew in importance through its position and status as a commercial center linking European trade with the network of the southern Ghana interior, indirectly extending all the way to the forest, the savanna, and the Niger and Sahel regions of West Africa.[12] With time, inland neighbors desired direct commercial contact with the Europeans for negotiable and favorable terms of trade, generating resentment of the increasing power and influence of Cape Coast as well as other coastal Fanti states.

Tension brewed between various coastal and hinterland Akan states on political and economic fronts. Wars between the Asante in the interior and the Fanti peoples on the coast occurred because of discrepant commercial interests. Fanti enclaves exploited their proximity to the Europeans on the coast and formed a buffer between the latter and the interior states. Fanti traders sold European goods in the interior, simultaneously acquiring and selling goods from the interior to the Europeans. As foreign items became increasingly expensive, the interior Akan peoples, particularly the Asante, demanded direct access to the European traders on the coast, an ultimatum that caused most of their wars with the Fanti states. The Asante quest for direct access to trade on the coast partly explains the subsequent growth and expansion of that kingdom toward the south. Politically, the Fanti people supported states such as Denkyira and Assin, both of which broke away from the Asante Kingdom. That opprobrious alliance further worsened the already rough relations between Fanti and Asante. Consequently, the Fanti states and Asante fought in 1726, 1765, 1777, and 1807, with the latter subsequently invading other states such as Akyem Abuakwa, Akuapem, and the Ga.

## COASTAL GHANA, CAPE COAST, AND THE TRANS-ATLANTIC SLAVE TRADE

All societies, peoples, and ethnicities throughout human history, across continents, have had, in one form or another, various systems of bondage and servitude. This phenomenon, often within the domain of people in positions of power, privilege, and prestige, hinges on claims to different degrees of ownership and control over certain persons as well as their labor or services. Whether individuals end up in these systems willingly due to desperate circumstances or were forced into them by such situations as failure to pay off debts, capture in warfare, or criminal charges, the ultimate rationale behind these practices invariably revolves around using them to turn a profit. As Cape Coast and, therefore, coastal Ghana expanded and became socioeconomically complex, systems of bondage and servitude became apparent even well before the late fifteenth century. Such socioeconomic arrangements, practices, and structures favored indigenous royal families, rulers, and well-placed families as well as individuals. Subsequently, designations such as *dɔn-kɔ* (plural *adɔn-kɔ-fo* or *ndɔn-kɔ-fo*) and *abaa-wa* (plural *mbaa-wa* or *mbaa-wa-fo*), all referring to enslaved people, came into usage. Although an issue not frequently discussed, well-informed elders could point to certain family houses and give names of individuals who benefited from those systems. These local systems found leveraging linkages with the trans-Atlantic slave trade when the emergence of plantation economies in the Americas unleashed the incessant labor imperative. In the history of Cape Coast, *Obrempong* Kojo often comes up as one beneficiary, quite well-connected and high in the realms of local power, who enjoyed unhindered access to the Europeans with whom he traded.[13] In other coastal Fanti towns, these individuals included John Kabes, John Konny, and Eno Baisie Kurentsi.[14]

While war captives heavily fed this trade, other sources included banditry, *panyarrring*, and *pawnship*.[15] *Panyarring*, meaning "seize or capture," is derived from the Portuguese word *penhorar*, quite like *penhor*, translated as "pawn, pledge, or surety." Hence, *panyarring* involved a trader or creditor temporarily seizing a person or persons from the household of a defaulter as collateral for the payment of debt. The practice of *pawnship*, alternatively, had to do with a principal person handing over a family member or other dependent as surety in advance of credit.[16]

Both Africans and Europeans practiced *panyarring* and *pawnship*. In 1775, David Mill explained the centrality of *panyarring* to both credit-advancing company traders and their African clients: "Every Dutch or English Chief makes a practice of trusting and selling Blacks with goods just as convenience suits him without regarding whether the people who make them are his subjects or not; and in case of not receiving payment, makes no scruple of *panyarring*: thus, the General at Elmina will sell or trust goods to a Cape Coast man and *panyar*, if not paid and vice versa. I will do the same ... the practice was always used."[17]

In the history of the trans-Atlantic slave trade, the role of coastal Ghana remains curious, perhaps (and justifiably so) given the fact that the country became preferred for the erection of European fortifications over any other site in West Africa. The shoreline of the country had thirty or so castles and forts that competing European trading nations built at different times beginning in the late fifteenth century. Fluttering flags of the Portuguese, Dutch, Danes, Swedes, Brandenburg-Prussians, and English identified the spheres of influence of their respective trading nations and companies.[18] These fortifications are inextricably associated with slave trade across the Atlantic to the Americas. However, the extent to which European trading entities obtained and maintained castles and forts along coastal Ghana equally accentuates the measurable economic significance and potential of this West African country. Before coastal Ghana became enmeshed in the trans-Atlantic slave trade in 1650, its possession of enormous gold deposits had become common knowledge among Europeans.[19] The "Gold Coast" as a nominal reference—along with other names such as "Ivory Coast," "Grain Coast," and "Slave Coast"—gained currency due to the tendency of early European traders to designate African shorelines according to the accruing principal commodities from the respective settlements. Indeed, these designations served as European traders' guide oblivious to indigenous place names. Furthermore, these convenient European names hardly precluded trade in commodities other than the principal ones commonly associated with each settlement. For instance, Europeans additionally secured supplies of ivory, pepper, salt, lime juice, and much more from southern Ghana.

The time-honored association of this part of West Africa with gold broaches yet another important strand in Ghana's long and tortuous history with the trans-Atlantic slave trade, as well as the emergence of an African diaspora across the continent itself.[20] Coastal Ghana served as a destination for captive Africans in the same way receiving ports in the Americas did. Portuguese traders brought captives from the Kingdom of Benin and other places in western central Africa to the country in response to the heavy labor imperative of their nascent gold mining operations. Gwendolyn M. Hall avers that "before 1650, the Gold Coast and the Slave Coast were insignificant sources of slaves for the Americas. The Gold Coast was a primary market for the sale of enslaved Africans within."[21] Hall adds that "in 1493, Portugal sent about 2000 Jewish children under the age of eight, both female and male, to Sao Tome.... Between 1595 and 1640, Portugal held the asiento (contract) to supply African slaves to Spanish colonies.... Greater Senegambia and West Central Africa were the only significant regions of origin for the transatlantic slave trade before 1650. Many enslaved Africans were brought from the interior, especially after 1650, when the Dutch, English, and French transatlantic slave traders became well established."[22]

After 1650, coastal Ghana consistently supplied captive Africans to the larger trans-Atlantic slave trade from some, if not all, of the many European fortifications on its shoreline. Often associated with this infamous trade are the Christiansborg Castle in Accra, Cape Coast Castle, Elmina Castle, and Anomabo Fort, as well as Fort Amsterdam in the twin towns of Kromantsi and Abandze.[23] Of all these places, Anomabo possessed preeminent record as the point of departure for more captives than any other coastal town.[24] Having found the best beach for landing purposes, the British Company of Merchants Trading to Africa constructed the sizable Anomabo Fort (also known as Fort Charles) in 1674, and after its destruction, the British built Fort William in 1753 exclusively to facilitate participation in the trans-Atlantic slave trade.[25] On the southern Ghana coast between 1662 and 1863, Anomabo and Cape Coast accounted for 76 percent of departures. With Elmina included, an estimated 83 percent went through these three towns.[26] On a larger scale, the country supplied about 11 percent of the total number of captives shipped during the entire duration of the trade, a majority of whom ended up in the Caribbean, particularly in Jamaica and the British West Indies rather than in North America.[27] Considering that coastal Ghana had a greater number of European castles and forts than any country in West Africa, the relatively small percentage of its supply of captives to the trans-Atlantic slave trade remains intriguing. Therefore, southern Ghana, relative to other places in West Africa, stood in the long run as a more significant commodity trade center than slave trading port. On both counts, the Cape Coast Castle, as well as other fortifications on the southern Ghana coast, became unmistakably prominent.[28]

As the plantation economy in the Americas unleashed an insatiable demand for labor, the trading posts, lodges, and forts that various European nations had built, some of which over the years received accretions and facelifts into castles as strongholds for residential and commercial purposes, became captive trading centers.[29] At Cape Coast, the Dutch sought and acquired the use of a rocky promontory on which the Portuguese had started a building project; subsequently, the English came to own this structure. The edifice eventually became known as the Cape Coast Castle, described then as the most beautiful building on the coast.[30] The structure had a unique triangular base with high, round towers projecting out at the three major points. Spacious rooms, halls, and courtyards gave the building a broad and imposing look from within and without. Basement spaces underneath the spacious rooms and halls, particularly facing the seaward direction, had originally been planned as storage and warehouses with neither windows nor provision for light. They subsequently found prominent usage as dungeons where captives would wait for ships to take them across the Middle Passage to the Americas and Europe during the trans-Atlantic slave trade. The high, round towers, thick walls, and heavy cannons facing the Atlantic Ocean added to the castle's almost impregnable construction. These ready armaments served the purpose of warding off enemy European maritime attacks and discouraging unwanted intrusions from competing traders. Two other forts, Victoria and William, situated on higher ground away from the beach, offered additional security from their commanding view of the ocean, town, and other interior approaches. These well-garrisoned forts also boasted towering circular walls armed with cannons intended as both intimidating and defensive mechanisms against local inhabitants and rival Europeans.[31]

Up to the eighteenth century, guns and gunpowder featured prominently in transactions between European merchants and their African customers, especially kings, chiefs, and states, as well as powerful individuals and groups. The prominence of this factor in the trans-Atlantic slave trade imposed a degree of heavy demand from merchants on European gun manufacturers.[32] Although English merchants supplied an annual quantity of between 150,000 and 200,000 guns, other European traders provided as many guns per unit of payment for goods purchased.[33] As the English controlled about 45 percent of the slave trade, the total number of guns imported into the West coast of Africa came to a quantity in the neighborhood of 333,000 and 444,000 per annum in the second half of the eighteenth century.[34] Many of these guns ended up in regions on the Guinea coast that particularly participated in the trans-Atlantic slave trade, especially the Senegambia, Sierra Leone, the Windward Coast, Bonny, Calabar, Cameroon, Congo, and Loango. The dynamic of preference for

Fig. 1.1 Front view of the Cape Coast Castle.

Fig. 1.2 The inland Fort William served as a lighthouse on a hill not quite one mile away from the Cape Coast Castle on the beach. Courtesy of Charles Ebow Jonah and Thomas Ekow Stephens.

firearms in these areas reified the strong connection between guns and the acquisition of captives. For instance, while Bonny (between the Bight of Benin and Calabar) expended 5.7 guns per captive, and the Windward Coast boasted 4.6 for the same, southern Ghana averaged 2.5 guns per enslaved person.[35] Along the southern Ghana coast, preferred firearms included square, round, and London muskets, as well as Danish, birding, militia, buccaneer, and tower guns.[36]

## A SOCIETY IN TRANSITION

Beyond being curious physical structures of great proportion in Cape Coast, the fortifications impacted the local population. The presence of these constructions eventually found expression in the local parlance, owing to their monstrous size and, later, political significance. The word *A-ban* or *Ban* in Fanti metaphorically refers to monumental and impregnable fortifications. *Aban* acquired another connotation as a metonymy of the colonial political establishment for which the castle served as the main headquarters. That the establishment would seek to regulate the everyday life of coastal communities, requiring considerable opposition on the part of townspeople, made the presence of those fortifications doubly impactful.

The initial relations between the people of Cape Coast and the English, as well as other Europeans, centered on the commercial imperative. The Europeans paid rent on their various forts, trusted in the goodwill of their hosts for peaceful trade, and often cooperated with them to fend off invaders. The Europeans depended considerably on the local people for a wide range of services, such as those of canoe men, laborers, and domestic servants, as well as for existential necessities including food, water, and fuel wood. The intensity of European commercial competition offered a strong bargaining chip to local traders, enabling them to take advantage of the situation just as the Europeans exploited local political divisions. In view of the enormous exigencies of trade on the coast, the blatant show of European military might initially had little application.

By the end of the eighteenth century, Cape Coast had become one of the few termini of the wealth that emanated from the exchange of hinterland southern Ghana commodities and foreign goods. Well into the nineteenth century, the town became the primary port of call for English merchants. In the absence of technically constructed harbors, sailing ships anchored some safe distance at sea, while local canoe men battled their way through intense breakers to reach them and help Europeans disembark.[37] Conveying goods to and from waiting ships proffered a lucrative venture for fishermen and others with requisite expertise. Moreover, in the absence of a network of paved roads and motor vehicles, goods needed to be carried on people's heads over narrow bush paths for long distances to desired destinations, often in the hinterland regions. This situation obviously provided diverse work opportunities and appreciable remuneration for the people of Cape Coast and neighboring societies.

In the last quarter of the nineteenth century, after the abolition of the trans-Atlantic slave trade, the introduction of legitimate trade led to intensive commercial cash crop production in the interior of the country. This trade further enhanced the economy of Cape Coast, as most exports passed through its port.[38] Specifically, these exports included dye woods, palm oil, peanut oil, kola nuts, animal skins, palm kernel, rubber, and cocoa. Ivory, gold nuggets, and gold dust remained perennial items of exports. Intensive cocoa cultivation in the first two decades of the twentieth century ensured the growth of economic activities in the port. Some imports into the country came through the town during the same period.[39] These imports included agricultural or gardening implements, ale, beer, porter, apparels, boots, shoes, caps, hats, bags, sacks, beads, beef, pork, brass, copperware, bread, biscuits, building materials, cement, lime, enamelware, flour, firearms (flintlock guns and ammunition), furniture, glassware, hardware, and cutlery. Other foreign items comprised machinery, aerated water, oils, kerosene, lubricating oils, perfumery, provisions, rice, silk goods, spirits, tobacco, cigarettes, cigars, vehicles (motor cars and lorry parts), and wines. Out of the country's the four principal ports, Cape Coast handled over 5 percent of the total import and export transactions close to the 1920s.[40]

Many people from the neighboring coastal towns and hinterlands traveled to and lived in Cape Coast, seeking employment opportunities in a variety of ventures, but mainly as porters. As a register of this emerging employment trend, the town acquired the accolade as a district "where so many carriers were employed."[41] Further evidence of trade as well as blossoming economic activities in the late nineteenth and early twentieth centuries manifested in the presence of commercial firms such as the Royal African Company, F & A Swanzy, and the Elder Dempster Shipping Lines, all of which did brisk business in the town.[42] This period marked the mercantile capitalism phase in the development of Cape Coast as a trading post of note on the West African littoral.[43] In addition to the European commercial presence, the town boasted many government departments and local firms. However, trading progressively became the predominant economic activity, making Cape Coast one of the oldest cosmopolitan centers in coastal Ghana. It accounted for the highest percentage—approximately 30.29—of people involved in buying and selling, with 24.04 for Accra.[44] Essentially, these developments accentuated the indigenous name for Cape Coast, *Oguaa* or *Iguae*, which means market.

With trade and locally accessible European educational opportunities, a new group of people emerged as the bearers of commercial and intellectual power in Cape Coast.[45] This group formed a growing and formidable alternative to the indigenous political elite, although not necessarily its rival (as the situation pertained elsewhere in southern Ghana). Small-scale indigenous traders who seized the new commercial opportunities comprised men and women possessing the capacity and requisite resources for obtaining credit from European merchants. Some of these traders gained great local political advancement through their connections and associations. This emergent group of traders included local women who became influential in their respective societies. Most of them depended on local kinship connections to benefit from their relationship with European merchants. Adept at trading as well as keeping accounts, several of these women took charge of businesses for months while their merchant partners traveled to Europe on vacation.

### ESTABLISHMENT OF FORMAL EDUCATION

Members of the indigenous commercial elite encouraged their children to acquire education in emerging European schools established locally, with all their associated benefits and opportunities. Acquisition of formal education became imperative after an economic depression between 1858 and 1860 caused a decline in the palm oil trade, a major component of the coastal Ghana commerce with Europe that had offered great means of social advancement. The need for formal education grew as the depression made it twice as hard for new entrants in the field to obtain credit from British traders on the coast.[46] This kind of education, however, rarely remained the exclusive preserve of children of the local commercial elite. Most, if not all, of the European traders who resided in Cape Coast also impressed on their progeny from unions and cohabitation with local women to seek formal education. The introduction and patronage of these schools laid the foundation for later developments in education throughout southern Ghana.[47]

Formal education originated as an unintended outcome of missionary activities in the country. For converts to grow as active Christians and exhibit meaningful commitment to the new faith, facilitation of literacy skills was imperative. Therefore, some early missionaries made provisions for this type of education locally. They later helped a few of the converts to travel to Europe for further studies to become missionaries themselves. In the middle of the eighteenth century, the Society for the Propagation of the Gospel (SPG) took Philip Quaque, a Cape Coast indigene, to England for missionary education and training to help with local evangelization efforts. He traveled in the company of two compatriots who died abroad. Quaque returned as the first non-European ordained in the Anglican religious organization in coastal Ghana.[48] In that context, his efforts laid the foundation for the expansion of formal education in Cape Coast. The outstanding contribution of Quaque enabled the reestablishment of the defunct Castle School that Reverend Thomas Thompson, the first resident English minister of the town, had started in 1750. After many difficulties, Quaque's sacrifices bore fruit; the number of schools increased in the nineteenth century. Eventually, the Wesleyan Collegiate School, established in 1876, further deepened the roots of formal education.

The first generation of beneficiaries of these schools in Cape Coast, though modest in number, had acclaimed achievement and influence. John Mensah Sarbah, the most prominent of this group, became the first professional lawyer in the town—and all of southern Ghana—in 1887.[49] His success set the standard for the next generation of formally educated individuals, including Joseph E. Casley Hayford and W. E. G. Se-kyi (otherwise known as Kobina Sekyi), both of whom became celebrated lawyers as well. Growing interest in legal studies opened another avenue for social mobility, partly because of the profession's absence of restrictions, as requisite conditions were based on aptitude and ability to pay for the education. Most lawyers in southern Ghana, like Mensah Sarbah, earned calls to the English bar because the growing tradition of obtaining an education in the country had hardly advanced to a professional training level. The growing number of individuals with certified legal knowledge became well placed to serve as the articulate mouthpiece of society. Legal training honed the capacity to read closely just as much as it proffered the skill to critically analyze documents, gazettes, and official correspondence. Furthermore, professional training, social standing, and reputation gave these individuals considerable confidence in engaging and contending with the fledgling colonial establishment.

The educated elite of Cape Coast increasingly cultivated a larger vision rooted in the need to devise a system of indigenous instruction that would meld formal education and specific local needs. Considering this inspiration, the acquisition of formal education, in a sense, hardly alienated beneficiaries from their culture and society. They believed that the quest for knowledge had great implications for cultural transmission—with the caveat that an indiscriminate adoption of a foreign educational system would be a disservice to their culture. Mensah Sarbah and others in his category founded the *Mfantsi* National Educational Fund for the purpose of establishing secondary schools in which liberal arts and technical subjects would be studied simultaneously, with an infusion of indigenous knowledge in the curriculum for students to learn to read and write Fanti.[50]

The founders hoped that indigenous studies would lead to the eventual creation of a Fanti literature and, at the national level, instruction in the nation's history and social institutions. Three years after creating the educational fund, Mensah Sarbah and his colleagues succeeded in opening a school in Cape Coast that later amalgamated with the Wesleyan Collegiate School under the new name Mfantsipim School, becoming the first of its kind in the provision of a competitive secondary school level education.[51] Well into the late nineteenth and early twentieth centuries, the town had the highest student population in the country.[52]

The subsequent intellectual ferment led to the formation, growth, and proliferation of clubs and societies for the enhancement of social commingling and the forging of common interests. Below are some of the instances of the increasing number of coteries. J. P. Brown and some of his friends formed the Try Company, a private literary club, in 1859.[53] The Reading Room Club, the first of its kind on the coast, opened in 1860.[54] The Gold Coast Debating Society came into existence, with the objective of educating members on the principles and tenets of cogent argumentation and critical thinking. Furthermore, some people started self-help and mutual improvement groups, leading to the establishment of the Star of Peace Society, a small study circle for young people, in 1895.[55] A few social groups for women also came into operation, including the Young Ladies' Christian Association and the Ladies' Mutual Club in 1904. This intellectual influence further became evident in the practice of book borrowing. A few avid readers managed to acquire personal collections and offered others the option of borrowing copies of popular and rare books. For a long time, these private collections and the kind gesture of their owners remained great resources for the burgeoning intellectual ferment.

Publication of newspapers became yet another factor enhancing social interaction and awareness through the spreading of information. Notable newspapers included the *West African Herald*, belonging to the Bannerman brothers (Charles and Edmund), and the *Christian Messenger and Examiner*, which had J. B. Freeman and Reverend H. Wharton as editors. James Hutton Brew launched the *Gold Coast Times* on March 28, 1874; the *Western Echo* became his second print media, with J. E. Casley Hayford, his nephew, as assistant. The Gold Coast Aborigines' Rights Protection Society (ARPS) founded the *Gold Coast Aborigines* newspaper with Attoh Ahuma and Reverend Egyir Asaam as editor and manager respectively. The *Gold Coast Leader*, one of the most popular newspapers, became associated with J. E. Casely Hayford, Herbert Brown, and Dr. Savage. Other publications included the *Gold Coast Methodist Times*, the *Gold Coast Methodist*, the *Gold Coast People*, and the *Gold Coast Nation*. For a considerable length of time, Cape Coast remained the place of choice for newspaper publications, deepening its track record as an outlet for popular opinion throughout coastal Ghana. The *Gold Coast Times* editorial of 1874 offers the best expression of the main objectives for the proliferation of these newspapers: "We shall always offer our adherence to the popular view of matters in so far as we can conscientiously believe that we are acting in their interest, advocating their rights but in instances where these rights and interests of the people are disregarded, and attempts are made to tamper with them, and to put them down with a high hand, we shall be found at our post, prepared to perform our duty fearlessly and independently, regardless of the frowns of the King or Kaiser."[56]

The raison d'être of these newspapers accentuated their uncompromising goal of protecting time-honored indigenous customs and institutions from the ravages of colonization. These sentiments engendered a strong sense of cultural consciousness among many recipients of European education, who garnered great respect and recognition among the larger portion of the town population, most of whom had not had such opportunities. To that effect, the *Mfantsi Amanbu Fekuw*, or Fanti National Political Society, came into existence in 1902 as an effort to mitigate and neutralize the demoralizing effects of certain European influences. Furthermore, some Fanti educated elite undertook a discussion and compilation of indigenous proverbs, customs, and laws together with important institutions. Series of articles on these subjects came up for publication in the newspapers, an effort that increasingly accentuated the determination of the educated elite to identify with local customs and institutions, earning the trust of their unlettered compatriots. This trust went a long way to enhance their authority and reputation among their people. Relatedly, well into the late nineteenth and early twentieth centuries, the seven *Asafo* companies of Cape Coast had an appreciable number of educated individuals as active members, with some in prominent positions.[57]

## THE GROWTH OF BRITISH POWER AND RESPONSE OF CHIEFS

Imperatives of trade came to underpin the expansion of British power that gained momentum after 1874 in Cape Coast. War never broke out between the people of the town and the British, making the typical victor-vanquished relationship largely inapplicable. Maintaining relatively peaceful relations was paramount, providing the conditions around which the expansion of British power in Cape Coast and other parts of coastal Ghana transpired. Captain George Maclean started his tenure in the town as an employee of local British merchants with the mandate, among other things, to secure British interest through uninterrupted trade. The strategy Maclean adopted, though not necessarily in conflict with his mandate, spelled doom for the indigenous political system of Cape Coast, laying the foundation for eventual tension and the concomitant local response. In the face of limited resources and ill-defined power, the diplomatic skills of Maclean, hinging on his charismatic and charming personality, came in handy.[58] As warfare proved antithetical to trade, and given the hinterland Asante prowess at waging war, Maclean brokered a peace treaty.[59] To balance the equation, he turned his attention to petty squabbles among the coastal societies and made them sign peace treaties revolving around issues of rules and regulations for the better protection and promotion of convenient commerce.[60] The crucial clause in that arrangement hinged on making the governor of the castle the arbiter in all matters among the signatory chiefs. Against this background of keeping the peace for the express purpose of maintaining trade, Maclean laid the foundation for what would become full British control of the country. His methods of putting in place an alternative system of justice would go a long way to detract from the power and authority of local kings and chiefs.

A pragmatic strategist, Maclean drew on his prior experience in coastal Ghana. In 1827, as an officer of the Third West Indian Regiment, he had accompanied Colonel Lumley, a commander in charge of British forces, to the hinterland as military secretary. Based on knowledge accrued during that time, Maclean understood how a single threat to peace could escalate and create a complex conflict because of various indigenous political alliances.[61] Using a small troop from the Gold Coast Corps, he gathered intelligence on potential disputes, no matter how small, that could disrupt trade.⁶² Maclean wasted no time in inviting disputing parties to settle issues and, in some cases, allowed commandants of other forts to handle cases within their respective areas of operation.⁶³ Even though this arrangement had long-term benefits for the British, some officials viewed it with great disapproval, particularly regarding the hearing of cases outside of the forts and castles. A British parliamentary select committee made the following observation: "A kind of irregular jurisdiction has grown up extending itself far beyond the limits of the forts... and that, magistrates are strictly prohibited from exercising jurisdiction even over the natives and districts immediately under the influence and protection of the forts... All jurisdictions over the natives beyond that point must, therefore, be considered as optional, and should be made the subject of distinct agreement, as to its nature and limits, with the native chiefs."⁶⁴

Accordingly, accusations and counteraccusations issuing from a small group of British officials in coastal Ghana stalled Maclean's administration and political career. The select committee that investigated these accusations, nonetheless, commended him: "We fully admit the merits of that administration, whether we look to the officer employed, Captain Maclean, or to the Committee under whom he had acted, which, with the miserable pittance of between £3,500 and £4,000 a year, has exercised from the four... forts... manned by a few ill-paid... soldiers, a very wholesome influence over... [the] coast, and to considerable distance inland... maintaining peace and security... We would give full weight to the doubts which Captain Maclean entertained as to his authority."⁶⁵

The committee reiterated that the initial jurisdiction of British law remained exclusively within the fortifications and that although the Maclean arrangement seemed irregular, Maclean had gained the consent and cooperation of chiefs without the interposition of force.⁶⁶ The committee further warned that the extension of British jurisdiction outside the perimeter of the forts must be an optional matter of expressed agreement with the chiefs, conducive to the conditions of the respective peoples and their settlements. Finally, the committee expressed the foreboding that any violation of its recommendations would unleash a new system bound to incur the displeasure of the various societies.

Based on that report, the British government confirmed Maclean as judicial officer with minimal extraterritorial jurisdiction, while Commander H. W. Hill became lieutenant governor over the castle. The appointment of Hill undoubtedly made Maclean a subordinate and, worse, consigned him to the background.[67] Commander Hill took advantage of a courtesy call from some chiefs to persuade them to sign what became the controversial Bond of 1844. In principle, the new bond amounted to nothing more than a rehashing of the agreement previously signed with Maclean. With a strict emphasis on cooperation and collaboration, the agreement stated that all consequential cases would be tried in the presence of judicial officers and chiefs, without any indication whatsoever that the latter might submit or relinquish their sovereignty. The bond essentially elaborated on ensuring peace for the purpose of maintaining the free flow of trade. The chiefs never gave up the responsibility and duty to hold their own courts. The pertinent questions or qualms unmentioned in the bond included the following issues: If the British, through the judicial officers, acquired rights of protection over them and their people, what would be the consequence of a chief repudiating the British rights of protection? What constituted the precise extent of the rights conceded to the British if anything of that sort happened? Did the treaties of agreement, trade, and protection mean a surrender of the right of the chiefs to govern their states according to accepted indigenous norms and practices?

Although the system that Maclean introduced would eventually limit the power and authority of indigenous rulers, it certainly had innocuous beginnings. Apart from King Joseph Aggery of Cape Coast, in whose territory the British operated, other chiefs of coastal Ghana appreciated the efforts of Maclean at ensuring peace.[68] The clause on magistrates consulting experienced British judicial officers who understood indigenous laws, beliefs, and practices made the proposition appealing to some chiefs. Most Europeans who acted as magistrates were long-time residents of the coast, proficient in Fanti, possessing notable (albeit differing degrees of) competence in indigenous laws, beliefs, and practices.[69] Initially, these British officials behaved respectfully toward the chiefs who sat with them on cases, demonstrating willingness to listen and learn. Francis Swanzy, a resident European merchant, indicated that his proficiency in the Fanti language and law gained currency among the local people. Additionally, given his competence as a magistrate, many ordinary people brought cases to him. A formidable knowledge of Fanti law, culture, and language remained crucial to make any sense of testimonies of witnesses in various cases. Notably, because Fanti men and women knew their indigenous laws and customs absolutely, they could assess the competency of European magistrates.[70]

## ENCROACHMENT: EVERYDAY LIFE AND CUSTOMARY RITE PERFORMANCES

The promising progress of local and European magistrates under the British judicial officers suffered a setback because ordinary people increasingly patronized English courts in Cape Coast. This patronage presented a welcome opportunity for the British administration to extend its influence on other areas of local life, resulting in an unprecedented encroachment on the power of chiefs. Still using the assurance of peace as a trump card, British judicial officers and their magistrates began to adjudicate cases emanating from everyday interactions. These infringements became incessant, since the English courts, unlike their indigenous equivalents, came across as inexpensive and convenient. The indigenous courts demanded strict observance of the local etiquette of gift giving to chiefs and palace officials in the form of drinks, sheep, chicken, and/or money, exclusive of fees as well as fines. These extra expenses stemmed from a local adage, *wɔ nn-fa nsa pan nn-kɔ Ahen-fie*, that advised individuals seeking adjudication at a traditional palace to bear gifts in hand. In comparison, English courts charged only the costs of summons, which invariably amounted to a small sum. The reasonable fees made the English courts attractive, particularly to the poor.

Records of court judgments in Cape Coast and Anomabu indicate that besides consequential cases, an overwhelming number of cases dealt with minor disputes, especially in the matter of debt settlement. Of the eighty-eight cases in one particular year, only seven involved serious crimes; sixty-one involved debts, with the remainder being miscellaneous issues. In subsequent years, the number of cases increased to one hundred twenty-eight, of which ninety-one involved debts, all involving small amounts of money.[71] Pertaining to the initial agreement the chiefs had with Maclean, such cases fell squarely within the jurisdiction of the indigenous courts. However, all these cases, in addition to domestic complaints, minor assaults, disputes over *adɔn-kɔfo na mbaa-wa* (people held in one form of bondage and servitude or another), including complaints of these people against their *ewura nom* (to wit, owners, lords, or masters), increasingly came up for determination in the English courts.

The preference of some ordinary people for this emerging alternative justice system resulted in the growth and influence of English courts, to the extent that a few people even forced the trial of local cases on the magistrates.[72] With the subsequent appointment of new British magistrates under Commander Hill, the good will and mutual respect among chiefs and European magistrates began to deteriorate. The new crop of magistrates simply lacked the requisite local experience; to make matters worse, they overzealously attempted to do their duty. Consequently, the British influence expanded, much to the chagrin of the chiefs. Cruickshank, one of the old group of magistrates, described the emerging system as a "new British establishment."[73] Given the increasing number of cases and the growing popularity of English courts, this new establishment knew no bounds. With the arrival of Colonial Office personnel following the departure of most of the old British residents, the English courts became equally colonial in character. Whereas English magistrates in the past had sat in judgment with the chiefs, and both groups had assisted each other in the administration of justice, a rather troubling system emerged under the new dispensation.[74] Instead of being assistants and advisers, judicial officers exploited their accorded deference to elevate themselves to the level of supreme judicial authority, even in cases involving purely indigenous customary laws.[75] The magistrates frequently held their courts without the presence of a single chief or indigenous ruler.[76]

This interference amounted to a brash usurpation and provided a ripe recipe for confrontation. The Draft Report of the British Parliamentary Select Committee on Africa elaborated on the curious shift in the original intention of judicial officers tasked with assisting chiefs in the administration of justice.[77] The report pointed out that the magistrates had indeed superseded the authority of chiefs through their unilateral decisions and judgments. That judicial office, initiated with the best of intentions, also led to the gradual introduction of needless technicalities with its attendant expenditure, such as hiring of attorneys in situations where people could conveniently speak for themselves. These emergent formalities made the British courts equally expensive. The select committee recommended that the chiefs be left to adjudicate within their own jurisdictions, with the potential of appeals to English courts as and when called for. It further stated that the use of advocates of the Queen seemed wholly unnecessary, with jury trials described as inappropriate in many cases. These recommendations scarcely saw the light of day, as the local British authorities abandoned them. James Swanzy, who had served as a magistrate under Maclean, later confirmed the shift in operation, observing that, during his tenure, he had considered himself an assistant to the chief. Unfortunately, the new dispensation clearly took power away from the chiefs. Swanzy opined that the usurpation emanated from a desire for power, coupled with an ignorance of the rights of chiefs on the part of the new group of British officials.

Another occurrence that marred the relationship between British officials and chiefs, together with the people of Cape Coast, revolved around the vexatious question of a poll tax that caused general uproar with widespread consequences in coastal Ghana. Worse yet for the people of Cape Coast, the colonial government flagged them as instrumental in the obstruction and subsequent abandonment of the tax.[78] To regularize and systematize his administration, Governor Hill convinced some coastal chiefs, along with others from the immediate hinterland, to agree to the levying of a tax of one shilling per individual. The proposed imposition earned classification as part of their responsibility for protection under the Queen of Britain and for infrastructural investment in the transportation, port, education, and health sectors.

The promise of these benefits, with their pivotal nature for the emerging times, persuaded the chiefs to consent to the proposal. They acquiesced in the understanding that power to impose the tax, determine the amount, and collect it would remain their sole responsibility, with minimal interference from the governor. The chiefs equally secured the promise of a small percentage of the tax for their efforts and support in the administration of the tax regime. However, for many chiefs, the most crucial clause hinged on the application of the net fund to "the public good in education of the people, in the general improvement and extension of the judicial system, in affording greater facilities of internal communication, increased medical aid, and in such other measures of improvement and utility as the state of social progress may render necessary, and that the chiefs be informed of the mode of its application ... entitled to offer suggestions on this point as they may consider necessary."[79]

Fraught with problems even at the planning stage, the poll tax encountered many difficulties. Governor Hill had envisaged annual total revenues well over £15,000. The tax managed to rope in a total of about £7,567 during its peak period, woefully less than the anticipated amount. At times, this amount shrunk to £3,625 and dwindled to a trickle in its worst years.[80] Hence, the taxes accrued fell far below the expected income, as collection expenses and compensation payments to chiefs eroded the real value.[81] Consequently, the governor and his officials took over the administration of the fund; this usurpation amounted to a clear violation of the rights and responsibilities of the chiefs as stipulated in the Poll Tax Ordinance.[82] The governor assumed sole responsibility and only informed the Colonial Office of the expenditures. Compensations to chiefs fell far behind schedule, and the fund had little to show in terms of the anticipated infrastructural projects.

To the extent that chiefs' consent gave currency to the tax regime, the cooperation and participation of the chiefs remained crucial for its sustainability. However, they became the first to oppose the scheme in view of its maladministration, even questioning the actual principle of taxation. When the chiefs of Cape Coast refused to pay the tax, their counterparts in disparate parts of the country followed suit. Admitting that they had originally supported the tax, the chiefs pointed out that they had acquiesced in the hope that it would be beneficial to the public good. They proceeded to list the miscarriages of the tax regime and reiterated the withdrawal of their participation in its collection.[83] Consequent to the pivotal influence of Cape Coast, similar opposition to the tax became popular across the country. The outbreak of general resentment irked Governor Andrew, whose reaction hardly escaped the attention of the chiefs. In a letter to the secretary of state for colonies, they observed that "because the whole country has reason to object to pay the Poll Tax any longer, the Governor is angry with us. But we will take care this time that no Governor makes us fools."[84] As though to taunt the administration about its failure to deliver on the numerous promises, they further released a litany of queries: "Where are the new streets that have been built of stone and lime? What had been the state of the roads between Cape Coast and Anomabu and their adjacent villages? Where is the European schoolmaster and his wife? How many ... have learnt to become physicians; and how many have been sent to England for education? What are the names of the chiefs and captains who were present before the proceeds of the taxes were distributed to the officers and commandants? Where is the wharf built? And where is the crane?"[85]

The establishment of the Supreme Court in Cape Coast for the purpose of dealing with British maritime cases and cases involving British citizens on the coast aggravated the situation, especially with the appointment of Chief Justice Henry Connor, who had little knowledge of Fanti laws and customary practices. Under the watch of Connor, the colonial authorities hauled residents of Cape Coast before the Supreme Court and tried them in accordance with British law. These arrests made the administration of the area more problematic and "occasioned discontent ... as native cases came before our courts which purely British tribunals ought not to entertain."[86]

The two systems of British judiciary in Cape Coast had become muddied and indistinct. Consequently, the indigenous courts hardly received any cases, making the chiefs suffer serious dents in prestige and income. James Bannerman acknowledged the seriousness of the situation for Cape Coast chiefs in his letter to Earl Grey. Because the town played host to British judicial officers, the Supreme Court, and several magistrates, ordinary people had ample choices in deciding where to take their cases. These opportunities meant fewer cases for the indigenous courts and dwindling sources of revenue for the chiefs. With the passage of time, chiefs endured trifling and irregular fees as well as diminishing judicial authority.[87]

The general attitude of the new crop of British officials, who became notorious for their lack of interest and readiness to learn, further exacerbated emotions. They had no time to interlace the customs of the country with British laws, as envisaged in the Bond of 1844. Poised to promote and enforce British laws, the new officials considered the indigenous culture irrelevant. Intolerant of the interests of others, some governors tried to regulate local practices that they or other officials personally found unsuitable and annoying.

The residential preference of William Hackett, as acting governor, acted as a catalyst for that kind of conflict. He moved from the English castle in Cape Coast to live within the precinct of the town, signifying a physical and spatial accretion of British power. Previously, British authority had remained strictly within the confines of the castle walls. In a letter to his superiors in London, Hackett observed that, although the relocation appeared questionable, he found it expedient not to seek the consent of the chiefs, described as "naturally suspicious."[88] Hackett's comment about governors of the castle having, for several years, considered the lands of Cape Coast as the property of the Crown come across as particularly revealing and portentous.

The blatant relocation of the British establishment within the precincts of the town created inviting avenues for officials to make interpositions in indigenous ways of life they deemed repugnant. Along these lines, local funerals rites described as "noisy and rowdy" came up for sharp criticism, regulation, and sanction. Celebrated with pomp and mourning, the duration of funerals depended on the socioeconomic status and connections of the deceased, not ruling out those of the bereaved families as well as their specific preferences for the departed. These considerations could mean three to seven days of mourning, drumming, singing, dancing, and elaborate gun salutes, particularly if the deceased belonged to the royal family, upper echelon of palace officials, or was a high-ranking member of an *Asafo* company. Governor Pine set out to reduce "noise making" with the application of rules and regulations to the organization of funerals. According to him, funeral rites for important chiefs should not exceed three days, with two days for subordinate chiefs. Funerals for ordinary persons had to be dismissed within a day and no more.[89] Regarding time specifications, Pine decreed that the written permission of a British senior officer "shall be obtained ... and no custom shall be made after 8 o'clock at night or before 5 o'clock in the morning."[90] The people of Cape Coast largely ignored the Pine proclamation; their observation of funerals remained a meaningful and revered way of honoring departed relatives, and so the celebrations went on with impunity. The chiefs unleashed a barrage of criticism against Governor Pine for failing to consult them, deriding that he issued the proclamation with great disdain for requisite mutual agreement.[91] They noted that the attempt to enforce these regulations, far from being a matter of law, bordered on the whims and caprices of a governor who had elected to live in the town instead of in the confines of the castle amid needless complaints of sleepless nights.[92] Local British authorities largely ignored these remonstrations—to the chagrin of the complainants, who equally disregarded attempts to regulate aspects of their time-honored customs.

Essentially, the reaction of the local British officials amounted to a definite degradation of the power and authority of the chiefs. When convenient, local officers took no notice of them at all. With time, the authorities subpoenaed eminent personalities of the indigenous political order before English courts, just like ordinary people, even on excusable charges. This treatment became so humiliating that even Governor Pine, who in his own way acted in abject disregard of the chiefs, frowned on it, observing that it constituted an assault on their persons and an undue interference with their authority, especially in matters of trivial offenses and cases.[93] When this treatment persisted, the chiefs expressed displeasure at being hauled before the courts "for trifling cause now and then [being] cast into prison by the officials which insures [sic] to them great disgrace, and places them on a par with their subjects."[94] In 1862, Governor Ross, who had just come into office, ordered the arrest of some Cape Coast chiefs for allowing funeral rites to go beyond the stipulated times, an offense that occasioned their confinement in one of the filthiest dungeons in the castle.[95]

## CONCLUSION

Under the emerging regime, chiefs who had been revered in times past became playthings at the hands of officials, who often pursued personal preferences. Onward of 1858, the power and authority of the chiefs had altogether atrophied in the main coastal towns.[96] The introduction of direct taxation in the form of the Poll Tax Ordinance and the failure to honor the anticipated promises spawned opposition on the part of the Cape Coast chiefs, who earned the support of their counterparts in coastal Ghana. The proliferation of English courts starved them of cases, causing loss of vital revenue sources and prestige—with chiefs being hauled before the English courts to boot. These developments gave the town a locus in the history of the country years after it had started as a *Fetu* fishing settlement and become a cosmopolitan commercial center on contact with the Europeans. In this context, the altercation lingered and continued for a long time. The town remained the epicenter of the indigenous political system, while at the same time being claimed as the stronghold of the emerging colonial order. The tension between these two identities leavened and led to other issues that had to be dealt with in this site of exchange, transaction, and power. As an emporium of exchange and transaction, the town encountered issues over who controlled the reins of economic activities—the kind of politics Cape Coast experienced in the engagement between the chiefs with their people on the one hand and the colonial officials on the other. In the same vein, the situation in the town reified the "urban problematique" revolving around the issue of molding the city—in what image, through what means, and against what opposition.[97] For the people of this town, the navigation of such challenges inhered in the reliance on indigenous ideas, systems, and institutions that had hitherto made their lives and world meaningful and valuable. These organized systems and cultural structures, such as the *Ebusua* and *Asafo* units, founded on the benefit of experiential knowledge, afforded a sense of pragmatism that included the ability to respond to new situations promptly, collectively, and decisively.

## TWO

# *EBUSUA* AND *ASAFO* SYSTEMS
*Gender, Complementarity, and Conflict among the Fanti*

AKAN GROUPS, QUITE IN LINE with other societies across Africa, developed varying yet similar sociocultural ideas and practices with a deep-rooted past. Indeed, these concepts and customs, which remained definitive of the Akan as largely related ethnic groups, impacted their sense of structure, order, organization, defense, offense, relationships, continuity, interaction, and so on—not excluding identity and belongingness, both of which determined necessary conditions for inheritance, along with requisite rights and responsibilities. To this end, the *Ebusua* and *Asafo* systems reified the indispensable foundation of the Akan peoples and their respective societies.[1] Among the coastal Akan, most prominently the various Fanti groups, the duality of *Ebusua* and *Asafo* structures developed to such a degree as to become synonymous with their maritime culture. Hence, the *Ebusua* and *Asafo* embodied the Fanti peoples whose cultures equally evoked these structures. The two systems became pivotal to everyday lives not only on the coast but also occupationally, on the beach and on the sea. Among various Fanti groups, the complementary nature of both systems stood as indubitable and visible, constituting a groundswell of resources on which groups drew to navigate their colonial experience.

The exclusively matrilineal and patrilineal *Ebusua* and *Asafo*, respectively, exemplified subsocial groupings that mattered in addressing issues and questions of identity: Who are you? Which house, family, or even family house do you come from? What is the root of your surname? Simply put, who are your parents or grandparents? The unraveling of these conjoined questions nearly always involved genealogical narratives and accounts starting as close to the roots as possible. Among Fanti societies, subsocial groups assumed complex usages given the pervasive coexistence of *Ebusua* and *Asafo* as discernible aspects of coastal culture. The two systems amounted to nothing more than intriguing expressions of Akan beliefs about the productive collaboration of the male and female principles. As a complementary entity, this duality had a complete complex impact on society. The *Ebusua* and *Asafo* subsocial groupings, reflections of the double descent system, simultaneously complicated indigenous social relationships and exhibited the capacity to hold society together harmoniously. This dynamic underscored a veritable dialectical relationship between the two indigenous systems. The double descent system further accentuated and underpinned a curious function of the paternal line in societies where kinship, inheritance of land and property, collective responsibility, and royal succession reckonings happened through maternal lines. Therefore, the double descent system rendered the individual, somehow coequally, a member of two distinct exogamous lineages.[2]

## EBUSUA: WOMEN, BLOOD, AND LINEAGE

The *Ebusua* system in practice comprised women, men, youth, and children whose lineages could be traced to a common ancestor—in most cases, a putative female accessed through their respective mothers. Various Akan groups expressed the conceptualization of blood as the sacred source of life traceable to women or mothers through statements such as *mo-gya yɛ dur sen nsu*, literally, "blood is heavier/thicker than water," and *wo dze mo-gya bɔ Ebusua*, "blood constitutes the essence of *Ebusua* membership." This system as a social support network had the semblance of an unwritten covenant that connected people who traced their origins (and therefore, identity) to a group of related female ancestors, sharing and bearing responsibility for their collective well-being. That commitment amounted to an ultimate belief in a shared destiny, grounded in the idea that the fate or experience of the individual had implications for the honor and dignity of the entire group (and vice versa).[3]

The unifying influence of the *Ebusua* system presents a somewhat measured expectation. Adages about this system proffer vague impressions of inherent subdivisions, or worse still, cliques. For instance, *Ebusua wɔ hɔ yi, egyi-na ekyir a ɔtse dɛ kwae, na sɛ ekɔ mu a dua bia-ra wɔ ne si bia* constitutes a lamentation about how the system presents a mirage of unity in being as impenetrable as a thick forest to the observer from a distance, but on entry the reality dawns that each tree (the individual female as the essence of the system) possesses her own marked space. It is a veritable warning that each woman and her direct descendants might, first and foremost, see to their immediate concerns, needs, and interest. Correlatedly, statements such as *sɛ wo na wu a nna wo Ebusua asei*, meaning that the relevance of the *Ebusua* for the individual vitiates on the death of one's mother, sought to puncture and upend the system.

Nonetheless, the inviolability and even sanctity of the *Ebusua* inhered in totemic beliefs with which the various groups commonly identified. Members believed that totems, in most cases sacred and revered objects, flora, or fauna, depicted the group's collective soul and well-being. Hardly claiming descent from these totems, respective groups averred that the purported flora or fauna possessed certain attributes, traits, and characteristics largely discernible among members. At the ultimate symbolic and visual level, each group had its totem carved atop a staff that designated individuals, most likely the *Ebusua Akyeame* (literally, spokespersons), would solemnly display at formal gatherings.[4] At the behavioral level, the group and, correlatedly, the individual had to live in a reverential relationship with the totem. If the totem happened to be an animal considered a delicacy for others, the members of that *Ebusua* could not under any circumstance partake in its eating. Should they chance on that animal in a lifeless condition, members had the obligation to bury it with full rites befitting an important member of the group.[5]

The broad structure of the *Ebusua* system could be conceptualized at three basic levels: *Ebusua-kuw,* local *Ebusua,* and extended family *Ebusua.* The first category involved the general concept that existed among various Akan groups of southern Ghana and some parts of Côte d'Ivoire. Akan groups espoused the idea of an extensive sibling relationship among members of a similar *Ebusua.* This relationship could be traced to an imaginary or putative ancestress hardly known to any living relatives or even those long dead. The second category, the local *Ebusua,* featured at a town or community level where the network of relationship and identity could be traced to that legendary ancestress. Membership to this group existed for all Akan peoples who claimed kin and therefore shared the same totem.[6] Essentially, even an Akan from Côte d'Ivoire or another part of Ghana could approach any of the Akan enclaves, introduce themselves to members of their *Ebusua,* and rightfully expect to be accorded the appropriate welcome and acceptance with all appertaining benefits. The third tier of the *Ebusua,* the extended family, functioned at the epistemological level. Membership thrived on directly traceable generations of descendants from an identifiable customary ancestress and her sister siblings, all of whom remained equally known to some of those living and deceased. At this level, reference to an *Ebusua-fie,* or family house, became a crucial locus of identity and belonging relevant for genealogical narrative and accounting.

The family house operated as the cradle for all *Ebusua* activities or celebrations, such as scheduled gatherings, funerals, marriages, and namings. An elaborate hierarchy of leadership existed among the largest and most influential families within the *Ebusua*. The *Ebusua-hin* (*Ebusua* chief) position had its complementary female counterpart in the *Ebusua-hin-maa* (*Ebusua* queen). The most elderly, honorable, or capable man, referred to as *Ebu-sua-pa-nyin*, wielded considerable power in the hierarchy. The female equivalent of that position included the *Ebusua Obaa-pa-nyin* (the most elderly and respectable woman) and, significantly, the *Abe-re-wa-tia*, usually the oldest surviving woman, nearly always diminutive and bent over with age.[7] All male and female positions constituted the representative high council of the various families, collectively referred to as *Ebusua mpa-nyin-fo*, "Council of Elders," within the third tier. The *Ebusuahin* and *Ebusuapanyin* took charge of the affairs affecting men, while the *Ebusuahinmaa*, *Obaapanyin*, and *Aberewatia* were responsible for matters concerning women.[8]

That division of responsibility hardly precluded collaboration, however, as a constant flurry of consultation always transpired among the leadership to determine the general direction of the group for the purposes of keeping it together. Accordingly, the *Aberewatia* remained the sure repository of *Ebusua* knowledge and wisdom. Given her widely acknowledged longevity, she knew nearly all the principal and significant female personalities of the lineage, their history, and the descendants who constituted the extended family. In other words, she knew where everybody belonged and indeed could be regarded as the ultimate or authentic narrator of the genealogy and family history. A fundamental moral obligation among the *Ebusua* accorded women at the top of the hierarchy the same deference given to their male counterparts. Some women in these positions, largely through sheer strength of personality and tenacity of purpose, exerted considerable influence.[9]

At the extended family level, the *Ebusua* functioned as a socioeconomic mutual support network. Members exhibited a strong sense of collective responsibility that remained largely binding. The nature of this support offered redemption and relief to members in dire straits because of indebtedness, sickness, disability, bereavement, orphanhood, and other such unfortunate life situations. Consequently, some strict definitions of the extended family *Ebusua* system describe it as a single unit of people who shared cost or debt. The network and scope of the extended family mutual support system were so wide, deep, and far-reaching that individual members, knowingly or unknowingly and in diverse ways and forms, became recipients of the dispensed beneficence. In keeping with that dispensation, beneficiaries had a somewhat unwritten obligation to give back to the pool. This expectation remained so strong that those who disregarded it risked being tagged as selfish, insensitive, and ungrateful.

Considering the purported descent from sibling ancestresses, marriage for members of the various *Ebusua* remained strictly exogamous. To avoid incestuous relationships, they married outside of the *Ebusua*, extended family, and even *Ebusuakuw*. Any marriage among members received general condemnation as decidedly unsavory, warranting some degree of ritual cleansing of the culprits and pacification of the ancestral entities. The stipulation for exogamous marriages constituted little loss to the various groups. Since membership to the larger Akan *Ebusua* remained matrilineal, children born to the women would ultimately take their rightful place in the system. Both local and extended family *Ebusua* ensured the veneration of ancestors, known and unknown. Rituals ordinarily included pouring of libation and, in some cases, sacrificing of animals such as sheep and cows. In rare cases, well-endowed *Ebusua*—in terms of resources and people—boasted internal celebrations and rituals that blossomed into full-fledged festivals.[10] All these gatherings would ideally start with the clarion call *"Ebusua mfrɛ yie,"* emphasizing their quest for collective well-being, eliciting the response *"yie mbra"* ("let prosperity be our portion").

Typical names of the *Ebusuakuw* among Fanti peoples included *Nso-na, Bre-tuo Twi-dan, Kon-na Ebi-ra-dze, Ano-na, Adua-na Abo-ra-dze, N-twea,* and *Adwin-da-dze*.[11] Totems for these groups presented an interesting array of flora and fauna. The *Nsona* identified with the crow and, in some cases, the fox. The *Bretuo Twidan Ebusua* upheld the corn stalk as its totem, and the *Konna Ebiradzi* touted the bush cow. The *Anona* identified with the parrot or hawk; the *Aduana Aboradze* claimed the use of the plantain and, in some instances, the antelope. The *Ntwea Ebusua* venerated the dog, and the *Awindadze* possessed the lion as its representative totem. In each *Ebusua*, members had specific appellations, greetings, and responses, both collectively and individually. Various stories of origin, often convoluted and contradictory, abounded among the coastal *Ebusua*. The core themes of these narratives trace origins to the major movements of larger Akan groups from their known enclaves, establishing them as slightly varying yet related peoples.[12]

### ASAFO: MEN, SPIRIT, AND POWER

Although the idea of *Asafo* remained common among the Akan peoples, the practice stood out as particularly prevalent and elaborate with coastal groups. All towns and villages in the Fanti enclave had two or more of these units—in their parlance, *Asafo kuw* or *Asafo dɔm*, "groups or following"—generally referred to as companies, militia, or troops in European colonial documents. Cape Coast preeminently boasted as many as seven units. In this town, the *Asafo* had added significance as a complementary institution to the *Ebusua* system. In this indigenous patrilineal organization, the father-child relationship prevailed as the determinant factor for membership. In the philosophy or discourse of various Akan peoples on the makeup and constitution of the individual,

Fig. 2.1 *Asafo* company members with their elders.

Fig. 2.2 A group of *Asafo* elders.

children derived their *sun-sum* (spirit), the essence of their personality and character, from fathers. Deemed stronger than the physical connection, the spiritual element endowed personality traits such as boldness, bravery, courage, and resoluteness. These essential characteristic features influenced and constituted requisite conditions for the *Asafo*'s quintessentially daring nature.

Etymologically, the word *Asafo* comprises two Akan words: *Asa* (the plural of the singular word *Sa*) and *fo*. The former has to do with war, whereas the latter refers to people; therefore, *Asafo* means "war people."[13] Essentially, such organizations represented the indigenous military institution as the main organized defensive and offensive mechanisms in times of war. The *Asafo* in the nineteenth and twentieth centuries boasted armory often based on gun ownership of individual members. Guns eventually became available to groups in coastal Ghana, trickling in with the advent of Europeans to the Guinea Coast during the trans-Atlantic slave trade, which ultimately supplanted the initial commodity transaction. Though individuals could acquire their own guns, the onus fell on fathers to provide weapons for their sons, whereas the *Aman-hin* (kings or chiefs) bore responsibility for the supply of gunpowder to the *Asafo* groups.[14] The militant posture and operations of these groups fell forcefully and fully within the orbit of concern of the colonial authorities, especially given their determination to regulate cultural institutions and everyday life. These same institutions, somewhat paradoxically, became major mechanisms for fending off colonial control. An inquiry into *Asafo* operation at the instigation of the colonial government in the twentieth century provided a description of its war formation. These included the *Twa-fo* (advance guard), *Ben-kum* (left-wing), *Don-tsin* (main army), and *Nim-fa* (right-wing).[15] The *Nkyi-dom* (rear guard) provided protection at the posterior for the army and particularly the *Amanhin*.

Elderly men and women among the *Asafo* constituted the prominent members, in addition to the young, strong, brave, daring people who unreservedly evoked the spirit of the organization. Consequently, in various Akan renditions and contemporary literature, the *Asafo* earned the description *mbrantse*, "young men," "youth," or "hotheads."[16] The terms "young men" and "youth" derived from the unit's place in the hierarchy of the town's indigenous political institution.[17] The three-tier structure, the *Oman-hin*, his council of elders, and the *Asafo* (in the various Akan parlance, *O-hin, na ne Mpa-nyin-fo, na Asafo*), underpinned the prominent placement of this organization in the larger indigenous political structure. The *Asafo* therefore comprised the "third estate," without whose support the legitimacy of chiefs could be considered dubious. Given the preponderance of young people, the *Asafo* constituted the largest base of society, as well as the most outspoken and influential component on whose shoulders rested communal political, social, and economic endeavors. This position conferred on the organization an appreciable degree of civic responsibility, manifested in possessing the power of the last word before the installation or removal of chiefs. That right made the *Asafo* instrumental in the determination of who became king, even though there existed an exclusive group of kingmakers. In view of this role, the organization acted as a systemic check and balance on the prerogative of the *Ebusua*, especially the royal *Ebusua*, which wielded the right to nominate the *Omanhin* (king or chief). During installations, the *Asafo* organization had the enviable role of parading the prospective ruler shoulder-high in a procession amid drumming, singing, and firing of musketry. The social and political stigma associated with refusal to carry a prospective *Omanhin* always compelled respective royal Akan *Ebusua* families to seek the consent of the *Asafo* before making the final choice. In the unfortunate event of deposition, the execution of that order was the sole responsibility of the organization. The essence of these roles in indigenous political processes enhanced *Asafo* influence over the *Omanhin*.[18]

Furthermore, the organization had other responsibilities, such as policing the community to maintain peace and security and helping with public building projects and other basic infrastructural development. During the colonial era, the *Asafo* bore the brunt of ordinances which the government eagerly enacted to enforce public projects, especially as colonial policies enjoined the administration to avoid committing the money of British taxpayers to any local project. The institution became a sure source of labor, again given the administrative imperative to optimize cost. In local civil emergencies, criminal cases, or natural disasters, the responsibility rested on the *Asafo* to enter the forest to apprehend elusive culprits or highway robbers and, when necessary, search for victims. The *Asafo* hunted down menacing wild animals in proximate bushes; in communities where occasional maritime accidents, such as capsizing of canoes or cases of drowning, occurred, it bore the responsibility of saving survivors and retrieving cadavers.[19]

Despite its usefulness and relevance, indications existed from time to time of negative associations regarding the *Asafo* because of inherent rowdiness and "hotheadedness."[20] Such general descriptions stigmatized the organization to the extent that its leaders had occasion to encourage members to fulfill family obligations and expectations. In everyday Akan parlance, the phrase *playing Asafo*, "being careless with parental responsibilities and obligations," became enduring evidence of that smirch. Careless individuals in general as well as those within the *Asafo* came across to their communities as a socially adrift, shiftless, and happy-go-lucky lot who consorted with like-minded friends.[21]

The *Asafo* quarter or ward system in coastal Akan towns and villages essentially indicated spatial demarcation and, therefore, appropriation of the entire community among the respective groups, with such spaces featuring conspicuous displays of *pu-su-ban*, "company grove," as landmarks. The original Cape Coast township, for instance, featured seven demarcated quarters, the

Fig. 2.3 *Asafo* company post or *pusuban*.

security, peace, and development of which remained the sole responsibility of the respective *Asafo* groups. Although individuals could come and go at will in any quarter, strict protocols applied to group entry, as no *Asafo* company could traverse the quarter of another without express permission.[22] The protocol enjoined the permission-seeking group to present alcoholic drinks to the company that owned the quarter. Violations of this arrangement, nearly always fiercely fought, could cause more than a few disturbances. As the central point or locus of *Asafo* company space and identity, the *pusuban* essentially comprised a walled edifice or structure emblematic of group spirit, nature, totem, and so on, all of which evoked awe and admiration in members and trepidation in nonmembers. These distinctive structures, more than anything else, stood in their power and glory as sacred sites for respective *Asafo* companies.[23]

The seven groups in Cape Coast and their corresponding ordinal designations were *Ben-tsir* (no. 1), *A-naa-fo* (no. 2), *N-tsin* (no.

3), *N-kum* (no. 4), *A-bro-fo-nkoa* (no. 5), *A-kram-pa* (no. 6), and *A-man-fur* (no. 7). *Bentsir* company, one of the earliest and largest, invariably insisted on its superiority over the rest. For its emblem, this company owned a flag made of a pure piece of blanket, signifying help rendered to men and women of other companies in the past.[24] Red remained the company's primary color, with black and white as secondary colors. Red represented the ability to face danger, accentuating the fact that bloody or life-threatening situations did not deter *Bentsir* company's members from doing what they set their hearts to.[25] Governor Charles McCarthy purportedly assigned the red ensign and a flagstaff to *Bentsir* prior to the fateful battle of 1824 against the Asante at Nsamanko for being the first company to respond to the call for troops. In that battle, *Bentsir* lost as many as ninety-nine men.[26]

*Anaafo* started as an offshoot of *Bentsir*, a history that explains a sense of kinship and cooperation that hardly meant an absence of disagreements as well as clashes between them.[27] More often than not, these two companies rallied together in the event of conflict with other companies. The primary and secondary colors of *Anaafo* included light blue and violet, respectively. The emblems approved for its exclusive use consisted of three gongs, a pistol, a long-necked bird, a snake, hands sticking out of a pot, and an equestrian figure.[28] These emblems, usually embossed on *Anaafo* flags, commemorated landmark events and processes in the group's history as an *Asafo*.[29]

*Ntsin* company, formed during the time of Nana Aggery I, remained the largest of all the Cape Coast *Asafo* groups. The formation of this unit commemorated the settlement of a dispute between *Obrempong* Kojo (a wealthy stepson of one of the kings) and a prominent woman in Cape Coast. Many of the original members came from the *Nkum Asafo*, while a cohort of *Obrempong* Kojo's friends and servants made up the rest. *Ntsin* earned the appellation *Abrempong Asafo*, literally, "company of the rich and famous," in reference to the status and reputation of

*Obrempong* Kojo in the town and because of its connections to several of the town's chiefs. The members derived an uncompromising sense of superiority from these royal associations. *Ntsin* used black as its primary color, with dark green and purple as secondary colors.[30]

*Nkum* company had the enviable history of being the first Cape Coast *Asafo* and one of the largest.[31] This pride of place and history derived from members' ancestors claiming the right of first settlement, tangentially signifying the honor of clearing the virgin bush for the foundation of the town. Consequently, members retained description as the landowners from original settlement rights.[32] Emblems approved for the group's exclusive use accentuated that claim; these included an elephant, a castle, and a palm tree, emphasizing the company's natural rights and robust nature and reiterating the fact that it had originally owned the land on which the Europeans built the Cape Coast Castle.[33] Its colors included white and yellow.

*Abrofonkoa Asafo* company counted as one of the smaller companies, if not the smallest. Known as the "artificers" or "builders of the castle," this group originally consisted of various enslaved people—indigenous as well as from neighboring West African countries—the Europeans brought over for the construction of the castle. The Swedes especially brought many men and women to the coast and eventually acquired others from Cape Coast. They trained the men as masons, carpenters, bricklayers, and in other skills necessary for the building of the castle. To reside near their masters, the servants, workers, and artisans secured plots of land close to the castle. Those who remained in the town after the completion of their construction duties constituted themselves into an *Asafo*, hence the name *Abrofonkoa*, literally, "servants of the Europeans."[34] The color of the company was light green, and its emblems included replicas of the implements used for the construction of the castle; its meaningful motto remained an emphatic *Hɛn Na Ye-si Aban Yi*, literally, "we built this castle."[35]

*Akrampa Asafo* company, quite akin to *Anaafo* and *Abrofonkoa*, numbered among the smallest. The original members of *Akrampa* were children of African and European parentage—direct descendants as well as servants. Thomas Edward Barter, otherwise known as Tom *Ewu-si*, formed this company. As a mulatto of great repute, he earned his fame through exemplary administrative and business acumen, overseeing aspects of British merchant trade interests on the coast.[36] As marriage and cohabitation became common among African women and European men, the mulatto population grew sizably, causing Barter to organize them into the *Akrampa Asafo*. The group's guiding principle, "defense and not defiance," accentuated its peaceful disposition as well as readiness to serve and promote the interests of the town. The group served as bodyguards of Sir Charles McCarthy in the battle of 1824 against the Asante. Consequently, King George IV of Great Britain granted military commissions to some of its members after the Katamansu War of 1826 in appreciation of their sacrifices. Evidence of the original group members' European connections was reflected in their use of uniforms and emblems, which included regimental dresses consisting of green tunics with cummerbunds, helmets, white drill patrol jackets, black pants with red side strips, green coats, and forage caps. Instead of standard African drums, they used European side drums to summon members. The use of these drums, among other things, is one instance of European influence on indigenous practices in the country.

*Amanfur Asafo* comprised artisans whom the Danes brought over to coastal Ghana from other parts of Africa mainly to assist in the building of Fort Fredericksborg, situated on a hill to the eastern approaches of Cape Coast.[37] These workmen, mainly from the eastern parts of the Bights of Guinea, included blacksmiths, goldsmiths, hat and cap makers, carpenters, bark cloth makers, ironworkers, and woodcarvers. Well into the 1660s, this settlement made up of artisans had a population of about fifteen hundred. Among the emblems registered for the group's exclusive use included those that underpinned the members' history as artisans, namely, the hammer, drill, file, and sandpaper. Use of the whale and turtle as emblems indicated that the original members came to southern Ghana from across the sea. Reverence of the crocodile as one of several emblems evinced the fact that the origins of a section of this group could be traced to the eastern part of the country, mainly from among the Ga people.[38] The *Amanfur Asafo* boasted gold or yellow as its primary color.

## ASAFO ALLIANCE SYSTEMS

*Asafo* companies in outlying towns and villages formed cordial relations with principal groups in larger towns over the years. Within the Cape Coast scheme of things, the *Bentsir, Ntsin, Nkum,* and *Amanfur* companies, together with the *Omanhin*, had the thirty-six towns and villages constituting the indigenous political area unevenly distributed among them. Members of the various groups in these outlying towns and villages, on the strength of these arrangements, received recognition as automatic members of their respective principal *Asafo* companies. *Bentsir* wielded direct control over five towns, namely, *E-kon, A-ma-ma* (or *A-ma-mo-ma*), *A-pe-wo-si-ka, Kwe-si-ibra,* and *Ko-kwaa-do. Ntsin* allied with twelve villages and towns, including *Siw-do, A-bo-ra, Ka-kum-do, M-pe-asem, A-ko-to-kyir, Ebro-bon-ko, Ami-yao, Dan-ko-krom, Bi-sa-krom, O-gua-krom, Kyir-akom-fo* (or Beulah), and *Ya-ya-kwa-na.* The *Nkum Asafo* had allies in eight towns and villages, namely, *Pe-du, Kwaa-prao, An-ka-fur, Esue-kyir, Anto-Esue-kyir, Sa-fo-ro, Mam-pong,* and *A-di-sa-dar. Amanfur* had, within its direct ambit, *Nkam-fua* and *Amoa-nda.* The remaining nine villages and towns—*E-ffu-tu, Tan-do-krom, Ku-be-kyir, Bi-bia-ne-ha, Be-ra-se, Ago-na, E-ssiam, Sar-man,* and *An-kwa-se*—fell under the auspices of the *Omanhin.*[39] Although the *Anaafo, Abrofonkoa,* and *Akrampa Asafo* companies barely possessed any satellite villages, the absence of alliances hardly precluded some of their members from living in outlying settlements.[40]

The advantages of these alliances for various groups included unwritten pacts of cooperation in defensive and offensive maneuvers. Alliances received reinforcement and a kind of mystical mien from *n-siw-dzi*, "the drinking of fetish," deemed as perpetually binding as oath swearing. The implications of these alliances manifested in diverse ways, as any affront to the principal company became an unmitigated attack against allied companies in the outlying towns and villages, and vice versa.[41] Correlatedly, an attack against a member anywhere constituted an attack against all members everywhere. Allied companies nearly always responded promptly, collectively, and forcefully to provocative situations in support of one another. Individual *Asafo* victories translated into collective achievements worthy of celebration, while defeats became disgrace demanding immediate vengeance. Consequently, these alliances aggravated simple and sometimes avoidable conflicts, as various groups exploited them in different ways for diverse purposes. The strength of the principal companies, among other factors, came to depend on the number of towns and villages under their control. The stronger companies often became the most belligerent because of their readiness to exploit numerical strength to their advantage. Within the Cape Coast *Asafo* system, the *Bentsir*, *Anaafo*, *Ntsin*, and *Nkum* companies stood out as the most fractious; indeed, *Ntsin* featured in nearly every conflict. Nevertheless, some smaller companies sprang surprises from time to time. Even though the *Anaafo* company, for instance, remained small and had no direct control over any outlying town or village, it fell fully within the category of the most belligerent.

## ASAFO HIERARCHY

The *Asafo* as an institution, and a mainly militant one at that, exhibited a structured regimen. In Cape Coast, the *Tu-fo-hin*, "king of the gun bearers," loomed large over all seven companies as the supreme head, with a corresponding responsibility for their general conduct and operations in the indigenous state (*Oman*).[42] Given this prestigious position in the organizational setup, the *Tufohin* represented the *Asafo* companies on the *Oman* Council and was revered as next in rank to the *Omanhin*. The significance and weight of this office was accentuated by the existence of a royal stool for the occupant, as for any high-ranking indigenous position of the Akan peoples. In Cape Coast, succession to the office of *Tufohin* purportedly happened through inheritance along the female line as the preserve of the Kwamina Edu family, a claim that remained vehemently disputed in some sections of the society.

The *Su-pi-fo*, or respective heads of the various companies, came next in the Asafo hierarchy and held allegiance to the *Tufohin*.[43] Each *Supi* was responsible for the general conduct of their respective group. Together, the *Supifo* and *Tufohin* formed the high council of the *Asafo* system; *Kwa-tɛ-kyi-rɛ-fo*, the officers who assisted with the administration of the various groups, came directly after the *Supifo*.[44]

Each company had subdivisions under the charge of divisional officers comprising male chiefs of the *Asafo* (referred to properly as *Asa-fo-hin-fo*) and their equally important female counterparts (*Asa-fo-a-kyi-rɛ-fo*). The number of *Asafohinfo* and *Asafoakyirɛfo* depended on the size of the company. Like all officers, the *Asafohinfo* and *Asafoakyirɛfo* embodied the soul and spirit of their group. They had to be fearless as well as daring, make bold decisions, and lead exemplarily. The reputation of these officers hinged on their ability to inspire these virtues in members under their charge. The *Asafohinfo* and the *Asafoakyirɛfo* equally retained responsibility for the general discipline of their subdivisions within the company.

The *Kyi-rɛ-ma*, "master-divine drummer," though not high up in the hierarchy, wielded considerable importance and prominence. His role of playing the drum remained crucial to the function and survival of the *Asafo* as an indigenous institution. Again, recognition of the *Kyirɛma* as a well-versed person, gifted and knowledgeable in the skill, art, and language of the drum, remained boundless. He knew the ordinary drum language that all members understood. On instructions from his superiors, the *Kyirɛma* could communicate urgent messages and call a gathering of the group through drum language. He played the common rhythm of *Asafo* songs and further distinguished himself through the ability to play drum poetry and other esoteric sound combinations powerful enough to communicate with the world of spirits in the air, land, and sea.[45]

The officers in charge of *Asafo* routine and mobilization included the *Fran-kaa-ki-ta-nyi*, *Asi-kan-mba-hin*, *Bo-mbaa*, and *Asafo Akom-fo*. The *Frankaakitanyi*, "bearer of the *Asafo* flag," had a pleasing place in the system, performing skillful and intricate dances while wielding the flag to the admiration of observers. In conjunction with other officers, he guarded the flags that epitomized the face, honor, and dignity of the group.

*Asafo* flags relied heavily on imagery, often evoking proverbial statements or warnings meant to make other groups or individuals pause and think deeply. A flag etched with the simple image of a crab and an inscription such as *A-nyan-ko-nyan-ko n-tsi* reminded people of the proverbial saying regarding the headless nature of that crustacean. In indigenous folklore wisdom, that condition stemmed from having friends in reckless abandon, and worse still, being overly liberal with the whole host of them. Other flags in this category could be fashioned to cast aspersions and innuendo. Standard *Asafo* flags, in most cases, exhibited the acclaimed colors and essential emblems for the exclusive use of the various groups.

*Asikanmbahin*, "the chief of the sword and knife bearers," had immediate oversight responsibility for maintaining order and ensuring that the group discharged its assigned duties. The *Bombaa*

Fig. 2.4 Simple flag exhibits such as this one strongly admonished the individual and *Asafo* groups against self-destructive actions, especially given their awareness of widely known precipitants. In this depiction, a person with a huge cotton ball protruding from his anal area risks a jump over blazing fire, quite akin to the following proverb: If you live in a glass house, do not throw stones. Photo by author.

supervised whip bearers in the group; the *Asafo Akomfo*, "priests and priestesses," together with the divine drummers, handled esoteric religious rites and practices. The *Akomfo* mainly played the role of facilitating meaningful communication between the physical and spiritual worlds. As indigenous priests and priestesses, they supposedly had the capacity to live in both worlds and therefore could communicate with otherworldly entities.

This hierarchy of senior and junior officers worked in concert to preserve the honor, pride, and spirit of the system. Although colonial authorities sought to portray the *Asafo* as a base institution whose existence fomented excesses, recklessness, and disorderly behavior, the commitment of its leadership to ensuring orderly and proper conduct of the various groups rendered

Fig. 2.5 *Asafo* flags exhibited complex images, such as the one above, that posed rhetorical questions to cornered and overpowered individuals or groups asking them to choose between options, either of which would be swiftly administered. Photo by author.

that view quite untenable. That sincere determination, however, hardly absolved the system from the stigma of conflict and acrimonious conduct.

### ASAFO, EBUSUA, AND CRUCIAL SOCIAL EXPECTATIONS

Despite the contemporaneous existence and functioning of the *Asafo* and *Ebusua* systems, as well as their complementary nature, these institutions created challenging and complicated situations in society while simultaneously holding it together. The patrilineal orientation of the former, as opposed to the matrilineal nature of the latter, presented difficult situations for men and women in society. An individual belonged to the *Asafo* of his or her father; if a man professed allegiance to *Bentsir Asafo* company, for example, his sons and daughters would become automatic members of that group. Given this mode of membership, a typical patrilineal household could consist exclusively of members of one *Asafo*, even if the children belonged to different mothers or came from multiple marriages. This situation complicated relationships in the *Ebusua* system, which functioned along matrilineal lines. One would find, in a matrilineal household, complex presences of *Asafo* membership.[46] With the number of *Asafo* companies in Cape Coast, the incidence of different memberships in a single household could be more convoluted than apparent. Children of the women in a matrilineal household would be members of the respective companies of their fathers, since these men rarely belonged to the same *Asafo*.[47] Obviously, this maze of group associations created problems quite notable to the critical observer. Conflicts among *Asafo* companies had serious repercussions for matrilineal group solidarity. The *Asafo* concept united men and women with their fathers' brothers and sisters, which often contravened general interests among mothers, brothers, and sisters, as well as, undoubtedly, between mothers and their children. The *Asafo* dynamic thus reinforced patrilineal group solidarity to the bane of bonds among matrilineal *Ebusua* kinsmen. Among the Fanti, attachment and commitment of the individual to an *Asafo* company took precedence over all other affiliations, making one likely to bear arms in group conflict against matrilineal kinsmen.

The potential for conflict due to *Asafo* and *Ebusua* dynamics was enhanced in cases of inheritance. In a town that gave nearly equal prominence to matrilineal and patrilineal alliances, a father often faced an overwhelming dilemma in his obligations to his *Ebusua*, mainly to the children of his sisters, as opposed to responsibility to his own children. The bond that held him to his sons and daughters hinged on affection infused with elements bordering on the spiritual; however, customary laws stipulated that when he died his property must pass on to the sons of his sisters. Complex kinship and marital relationships existed in most Fanti households as well as among various Akan groups.

The dilemma confronting men of various *Ebusua* groups added another shade of complexity to the situation, especially when men started their own families after getting married. Social and kinship obligations compelled married men to offer lodging and other kinds of assistance to needy maternal relatives, notably the children of sisters (nieces and nephews). Wives, in some situations, would be expected to live with their mothers and sisters in family or *Ebusua* houses. Married men often had to carefully negotiate their way through this maze of expectation to satisfy the equally demanding and contending parties.

Mature sons encountered similar conundrums. Though they lived with their fathers and served them all the time, their economic well-being, obligations, responsibilities, and crucial family ties lay with their *Ebusua*, enjoining them to ensure its collective good. Wives became equally entangled in this complex web of social and cultural complicity, as women had to look up to their brothers for social and economic security in critical times within the purview of the *Ebusua* system. They often found themselves torn between commitments to husbands and kin, particularly their mothers and brothers. These conditions and situations spawned tremendous quandaries, conflicts, as well as mistrust between the sons of a man and the sons of his sisters, as well as between his wife and or wives and his sisters, with their daughters in tow.[48]

Although these seemingly confounding conditions occurred across various Akan communities, incidents among the coastal sections of this larger group became aggravated to a greater extent. In Cape Coast, for instance, conflicts hardly escaped attention because of the heavy concentration of *Asafo* and *Ebusua* groups. This dynamic often laid at the heart of petty squabbles and serious political conflicts, most of which found expression in documents and oral tradition. The phrase *Guae wɔ-nnyɛ*, in everyday or casual parlance, gave an intimation of the propensity of conflicts in Cape Coast. This proclivity found further expression in local imagery of crabs trapped in a bucket. To free themselves from confinement, these crustaceans climb on each other's back. But when the topmost crab reaches the point of escape, the rest at the base slip out of place, causing the entire heap to tumble back down into confinement. Again in this town, incidences of petty squabbles, tension, and mistrust became rife among households. Nonetheless, given Fanti philosophical expressions regarding the unavoidability of conflicts among siblings and even within the individual, this seeming propensity for conflict and mistrust should be least surprising. These thought-provoking assertions illuminate the nuances of custom and tradition that breached social equilibrium while exhibiting the capacity to hold society together. Indeed, the sociocultural provisions of various Akan groups ensured that every individual benefited from entrenched and enduring affiliations through female lineage.

## CONCLUSION

Despite their apparent contradiction and opposition, the patrilineal *Asafo* and matrilineal *Ebusua* systems expressed the ideas of gender complementarity among Akan groups. This parity hardly precluded operational complications and conundrums, as both systems manifested a kind of dialectical relationship in a social sense. Aspects of these indigenous perspectives on conflict, in many ways, provided the seedbed that nurtured responses and reactions to sensitive situations emanating from the determination of the colonial government to control and regulate everyday life.

# THREE

## COASTAL COMMUNITIES, INTERGROUP WRANGLING, AND ASPECTS OF THE COLONIAL EXPERIENCE

*Historical Undercurrents*

A HISTORY OF CLASHES AND confrontation revolving around issues of everyday life prepared coastal communities to engage the colonial government on all fronts. These incidences emanated from routine interactions, exigencies of social obligations, and more specifically, intergroup relations. In the same vein, social settings, organizations, and collective worldview informed the lived experiences of these communities, offering them diverse systems as well as strategies for responding to disruptive situations from within and without. As Michael Pearson and, to some extent, Fernand Braudel argue, shore life transcended the manifold influences of geographically and culturally diverse inland settings—which are manifestations of the interplay of natural and social processes.[1]

Coastal Ghana communities lived close to the sea, which influenced nearly all aspects of everyday life. These influences impacted interactions within and among the communities, as well as with their nonmaritime neighbors. Alfred Crosby, for instance, reiterates the impact of some of these circumstances. He upholds the view that the biological nature of human life, its interaction with the environment, and its exploitation of natural resources necessary for survival all constitute focal elements in history.[2] Hence, contemporary studies of societies have increasingly focused on "the totality of the natural environment or upon geography as an element of history."[3] Furthermore, to reprise the environment's relevance within the African context, Emmanuel Akyeampong points out how the environmental history of the continent in the past focused solely on land as a factor of production and historical space. It neglected water resources, irrespective of the fact that an eco-social relationship existed between the sea and the people who lived close to it, particularly in terms of the sea's impact on social identities.[4] Certainly, these manifestations impinged on cultural identities. Land as a category of historical analysis remains relevant because the landscape encompassed the physical layout, the inhabitants, and the culture or range of everyday life through which they worked out all the possibilities that the available natural resources rendered, as Klein and Mackenthun argue.[5] Alternatively, the oceans and seas as geographical entities had everything to do with the existence of humanity. The space between the land and the sea encompassed the shoreline, the people on it, and their culture—created and inherited—which ensured effective functioning as masters of their world. Correlatedly, the dynamic relationship between the coastal communities of southern Ghana and their environment manifested in social structures, accumulated practices and processes, economy, livelihood, knowledge, belief, and ideas of power, bravery, and defiance, all of which went a long way to inform various modes of response to situations.

These coastal communities exuded pride, strength, and bonds that received reinforcement from shared connection with the Atlantic Ocean to the south of the country. However, the sea served not only as an economic resource but also as an express freeway across which came the European contact that would equally be impactful from the late fifteenth century onward.

## AFFINITY WITH THE SEA AND THE ACQUISITION OF FISHING SKILLS

In relation to landmass, the sea as a larger component of the hydrosphere, in many ways, touched those who lived close to it in the general situation of coastal Ghana communities, and particularly Cape Coast. Among other things, this vast stretch of salt water provided a cosmological blueprint for understanding the situation of society, everyday life, and even relations with hinterland neighbors. This briny water body had a broader conceptualization in religious terms that also necessitated elements of ritual performances. Besides their strong knowledge of the sea as a physical entity, coastal communities, especially the fisherfolk, upheld its spiritual nature, which defined the connections between them.[6] The chief fisherman of Cape Coast, locally referred to as *A-far-fo-hin* (also known as *Pu-fo-hin*), would describe the sea as *Nana Bo-sum-pu*, reiterating elements of the spiritual and even assigning it an emphatic deity status that necessitated occasional pouring of libation and other rituals.[7] These ceremonial customary rites, in the estimation of various coastal communities, ensured peaceful coexistence with the hydrosphere, safe fishing expeditions, and ultimately, abundant catches. On the economic front, coastal communities earned differing degrees of income from the sea's enormous resources, with which people met both familial and nonfamilial obligations. The boundlessness of the hydrosphere, with its unlimited beneficence, manifested in surprising ways.[8] Often, the sea served as a sanctuary or haven for fisherfolk and their families who had broken the law in diverse ways. Some would take refuge on the sea when warrant-wielding police officers pursued them. To this end, "facing the sea," "breathing the smell of the sea," and "the sea being their all in all," as expressed in everyday parlance, appropriately characterized this rewarding relationship.[9] Indeed, the consequent culture provided dispositions that enabled fishermen to endure the exigencies of traversing the sea and living off it.

In Cape Coast, centers of operation serving as takeoff and landing points for canoes as well as beach fishing were set up at selected sections within the confines of the distance between Amanfur, the castle vicinity, and beyond.[10] Initial fishing community settlements, mainly made up of round wattle and daub huts with thatched and coconut palm frond roofs, expanded.[11] With time, particularly in the late nineteenth century, and amid both local and foreign architectural influences, four-sided, specifically rectangular walls supplanted the round huts. Further expansion and the relative urban sprawl ensured the availability and use of corrugated iron roofing sheets. During this phase of growth and expansion, some of the mud houses received reinforcement with cement-based mortar, while many newer houses in the early twentieth century boasted cement block and mortar solidity. Cracks in walls resulting from the use of iron rods and corrugated iron sheets, rusty to differing degrees, became perpetual evidence of living close to the sea, with its ubiquitous saltwater breeze.

Narratives on the acquisition of maritime acquaintanceship and fishing expertise among the people of Cape Coast, generally attributed to *hɛn na-na-nom*, "our ancestors," scarcely explained the originality of said skills.[12] At best those claims only accounted for transfer of know-how along lines of apprenticeship done through observation and participation. Lagoons and smaller inland water bodies served as long-lasting laboratories for experimentation in the development of canoe and fishing techniques later transferred for use on the sea.[13] This seeming ease of transfer did not discount the significant differences between lagoon and maritime navigation. Indeed, the tempestuous currents and heavy surf of the sea required distinctive types of canoes and special skills. However, the calmer inland water bodies augmented familiarity with the turbulent ocean, making inhabitants of these neighborhoods strong swimmers before they acquired marine navigational skills. Lagoon fishing and salt making supplemented other occupations, with the experience and expertise garnered in lagoon exploits later invested in sea fishing.[14]

The Fosu Lagoon, located a short distance west of the fishing settlement, with its stable, tender, and temperate waters flowing into the sea, served as a medium for honing basic water-body maneuvers for inquisitive and would-be seagoers and fishermen of Cape Coast. The Brenya Lagoon offered similar utility for their Elmina neighbors to the farther western approaches. Yet for the people of Cape Coast, as for all Fanti groups of coastal Ghana, knowledge and experience of water bodies was rooted far in the past and in distant places.

The *Etsii*, generally seen as the first inhabitants of the shoreline of southern Ghana (especially the section stretching from Keta to Elmina), arrived in the late thirteenth century, supposedly from the Niger Bend. They have received great acclaim as the original bearers and transmitters of maritime fishing skills in the country,[15] having benefited from experience in the Niger River and other smaller bodies of water in that part of West Africa. The *Etsii*, according to Meyerowitz, moved from the Niger Bend because of war and famine, settling on the land abutting the Benue, a tributary of the Niger River. Here, they led quiet and peaceful lives, fishing and sailing to nearby places. The *Etsii* additionally acquired indigenous technology for traversing larger water bodies through borrowing of ideas as well as improvisation. They learned how to build large canoes from huge pieces of wood—a process that improved on an earlier practice of making canoes from two pieces of wood, laboriously assembled. The *Etsii* made sails from bark fiber cloth fashioned into mats and fastened to bamboo poles, with the introduction of triangular oars eventually coming in handy.

The presence of the *Etsii* on the southern Ghana shoreline proved beneficial in many ways as various Fanti peoples, who arrived much later, learned maritime skills and technology from them. Well into the early eighteenth century, Cape Coast fishermen, as part of larger, dominant Fanti groups, came into their own as formidable fishermen. A German chaplain at the Danish Fort Frederiksborg (in the vicinity of Cape Coast), Wilhelm Johann Muller, had this to say about Fanti adeptness at weaving fishing nets: "Their principal fishing tackle consists of a net, hooks, and barbed spears for throwing or stabbing with, generally harpoons.... They make their fishing nets out of tree barks ... beating long leaves such as those of benninas [sic] or palm tree with a club, plaiting twine from the veins of the leaves, winding it on to a spindle and then preparing nets with large and small mesh, after the manner of the European fishermen."[16] Subsequently, the Fanti peoples earned an enviable place in the oral tradition of the Ga of Accra, their eastern neighbors, as masters of the fishing craft who taught the people of Labadi to fish.[17] This lasting legacy of bequeathing fishing know-how along coastal Ghana received great citation in the 1774 Danish governor's Agricultural and Trade Report on the spheres of influence of his country along the Guinea coast.[18] Specifically on fishing, Governor Aarestrup offered an accurate account of local net making in the Volta Delta area, giving an inkling of the Fanti influence, especially on those who lived at Anexo, as he reported:

> [They] make a kind of thread, both for sowing and for making nets. They take the largest pineapple leaves they can find, soak them in water for twelve hours, and then beat them on even piece of wood or stone, with a ... straight or even hammer until the green part of the leaves disappears and they become quite moldy. After that they pull the leaves through a wooden knife on the piece of wood until nothing, but the strings of the leaves are left. These they wash in fresh water until they become quite white. When dry, they twist them on their right thigh till they become as thick as they want them.[19]

Successive accumulation as well as accentuation of knowledge, skill, and technique earned the Fanti peoples a respected tradition of maritime accomplishments. They ventured out in canoes over long distances, some for the purpose of permanent settlement, both up and down the familiar coastline, to Accra, Anexo, Keta, and so on, and along the Gulf of Guinea coast as far as Liberia to the west. A daring few navigated their way southeast to Angola.[20] Most of these journeys involved not only visiting proximate and distant lands but also conveying traders with their wares to some of those places. European merchants who lacked adequate numbers of canoe men to transport goods to farthest forts at distances of 350 to 450 miles relied on local Fanti experts, who received various fees for their services. Hence, coastal societies of southern Ghana, particularly the Fanti peoples, had a highly developed maritime culture of their own, including adeptness at protecting their shores using specially designed and maneuverable canoes capable of withstanding all manner of wind conditions.[21]

### THE BEACH: GROUPS AND ACTIVITIES

The beach (*mpu-ano* or *ɛpu-ano*), that sandy space between land and sea, likewise the marketplace for many an African society, stood out as a peculiar place to coastal communities. Besides being an arena for economic activities, the beach remained in its entirety a social, political, and cultural sphere, assuming the semblance of a sacred space. Among other things, canoes were visible features of beaches belonging to fishing communities along coastal Ghana. The canoes commonly used within the coastal stretch consisted of dugouts from soft, creamy-white tree trunks known in local parlance as *wa-wa*.[22] The canoe—*hyɛn-ba*, as generally known among the littoral Fanti peoples—stood out for all fishing communities along coastal Ghana as indispensable to their existence. Its economic importance as a rare resource imbued it with a somewhat religious relevance. This sanctity played a revered role in ensuring its productive utility. Consequently, identifying a suitable tree for a canoe, felling it, digging it out, conveying it to the coast from the interior, and launching it all constituted religious routines steeped in ritual, as evidenced extensively in the pouring of libation. The canoe in many ways remained central to all facets of everyday life on the coast, a consummate cultural symbol among owners and nonowners alike. Besides its indispensability to fishing expeditions, the canoe constituted a trusted means of transportation to and from distant neighboring coastal communities. Ultimately, it served as a great symbol of social status for its owners.

Generally, the canoes used along coastal Ghana featured bows and sterns rallying to a rounded point, both considerably elevated above seawater at angles enhancing those projections. The semi-rounded underbelly improved stability, as the thoroughly worked sides gave the hull a V shape. Even when overflowing with weight, their heavy draft facilitated navigation in shallow depth of less than one foot.[23] Some European accounts provide descriptions of impressive canoes in coastal Ghana. A keen yachtsman observed that the "Gold Coast ... canoes are ... well adapted to their [fishermen's] work. They [are] ... light but seaworthy, fast, [and] when running with the wind, exactly ... [what is] needed for working from a steeply shelving sandy beach[es] in heavy surf. The men ... [are] wonderfully skilled at handling them in the critical moment when this canoe [sic] came flying up the beach on the crest of a wave and took to the ground as the wave receded. With their rounded bottom, they settled flat and easily hauled up the beach."[24] Relatedly, Pieter de Marees opined that Grain Coast canoe makers made "fine canoes," but "those of the Gold Coast [were] ... the best."[25]

The enduring salient significance of the canoe formed part of the knowledge in the training of novitiates for the acquisition of requisite skills in canoe handling. Essentially, initiation into fishing as the main occupation of coastal communities comprised a paramount phase of rites of passage. During this period, beginning learners honed their skills in swimming, diving, paddling, and identifying various schools of fish and the appropriate nets for harvesting them. These accomplishments came with what could be described as routine instruction in rudimentary astronomy. Trainees would have to understand astronomical changes such as phases of the moon and star movement.[26]

In Cape Coast, as in other coastal communities, parked canoes remained along the beach; to get them across the sand onto the sea, fishermen would use wide cylindrical metallic or wooden rollers. In most cases, several of these rollers would be placed under the canoe as a group of men maneuvered it in the front and rear. As the canoe inched forward, the rollers at the rear would be removed and placed in the front, with the process being repeated until the canoe floated on the sea.

The earliest group of fishermen on a regular day would leave a couple of hours after *es-suem* (midnight). Other fleets left at different times up to *dɔn n-kron* (approximately nine o'clock) in the morning. Depending on the kind of fish being pursued, a fleet could be away for a few hours or several days. The kind of fish a fleet targeted also dictated the technique and equipment used. During the *ɛ-ban* (herring) season, the net-casting technique was preferred, whereas line fishing dominated in the *wii-wi-riw* (redfish) season.[27] Beach fishing, done at different times and spaces, remained the most visible method of fishing to the casual visitor. Even this type of fishing required fishermen to "climb the sea," *fow po*, which involved going over the high tide to cast nets that would later be dragged from the beach.

Dragnet fishing on the beach usually happened to the accompaniment of a slew of songs and occasional theatrical performances from small groups playing tunes on improvised musical instruments. The din of songs and yells might sound cacophonic to the untrained ear, but to the indigene, that seeming noise constituted a merry melody meant to add rhythm, tempo, and ease to the otherwise arduous task of dragging nets for hours on end.[28] The songs comprised common indigenous secular and religious tunes, or an admixture of both. In a bid to endure the otherwise monotonous task at hand, some work-related songs were heavily onomatopoeic to the extent that meanings of the words hardly mattered as much as the beat and rhythm. Some of the songs sought to address social issues or conundrums. Typical among these was the following folk song:

> Me tse a-se m'ennya a-dze
> Me re bo wu m'enya a-dze oooo!
> Yaa ya nko-ba!
> Nko-ba nko-ba nko-ba nko-ba eeeiii!
> Yaa ya nko-ba![29]

This song remained prominent, sang for and on behalf of people who had ready reasons to lament their destiny and lampoon society, clan (*Ebusua*), and extended family for lack of sympathy and abject neglect of the needy in the face of everyday woes. Justifiably, the aggrieved individual in this song poses thought-provoking questions regarding why the likelihood, or even the reality, of being showered with money and material things happens more often after people die than when those things were necessary for their survival. Society in this song stands accused of the futility of caring more for the dead than the living. Such a degree of care for the dead seems senseless and useless, amounting to a blatant show of callousness and wickedness. Some of the men responsible for dragging the nets on the beach would be bare chested, wearing only *dwo-ko-to* (big and often baggy underwear) and, in some cases, shorts. Fishing on the beach often happened with the assistance of some casual workers, who would work well in hopes of receiving a take-home share of the catch. Although net dragging featured as the main activity on the beach during these times, it happened among other activities.

Petty traders practically turned the fishing grounds into marketplaces amid shouts and sounds to draw the attention of potential customers to the items for sale. These activities added

Fig. 3.1 Onshore or drag net fishing: Fishermen getting ready to reel in their catch. Courtesy of Charles Ebow Jonah and Thomas Ekow Stephens.

to the din of fishing crews and small groups of music makers, rendered even louder in obvious attempts to drown and neutralize the booming sounds of the waves. Women who handled fish, either as traders or porters—largely comprising wives, concubines, relatives, and friends of the fishermen—participated in differing degrees of productive and enterprising ventures on the beach. Some of them, as processors and distributors of fish, enhanced their agency in commercial and artisanal fishing. Two significant groups of women whose activities presented fishermen with a conundrum included fishwives maritally related to fishermen and commercial fish dealers, not necessarily relatives but appropriately described as business partners.[30] These groups

Fig. 3.2 Onshore fishing: Fishermen dragging their net. Courtesy of Charles Ebow Jonah and Thomas Ekow Stephens.

remained indispensable to the extensive and expansive network of processing, distributing, and marketing of fish along the coast and in the hinterland regions.

The latter group of women wielded an added advantage given their capacity to offer loans, cash, and credit to fishermen, a service that few in the fishing communities could provide. These women had the wherewithal and resources to handle larger quantities of fish than the fishwives during peak seasons, given that their operations spanned local and distant markets. Occasionally, fishermen faced the dilemma of choosing between doing business with the large-scale dealer, who provided ready cash, or with a wife, who would take several days, if not weeks, to turn a profit from the sale of fish. Invariably, fishermen had to turn to the large-scale or commercial fish dealer in a credit relationship, giving those women some sustained sense of control over the supply of fresh fish and assurance of favorable terms of trade to the near exclusion of relatives, especially wives.[31]

On nonfishing days, the beach became a recreational ground for all kinds of leisure activities, such as swimming, racing, and organized competitions. Occasional wrestling bouts among different groups constituted one of several kinds of enduring entertainment for folks in coastal communities. These competitive wrestling bouts pitted *Asafo* groups or even fishing groups against another, sometimes casually among friends. Tug of war contests involved two lead contestants trying to pull each other with their hands as a chain of supporting people pulled from the waist level. These competitions and many more happened amid a convivial atmosphere heightened by breathtaking drumming, singing, and dancing.

### TUESDAY: A DAY OF REST, RECUPERATION, AND REVITALIZATION

The overwhelming diligence and sense of strong work ethic among coastal fishing communities would generally be tempered with an imposed resting period on Tuesday, when no one might venture seaward. For instance, Wilhelm Johann Muller, in his description of the *Fetu* country (Fanti or Cape Coast in this context) between 1662 and 1669, noted that "every day except Tuesday (which as mentioned, they celebrate in honor of their sea gods) they go in large numbers 2 or 3 miles out into the open sea to fish."[32] Traditionally referred to as *Be-na-da da bɔn*, Tuesday was touted as a day that foreboded evil or ill omen; violation of the prohibition of work not only attracted a fine but also the general expectation that violators would propitiously and miraculously escape a near-fatal experience as the elements, or some vindictive spirit, might strike them down. Beliefs and thoughts such as these, invoking trepidation and caution on a superficial level, had the unspoken scientific undertone of ensuring rest and recuperation for the sea and the fishermen, as well as providing ample time to mend nets and other fishing accoutrements, including canoes in dire need of repair.

The observation of this general work prohibition happened not only in coastal communities but also across the hinterland regions. Just as fishing communities in the coastal belt remained mindful of the ban, farmers in the rural areas hardly entered the forest to do any work whatsoever on Tuesdays. The conventional indigenous religious thought behind these work prohibitions considered this day as the period when the nature spirits ventured out, presenting high risk of a defiant individual encountering them. Amid the many indigenous religious restrictions or taboos, the alternative explanation for these rules, which rarely came up in discussion, hinged on providing rest not only for the individual but also for nature. Both the sea and the forest might not be disturbed for the assurance of a kind of natural regeneration and revitalization. That occurrence equally implied, especially for coastal fishing communities, bountiful catches on workdays following the prohibitions. Hence, the exigency and practice of traditional religions to some extent impacted productivity. Public health personnel and colonial government officials who desired direct policy dissemination in these communities would choose Tuesdays—convenient for the people and assuring impressive community turnout and participation.

### HIGH-SEA EXPERIENCES

The diverse and differing high-sea experiences of fishermen, including omnipresent risk, stemmed from natural occurrences such as thunderstorms, strong winds, and other weather-related hazards. The precariousness of high-sea fishing worsened with the use of small, narrow canoes. The apparent absence of space became increasingly obvious in the nearly full state of the canoe, stocked with necessary accoutrements and supplies such as massive fishing nets, fuel, water containers, food, coal pots, pots, and pans. Consequently, the continuing competition for space away from the shore presented two basic paradoxes: first, the individual fisherman, crammed together with his cohorts yet collectively isolated from the rest of humanity, and second, fishermen working on the high seas while confined to what amounted to wooden walls.[33] A fisherman could be separated from the rest of the world and simultaneously feel the physically pressing presence of other folks on the expedition. Equally, at some points, he could see panoramic views of landscapes without enjoying the immediacy of experiencing any of them. These circumstances constituted the character and constraints of life at sea, providing prompts to understand the mentality of those who traversed it.[34]

No sooner did fishermen make their way up the high seas than they encountered yet more difficulties. Both experienced and amateur fishermen battled differing degrees of seasickness, that ubiquitous, recurrent, and unavoidable momentary malaise. For the amateur, seasickness remained an unpleasant experience that worsened with lack of sleep, rendering him a bundle of testy trouble. Under these conditions, fishermen could nag as much as they suffered nagging. Petty fights among fishermen in a canoe at sea stemmed from impatience and immediacy associated with group work, the productivity of which hinged on synchronized efforts. Consequently, a break in rhythm could cause confusion and, in some instances, scuffles. Empty threats would precede confrontations, often acted on in the spur of the moment. Some fishermen would unleash a barrage of insults at one another, which would often degenerate into near fights. In the process, they would shout vulgarities not only at whoever worried them but also at their parents, wives, and other relatives, with sarcastic statements being introduced into the fray. These kinds of altercations and fights would occasionally happen during fishing on the shore.

Furthermore, intemperate weather conditions often plagued the work of fishermen at sea, resulting in work-related accidents such as canoes capsizing or sinking. At best, canoes ran adrift, and fishermen would be confronted with the tedious option of maneuvering to change course or getting back to the original direction despite the turbulent winds. They equally endured storms amid thunder and lightning in the middle of the ocean. In such situations, fishermen would work against nature as well as time to empty their canoes, which flooded freely and quickly under such conditions. The powerful elements stood out clearly relative to the fragility of the human frame in these severe situations.[35] These dynamics informed the robust nature and character of maritime life in coastal Ghana.

Fishermen and other men of the sea do not easily comply with being ordered about, and their conduct in coastal southern Ghana, where they constituted the core of the *Asafo* institution, was no different. Men of the sea exhibit enormous disposition to instigate confrontations with power and authority structures in the same manner as other workers, such as miners, who also labor in difficult and dangerous physical conditions isolated from the rest of society.[36] Many fishermen appeared intolerant, fractious, daring, and not easily intimidated because they considered themselves one of the few groups of humanity whose major productive activities exposed them to ever-present fatalities. These exposures, in the coastal worldview, put fishermen a notch above average human beings, and they would therefore scarcely suffer weaklings trifling with their otherworldly lives. This perception invariably influenced the engagement and interactions of fishermen with people outside the fishing occupation. With most of these men and women constituting the quintessential membership of the *Asafo*, that temperament manifested among several groups and not infrequently in controversies with the colonial government.

## COASTAL COMMUNITY *ASAFO* AND CONFLICT: ACCRA

The preponderance of fishermen and women within the membership of *Asafo* groups in Cape Coast, Accra, and Apam underpinned the recurrent history of intergroup rivalry and contestation of colonial authority. From the late nineteenth century onward, authorities in coastal Ghana increasingly came to terms with the occurrence of *Asafo* conflicts and clashes. The form and frequency of these altercations overwhelmed the colonial officials not only in Cape Coast but also in Accra, Apam, and other places along the coast. Between 1924 and 1925, *Asafo* groups in Accra led a formidable fight against the introduction of a fully elected and self-sustaining town council. As grassroot organizations conversant with the ebb and flow of everyday life, the *Asafo* quickly pointed out the financial implications of the new scheme on an already overburdened urban poor. Basic tax rates, if the proposal passed, would increase roughly 20 percent; the tax net would be cast widely enough to drag in a greater section of the population, including drummers who, additionally, had to acquire license fees, which would boost revenue income collection for the government. For traders, including those who had stalls in markets and petty traders who purveyed their wares around neighborhoods, license fees would go up close to 50 percent.[37] In its rejection of the new plan, the Accra *Asafo* decried the difficult economic circumstances of the period and the effects on ordinary people. The disparate financial situations of the inhabitants of the town of Accra would make it impossible to endure the fresh hardship of the tax impositions of the new scheme of municipal governance.[38] The local economy was already reeling from global depression at the time; most people found themselves in arrears on their taxes, with nearly all the major activities at Salaga, one of Accra's many markets, grinding to a halt.[39]

The colonial government contributed, in part, to the prevailing, widespread economic hardship. Instead of allowing local women to continue providing prisons in Accra with meals for a fee, the government pressed prisoners to prepare their own food to cut costs. This decision produced a pecuniary effect on many women, who had barely profited from the previous arrangement. Worse yet, the government extended cost-cutting measures to the building and construction sector, frustrating workers such as bricklayers, carpenters, and other artisans in the process. The *Asafo* promptly pointed out these occurrences and took action to counteract them.

Furthermore, the growing number of both European and Levantine export-import businesses adversely affected traders of Accra, who had previously dominated the sector. In the past, a good number of young men would go to the hinterlands, buy cocoa, and resell it to foreign firms, barely turning a profit. Then, some expatriate traders started going directly to the farmers in the distant districts, circumventing the local middlemen.[40] The foreigners continued their penetrating course, gradually setting up stores in every village of importance and even in smaller and more obscure places throughout the country.[41] With the mushrooming of these foreign stores all across southern Ghana, local women in the business of buying and selling suffered severely, especially when they had previously bought textile at, say, ten shillings, taken it up the railroad into the interior, and retailed it at eleven shillings six pence. The growing number of these stores in the villages caused the same pieces of cloth to sell for nine shillings, burying these women in deep debt with the supplying firms. Several faced court action aimed at compelling the retrieval of outstanding amounts owed.[42] Despite these frustrations and hoping to turn the situation around, the women continued to trade in cloth and beads, albeit at the expense of their independence, on account of increasing indebtedness to their creditors, the expatriate-owned wholesale businesses.

The Accra *Asafo* equally took cognizance of increasing unemployment, which worsened because of the introduction of vehicular conveyance of goods to and from the Accra railroad termini, especially at the port. The hauling of goods had constituted a booming business for men and women who used carts to convey merchandise or carried it on their heads to distant destinations. With the dwindling of that income-earning opportunity, they and their families, as well as other dependents, came off worse. Moreover, the population of Accra doubled within the period, pushing unemployment levels in the city to critical proportions.[43] *Asafo* leaders blamed the colonial government and foreign firms for the impoverishment of many inhabitants.

The *Asafo* leaders reiterated the preposterousness and insensitivity of the government imposing the new measures. Raising taxes on already overburdened people amounted to a punitive measure, pure and simple. Given its determination to prevail, the *Asafo* set about harassing the chiefs and educated elite perceived as being supportive of the new municipal and town council arrangement. It gained considerable backing from disparate inhabitants of Accra and staged a highly effective opposition to the new measures. J. D. Garshong, a leader of the group, managed to get a copy of the ordinance in question and submitted it to other leaders, who backed the immediate scuttling of the government action.[44] At a large public gathering, Garshong reiterated the severity of the proposed measures that had already become common knowledge. He proceeded to read the details to the meeting in the Ga language, consciously drawing attention to the opprobrious and oppressive provisions. The incensed and agitated gathering rejected a suggestion from the Ga *Man-tsɛ* to consult with the Accra branch of the Aborigines' Rights Protection Society (ARPS).[45] The rejection hinged on the suspicion that some of the educated elite who formed the ARPS exhibited an informed inclination toward supporting the municipal arrangement. Accordingly, tempers rose as the boisterous section of the gathering pushed for radical responses.

The *Asafo* leaders initially advocated for a formal approach, with the recommendation of an immediate telegraphic dispatch to the secretary of state for colonies in London. The Ga *Mantsɛ* refused to endorse the telegram, but the leaders sent it regardless, arguing that not a single moment should be spared in opposing the ordinance. Gauging the sentiments of the people at meetings, the leaders felt empowered to take all necessary steps to prevent the implementation of the Municipal Corporations Ordinance 1924 in Accra and its environs.[46] Between August and October 1924, the Accra *Asafo* dispatched three more petitions to the Office of the Secretary of State for Colonies. They brought pressure to bear on two prominent chiefs of Accra, the Osu and James Town *Man-tsɛ-mei*, to act accordingly.[47] These telegraphic petitions gained some attention within the corridors of power, given the appointment of a commission of inquiry under H. S. Newlands to assess the viability and applicability of the proposed plan. The *Asafo* leaders remained unrelenting in their protest as they reiterated an absolute rejection of the Corporations Ordinance.

In addition to using official means to achieve their motives, the *Asafo* leaders employed unprecedented moves whenever the opportunity presented itself. They dealt with the Ga *Mantsɛ*, whose ambivalent conduct with respect to the issue had become widely known. He became known in official colonial circles as personally eager for the success of the municipality idea.[48] As suspected about the educated elite of Accra, the rumor that the Ga *Mantsɛ* had indicated his approval of the municipal plans spread far and wide.[49] His failure to endorse any of the petitions that the *Asafo* presented confirmed suspicions of him as a supporter of the colonial government. The perception that the Ga *Mantsɛ* had betrayed his own town to an iniquitous law grew exponentially.[50]

The *Asafo* leaders defied the authority of the Ga *Mantsɛ* and instigated the town to boycott any meeting he called. The leading advocates of this defiance required people to attend only meetings that the *Asa-fo-atsɛ-mei* or *Asafo* leadership called. After the Ga *Mantsɛ* refused to give his consent to the petitions, the *Asafo* declared him suspended for daring to file a lawsuit against its leaders and went a step further, announcing with gongs that he had been ousted as king of the town.⁵¹

The politically sensitive nature of the deposition compelled the colonial government to constitute a commission of inquiry to review the case.⁵² Secretary of Native Affairs C. W. Wellman, who chaired the commission, declared the dethronement of the king as an improper and abject contravention of customary rites.⁵³ The colonial government attempted to reinstate the Ga *Mantsɛ*, which generated general uproar as the *Asafo* mobilized immediately and decided on the next line of action. Members demonstrated along the road from the Accra town proper to the Christiansborg Castle, the seat of government, shouting insults and singing songs of defiance. The *Asafo* embarked on this noisy protest, with women singing, shouting, and dancing beneath the windows of the office of the governor. The protesters proclaimed that no matter what the governor said or did, the *Asafo* would not serve Tackie Yaoboi, the suspended Ga *Mantsɛ*.⁵⁴ In the end, the government dispatched a contingent of eighty policemen to disperse the men and women, arresting fifty-five and charging them with illegal entry into the precincts of the Christiansborg Castle.⁵⁵ The presiding judge kept the arrested men and women in custody for a little over a month, refusing them bail because of the general temper that disturbed the political stability of Accra.⁵⁶

Still pursuing a radical route, the *Asafo* managed to mobilize the market women of Accra with the assertion that taxes, anywhere in the world, signified a kind of hardship and were therefore never a pleasant experience. The women came out en masse to protest the imposition of taxes, and the ensuing commotion became no small matter.⁵⁷ The aggregate effect of the diverse means of protest that the Accra *Asafo* deployed against the proposed town council was profound. Eventually, Governor Guggisberg came to terms with the inadvisability of moving the new measure forward and abandoned the plan, albeit for only a season.⁵⁸

## COASTAL COMMUNITY *ASAFO* AND CONFLICT: CAPE COAST

The Cape Coast *Asafo* had a history of peculiarly recurrent intergroup conflicts and, notably, of contesting colonial authority. These occurrences exhibited complex manifestations, especially given that the town had seven *Asafo* groups.[59] Their confrontation of the colonial government accentuated the uniqueness of Cape Coast, which in many ways epitomized the political temper of coastal Ghana in the late nineteenth and early twentieth centuries. Nearly all the *Asafo* companies of Cape Coast were, at one time or another, responsible for or involved in the contestation of the administration on several scores.[60] Colonial officers often had to deal with troubling situations involving intercompany engagements that led to sporadic clashes and noncooperation with the government. Many such engagements and disturbances were rooted in enduring expressions of rivalry and conflict among various *Asafo* groups.

By 1909, these disturbances had persisted for over fifty years and posed a serious threat to the internal peace of Cape Coast.[61] For instance, in 1859, a consequential affray broke out between the *Bentsir* and *Ntsin* companies; a similar situation occurred ten years later, in 1869. Then, in 1877, the *Bentsir* and *Anaafo* companies engaged each other again. The severity of the punishment meted out to leading participants provides an inkling of the seriousness of the scuffle. The courts tried about fifty men, and four of them received a death sentence.[62] The year 1885 saw yet another conflict in which the *Anaafo*, *Ntsin*, and *Nkum* companies fought against *Bentsir*; the *Ntsin* and *Nkum* companies pitched battle in October 1899. These disturbances continued in the twentieth century. Again, 1904 saw a bloody scuffle between the *Bentsir* and *Ntsin* companies.[63] Just the following year, in December 1905, a four-day altercation occurred between the *Anaafo* and *Ntsin* companies. On February 27, 1915, the *Ntsin* and *Nkum* companies fought again, resulting in the former losing a member and seven people sustaining injuries.[64]

A causal analysis of these disturbances reveals an intriguing pattern that includes, among other things, blatant exhibition of objectionable flags. *Asafo* flags ultimately represented the honor and spirit of each group, having everything to do with dignity—the veritable embodiment of companies, held high and defended in any situation. During parades, specially trained members would display flags and wield them in spectacular fashion. Flags often exhibited signs and symbols that recapitulated *Asafo* history with images emblematic of perceived or purported superiority relative to other companies. Hence, any seizure or vandalization of a flag amounted to the capture and denigration of company honor. Companies created flags in response to objectionable actions of rival groups in equal measure. In this dynamic, symbolic language and other implied communicative techniques came into play, and since all groups knew the meaning of aspersions involving *Asafo* flags, they responded appropriately. Flags extolling the honor of companies intriguingly became useful in demeaning rival groups.

The use of objectionable flags caused the contention between the *Bentsir* and *Ntsin* companies in 1859, as well as in the 1885 conflict, during which *Anaafo*, *Ntsin*, and *Nkum* companies fought against *Bentsir*.[65] In the latter incident, *Anaafo*, *Ntsin*, and *Nkum* companies exhibited flags that infuriated the *Bentsir* group. These companies touted their achievements and superiority in provocative ways. *Bentsir*, in turn, displayed an unusual flag made of a pure piece of blanket, implying that it had in the past fended for and been of great help to members of those offending companies, just as mothers often use blankets to swaddle babies, an important action in caring for them. In other words, this group insisted that those companies in the past had found themselves in desperate degrees of helplessness and hopelessness, to the point of becoming considerably dependent on the magnanimity of the stronger and superior *Bentsir* company.

The other groups collectively took exception to that attempt to demean their dignity, sense of achievement, and history, hence the fight.

The singing of defiant and provocative songs featured as a constant cause of inter-*Asafo* conflict. *Asafo* company songs could be described as characteristically intriguing and interesting. In addition to standard repertoire, companies improvised songs on the spur of the moment to wrangle with opponents and goad members in exigent experiences. Songs of this nature directed taunting, defiant, and insulting remarks at enemy companies. The rhythms often had nonphonemic Akan vocative punctuations, such as *a-yee, yee, a-yoo, ooo, eeeiii, nyoo,* and *a-woo*, used as refrains or fillers to create suspense and nuanced emotional effects.[66] The technique of call and response in songs proffered occasion for dramatic as well as provocative performances in sensitive situations. *Asafo* songs came in fast-paced militant call and response modes, accentuating situational exigencies. A song leader or any inspired member would raise a tune and go through the main verses as the rest sang the chorus intermittently. The rise and fall of cadences would allow for the manipulation of moods commensurate with the occasion, preparing members mentally and emotionally for action. The most definitive song for the *Asafo* of the various Fanti groups was as follows:

> *Oburumankoma eeeiii Oburumankoma eeeiii*
> *Oburumankoma eeeiii eeeiii*
>
> *Oburumankoma Ɔdapagyan eeeiii*
> *Oburumankoma Ɔdapagyan eeeiii*
>
> *Ɔson eeeiiii eeeiii*
> *Ɔson n'ekyir nnyi aboa!*

Basically, the words in this song invoke the names—*Oburumankoma, Ɔdapagyan,* and *Ɔson*—of putative, iconic leading figures of the Fanti peoples during migrations from the Akan cradle to their current places of settlement. The popular chant remained the general battle cry for this indigenous organization in most charged circumstances.

In the 1885 conflict concerning the objectionable blanket, the *Bentsir* company not only used etched devices and emblems on the flag to convey its message but also repeated the meanings and implications of those symbols in songs infused with vocative punctuation.[67] This provocation produced a bellicose and militant atmosphere conducive to the operation of the *Asafo* as a massed unit of people ready for action. Against this background, the aggrieved company reminded the provoking allied group through song that they had been beneficiaries of *Bentsir* benevolence and therefore knew how to conduct themselves as leeches. The company extolled its own deeds of valor in songs to further demean its opponents. Some *Bentsir* members in the front of the dramatic procession indulged in obscenities and vulgarities directed at the allied companies.[68] These actions drove the message home to the targeted companies and achieved the desired effect of provoking them to come out and fight *Bentsir*. Since *Asafo* companies jealously guarded their prestige, privilege, power, and pride, the clash happened as anticipated.[69]

Additionally, trespassing on *Asafo* company quarters precipitated intergroup conflict; one such violation caused the 1904 *Bentsir* and *Ntsin* fight.[70] On this occasion, the *Supi*, or leader of the *Bentsir* company, ignored the customary protocol arrangement of a notification, drink, and fee to *Ntsin*. He, however, had presented the drinks and fees to all other groups, indicating the intention of his company to parade through their respective quarters. On the day of the parade, *Bentsir* company changed the route and deliberately marched through Commercial Road, clearly within *Ntsin* territory. The ensuing clash lasted for just twenty minutes due to prompt police action; however, the fury of these two companies caused injury to many people. *Omanhin* Mbra, who had rushed to the scene with his men to prevent the disturbance from getting out of hand, fell several times after being violently pushed.

The police arrested nineteen of the principal actors and helped transport the wounded to the hospital.[71] The underlying cause of this fight had to do with the *Bentsir* company still feeling quite irritable about the 1885 conflict, in which the other companies questioned its claim to superiority. With *Ntsin* being the largest rival that had questioned its superiority, *Bentsir* decided to take the former for granted just to spite *Ntsin* and to prove itself stronger and superior in provoking the largest group.

Provocative drum language underpinned many *Asafo* fights and clashes.[72] The poetry of the *Asafo* drum (*Asafo kyin*) remained highly revered, and company members could decipher its implications. Drumbeats and sounds, when performed, had a life of their own, infused with a stimulating language. The tonal and pitch differentiation of both the female and male drums accentuated the meaning as well as implication of the language. The type of animal skins and tree trunks used for making these drums ascribed their gender and enhanced the nuances of drum language. A company might use drum language to extol its achievements and simultaneously provoke other companies. In the 1904 riot between *Bentsir* and *Ntsin*, the drummers of the former group kept sounding the battle charge, referring to the latter as cowards.[73] Inaction or lack of response meant a confirmation, or worse yet, a justification of the insult; since cowardice remained an ignoble trait that no serious *Asafo* company would countenance, *Ntsin* in the usual *Asafo* scheme of things accepted the *Bentsir* stance as a clear call to action. *Bentsir* vilified members of the *Ntsin* company, calling them leeches, effeminate, and ingrates. The *Bentsir* allusion to these affronts using drum language ignited an already volatile situation and incited young men of both companies wielding old guns, knives, clubs, and sticks to attack one another, as the rest engaged in a stone fight.[74]

Excessive consumption of alcohol endured as a constant factor in *Asafo* scuffles and rows.[75] Alcohol as a powerful, intoxicating liquid remained pivotal to the operation of the organization.

This indispensability found expression in the saying *Asafo wɔ-dze nsa bɔ*, literally, "it takes alcohol to play or perform *Asafo*." The fundamental meaning of *Asafo* emphasized warfare, bravery, fortitude, resoluteness, and even manliness. Companies envisaged an overwhelming connection between these attributes and alcohol usage. Alcohol—or better still, spirits—the king of all drinks, stimulated aggressiveness and the desire for dominance, both reminiscent of power as a necessary condition for war. At best, the *Asafo* stood as a metaphor for popular power; alcohol equally cast itself as a metaphor for power because it encapsulated a spectrum of dynamics. Given its nature as a sharp, mood-influencing fluid, alcohol was a potentially dangerous substance. Yet, as a liquid that possessed power vital for communication with entities in the spiritual realm, alcohol dethroned reason.[76] The power dynamics of alcohol also entailed its potential to endow extraordinary ability. Warfare, one of the essences of the *Asafo* raison d'être, emphasized animal blood offerings and ritualized usage of alcohol. As purveyors of war, companies acquired specific "war medicines," religious strongholds, and objects that required ritual use of alcohol.[77] Religious use of alcohol hinged on its perceived potential to make the physical world confer with the supernatural realm. In line with various Akan social and religious belief systems, *Asafo* members asserted that success in their activities as an indigenous institution could be enhanced through the cultivation of the supernatural forces that inhabit the spiritual realm, access to which laid in alcoholic spirits.

For the *Asafo* companies, these supernatural forces included the spirits of their war medicines, *mpa-nyin-fo* (departed leaders), and *nananom* (ancestors). The spirit within alcohol accentuated its mood changing or intoxicating essence. Because both ancestors and war medicines dwelled in the spiritual realm, alcoholic spirits provided the larger link between them and the organization through the performance of libation (*nsa-gu*). After the proper observation of these rituals using alcoholic spirits, members indulged themselves liberally to revive their individual and collective spirit with the remaining substance. The ensuing group drinking happened with the passing around of a single—or better yet, a couple—tumblers for members to gratify themselves according to individual taste and capacity. During these drinking sprees, participating members frequently received commendation as "unusual men" for their impressive capacities for copious consumption. The consequences of these demonstrable *mba-nyin-dze*, "manly acts," portended trouble in most cases. Yet alcohol usage among the *Asafo* had a paradoxical dimension. As much as it had a notorious association with conflict, alcoholic drink played a prominent role in facilitating the settlement thereof. After requisite deliberations at gatherings, the peacemakers would ensure the liberal circulation of spirits or alcohol as *asomdwee nsa* (peace drink) to cement the fresh bond of good feeling among hitherto disputing companies.

Excessive consumption of alcoholic drinks factored prominently in the clashes between 1859 and 1915. The 1905 conflict between *Anaafo* and *Ntsin* companies could have been avoided but for the excessive consumption of liquor among the young men, a common phenomenon in the early twentieth century.[78] On Tuesday, December 5, a considerable number of young *Anaafo* men with "rum inside them" advanced up *Ntsin* Street, trespassing the quarter of that company.[79] They desecrated a sacred stronghold belonging to the group, retiring with an iron emblem (*da-dze-kur*) and a bamboo fiber.[80] Earlier in the day, the *Ntsin* company had resisted *Anaafo* attempts to traverse its quarter to get to the cemetery for the solemn purpose of burying a deceased colleague because the latter had insisted on practicing the custom of dancing on the coffin. The former company objected because that custom normally involved some sort of mischief, as the performing company used the ritual to offend people along the road with covert terms and signs of contempt. That custom, again, happened mostly with gestures generally understood among the various companies. *Ntsin* allowed only the bereaved family to pass through their quarter to gain access to the cemetery. The *Anaafo* company considered this denial of passage an affront to their pride and reputation, particularly given the fact that the deceased happened to be an old drummer and therefore an important member.[81]

*Anaafo* company orchestrated the attack to disparage the pride and reputation of *Ntsin*, who reacted because sacred strongholds were highly revered and sensitive spiritual spaces for the *Asafo*. That sacrosanct space in particular stood as powerfully meaningful because *Ntsin* had built it on the remains of a member of the *Bentsir* company whom they had captured in 1869 on *Ntsin* Street.[82] The police, under the command of Superintendent Webb, in concert with prominent personalities such as J. P. Brown, *Safohin* O. Cromwell, and *Safohin* Thomas Aggrey, had a horrid time containing the situation on each day of the clashes. The tension generated hardly subsided until 1909, when local colonial officers decided to ensure peaceful coexistence among companies.[83] During a durbar of companies held on March 6, 1909, at Victoria Park, Commissioner Eliot spoke critically of young men and their drinking habits. He intimated that men often acted foolishly with "rum inside them," and under the influence of competitive company customs, they became even more disagreeable than usual.[84] He explained that excessive drinking caused young men to lose their heads and become carried away, leading to the loosening of tongues. In this state, they spoke unguardedly and committed acts that insulted other companies. Consequently, the offended company would conclude that the untoward action on the part of a few ill-behaved individuals meant an insult to the entire group.[85] Yet, at the same gathering, liberal drinking of alcoholic spirits took place, this time as a peace drink (*asomdwee nsa*) to promote good relations.

Women of *Asafo* companies played just as significant a role in impacting the outbreak of conflicts by either acting of their own accord or standing with their men, supporting them in victory and defeat. The public perception generally frowned on women insulting men, considering it ignoble for a man to countenance the insults of a woman. *Asafo* women, among other things, possessed a special ability to use bitter and acerbic words, innuendo, and imagery. Besides their ability to compose improvised provocative songs vividly conveying blunt messages to taunt and incite men to fight, they could, to a considerable extent, cause conflicts independent of their men. Farcical skits and dramatic performances featured women wearing male costumes that exaggerated visible disabilities or deformities among members of rival *Asafo* companies.[86] These factors accounted for the 1904 scuffle between *Bentsir* and *Ntsin Asafo* companies. The women of *Bentsir* urged their men to act when *Ntsin* trespassed their quarter.[87] In the following year, a conflict between *Anaafo* and *Ntsin* degenerated into a dangerous fight in which women of both factions supplied stones for strategic use by their men.[88] The power, courage, or capacity to cause altercations, though considered a masculine prerogative, in practical terms manifested a unique feminine parallel in southern Ghana. Just as the complementarity of men and women remained vital to community survival, power equally possessed both masculine and feminine principles.[89] Besides a few women who might join men on battlefronts, the majority remained behind and performed *mmo-mo-mme*, a mainly female form of spiritual warfare, at the home front. In this ritual involving singing, moaning, and groaning in varying states of nudity, women traversed one end of the town to the other.[90] The women would continue this ritual procession until the men returned. This feminine form of spiritual warfare supposedly protected their masculine counterparts and goaded them on to victory.

## CONCLUSION

All told, the overwhelming superiority complex among the *Asafo* manifested in unbridled displays of bravado, rivalry, and an uncompromising tendency to outdo one another, aggravating intercompany relations—especially among the groups in coastal Ghana, whose maritime culture reified that system. The dialectic of bravery and cowardice came into play in this dynamic, emphasizing the concept of "self" and "other" within the context of conflict. The "self and bravery" opposed the "other and cowardice."[91] Bravery became a quality for the self to establish its identity. Feats of bravery often remained expressed in the present tense even if they had occurred in the past. Boasting also manifested in rallying calls, appellations, and motifs on flags, often in a competitive relationship with other companies. The diverse circumstances of coastal Ghana communities, especially in social setting, occupation, indigenous institutions, and worldview, ran through everyday experiences. These experiences became reliable resources on which to draw to navigate challenging social and political situations. Combined with a local history of *Asafo* company rivalry, clashes, and confrontations, coastal communities became predisposed to engage plans and actions of not only indigenous power structures but also colonial authority. Such tendencies, especially toward the latter, were heightened with the interplay of indigenous ideas about ownership.

## FOUR

# ART, SYMBOL, AND THE WRITTEN WORD

*The Audacity, Dignity, and Sovereignty of Private Property Ownership*

COMMON STATEMENTS WITHIN AFRICAN SOCIETIES such as "I am because we are, and because we are, I am"—alternatively, "a person is a person because of other persons"—have often been touted in the reiteration of characteristically communal orientations across the continent.[1] Nonetheless, against the social spectacle of communal, family, or group ownership, coastal Ghana communities, like other societies, equally exhibited a strong sense of individual or private property acquisition. The individual certainly remained relevant, both respected and remarkable within the group. To reiterate the sense of power, potential, dignity, and responsibility of the individual, various Fanti societies had sayings such as *Ɔ-bra nye w'ara-bɔ*; this heavily loaded statement, taken literally, means "the essence of life came down to how the individual lived it." Essentially, these words constitute a candid expression of self-responsibility. Mature adult individuals become responsible for choices or actions that impinge on self-improvement and, ultimately, destiny. This hint of an individualized sense of self played out in coastal Fanti ideas of ownership, as in the possession of a wide spectra of material things—including canoes, the salient and most indispensable resource among established fishing communities. The pride that exuded profound audacity, dignity, and sovereignty in property acquisition and ownership found expedient expressions in speech, art, and symbols, as well as designs and meanings, the implications of which became widely understood within contiguous cultural locales. While general and direct meanings could rarely be misconstrued, other connotations were abstract and, therefore, open to all manner of interpretation. These ideas and practices remained essential components of various related Akan cultures and became quite elaborate after initial Akan settlements. Certainly, such practices continued and changed with equally changing circumstances and accompanying experiences, as in all dynamic human societies. Indeed, with the passage of time, these practices became far more subtle, complex, and purposefully directed than when they started.

### ARTISTIC SIGNS AND SYMBOLS

The precontemporary literacy and numeracy period in coastal Ghana witnessed the use of simple signs, symbols, and motifs as markers of ownership (*a-hyɛ-nsiw*) to delineate uniqueness (*so-ro-nko*). For instance, plain drawings, paintings, or sculpture in wood, stone, or metal depicting an individual eating from an earthenware bowl while another seated person merely stares on succinctly encapsulated the sense of pride, audacity, and sovereignty that came with ownership expressed in the emphatic Fanti statement *a-dze wu-ra n'o-dzi nn-yɛ ma kom dze no bi*. Particularly in indigenous royal parlance, this statement emphasized the absence of inhibitions with the authentic owner deciding to eat whatever without regard to the hungry other. Similarly, the statement *a-dze nye w'ara wo-dze* implied that the essence of property ownership derived from the category of things that individuals could unquestionably claim or identify as not being co-owned—especially within the domain of assets that one toiled for and therefore personally acquired, a verifiable incontestable ownership. These statements could apply to the collective, given the purported communal nature of societies in these parts of the continent; the ideas inherent in these statements also resonated with insightful individuals who cherished the absolute authority, freedom, liberty, and dignity that came with having a generally well-known sole ownership of all manner of possessions. In everyday discourse, then, statements such as *pɛ wo dze*, literally, "seek your own property" (that which genuinely and unquestionably belongs to you), sought to admonish the individual to avoid leeching off others and endeavor to acquire personal possessions to enjoy the contentment of private ownership with its undisputed rights of administration. In similar renditions, an individual with any kind of effects could boldly retort *me nn-ye o-bia-ra mm-bɔ-ho hyi* (my personal property) to any direct or indirect intimation that they co-owned a certain item of property. Essentially, that assertion authoritatively pointed out that the speaker did not share the right of ownership of that asset with anyone else and that the property in question remained subject to their whims and caprices. Submissions such as *ma-ra na me tɔ an-saa-na m'e-dzi* reiterated self-reliance and independence, evoking an emphatic distance between the speaker and any unwarranted suspicion of dependency syndrome. Alternatively, the foregoing assertion could be stated *ma-ra me tse m'a-se*, literally, "I live under me or live on my own" (precisely, I am independent), as in the matter of the provision of essential existential everyday needs. With such statements, the speaker echoed the beauty and dignity inherent in fending for oneself.[2]

Set against the spectacle of various cultures that thrived on decorative and visual dynamics, this idea of the pride of ownership assumed intriguing dimensions. Diverse signs, symbols, as well as other expressive artistic forms appeared on all kinds of property, big and small, including royal paraphernalia or regalia, buildings, canoes, and many others. These culturally influenced artistic portrayals amounted to what could be described as silent yet loud expressions of self-assertion and status in community interactions and interrelations. Images and representations cut across a plethora of flora, fauna, celestial bodies, regalia, and weapons, including human depictions.

Fauna illustrations mainly derived from the various totems of individual property owners' respective *Ebusua*, or merely from fanciful and appealing ones in that category of animate beings. These artistic impressions commonly included crocodiles, crows, parrots, hyenas, tortoises, lions, elephants, and so on, as flora representations showed different kinds of trees and plants, often with imposing features. Other property owners would depict sea creatures such as whales, sharks, turtles, or octopuses. The rationale for the use of these flora and fauna illustrations, in nearly all cases, was to uphold the generally well-known, definitive characteristics that property owners might identify with (wholly or partially) and remain unabashedly proud of. Clan totemic symbols or pictograms would—on face value—indicate the group identity of individuals by showcasing the qualities of animals and objects that appeared meaningful to the property owner. Besides obvious characteristic semblances, these depictions sometimes included revered animals because of some purported help the group had received from those creatures as expressed in legends and myths of migration from various places of origin. Along these lines, the image of an elephant, deemed the largest of all animals, implied stability, strength, power, and majesty incomparable to that of any other animal (*Ɔson n'ekyir nnyi aboa!* Literally, there is no other animal beyond the elephant). A family or an individual would use the lion to symbolize fearlessness, fearsomeness, boldness, smartness, stateliness, and majesty or to showcase royal heritage in the sense of the lion being the king of the animal world. For others, the image of the leopard evoked pride in independence and solitude.[3]

In other scenarios, the sun, stars, or moon (depicted in its most recognizable quarter and half phases) featured prominently.

The use of these light-emitting celestial bodies as symbols emphasized great reverence and uniqueness, intimating that those qualities underscored their glorious brightness during the day—as in the case of the sun—or at night. To this end, canoe owners would use images of these bright bodies to emphasize their importance in helping with guidance and direction during navigation on the high seas. These images etched on the surfaces of a wide variety of property might, in other ways, reminisce the characteristics and belief systems of the respective property owners. Other delineations on canoes reflected impressive sea creatures such as whales, sharks, and octopuses, highlighting unique attributes adjudged relevant to the individual or group owners of the seacraft.

Some members of royal *Ebusua* houses—alternatively, *a-de-hye* (people of royal heritage and hence the right to rule)—with their loyalists would use, among other things, silhouettes of stools (*ase-sa-gua*), state swords (*a-ko-fe-na*), and royal umbrellas (*a-hin-kyin*), all of which constituted indigenous political regalia. Often these royal images appeared concurrently with implements of war and state building, *Asafo* symbols, or *Adinkra* motifs as evidence of authentic ownership of land, power, and authority.[4] Other *Adinkra* motifs appeared as impressions on fabric or designs on buildings and canoes. The image of two crocodiles conjoined at the belly area referred to dire situations associated with unity in diversity, the management of which required great caution, as any misjudgment or misstep might have extensive repercussions for perpetrators and victims alike. That depiction, therefore, implied a kind of sensitive shared destiny. Although some might use the traditional stool and sword symbols to accentuate royal status, others, including nonroyals, preferred the former to signify stability, power, and authority. The latter evoked bravery and honor, with the bow and arrow, among other things, representing swiftness and directness.[5]

## IMPACT OF FORMAL EDUCATION AND LITERACY

In all its manifestations, the use of figures, signs, and symbols preceded the writing of inscriptions or statements that occurred well after the introduction and spread of formal education in the nineteenth and twentieth centuries. Many who became proficient in English, the main medium of instruction, benefited from the utilization of their respective first languages, marshaled with the full complement of inherent folk tales, proverbs, circumlocutions, exaggeration, sarcasm, and other literary devices. Despite linguistic complications from the interface, these vernacular literary forms served as a seedbed for nurturing English as a second language. The circumstances leading to the acquisition of a foreign lingua franca eventually presented the need to reduce several local languages into written forms for the first time.

European education in coastal Ghana, as in many other places in Africa, started as a Christian missionary effort. Although missionary groups hardly set out to establish schools, the reality dawned sooner than later that their converts needed rudimentary reading and writing competencies to become well-grounded, active Christians. The Dutch West Indian Company School that started at the St. George Castle, Elmina, in 1644 became the precursor to those missionary endeavors in the country.[6] The castle school system gained currency with the missionaries in Cape Coast and Osu, where reading, writing, and catechism formed the bedrock of the emerging European educational system from the mid-eighteenth century onward. These initial schools transcended the European fortifications on the coast with attachments to the few available churches, as Christianity spread from the coastal areas into the hinterland. The expansion and growth of schools came with the eventual participation of the colonial authorities, who began to appreciate the utility of having Africans equipped with basic literacy and numeracy capacities to work as clerks, messengers, support staff, servants, and other auxiliary workers for the administration and expanding European establishments.

The entrenchment of the British-oriented educational system implied not only an unhindered spread of the English language but also the appearance of indigenous languages in written forms. Building on modest precedents, the most extolled efforts in that direction were those of Johannes Gottlieb Christaller, a missionary with a profound flair for languages, as well as his southern Ghana colleagues David Asante and Theophilus Opoku, both of whom had established themselves as masters of the variant Akan linguistics. Long before the instrumentality of Christaller, missionary Andreas Riis had demonstrated great interest in learning to speak Twi, the generic dialect of the hinterland section of the Akan peoples, throughout travels that took him to Akuapem Akropong, Akwamu, Akyem Abuakwa, Cape Coast, and Kumasi, the Asante capital. In the process, he compiled a seminal Twi and English dictionary that became a modest template for his nephew, Hans Nicolaus Riis, to work with. Equally working as a missionary, H. N. Riis took the unprecedented effort of his uncle a step further, churning out two impressive publications.[7]

Christaller applied his familiarity with Riis and these publications to good effect. At home in Germany, his linguistic aptitude had already made him proficient in English, Hebrew, Greek, and Latin. In addition to these languages, he started learning Twi under the tutelage of Riis. This impressive linguistic proficiency persuaded the Basel Mission to send Christaller to southern Ghana to work on the Twi language, the rudimentary grammar of which he had helped edit at home in Germany before he went to Africa. With the support of local language specialists, Asante and Opoku, he settled on *Akuapem* as the most median and composite of the varying yet mutually intelligible Akan dialects worthy of serious attention in the effort to produce a standardized written form.[8] Christaller became so knowledgeable in the Akan language and its grammar that his authority and opinions gained respect as well as consideration in subsequent efforts to write various Fanti dialects.[9] All told, he expertly wrote Old Testament stories in Twi and eventually repeated the same feat for nearly all of the New Testament.[10] Given the increasing need for clerks, messengers, recruits, and supporting staff for the burgeoning European establishments, the colonial administration subsequently built on the formidable educational foundation that the missionaries had laid.

## SCRIPTED FORMS: VERNACULAR AND THE HEAVY INFLUENCE OF CHRISTIANITY

Well into the twentieth century, not only had literacy and proficiency in the English language spread, but knowledge and dexterity in the writing of most indigenous languages together with their various dialects had also become increasingly common, particularly among those who went to school and acquired some rudimentary formal education. This emerging trend received great boosts from the impressive assemblage of missionary printing presses, book depots, and bookstores that shored up the developing print culture, making these services available to those who could afford them.[11] Furthermore, the springing up of newspapers, both Christian and secular, in English as well as in local languages, was evidence of the emergent print culture.

In coastal Ghana, the indigenous languages, with their clearly defined ideas about what constituted eloquence, elegance, and beauty, came up in various forms of writing, to both good and bad effects.[12] At the local or community level, individual letter writers, sign writers, teachers, and students took pride in serving sections of the population left behind in the era of growing literacy. This privileged few took charge of facilitating social and official communication, both domestically and internationally, for as many as needed help along these lines. Another group of semiliterate individuals became available for the writing of signs, inscriptions, and popular expressions on all manner of surfaces that had originally exhibited symbols and other artistic forms. In most cases, this revolution in style reflected combinations of both, as symbols and artistic forms flamboyantly occurred with written inscriptions. Others sought to abandon the use of the former with a preference for the latter as evidently fashionable and therefore impressive.[13]

The late nineteenth and early twentieth centuries witnessed an increasing appearance of exciting, intriguing, and interesting words, phrases, and brief inscriptions, all of which amounted to salient statements of power, privilege, and prestige in ownership. As the era of literacy in both indigenous and English languages began to blossom, inscriptions along these linguistic frames popped up on all kinds of property surfaces. Initially, vocabulary on surfaces remained predominantly written in indigenous languages for the perusal of the local community, especially targeting those who had acquired differing degrees of literacy. To this end, all manner of surfaces became awash with words and phrases as property owners sought to tout their lifetime achievements and make a claim of significant status in society. Words such as *Ebusua* extolled the clan, as did *Ebu-sua-pa-nyin*, if the property owner happened to be a leader or elder of the same. Alternatively, an individual who appreciated the leader or elder of his clan could use such words. Others might simply use names of their respective clans, as in *Anona, Nsona, Aberadzi, Awindadze, Bretuo*, and many more. In the same vein, an owner might have inscribed on his or her property words such as *Na-na-nom, M-pa-nyin-fo*, or *Nananom Mpanyinfo* conjointly in acknowledgment, honor, or appreciation of the ancestors for their sacrifices and achievements as forebearers and culture bearers. Similarly, individual owners who happened to be leaders of the *Asafo* might prefer titles such as *Tufohin, Supi, Safohin*, or *Asikanmba* on their respective property. Ordinary members, like these leaders, might want to demonstrate commitment to their various groups in the use of names such as *Anaafo, Ntsin, Bentsir, Nkum*, and others. Canoe owners who, in many ways, revered the sea and even ascribed some deity status to it would have a word like *Bo-sum-pu* written on their canoes; others might make references to various celestial bodies, signs, and symbols such as *E-wia* (sun), *Bu-sum* (moon), *N-su-ru-ma* (stars), *N-yan-kon-tɔn* (rainbow), and other related things, all of which were pivotal to the plying of their trade on the high seas.[14]

With the spread and entrenchment of Christianity, inscriptions reflecting beliefs, faith, gratitude, hope, and aspirations of converts occurred prominently. Along these lines, a Christian who had come into property ownership and was of the strong conviction that those asset acquisitions amounted to divine provision would make emphatic statements such as *O-nya-me na o-dze ma*, *Dom-fo Nya-me*, *Nya-me Yε O-dom-fo*, or *Nya-me-kyε*, touting the goodness and beneficence of God. On issues of salvation, preservation, protection, and provision as aspects of the providential plan of God, a good number of property owners preferred words and expressions such as *A-dom* (grace), *Nyame n'A-dom* (the grace of God), *E-gya Gye Me* (Father save or deliver me), *Fa-kyε Hεn* (forgive us), *Nyame Ban-bɔ* (divine protection), and *E-nyim-pa* (favor).

Words and expressions bearing on existential issues, dealing with challenges in life as well as opportunities, also abounded in inscriptions on private property. Along these lines, individual or group owners of property would opt for words and expressions such as *Ɔ-bra*, which in a simple sense emphasized the intriguing vicissitudes of life, or *A-bra-bɔ*, pertaining to life on earth with all its uncertainties. In reiterating the uncertainties of life, other inscriptions might read *Da-bεn*, willfully wondering when and how expectations of the individual or the group would be achieved or how soon a certain life situation or problem would take a turn for the better. *Dzin Pa* in most cases signified the beneficence of a good name, while others might prefer *A-kwan Pa*, an extension of the concept that emphasized good ways, means, and manners.

Fig. 4.1 Canoe with inscription *Nyame Nye Me Boafo*, "God is my helper." The one in the background reads *Nyame Nye Boafo*, "God is the ultimate helper." Courtesy of Charles Ebow Jonah and Thomas Ekow Stephens.

*O-ye* was a generic word that evoked enduring goodness and, in most cases, the goodness of God, life, people, a system, or even preferred as a simple answer to a form of greeting, a response to a simple inquiry about the health or life circumstances of someone. Additionally, *Pa-pa Yɛ* stated the blessing and beneficence that came with doing good or kind deeds.

Amid this culture of expressiveness, themes of conflict or innuendo came up prominently in the plethora of inscriptions on property, as owners chose to cast insinuations and aspersions against perceived, real, or imaginary enemies and detractors. This category manifested strongly in the use of words such as *A-tan-fo*, *Ɔ-yɛ-fo*, and *Ɔ-tan-hun*. All these words essentially dared others to do their worst, as the owners in question would prosper despite (and possibly because of) pervasive negative expectations. Other property owners would choose to focus on good, helpful, as well as influential people, friends, and relatives and the impact these personalities had on their lives. Owners with this frame of mind preferred expressions such as *Ɔ-yan-ko Pa, Ebusua Pa, Na Pa, Egya Pa, O-nua Pa,* and *Wɔ-fa Pa* or expressed thanks more explicitly with a simple inscription such as *Ase-da*. Individuals or groups of people who appreciated the dignity in being productive would tout ideas of hard work and strong work ethics with inscriptions including *E-dwu-ma Pa, E-dwu-ma Dzen*, or even refer to *Bo-tae Pa*, pursuing an innovative purpose and vision for themselves and posterity. As general advice to all and sundry, some would inscribe the expression *Da Dwin*, an admonition for people to hone their critical thinking capacities and be reflective even in their sleeping state.

### SCRIPTED FORMS: ENGLISH AND COMPLEX COMBINATIONS

The inscription of English words and expressions mimicked indigenous types, with occasional incremental sophistication. In addition to the translation of many indigenous inscriptions into English, some preferred direct anglicized forms such as "good people," "good character," "hard work," "love," "hope," and "time changes." Canoe owners especially preferred other fascinating written forms that included, but were not limited to, "sea man," "sea obeys," and "sea never dries." All these categories emphatically suggested that these owners plied their trade and made a living on the high seas, simultaneously intimating the immensity and power of that invincible hydrosphere.

A section of the diverse Christian property owners equally exhibited a great fancy for writing names of the books of the Bible, with their relevant chapters and verses. In this category, the books of Psalms, John, and Revelations remained quite popular. Besides the inscriptions of books, chapters, and verses, brief Bible verses featured, shorn of their specific references. In most cases, these quotations reflected popular parts of scriptures evocative of the beliefs, hopes, and aspirations of the property owner. To this end, "walk by faith," "the Lord is my shepherd," "I shall not want," "grace of God," "our Father," "Jesus wept," "Jesus is Lord," "thanks

Fig. 4.2 A canoe with a biblical inscription reflecting influences of Christianity. Courtesy of Charles Ebow Jonah and Thomas Ekow Stephens.

Fig. 4.3 Canoe with English inscription evoking a Christian theme. Courtesy of Charles Ebow Jonah and Thomas Ekow Stephens.

be to God," "the Good Shepherd," "signs and wonders," "fishers of men," "peace be unto you," "Israel," "amen," "faith," "hope and love," "bread of life," and many more became the preference for Christian property owners.

Another prominent and captivating category combined English and indigenous languages or used pidgin English. Some such combination might, on face value, seem hilarious, yet many were

Fig. 4.4 English inscription with a biblical or Christian theme. Courtesy of Charles Ebow Jonah and Thomas Ekow Stephens.

quite philosophical statements of intent or conviction.[15] English and local language combinations such as *O-ni-pa Yɛ Bad, Si-ka Mm-pɛ Rough, A-bra-bo Yɛ Hard*, and *Fie Na School* dealt with issues of trust, management of money, difficulties of life, as well as life at home and school, respectively. Additionally, "money swine," "chop money," "one man no chop," as well as "travel and see," referred to the reckless spending of money, money for daily upkeep, the ill-advisedness of a few people gorging themselves with superfluities as many lacked necessities, and how traveling bestowed cosmopolitan perspectives but not without an attendant social cost or bitter experiences, respectively. A pidgin expression such as "skin pain," a transliteration of the Akan word *A-ho yaw*, taunted and admonished individuals or groups of people supposedly envious or aggrieved because someone had come into property ownership and was, therefore, prospering in life.

## SCRIPTED FORMS: THE HINT OF ISLAMIC INCLINATION

Some property owners in southern Ghana and much of the coastal belt who had professed Islam preferred inscriptions, words, and symbols resonant with their faith. The north-south religious dichotomy across Africa vis-à-vis Islam and Christianity respectively also cast its shadow in Ghana. Between 639 AD and 708 AD, the Arabs conquered and occupied most parts of North Africa; the activities of traders and devout Muslims who came later facilitated the slow but steady spread of Islam from the north to the Sahara and Sahel regions well into the tenth century. This gradual north-south spread of Islam saw it take root in the savanna and forest fringes of West Africa close to the end of the sixteenth century.

From these regions, various converts among the Mande or Wangara, Malinke or Malinka, Fulani, Dyula, and Zamarama peoples, especially the traders among them, not only sold and bought items as participants of the trans-Saharan caravan trade but also carried Islamic faith into the forest kingdoms, states, and societies, with a few reaching the coastal belt of West Africa. This trend, especially through the instrumentality of long-distance traders, planted Islam in the Dagomba and Gonja areas in the northern part of Ghana toward the end of the sixteenth century.[16]

Given that Islam entered Africa from the north of the continent, accepted by peoples and societies scattered across these parts, and that the religion equally entered Ghana through the north, southern Ghana peoples commonly regarded the Islamic faith as a northern religion. Because of its prevalence among the northern part of the country—especially within the savanna or grassland belt, translated in the Akan language as ɛ-sra-mu or ɛ-sra-mu-fuɔ for the people living on the grassland—the Islamic faith tangentially became ɛ-sra-mu-fuɔ som, "the northern faith," or N-kra-mo som.[17] Nkramo or Kra-mo stemmed from the loud cry or call to prayer performed five times a day, one of the principal pillars of Islam, as well as the preparatory ablution and manner in which Muslims say those prayers.

With larger Akan groups occupying the middle or forest belt, as well as the coastal section remaining predominantly inhabited by practitioners of traditional religions, and many professing the

Fig. 4.5 A canoe with a misspelled Islamic inscription: "Masha Allahu" instead of "Insha Allah." Courtesy of Charles Ebow Jonah and Thomas Ekow Stephens.

Fig. 4.6 A canoe inscription showing Saudi Arabia, a country connected to Islam, with Mecca as the mainstay of the religion. Courtesy of Charles Ebow Jonah and Thomas Ekow Stephens.

Christian faith after the Europeans helped spread it from the south, the few Akan who converted to Islam identified as Akan *Kramo*. Specific terms of reference for these people included variants such as Asante *Kramo* and Fanti *Kramo*, if the persons involved spoke Twi or Fanti, respectively.[18] Despite their minority status, Islamic adherents in southern Ghana, especially along the coastal belt, found it necessary to tout and showcase their religion in the expression of pride in the ownership of property. Bold inscriptions such as "Allah," a name so central and sacrosanct to Islam, "Insha Allah," meaning if Allah allows or permits, "Saudi Arabia" or "Mecca," names fundamental and reminiscent of Islamic sacred sites, all gained popular usage. Often, these inscriptions occurred along with symbols including the crescent moon, which would later become heavily associated with the Islamic faith.

## CONCLUSION

Although the individual passed as a person within community in coastal Ghana, that predominant sense of communal belonging hardly hampered personal assertiveness in all facets of life including property ownership. The liberty, pride, and underpinning dignity and audacity of individual ownership found full expression in the emerging age of literacy initially brought through the facility of European missionaries and their local associates, as well as the colonial government. The intriguing array of words, inscriptions, and expressions—and the availability of people who could write them on property surfaces—knew no bounds. Those who used these services had no inhibitions whatsoever in making their hopes, beliefs, aspirations, and intentions known in their respective societies. Inscriptions of words and expressions appeared in indigenous languages, English, pidgin English, or fascinating combinations of these three languages, not excluding intricate religious undertones drawn heavily from both traditional beliefs and Christianity, with scant Islamic inclusions. These hybrid scripted forms essentially acted as enhanced reinforcements of entrenched expressive artistic and symbolic precedents in the indigenous culture. This strong sense of individual and group property ownership, as well as the attendant empowering pride, dignity, and audacity, served southern Ghana well in the efforts to obstruct colonial government land policy.

# FIVE

## "HƐN-ARA HƐN A-SAA-SE NYI"

*Land in Everyday Life, Colonial Policy, and Indigenous Resistance*

AMONG SOUTHERN GHANA SOCIETIES, THE significance of land endured at multiple levels. It constituted an exclusive economic as well as political resource and a crucial cultural and religious entity. Further, the essence and meaning that land elicited, as with other African cultural practices and institutions, exhibited a considerable degree of fluidity and dynamism. Generally, land stood as communal property; and the right to occupy, farm, or develop a plot derived from recognized membership of people to a family, *Ebusua*, or society.

Among the various Akan groups, for instance, family, *Ebusua*, and stool or royal statuses signified several types of land ownership with concomitant rights and responsibilities. Each of these manifold strands of land ownership had internal regulation systems and arrangements that ensured a generally accepted sense of equity and justice. Stool lands, in the indigenous political, economic, and cultural wisdom, existed for the purposes of enhancing the upkeep of occupants such as kings, chiefs, and queen-mothers, accentuating their power, privilege, and prestige.[1] These indigenous offices, the power and authority of which changed through strains of colonial administrative intervention, stood their ground and retained their dignity in nearly all cases.

Additionally, population pressure, development of the modern monetary or contemporary economy (with the consequent liquidity of land), and ever-expanding built environments enormously increased the demand for that rare resource as a major factor in production.[2] Given this pressure, conflict in the matter of land management in southern Ghana was unavoidable, and the nature of these disputes portrayed profound degrees of sophistication. When the colonial authorities formulated and endeavored to implement policies with planned appropriation of certain categories of land, the people touted indigenous conceptualizations of land as justifiable cause to contest those attempts, regarded in their entirety as clear violations of time-honored property rights.

Against this local stance, and despite the advice of a couple of perceptive officers, the colonial authorities encountered difficulties in their bid to implement economic and political control of land as part of the larger scheme of empire building. In all these endeavors, they proceeded on the premise that power over land remained essential to support foreign private enterprise, particularly in the gold mining industry. According to the authorities, southern Ghana, like most African colonies, had auriferous lands and considerable natural resources but lacked capital and enterprise, which could only be harnessed with great infusion of foreign investment.[3] Joseph Chamberlain, the British secretary of state for colonies, described the entire colonial empire as pristine estates that could hardly be developed without imperial assistance and incremental injections of foreign capital.[4] In the late nineteenth century, the government sought to remove every conceivable obstacle to a fruitful exchange between the colony and England through the provision of infrastructure and basic services, with the hope of creating favorable conditions for foreign investors. That approach led the administration, consciously or unconsciously, to overemphasize foreign capital and neglect time-honored, internal indigenous enterprise.[5] Given this exclusive official stance, efforts evolved to encourage foreign investment in the gold industry through land concessions—attempts at which occasioned contentious issues.

Southern Ghana has had an undeniable, long-lasting association with gold and the production thereof.[6] Gold mining remained a formidable sector of the indigenous economy from ancient times. On a larger scale, the country contributed considerably to the quantum of gold supply, among other commodities, that fed the trans-Saharan caravan trade, which formed the vital economic network extensively linking the western as well as northern halves of the continent of Africa to Europe and Asia. Southern Ghana became a great source of gold on initial direct European contact with West Africa, earning the nomenclature "Gold Coast" from that score. However, in the nineteenth century, the colonial government thought that because indigenous methods proved inefficient for deep mining production, modern machinery was necessary for the development of an increasingly competitive global gold mining industry. The larger motivation for this line of thought hinged on the view that the great demand for gold on the world market could only be met by the combined incentive of foreign private investment and commitment, both indispensable for mechanization to materialize.[7]

The survey and geological reports of the administration forecast £40 million worth of gold accruing over ten years. These projections emphasized the imperative of official support in the bid to mechanize gold mining in southern Ghana. In the early 1870s and 1880s, several factors frustrated initial attempts on the part of European investors to effectively participate in the gold mining sector. Scanty infrastructure made it difficult and expensive to transport machinery. The only pragmatic mode for the conveyance of machines and materials involved individuals laboriously carrying disassembled parts on their heads over long distances to desired destinations. Differing degrees of foreign investor participation became successful only after the construction of railroads enabled cheaper transportation in the twentieth century. The government also assisted European entrepreneurs who had the requisite capital to obtain labor, albeit to a lesser degree than elsewhere in colonial Africa. Across the continent, most colonial governments, through stringent policy and action, considered it essential to intervene in the labor market to assure an adequate supply and boost production within the export sector of the various economies.[8] The administration in southern Ghana initiated efforts in this direction, with the usual excuse that "one of the most serious problems is the dearth of labor to which the character of the inhabitants largely contributes."[9] When simultaneous demands for labor in gold mining, railroad construction, and cocoa cultivation caused a severe shortage of labor in the nineteenth and twentieth centuries, the government established a Transport Department to alleviate the conditions under which "exorbitant rates had for some time been demanded . . . which the mining agents paid."[10] The government made efforts to recruit Asian laborers; however, only a small number arrived. The administration arranged meetings between labor agents and chiefs to help the gold mining industry, not so much out of coercion but rather through the application of benign pressure.[11] However, the colonial government could scarcely do much in this regard because it did not control the labor market fully or effectively. Moreover, given the nature of pertaining contractual arrangements, the government found it awkward to brazenly seize mineral rights to help European mining concerns. Those rights required, for most part, working through a maze of tedious and time-consuming private negotiations between prospectors, agents, and local chiefs who, essentially, remained the rightful custodians of the land.[12] However, given its commitment to becoming an effective and relevant stakeholder in the concession-granting process and expecting to eventually assume total control for the benefit of European gold prospectors, the administration introduced the Crown Lands Bill.[13]

## "WASTE LANDS": THE CROWN LANDS BILL OF 1894

The Crown Lands Bill of 1894 sought to deprive kings, chiefs, queen-mothers, and headmen of the right to award concessions, reposing all powers over "waste lands," defined as unoccupied and/or uncultivated forests with all their rare resources (including water bodies), solely in the British Crown.[14] The government anticipated that the bill would put an end to protracted land disputes resulting from rival kings, chiefs, or queen-mothers granting mining as well as timber rights over vast and variously defined tracts of land without the strict regulations of due process. The colonial administration hoped that the new land management regime would facilitate accurate demarcations of concessions and require concessionaires to work within reasonable time frames.

The administration in its attempt to rationalize the proposed bill pointed to the alarming rate at which European mining companies and, in some cases, timber firms secured large land concessions from kings, chiefs, and queen-mothers of southern Ghana, hence the urgent necessity to instill some sense of order and sanity in the acquisition process.[15] Long before 1894, when the British government contemplated the introduction of the Crown Lands Bill, Governor Stanford Freeling had apprised the Colonial Office in London about his misgivings should the government attempt to claim ownership of certain southern Ghana lands. Freeling, who of all his contemporary colonial officers had a relatively appreciable knowledge of customs with respect to land, remained particularly apprehensive about the designation of mechanical and industrial gold mining as a new field exclusively for European enterprise. Though Freeling's knowledge about local customs was hardly exhaustive, he came across as an objective senior colonial officer. In April 1877, Secretary of State Henry Howard Herbert, the fourth Lord Carnarvon, inquired whether in the changing circumstances of the protectorate some serious consideration might not be accorded the mining companies.[16]

Freeling raised a red flag indicating the need for conscious caution in the promotion of such a venture.[17] According to him, the influx of Europeans into the country for the purposes of mining would necessitate some direct and drastic land takeovers on the part of the colonial government. In the same breath, the governor noted that land remained inalienable in local thought and practice, warning that no subject spawned as much local acrimony as the issue of land. He perceptively explained that

> the rightful owners of the soil in the Protectorate are the Kings and Chiefs and their people, and not the colonial government. I consider that her Majesty's Government have no territorial rights whatsoever over the various districts of the Protectorate. The limits of British territory are even now somewhat indefinite, and had better remain so ... The right of jurisdiction exercised by the Crown does not rest upon any claim of sovereignty, but upon a course of long-continued general and undisturbed usages and acquiescence and no similar usage has established in the Crown any seigniorial rights over land.[18]

This utmost understanding of the legal and cultural complexities of the issue at stake cast Freeling, a governor with a commission to champion the Victorian cause of establishing the influence of the Crown over the colony, in quite a remarkable light. He warned that the colonial administration had no rights to land and that even the plots it did control and use hinged on the kindness and friendship of the kings, chiefs, queen-mothers, and their people. Even more notable than the preceding view, the governor averred that among the various Akan groups, the concept of "waste land" did not exist. Land remained the property of the ancestors and the people, overseen by occupants of the stools, other indigenous political leadership, and family heads. The chiefs could allow others to occupy and work plots of land following payment of a certain portion of the yield in gold or agricultural produce. Furthermore, occupiers obtained no fixed tenure, and duration of occupancy hinged entirely on the discretion of landowners. Royal or stool lands could be leased or put to any use during the incumbency of the king, chief, queen-mother, or any indigenous political leader; however, on their demise or removal, the land reverted to the stool and subsequently their successor. Freeling in the expression of these concerns raised further pertinent issues that might crop up should the colonial administration follow through with its plans. Government takeover of land in support of the gold industry would necessarily call for protecting the mines as well as securing ground and water rights. He pointed to the need for facilities to shield the gold mines from the whims and caprices of aggrieved indigenous political authorities or individuals, as most of the targeted lands would without question already be immersed in litigation.

Notwithstanding these thoughtful insights and misgivings, the British government pressed ahead with determination to get the bill through the Legislative Council. In the 1890s, the general official opinion strongly favored vesting all waste lands in the Crown. Accordingly, active attempts at the implementation of the new land policy happened under the watch of Governor William Edward Maxwell, a committed empire builder in the service of the government of Her Majesty, Victoria, the Queen of Britain.

Discussions on the matter of land policy within government circles leaked into various southern Ghana communities in the form of rumors sparked by indigenous waiters, maids, servants, attendants, messengers, cleaners, and other support staff for officials of the administration. These locals reported what they had heard during the performance of their daily duties near and around the venues of various official meetings on the matter. Given the profound indigenous conceptualization of land, communities across the country took these rumors seriously and prepared to obstruct efforts of the colonial government to roll out the infamous land policy. As soon as the bill reached the floor of the Legislative Council, the educated elite officially started the protests. James Hutton Brew, a solicitor, editor of the *Western Echo* newspaper, and assistant secretary of the Fanti

Confederation, then residing in London, made representations to the Colonial Office on behalf of the people. Like Freeling, the former governor who had sought to abort the policy from within, Brew did not hesitate to remind the British government about the unique nature of its relationship with southern Ghana. In a letter to Secretary of State George Frederick Robinson, the Marquis of Ripon, he wrote that "it is historically true to say that the Gold Coast Protectorate stands on a footing different from that of any dependency of the British Crown. Its position is unique. It has not been acquired either by conquest, cession, or treaty; and although the British Government have exercised certain powers and jurisdictions, it possesses no inherent legal right to deprive us of our lands, as is contemplated in the proposed Bill, whatever it may have done in countries such as South Africa, Tasmania, New Zealand, East Africa, and elsewhere."[19]

Brew, for all intents and purposes, argued that the people of southern Ghana had the capacity to manage their land barring any British supervision, direction, or legislation. They could manage land transactions, including the handling of manifold issues regarding clients and concessions, and judiciously disburse any accruing rents as well as royalties. He responded to Governor William Bradford Griffith's purported remarks that, in 1874, all the lands of the southern Ghana colony had become the property of the government through the right of conquest.[20] Strongly objecting to that notion, Brew charged that a high official of the caliber of Governor Griffith should not utter such statements in earnest. He affirmed that the British hardly owned an inch of the land mass but conceded that the government possessed some land acquired through purchase. Accordingly, Brew concluded that the jurisdiction, rights, and power the government had exercised over the protectorate had only come from usage, sufferance, or usurpation and not because of cession, treaty, or conquest.[21]

The popular protest to the Crown Lands Bill hardly remained limited to individual intellectuals. Newspapers, mostly published in Cape Coast, became inundated with reports of meetings, strategies, and petitions, not excluding featured articles, letters, and editorials. The land issue came to revolve around everyday matters so much that, for instance, the *Gold Coast Methodist Times*, originally a missionary newspaper under the editorial guidance of Reverend Attoh Ahuma, did not restrict its publication to evangelical content because of the "fiery indignation likely to devour the Colony, on account of the Bill entitled Crown Land Ordinance."[22] The *Gold Coast Chronicle*, on the other hand, reported that if the bill passed, the people of southern Ghana would leave the country en masse. These and other newspapers averred that clauses in the bill sought to vest waste and forest lands in the British Crown and claim them for the designs of the colonial government. They further charged that, having failed to identify with the indigenous people, the administration was adding insult to injury by seeking to push through a bill that surreptitiously and in practical terms abrogated their rights to land. The newspaper editorials observed that the colonial authorities appeared desirous of concealing their real reasons for pursuing the bill.[23] Remonstrations against the bill became far more widespread than the authorities had imagined or anticipated.

Indigenous political authorities in the central and western parts of southern Ghana, as custodians of the land, made their voices heard in widespread denunciation of the bill. The chiefs, queen-mothers, and people of Elmina and its environs sent delegations to the governor in Accra officially decrying and declining to consent to the bill. Equally aggrieved, the king of Abura with his chiefs, headmen, and counselors went to Cape Coast to confer with the district commissioner on the matter of land. In his interpositions during the discussions, the king pointed out that none of the former great and good governors who had lived with his ancestors for a long time in the past had ever made any such propositions with respect to land.[24] In their petition to the secretary of state for colonies in London, the chiefs, queen-mothers, and people of Cape Coast cited the details of the Bond of 1844 and the eventual 1874 Proclamation that defined colonial jurisdiction in the country. Neither of these historic documents explicitly declared land as the property of the Queen of England; the people of Cape Coast had been told repeatedly that the Queen possessed no claim whatsoever to any land outside the walls of the European fortifications. The Cape Coast petition averred that, considering the growing gold industry and consequent appreciation in the value of land, the bill definitely sought to deprive the people of their inalienable natural rights to property for the sole benefit of the colonial government. The indigenous leaders of Cape Coast pointed out that they and their people hardly had a hand in the establishment of the colonial administration and scarcely any say over its formulation of policies. Therefore, the administration remained an alien entity that could not be entrusted with a seminal cultural resource such as land. The kings, chiefs, and queen-mothers of Anomabo and Heman joined the chorus of dissent, expressing the foreboding that, to the best of their understanding, the Crown Lands Bill would orchestrate the ousting of men, women, and families from the land of their ancestors. Nearly all the petitioners argued at different times and in diverse ways that the bill was unnecessary, as the extant Public Lands Ordinance of 1876 gave the colonial government adequate allotment to secure land for any legitimate general good. Considering that ordinance, the petitioners reiterated that the Crown Lands Bill bore a cloud of suspicion around it, especially given its inherent potential to disrupt everyday life. Petitioners from the disparate regions of southern Ghana unanimously challenged the nebulous official concept of "waste land," affirming that the land belonged to kings, chiefs, queen-mothers, headmen, family heads, families, and individuals; hardly any plot or piece existed without owners.

Governor Maxwell took a strong stance against the barrage of dissent and discord surrounding the land bill. He insisted that the

Chiefs enjoyed British protection and needed, therefore, to give up some of their rights over land because of the impracticability of receiving every conceivable benefit from the relationship and not yielding anything in return.[25] According to the governor, the theory regarding protectorates implied some element of relinquishing or ceding sovereign rights to the protecting power. Quick to draw on the British experience in the Malay Peninsula, he lamented that the colonial government had made sacrifices in freeing the protectorate from Asante invasion between 1873 and 1874 for "petty Chiefs" to remain sole beneficiaries of full sovereign rights over forests, waste lands, and minerals. Maxwell appeared conveniently oblivious to the fact that the British had used armies of men drawn from southern Ghana during the invasion and that the sacrifices remained inherently mutual, as the inhabitants had paid for the war in more ways than one. He nonetheless deemed it proper to rein in the powers of kings, chiefs, and queen-mothers to grant concessions to European mining prospectors, making the colonial government privy to and ultimately the determining agent in any such sensitive arrangements. The governor was frustrated with the tedious legal process through which the colonial government found itself having to go to bring closure to compensation concerns. Governor Maxwell frowned on the reality that the administration could not get land without applying to some native authority for permission. In the process, he vented his displeasure on Africans and their "wasteful" agricultural practices of shifting cultivation, as practiced in India.[26] Ironically, the governor diplomatically refrained from criticizing indigenous cultivation practices in a speech on the matter at the Legislative Council.

Overall, however, the colonial administration conceded that the petitioners had stated their case so compellingly and convincingly that it would withdraw the bill in hopes of reenacting formidable legislation on the issue. To this end, the government came to terms with the need to restate its case to the people of southern Ghana.

## THE CROWN LANDS BILL OF 1897 AND "PUBLIC LANDS"

Unrelenting in the desire to have control over land in the country, the government took account of the resistance and modified the controversial bill somewhat. Essentially, the new Lands Bill of 1897 was different in letter but unambiguously same in spirit. Laid before the Legislative Council in March 1897, the bill categorically stated that the intent of vesting the so-called waste and forest land in the Queen had been abandoned. The Crown would have rights of administration, not ownership. In place of "waste land," the new bill touted "public land," which the colonial government would administer for the general good.[27] Kings, chiefs, and other traditional leaders would still have all reasonable and justifiable authority, but, in order to prevent prerogatives being improvidently created over so-called public lands, the power to award private rights inhered in the colonial government. The right of the people to ownership of land would no longer be automatically recognized; therefore, present occupiers would be entitled only to settler rights, leading to a permanent, heritable right of occupancy that could be transformed into an absolute one on application to the governor, who would ensure the issue of a grant of land certificate. Furthermore, the new land bill gave the government the right to declare that a piece of land had no owner and authorize occupation. The people of southern Ghana could make land grants and concessions to other Africans but not to any European, except with express approval, again, of the governor.

The government, basking in the full expectation that these changes to the letter of the first bill would appease the people and dissipate the earlier remonstrations, received a rude shock. The intellectuals quickly realized that the two bills, old and the new, hardly differed considering the wide powers ceded to the governor. They refused to fall for the superficial offers made to the inhabitants in the new bill. Newspaper editors and contributors, among the intellectuals, again wasted no time in calling for a rejection of the bill and unanimously challenged the excessive powers placed within the purview of the governor.[28] With screaming editorials, the *Gold Coast Methodist Times* and *Gold Coast Chronicle* both called on the people of southern Ghana to give the new bill unrelenting condemnation.

Back in the Legislative Council, the few educated indigenous representatives similarly protested the bill, to the chagrin of the governor.[29] Charles J. Bannerman, who had emerged as the lead counsel in the protest, reiterated that the kings, chiefs, and queen-mothers had immemorial rights to their land; therefore, it remained well within the ambit of their power and authority to do with it as they pleased. He further observed that the Supreme Court had always recognized the rights of the kings, chiefs, and queen-mothers to grant land to whomever they wished and that the new bill, among other things, sought to abrogate those inalienable entitlements. To him, the proposition amounted to a violation of the tenuous trust the people had reposed in the government. Bannerman pointed out to the governor that despite claims that the old bill had been abandoned, no one could in any conceivable way deny the similarity in intent between it and the new Lands Bill of 1897. That strategy, he averred, metaphorically amounted to the administration seeking to barge into a room through the window when it found the door firmly locked.

The governor insisted that the new bill would hardly take away the rights of the kings, chiefs, and queen-mothers; rather it unambiguously clarified the distinction between public and private rights to land. He strongly expressed the opinion that stool lands translated into public lands, which should be administered for the benefit of the people. The bill would only allow the governor concurrent rights to help achieve that goal as well as work with the kings, chiefs, and queen-mothers.[30] According to Maxwell, indigenous authorities would retain their power to authorize the occupation of public lands as sites of habitation or for permanent agricultural purposes. Only in their dealing with Europeans in the matter of concession granting could it be said that some rights had been curtailed: the kings, chiefs, and queen-mothers would hereafter be denied the power to grant a foreigner private rights in public lands without the written consent of the governor.[31] He lamented that the preposterous practice of shifting cultivation, resulting in land being left to fallow for a long time, could be tended as a claim to ownership, arguing that it would be monstrous if such a system gained any legal assent. With the governor seeking to superimpose English law over the customary practice of southern Ghana, Bannerman countered that shifting cultivation endured as an established practice of laying claim to land and must be left intact. He explained that various pieces of land belonging to different people might, at some given time, be found lying seemingly idle; all those parcels were practically left to recuperate after extensive periods of cultivation, with the owners working on other plots in different locations. To this end, ostensible "idle lands" could hardly be deemed vacant but rather properly and effectively owned.

Given the entrenched positions and the resulting stalemate, the Land Bill of 1897 worsened the uneasy relations between the colonial administration and the people, paving the way for the formation of the Aborigines' Rights Protection Society (ARPS) in Cape Coast. The intellectuals of the town managed to secure a copy of the bill after the process of consideration started in the Legislative Council. At a meeting that included John Mensah Sarbah, J. W. DeGraft Johnson, J. D. Abraham, and J. P. Brown, all formally educated and of great influence in Cape Coast, the group decided to pursue a persistent and sustained official protest to the Land Bill of 1897. Other intellectuals began similar movements across the country and decided to affiliate with the original movement founded in Cape Coast. This large umbrella organization became known as the Gold Coast Aborigines'

Rights Protection Society (GCARPS), with the shared objective of obstructing colonial land policy. Among other things, the members set themselves the tall task of helping the indigenous population of southern Ghana understand the machinations of the colonial government. This became the first movement in the colony to approach the similitude of a national organization, albeit doing little to make a good proportion of the ordinary folk effective members. Its first public statement resolutely rebuked the colonial government:

> Whereas in former times, all measures intended by the Government for the whole Protectorate were brought before a meeting of the various Kings and Chiefs of the Protectorate convened for the purpose, and who in turn communicated them to the people of their respective districts by gong-gong. And whereas the time-honored and effective custom has for some time [been] set aside and superseded by the Gazette. And whereas a very large majority of the population of the Gold Coast Protectorate are still unable to read, and whereas even the greater part of those able to read cannot well comprehend the meaning of the Bill passed from time to time by the Government, the above Society of which natives and residents alike can be members, has been formed to discuss the various Bills intended to be passed by the Government from time to time, with a view to fully understand the meaning, purport, object and effect thereof that every person may have the opportunity of understanding the same.[32]

These pursuant plans and purposes left the colonial government in no doubt about being confronted by a different kind of political movement. The ARPS pointed out that contrary to previous practices, the infamous bill undermined relations between the people of southern Ghana and the colonial government. The bill made people suspicious of the administration's intentions, which were charting a course far removed from precedent situations where all policy proposals happened in a palaver with the various kings, chiefs, and queen-mothers.[33] After these discussions with the government, the chiefs would inform their people about final decisions, with occasions made for comments, suggestions, and questions. The ARPS observed that the administration had gradually replaced that enduring and effective consultative system with the arbitrary publication of gazettes.[34] With great concern, the members noted that the new system was ineffective given the low literacy rate in the country at that time. Even literate individuals sometimes struggled to grasp the nuances of legal language used in the crafting of bills and gazettes. To counteract this situation, the ARPS declared that one of its purposes pivoted on helping the ordinary people of the country understand such bills and gazettes in information and discussion sessions.

The colonial administration had long been suspicious of the educated elite and consequently refused to work with them, yet the essence of the mission statement of the ARPS raised critical questions in the minds of the officials.[35] Did the existence of the educated elite as a group amount to usurpation of the roles of kings, chiefs, queen-mothers, and other leaders of the indigenous political system? Could the formation of the ARPS be interpreted as the intellectuals taking undue advantage of their education to impose themselves on the colonial establishment as the rightful representatives of the people? To what extent could the glaring private and personal interests of individual members of the ARPS be cast in the framework of the general good? Convinced that these concerns constituted the main motivation of key members of the ARPS, colonial officials alleged that the membership of the organization sounded spurious, exhibiting an admixture of aptitude and foolishness. For instance, some officials referred to Charles Bannerman as a "talented native" advocate, albeit devoid of principle. Others suspected the intellectuals, particularly the Cape Coast cohort, as the real sponsors of obstruction to government policies and actions. They insisted that the administration never consent to handing over power to a few scheming, needy, half-educated natives. The governor, expressing his views on the intellectuals, stated that they were the real culprits in all the difficulties, including the frustrations the British had hitherto encountered in the southern Ghana colony. He stated categorically that the intellectuals remained artful and crafty men who had made chiefs a source of constant danger.[36] Altogether, the colonial administration perceived the intellectuals of the ARPS as political schemers attempting to either displace or use indigenous political establishments to become important players in the British policy of indirect rule.[37] Contrary to such claims, the intellectuals and indigenous political authorities in Cape Coast had long enjoyed a cordial, and collaborative relationship that stood out in comparison with alliances elsewhere in the country.[38]

The reluctance of the colonial government to heed the numerous petitions regarding the proposed land policy incited some market women and fishmongers in Cape Coast to take matters a step further in their own way.[39] When Governor Maxwell arrived in the town on a routine official tour, they confronted him in a furious demonstration. Women at the head of the demonstration displayed a red banner with the inscription "We Protest the Land Bill!" A long procession of women followed, chanting dirges and singing hymns.[40] The governor later dismissed the demonstrators as "a noisy crowd of women and boys" with a banner bearing words of resistance, suspecting the instigation of men "too prudent to risk anything" themselves.[41]

Further, the governor accused some of the intellectuals of pursuing private business interests by obstructing the Lands Bill of 1897.[42] According to him, regulations and sanctions in the bill threatened their operations as land speculators. They feared that the bill would render their concessions and activities invalid. Maxwell, for instance, accused both J. W. Sey, the president of the ARPS, and Brew, one of the most outspoken critics of the bill, of being connected with the Gold Coast Native Concessions Purchasing Company established in 1882.[43] J. P. Brown, vice president of the ARPS, counted among those who had helped with negotiations in the lucrative Adansi concession, which later became the property of the Ashanti Goldfields Corporation. Significantly, regardless of the compensation these men received for their roles in previous land deals, it remained an undisputable fact that African brokers hardly gained as much from such transactions as their European counterparts. Notwithstanding the criticisms the colonial government leveled against them, these intellectuals insisted that they were acting well within their rights as concerned indigenous individuals first and foremost in helping to obstruct the bill on behalf of the public interest. Moreover, the kings, chiefs, and queen-mothers preferred well-informed local people negotiating land dealings on their behalf instead of a colonial administration with a downright remote and foreign posture. The southern Ghana press chastised the governor for casting personal aspersions against the intellectuals and denouncing them as firebrands in the popular movement against the Land Bill.[44]

These aspersions and innuendos barely daunted the ARPS as it continued to coordinate scattered protests across the country against the proposed arrangement. The executive members pursued this coordination first through personal contacts with prominent kings, chiefs, and queen-mothers. They then resorted to newspaper publications; to this end, the *Gold Coast Methodist Times*, for instance, continued defying rumors of press censorship, taunting and warning the colonial government with statements such as "thank God, we are not in Russia ... if the Legislature so far forgets itself as to descend against public rights conceded to us by the Constitution of England, we will resist unto blood."[45] The newspaper further energized the general public, stating that "while we have breath and while the Governor is bent on forcing this measure on us, we must not tire in our efforts to destroy the pernicious Bill."[46] The ARPS relied heavily on the *Gold Coast Methodist Times* until it started publishing its own newspaper, the *Gold Coast Aborigines*. When the new Lands Bill came up for a second reading in the Legislative Council, the opposition had grown exponentially. At this stage, John Mensah Sarbah was the lead counsel with the assistance of P. Awoonor Renner for the kings, chiefs, and queen-mothers. Like Bannerman before him, Mensah Sarbah reiterated that there existed no significant difference between the bills of 1894 and 1897, further expatiating that "I am specifically instructed to say that this Lands Bill is an elaborate and expanded form of the Crown Lands Bill of 1894. That Bill refers only to what is termed waste and forest lands whereas this Bill refers to the whole land of this country, depriving the aborigines of their rights in the soil of their native land."[47] In substantiating his arguments, Mensah Sarbah referred to the 1895 report on land tenure and insisted that every plot in the country had an owner, irrespective of vague descriptions of some as "waste" in government rendition. Family land remained the property of the same under all conditions, whether cultivated or uncultivated. The only condition under which a family might lose its land would be the unlikely event of the failure of successors to maintain it properly. In that improbable scenario, land would revert to the common property of the village, community, or town, subject to the control of kings, chiefs, queen-mothers, headmen, and elders. He pointed out that southern Ghana indigenous political authorities had unanimously rejected the bill that sought to change their inalienable natural rights of absolute ownership into those of disinherited holders and settlers. Furthermore, the removal of the generally accepted distinction between individual, family, and communal lands as rendered in the bill would tamper with the time-honored governance the indigenous political authorities had hitherto exercised over families, villages, and towns. Consequently, Mensah Sarbah observed that the bill, as it stood, could disrupt social bonds and familial ties, portending serious implications for everyday life to the detriment of societies across the country.

He went on to brief the council on other issues as well as potential unforeseen consequences of the bill. The forfeiture of rights of owners to plots of land unutilized for three years would bring untold hardship on clerks, artisans, and traders. Individuals in these categories, given the nature of their jobs, traveled over long distances to live in other parts of the country—sometimes for years.[48] Absence from their villages beyond the stipulated three years would cause them to lose their title and rights to individual and family lands. Mensah Sarbah equally raised objections to the definition of "natives" in the proposed bill, which excluded mulattoes.[49] The bill took away the rights of mulattoes as recognized and reputable members of their various communities. Failure of the bill to recognize the practice of shifting cultivation as a title or claim to land ownership also came up for questioning in his deliberation on the Lands Bill.

Mensah Sarbah affirmed that as a religious resource, land had deeper implications than could be fully articulated for people across the country because it connected them to their ancestors in many ways. To the extent that departed and venerated forebearers bequeathed it, land had gained elevation as an inalienable, revered resource.[50] The ancestors acquired their land allocations through settlement and war, ultimately implying the shedding of blood. The sanctity of those various modes of acquisition enjoined the living to treat and regard land in the same sense as they would ancestors or family heirlooms. Any alienation became an irreparable infraction bound to incur the displeasure and sanction of the ancestors, who, like all spirits, could be vindictive.[51] Furthermore, land remained the sacred resting place of the ancestors and, therefore, could not be given away indiscriminately. The practice of libation, a long-lasting communication mechanism across societies in the country, amounted to an affirmation of the importance of land in the relationship with ancestors. Relatedly, the ancestors in their beneficence gifted treasure troves through inexplicable deposits on and in the land, along with its rivers, sea, and other water bodies. To this end, according to Mensah Sarbah, the societies across the country had ready reasons not to relent in their bid to prevent the colonial government from passing the Crown Lands Bill.

The refusal of the lead counsel to accept a retainer fee of four hundred guineas from the ARPS for his services launched him to greater heights of fame and reverence, adding a gracious gravity as well as solemnity to the issue at stake. Mensah Sarbah emphatically assured that he had been touched and moved to decline the offer because of the widespread determination on the part of the people of the country to preserve their right to land. In his own words, "when... I was fully convinced in my own mind that they [were]... so determined in all parts of the country, I left home to do their bidding."[52]

The governor and colonial administration continued to press for the passage of the bill through reformulation and reconceptualization, providing additional fuel to the already sensitive situation. When Governor Maxwell died at sea in 1899 on his way to London, the press had no tear to shed for him, perceiving some element of divine intervention and retribution. One newspaper referred to the ability, energy, and advanced views of the deceased governor in pushing "the tyrannical land grabbing and rotten policy marked out for him." He allegedly pursued that goal with a cold, unsympathetic spirit and with abject "contempt... characterizing most of his measures."[53] The kings, chiefs, and queenmothers of various Fanti groups at a meeting in Cape Coast sent a telegram on the death of the former governor to Queen Victoria asking for a new understanding official quiet sympathetic to their cause.[54] They had no such luck—Governor F. M. Hodgson, equally enthusiastic to get the bill passed, replaced him.

In his assessment of the situation, Governor Hodgson erroneously assumed that the indigenous political authorities had become resigned to the inevitability of the proposed bill. Given this perception, he sought to get it through the Legislative Council quickly after the necessary changes—before the supposed feeling began to wane. Gradually waking up to the enormity of the discontentment toward the Lands Bill and the need to accurately assess the situation, the Colonial Office nonetheless opted to use the unfortunate demise of the former governor to temporarily stay the passage of the bill. Furthermore, ample official notice was served that a delegation had been put together to travel to London to oppose the bill; therefore, the Colonial Office saw reason to be doubly cautious.

The ARPS continued to encourage kings and chiefs to attend regular meetings to sustain the widespread protest against the Crown Lands Bill. Members unanimously advocated for branches to open in other parts of the country for the organization to gain government recognition as the veritable voice of the nation. The group equally sought legal advice in London, imploring Joseph E. Casely Hayford to gather legal and historical evidence for the consideration of appropriate authorities in London. He and his traveling colleagues collected more than thirty parliamentary reports, Legislative Council debates, and government blue books, which they submitted to their London solicitors to reinforce their case.[55] The ARPS eventually managed to raise funds through solicitations and contributions from kings, chiefs, queen-mothers, and ordinary people to finance the travel of the delegation to London. Consisting of three prominent merchants, the contingent took along indigenous state swords and the insignias of kings, chiefs, and queen-mothers from across the country to accentuate their accredited authority and emphasize the cultural and religious significance of land. With the aid of their British legal counsel, Secretary of State Joseph Chamberlain granted the delegation audience at the Colonial Office.

The delegation argued that the Lands Bill of 1897 remained flawed in principle because of its basis in the widely challenged premise that unoccupied lands in the colony belonged to no one. Ignoring essential customary practices altogether, the governor had defiantly denied community members an audience to argue their position. The deputation affirmed that those lands, along with their mineral resources, rivers, sea, and other water bodies, belonged to kings, chiefs, queen-mothers, towns, villages, families, and in some cases, individuals. Indigenous land ownership and management had been structured such that no one (whether they came from another family, a different ethnic group, or were a foreigner) could occupy without the express consent and permission of kings, chiefs, queen-mothers, and respective families. These arrangements irrevocably underpinned the everyday lives of various peoples. Any attempt to tamper with local customs would lead to a severe social breakdown. In other words, the vast expanse of land without question remained completely owned, with owners in full possession of the knowledge of their respective boundaries.

The group equally rejected as arbitrary the proposal that governor-appointed commissioners would have the power of dealing with every concession without specific procedures or regulations. In their view, a workable alternative would be to make the whole procedure judicial rather than administrative. Another important objection concerned a proposal in the bill that subjected the issuing of land certificates in accordance with English law instead of customary local practice.[56] The delegation insisted that all such certificates should be based on indigenous laws that were culturally acceptable, meaningful, and worthwhile to the people of southern Ghana. They pointed out that while the kings, chiefs, queen-mothers, and others had no problem giving up land for the general good, the purposes for which the supposed unoccupied lands could be released remained loosely defined in the bill; the delegation therefore demanded that these purposes be specified to avoid any doubts whatsoever. Moreover, they observed, arbitrary notices in the government gazette would scarcely secure the meaningful consent of landowners affected by the new concession procedures. The delegation demanded that proper notifications be personally delivered to the kings, chiefs, queen-mothers, families, and individuals concerned through the facilitation of competent interpreters.

To the delight of the delegation, Chamberlain attested to the soundness and cogency of their concerns and arguments;

consequently, he gave steadfast assurance that they would receive what they wished for. The secretary of state equally expressed his commitment to having customary law prevail in all indigenous matters, with the fervent assurance that such questions would be determined and decided in competent courts of adjudication.[57] As a much-needed face-saving gesture, the Colonial Office used the demise of the former governor as an excuse to call for the withdrawal of the bill; as the main architect, his unfortunate passing created missing links without which the Crown Lands Bill could barely be carried through—albeit to the chagrin of the new governor and his supporting cast of colonial officers.

### CONCLUSION

In all these obstructions to the passing of the Crown Lands Bills of 1894 and 1897, southern Ghana communities, especially along the coast, reached into their treasure trove of customary ideas and practices. The general chorus of dissent hardly abated in the face of frantic efforts on the part of the administration to reconceptualize and reformulate aspects of the bills. In their constant contestations, the communities, with indigenous political leaders and educated elite as their spokespersons, reiterated that besides its economic, social, and political significance, land—along with its minerals, rivers, sea, and other water bodies—was an enduring religious resource. All these entities conjointly allowed for proper connections with the ancestors who had acquired the land with their blood as well as sweat and who remained interred therein. Insofar as the ancestral connection proved indispensable to everyday life, land and its accompanying rare resources personified the ancestors to these communities, rendering its ownership and the appertaining rights inalienable. Primed with recurrent issues from the past, these remonstrations proved costly to Cape Coast because of the pivotal role its representatives played as outspoken advocates against the Crown Lands Bills of 1894 and 1897.

# SIX

## THE POLITICS OF MODERNIZATION AND CLASH OF OFFICIAL AND INDIGENOUS INTERESTS

*Judiciary, Military, and Urbanization*

SUBTLE ADMINISTRATIVE DISPENSATIONS UNDER THE watch of successive British mercantile officials preceded the emergence of full-fledged colonial rule in southern Ghana, a process that benefited immensely from the largely accommodating and unsuspecting local communities. That fledgling, informal beginning had its own challenging and difficult moments with rude awakenings on both sides. The fractious relationship delineating these broad phases of the developing system reifies the notion that the colonial enterprise, especially in this context, was hardly a one-sided narrative in which officers always had their way; it was a peculiar one with many often surprising outcomes compared to situations elsewhere across the African continent.[1] Coastal communities in southern Ghana persistently took steps, over time, to contest colonial policy and action, often compelling the administration to take intriguing measures. These communities would generally grow suspicious of the officials, draw on a repertoire of indigenous ideas to confront them, suffer the consequences, and yet remain defiant. In the coastal communities, particularly Cape Coast, persistent and resilient agency against the administration resulted in certain official responses, several of which the local people suspected of being conspiratorial.

Increasing local wariness and discontentment with the policies of the administration played out in a variety of judicial matters and economic issues that muddled already uneasy relations. In 1853, the educated elite of Cape Coast convinced *Omanhin* Kofi Amissah to create a single, overarching indigenous court instead of the numerous tribunals that operated variously under his authority in private homes throughout the town.[2] The single system gave these numerous and scattered trial places an enduringly genuine and formidable power that the proponents thought would ensure some degree of standardization in the administration of indigenous justice. The indigenous authorities appointed James Robert Thompson as the magistrate of this centralized court. During that year, James Coleman Fitzpatrick, judicial assessor of the English court, on receipt of a civil action, compelled Amissah to appear before him. In response, a group of traders and the educated elite submitted a signed petition in condemnation of the judicial assessor for bringing the *Omanhin* to trial. The action, according to them, amounted to gross disrespect of not only the person but also the high office of the indigenous ruler. The acting governor showed his softer side, sympathizing with Amissah and the petitioners and suspending the judicial assessor, to the chagrin of the Colonial Office in London.[3]

Barely a year later, in 1854, Amissah had a brush with the indigenous law when he attempted suicide for personal reasons. His accusers argued that attempting to take his own life negated proper codes of conduct for a person of his rank; therefore, along customary lines, Amissah could not continue in that office. Consequently, some of the subordinate chiefs decided to depose him, but Amissah would not go without a fight. Given the gravity of his personal problems with indigenous law and having nowhere else to seek redress, the beleaguered *Omanhin* under great compulsion appealed to the English court based in Cape Coast—the jurisdiction of which he, in conjunction with his subordinate chiefs and some of the educated elite, had previously challenged.

Regardless, the chief justice ruled in favor of Amissah, declaring that he could hardly be removed without the consent of the governor.[4] Accordingly, the colonial government refused to recognize the deposition. The judgment questioned the authority of the indigenous court that had deposed Amissah, who at this time was generally suspected of being in collusion with the administration, especially given the perception that the governor found him malleable and compliant. Considering these suspicions, the colonial authorities' trivialization of the charges against Amissah and the counter faulting of his accusers for overindulgence in alcohol surprised not a few people.[5] The accusers of Amissah consisted of a determined lot who would barely budge given the stance of the government. A demonstration protesting the recognition of Amissah as *Omanhin* became disruptive, compelling the governor to commission a special inquiry. In his attempt to defuse the acrimonious feelings among the people, the governor made a quick volte-face and declared Amissah deposed but refused to let the principal demonstrators go unpunished. The governor fined them and used the money to compensate those who had suffered injuries from the disturbances.

## *OMANHIN* AGGERY AND THE ENTRENCHMENT OF COLONIAL ADMINISTRATION

Although the government persistently pushed its power and authority beyond the forts and castles, it reneged on its obligation to protect the coastal communities. This dereliction of duty became obvious when the Asante invaded the coast in 1863; heavy losses for the Fanti societies caused their confidence in British protection to waver and wane. In actuality, the promise of protection in the face of attack suffered a setback from the Colonial Office's insistence on noninterference in any local quarrels with the king of Asante and on the kings and chiefs being left to settle their own scores.[6] As if that denial of protection proved unprovocative enough, local colonial officers decided to impose an annual license fee of £2 on all wine and spirit traders. According to the government, the proposed fee would check the trafficking of these alcoholic beverages rather than increase government revenue (as people alleged). Similarly across Africa, consumers of alcohol considered the imposition, with the potential rise in the retail price of wines and spirits, as an indirect tax meant to garner additional revenue for a government that did little or practically nothing to protect them.[7] The chiefs and people of Cape Coast stood against this fee, arguing that as non-British citizens, they should hardly be taxed when the government had done no meaningful or convincing consultation with them.[8] In his defense, Governor Richard Pine insisted that the government had followed due process in consulting some of the chiefs, a council of influential men, and traders who, in turn, should have consulted with their respective constituencies. Subsequent local investigations by those opposed to the annual license fee revealed, however, that the governor had overstepped his bounds by not properly seeking the explicit consent of all the chiefs. To avoid disgrace, the British secretary of state delayed implementation and kept the proposed fee suspended.[9] These events constituted the immediate circumstances preceding a major confrontation between the colonial administration and the people of Cape Coast, leading to decisions that the latter construed as decidedly punitive on the part of the former.

Although the colonial administration exhibited occasional confusion and uncertainty, its presence in the town posed a formidable challenge to the indigenous political order. Through sheer tenacity, the chiefs and people stood their ground and contested the administration whenever any such opportunity presented itself. This obvious struggle between the two opposing political structures was not without consequences for both. John Aggery, who became *Omanhin* of Cape Coast and maintained a deep commitment to the indigenous mandate, lost no time in indicating that he viewed the fledgling British administration in a bad light.[10] As king, Aggery represented the ultimate embodiment of the local political order, an ancestral heritage that his oath required him to revere, support, and defend.[11]

He succeeded in going down in history as one of the leading and loudest challengers of British power in West Africa.[12] Compared to King Ja-Ja of Opobo, Nigeria, Aggery bore discrete motives and lived in equally different circumstances. Although the former had a more dominant character with stronger economic reasons for confronting the British, the latter defended the indigenous political order and castigated colonial rule in West Africa as nothing but a blatant use of military power. Aggery received enormous support from the growing educated community, some of whom became his main mentors during his short reign in the nineteenth century. This kind of cooperation proved pivotal at the peak of colonialism in the middle of the twentieth century. Although hardly the only one to discern threats in British colonial encroachment, Aggery became the first, given his position as *Omanhin* and his persistence, to prominently call out all covert and overt moves.

The circumstances surrounding the assumption of office of *Omanhin* Aggery stood out as intriguing. After the indigenous kingmakers of Cape Coast administered all the requisite rites and procedures, the British authorities decided to hold a coronation ceremony for him. This decision was significant in the estimation of Aggery, who perceived it as an accentuation of his claim to full sovereignty and equal status with his royal counterpart in Britain. During the ceremony, British troops in Cape Coast fired a twenty-one-gun salute as Aggery had the rare prestige and privilege of inspecting a guard of honor. Seemingly slight yet significant, the administration failed to administer the oath of allegiance to the British Queen. All of these official acts of commission and omission reinforced the expectation of Aggery that the prominent kings in southern Ghana should prepare for self-governance to relieve the British government of a task they appeared quite anxious to abandon.[13] Indeed, as a well-informed man, he followed British political discourses published in the *African Times*, a journal belonging to the African Aid Society in London.

Avidly perusing these critical publications, Aggery learned about anticolonial advocates as well as African advancement groups and their influence on British public opinion. These pressure groups managed to get their government to insert a clause in the British Parliamentary Report of 1865 regarding eventual self-governance for colonized peoples. Considerations that led the select committee to this conclusion included the general perception that the southern Ghana protectorate had become an indefinite British responsibility without adequate advantage to the inhabitants.[14] The prevailing arrangement atrophied the power and authority of the chiefs, giving them the inclination to simultaneously depend on and frustrate local colonial officials. According to the committee, the most reasonable thing to do in these circumstances was to halt all further extensions of territory in West Africa. In its final report, the committee resolved that the objective of British policy should be to encourage inhabitants to exercise those qualities that would enable a convenient transfer of governmental functions to them prior to an ultimate British withdrawal. Strategically following, imbibing, and relishing these arguments, Aggery eagerly anticipated the eventual withdrawal of colonial rule that would pave the way for kings and chiefs across the country to assume complete control. After the coronation ceremony, the governor received him at the government house with great honor and dignity as a "Christian king."[15]

### DISAGREEMENTS OVER LIMITS: *ASAFO* CEREMONIES, MISCELLANEOUS ACTIVITIES, AND FISHING LOCATION

No sooner had the celebrations ended than the first confrontations set off as Aggery systematically frustrated the colonial

Fig. 6.1 A fishing community with its center of operation adjacent to one end of the Cape Coast Castle. Courtesy of Charles Ebow Jonah and Thomas Ekow Stephens.

administration at nearly every move. Initially, he gave commands counter to those of the governor and contested him directly whenever the opportunity presented itself. In 1865, *Omanhin* Aggery and Governor Conran clashed over issues of limits to aspects of *Asafo* ceremonies, particularly displays and firing of musketry. Conran insisted that these activities be done within the confines of either the military parade grounds or the salt winning compound; both places, he opined, were reasonable distances from the town center.[16] Aggery objected to this order, arguing that those locations had antipathy associated with them as both had served as scenes of traumatic battles for the *Asafo* companies. Accordingly, when the *Omanhin* advised that displays and firing should not be done at all, the companies obeyed him rather than the governor.[17] With time, Conran decreed that markets should not open on Sunday and banned free-range animal rearing to rid the streets of coastal Ghana, particularly in Cape Coast, Accra, and Anomabu, of pigs, cattle, and fowl.[18] Aggery objected to that official order, arguing that it would adversely affect the poorer people who raised animals as their only means of livelihood.[19]

Furthermore, the Governor sought to regulate the activities of fishermen with a ban on fishing activities within the precincts of the castle. When he took action to enforce the ban, the *Omanhin* accused him of confiscating canoes belonging to fishermen and appropriating public economic spaces for his personal purposes. Aggery averred that the beach near the castle had, from time immemorial, been the main fishing grounds; moving operations from that vicinity was inconceivable. These initial confrontations led to an irreversible gulf between the two leaders and the institutions they represented.

## THE CLASH OF COURTS

The most far-reaching conflict between *Omanhin* Aggery and the colonial administration involved the recurrent issue of competing court systems. The administration continued to establish new courts despite the existence of similar indigenous trial places, giving rise to great confusion regarding the nature and extent of the respective jurisdictions of these incongruous legal institutions.[20] Whether fortuitously or purposefully some ordinary people in society, particularly the poor, relished the prevailing ambiguities and tension that the simultaneous operation of indigenous and colonial courts created. Illustratively, the indigenous court gave an imprisonment sentence to Kojo Esuon for attempting to poison his neighbor. He escaped and appealed to the English court in the castle, which found the magistrate of the indigenous court, Joseph Martin, guilty of technical assault and fined him £5. The *Omanhin* came under enormous compulsion to settle that fine on behalf of the magistrate of his court, which he did, albeit reluctantly. In 1865, the indigenous court sentenced Blankson Wood, a clerk in the employ of W. C. Finlason and Jamaican resident in Cape Coast, on account of disrespectful language and blatant contempt. Finlason reported the matter to the governor with the explanation that his clerk did not acknowledge any authority besides that of Her Majesty, the Queen of England, and to her, he confidently appealed for redress.[21] The proliferation of such defiant and daring occurrences became increasingly concerning due to the growing urban status of Cape Coast, then the seat of the burgeoning colonial administration, and its concomitant cosmopolitan outlook. As a consequence of the booming trade, merchants and individuals from virtually all major parts of the world had some business or other activity to attend to in the town. The action of Finlason on behalf of Wood amounted to clear contempt and disregard for the indigenous court.

Governor Pine lambasted the operation and proceedings of the indigenous court, describing them as unlawful, unconstitutional, unwarrantable, and palpably in conflict with the understanding, spirit, and usages existing between the government and the people under its protection. He further charged that the indigenous court remained annoyingly authoritative and, above all, could barely be recognized because it neither encouraged nor supported appeals to the British judiciary system. The governor arbitrarily ordered the annulment of all proceedings and the immediate transfer of pending cases to the English court.[22] Additionally, he required Aggery to hold discussions with him on the constitution of a court the operations of which would be acceptable to the colonial administration. The latter disregarded the requirement, which he considered insulting to his person and office of *Omanhin*.

In response to the complaints and accusations of the governor, the *Omanhin* unleashed a vitriolic attack on the administration, describing it as an intruding and invasive political establishment that had arrogated an unreasonable degree of power to itself. He charged that the nature of British jurisdiction had become so nebulous and nondescript that he, as *Omanhin*, remained in grave doubt regarding its extent.[23] As a fully constituted king, Aggery asserted that it was unthinkable for a third party to direct what he could and could not do on his own land.

Relatedly, the *Omanhin* expressed his disapproval of the questionable Bond of 1844, the supposed basis of British power and authority in southern Ghana to which Captain George Maclean and those who supplanted him had coerced a group of chiefs to append their thumbprints. In the opinion of Aggery, that bond had wrenched power from the hands of the kings, chiefs, and other indigenous political leaders in a bizarre manner. He charged that the main architect of the bond, Maclean,

> in a very peculiar, imperceptible, and unheard-of manner, wrested from the hands of our Kings, Chiefs, and head men, their power to govern their own subjects. The Governor, placing himself at the head of a handful of soldiers, had been known himself to travel to the remotest parts of the interior, for the purpose of compelling Kings, Chiefs, and head men (through fear of man or other feeling) to obey his Excellency's summons or to comply with His Excellency's decrees. A blow was thus firmly, slowly, and persistently struck ... A white face, a red jacket ... countenanced to throw off with impunity their very allegiance, an allegiance which could not well be disowned and ignored and denied without endangering the security of the King.[24]

This perception of the British colonial enterprise amounted to a profound indictment. The *Omanhin* reiterated, in no uncertain terms, that the British dispensed force, fear, and fright systematically through a body of intolerant soldiers.

## COLONIAL MILITARISM AND INDIGENOUS MILITANCY

The military as a formal regimental institution in southern Ghana emerged from a preexisting crop of energetic men who started two irregular troops, later referred to as the Gold Coast Corp, as well as the militia and police in the early nineteenth century.[25] The Gold Coast Corp consisted of a formidable group of men drawn from a detachment of the West Indian Regiment; largely unfamiliar with local languages and ways of life, they remained downright ruthless and uncompromising in carrying out orders. That unit provided the colonial government with an intelligence service, kept the population in check, and suppressing and repelling rebellions. Over time, the need for convenient communication with the people became unavoidable, leading to the recruitment of a few local men as well as others who could speak the language and were conversant with general ways of life. The old corps eventually became the Gold Coast Militia and Police. Their uniforms comprised duck outfits, coatees, forage caps, and half-boots; they later enhanced their apparel with blue pants, red coats, blue collars, and the standard forage caps. Brass buttons on the uniforms exhibited etched crowns with the name of the unit boldly displayed. The main detachments of the militia and police had their base in the Cape Coast Castle. The possession of arms such as muskets, bayonets, and truncheons accentuated their power and authority, especially given the fear that these weapons evoked among the local population.

The establishment of a Gold Coast artillery with definitive, rigid military training and composition raised the level of terror that government forces struck among inhabitants. Given the enduringly negative local perception of that sort of stringent training, people of prestigious social backgrounds avoided recruitment, leaving those who readily elected to join the artillery—mainly individuals who had been freed from diverse systems or arrangements of bondage and servitude. The opportunity to become a government operative in the artillery force, fortunately or unfortunately, proffered such people with an outlet for the expression of their newly found freedom. In view of lingering bitterness against their former masters—and a strong desire for revenge—these recruits became a somewhat difficult lot for their officers to control. The military force offered them a platform of power and authority for enforcement of law and order to the detriment of their former masters.²⁶ Because most of the chiefs had kept several persons in bondage and servitude, a good number found themselves at the receiving end of these enforcers of the law, who used the slightest excuse to settle personal scores.

The use of persons freed from bondage and servitude in the police force created other severe social problems. Because these men had the tendency to exhibit ruthlessness in the discharge of their duties, they created considerable bad press for the government. Their low perceived social status made it impossible for most people who boasted reputable pedigree or social standing to respect their authority, especially given the peremptory manner of its expression; this stalemate caused considerable uproar in society. The existing police force, made up in part of local men, remained ill-trained and unreliable. The acting inspector general of police, in his evidence before the Legislative Council in June 1868, lamented the liability of the police in keeping order in Cape Coast on account of several factors, most prominently their inadequate numbers, local origins, and overfamiliarity with the townspeople. These factors made some of them timid, rendering them inefficient for active duty because of the general prejudice against the police.²⁷

The colonial government anticipated the effectiveness of the police force in keeping order, hence reserving the deployment of soldiers for the most severe situations. Further, the administration had previously justified the use of a tolerant police force as a measure more in keeping with the character of southern Ghana, fearing that the evident aggressive tendencies of soldiers would provoke the people. Troops of soldiers had been used to perform police duties before the establishment of the latter unit, but that had generated a considerable degree of disagreement between the War Office in London and the local commanding officer. Consequently, the colonial government anticipated a convenient compromise in establishing a police force under its exclusive control.

In 1860, the colonial authorities established the Gold Coast Armed Police Force. Given past difficulties and concerns with troop composition, the government decided to limit membership of this force to the Hausa, arguing that the success of these troops in Lagos, Nigeria, provided a model for southern Ghana. As a language, Hausa passed generically as a term for diverse ethnic groups that straddled the middle northern belt of several West African countries, with their core concentration in Nigeria. Their reputed intelligence, determination, and uncompromising commitment to execution of orders made them particularly suitable for the task of keeping law and order in colonial West Africa. The conduct and bearing of the Hausa confirmed perceptions, already rife in many quarters, of their high-handedness. In southern Ghana, their origins in the northern territories of the country and in Lagos, Nigeria, assured neutrality for the colonial administration, as they had hardly any family relations or cultural connections with the people. Uniforms for the Armed Police Force consisted of blue baft with red facings, blue fezzes with red bands, blucher boots, and bands. Others wore flannel shirts and pants with suave jackets, red woolen sashes, black leather, and fezzes with blue tassels mimicking those of their Lagos counterparts. The officers used blue flannel with Norfolk jackets, Hausa trousers, red silk sashes, white helmets with red puggaree or fez, and brown leather belts.

In 1875, the Armed Police Force became the Constabulary Unit, charged with additional duties comprising constant patrols and handling minor skirmishes. Eventually, constabulary operations extended to most parts of southern Ghana. Colonel McInnis—a man of strong character, impatient with difficult people, and ruthless in handling disturbances—served notoriously as an inspector general.[28] After his term of command, the governor eulogized the impressive class of courage, loyalty, efficiency, and success that he had brought to the constabulary. These qualities, according to the governor, changed the establishment into an irregular regiment, laying a strong foundation for the eventual formation of the West African Frontier Force Battalions.²⁹

Unfortunately, incessant cases of indiscipline, drunkenness, terrorizing, and extortion, especially among the rank and file, surfaced in the process of establishing military and police forces in southern Ghana. The mere introduction of regimental colonial institutions with repressive and oppressive tendencies immeasurably increased the potential for backlash in relation to local communities. Various manifestations of indiscipline, terrorizing, heavy-handedness, extortion, and drunkenness acted as catalysts for the outbreak of frequent clashes.

Aggery, out of personal conviction and in his capacity as *Omanhin*, was one of numerous people who expressed constant concern about the nature of regimental institutions. In his estimation, these institutions evoked fear and terror not only among his people in Cape Coast and the surrounding villages but also in the entirety of southern Ghana.³⁰ Accordingly, many peace-loving subjects felt greatly compelled and intimidated to throw off their allegiance to the indigenous authorities, a development that in no small measure endangered the security of the *Omanhin*. Aggery reiterated his assertion that colonialism amounted to an unmitigated military rule. This regime, in his assessment, thrived on the deployment of soldiers and battalions of red-jacketed policemen who, in most cases, swiftly carried out not only the orders of the governor and the larger colonial agenda but also their personal interests. Indeed, an earlier statement by Governor Pine confirmed aspects, if not all, of what the *Omanhin* implied in his statement. In his frustration over the comments Aggery made on the case involving Blankson Wood, Pine expressed his frustration and retorted that, if the matter had occurred during the tenure of Governor George Maclean, it would have been settled with the dispatch of a few forces.³¹ Aggery accused the colonial administration of arrogating to itself power and authority not granted in the Bond of 1844. Although he had only been a minor during that signing ceremony, the *Omanhin* claimed he had understood the altercations between the representatives of indigenous political authority and Maclean, who authored the document. Aggery insisted that the people of southern Ghana scarcely constituted the subjects of the Queen of England. With respect to territorial extent, he averred that the British had their limits set within the walls of the castle and two other forts. Given the expansion of British influence beyond the original agreement, Aggery charged that the colonial administration, through military mobilization and superior mechanical might, was engaging in territorial aggrandizement.

Aggery served notice that correspondence with the administration would be unproductive until he received redress from the government in England on these pressing issues.[32] Pine threatened to withdraw official recognition of Aggery as king of Cape Coast on account of what Pine described as insolent and combative communication. Perhaps to show the resoluteness of the administration, the English court awarded Blankson Wood damages and costs despite the vehement protestations of Aggery and his supporters.

The last straw that offered Aggery the opportunity to call the bluff of the militant colonial administration happened when West Indian soldiers stationed in Cape Coast clashed with some local young men. The soldiers were on a drinking spree in town when the clash occurred, resulting in the death of two young men and the disappearance of one soldier. As usual, the soldiers had swiftly resorted to their military and mechanical might in the clash with the young men. Aggery officially protested with characteristic vehemence to Conran:

> [a] frightful tragedy has been enacted in this town ... soldiers of the garrison have suddenly issued forth at night with some officers, and have treated this town as if they had taken it by assault in time of war ... we have a right to expect that the government will cause the most searching and complete judiciary inquiry to be made ... how

it came to pass that the troops in garrison at Cape Coast were rushing about the town in detached bodies, some with, some without officers, armed with muskets, bayonets and clubs, forcibly entering houses of sleeping persons, slaughtering the "Queen's subjects," taking away property, beating peaceful citizens, dragging human beings about like dead cattle, and creating such terror and confusion as will never be forgotten here ... it was not a riot on the part of the people; it was an attack on the town by the garrison.[33]

The indictment of the militaristic nature of the colonial administration and its penchant for the use of force recurred in the town and other places in southern Ghana. Aggery averred that soldiers armed with muskets and bayonets ran amok, with or without officers, sending frightening signals to defenseless people. Not unexpectedly, these developments made the people of Cape Coast further averse to the presence of the colonial administration.

The administration, without question, acted conciliatorily and protectively toward a private in the army found culpable of the murders in the clash, whom the acting chief justice of the English court had sentenced to death. Exercising executive prerogative, the governor commuted the sentence to life imprisonment with hard labor on the advice of the Executive Council, postulating that the soldier had dutifully acted to suppress a dangerous disturbance.[34] He criticized Aggery and his advisers for endeavoring to use the incident, as well as the funerals of the victims, to incite inhabitants against the administration. The *Asafo* had paraded the coffins of the deceased through town amid drumming, singing, and firing of musketry within the precincts of the castle, where the government held most of its deliberations and operations. The governor used the event as an excuse to blame the *Omanhin*, even though the practice was a time-honored indigenous warrior funeral ceremony.[35]

Suspecting the colonial officials of using legal and administrative technicalities to get their way, Aggery wrote a letter to Conran's superior, William Blackall, governor-in-chief of Sierra

Fig. 6.2 *Asafo* No. 5 Company parading in front of the Cape Coast Castle during its annual custom.

Leone, then on a visit to southern Ghana. He requested that Blackall "respectfully define the relationship between the court of the *Omanhin* and the English court, between him as *Omanhin* and the Governor, and between the English King and his brother Kings on the Gold Coast."[36] Fed up with the undue interference with his power as head of the indigenous political order, Aggery complained that compared to other kings, chiefs, and indigenous leaders in southern Ghana, the efforts to perform his duty met constant barriers because his town hosted the seat of government. This pernicious presence also stifled his financial base, as the administration actively raked in all customs, excise, and other revenues with which his predecessors had operated.

Besides giving a litany of past grievances, Aggery served notice that in view of the unnecessary show of force on the part of the colonial administration, he would hardly hesitate to constitute his own army to confront the government in equal measure as a defense mechanism.[37] He threatened to transform the *Asafo* into a professional, well-armed band to meet the army of the administration squarely. The colonial government, exhibiting the characteristic intolerance of military regimes, described Aggery's language as manifestly seditious.[38] Conran, accordingly, took serious exception to his threat and requested the support of Blackall in putting down this "insolent, ignorant, and stubborn man" suspected of a determined desire to overthrow British rule and substitute it with his own.[39]

Reports of these occurrences reached England through regular correspondences, dispatches, and telegrams, starting spirited debates about the worth of the colony in relation to the incessant problems and high annual costs of its administration. Authorities in London opined that if the administration remained in southern Ghana, colonial officers would suffer perpetual frustration from the kings and chiefs. Others argued that in the event of the colonial agenda being carried through, kings such as Aggery would need to be prevented from setting up armed forces certainly made up of incorrigible characters and, therefore, difficult to control. Blackall appeared equally intolerant of Aggery's defiant posture against the administration and, not unexpectedly, showed strong support for Conran. He regarded Aggery's warnings as mischievous and his claim to a share of revenue as inadmissible. In the view of Blackall, such pretentious behavior must be effectively checkmated. Despite the adamance of the colonial authorities in their dealings with Aggery, they worked frantically to forestall or at least mitigate local opposition in Cape Coast by moving the seat of judicial authority to Freetown, Sierra Leone. Unfortunately, there was so much bad blood between the administration and the people that this effort proved too little, too late.

To make matters worse, Conran refused to cooperate with Thomas Hughes, an official of the palace of Aggery in charge of assisting the indigenous political establishment with maintaining order, development, and welfare of the people. This denial sparked a complete crisis, and leaders of the seven *Asafo* companies of

Cape Coast organized a number of protests to express their discontentment with the administration.[40] The *Omanhin* unleashed yet another condemnation of colonial governance, describing the refusal of the administration to work with Hughes as an attempt to withhold civil liberties from the people in a manner unprecedented in any civilized country no matter how despotic the sovereign.[41] Conran, in his attempt to dismantle the judicial authority of Aggery, released a number of people that the indigenous court had sentenced to various terms of imprisonment on their submission of private petitions, citing cruelty of sentences that contravened the letter and spirit of British law.[42] A large public gathering in support of the *Omanhin* encouraged him to send Conran an official letter of protest even more scathing than usual:

> The time has now come for me to record a solemn protest . . . the perpetual annoyances and insults that you persistently and perseveringly continue to practice on me in my capacity as legally constituted King of Cape Coast. I presume your object is . . . to incite me and my people to enact more of those fearful things that took place in Haiti that I have heard of . . . however much you may wish to have me and my people under martial law, you will never have that pleasure . . . the Earl of Carnarvon has laid it down in his speech on the 2nd August last, that we are all entitled to redress at his hands as the Colonial Minister. To that quarter I shall appeal for the last time, and then if some tangible satisfaction is not accorded to me and those whose interest I am bound to protect, it will be time enough for me to adopt those measures which will ensure to me and my people something unlike the slavery that you are endeavoring to place us in.[43]

Moreover, Aggery referred to previous grievances, particularly those regarding the harsh treatment of his people at the hands of the colonial forces. He recalled instances when the soldiers had "butchered" his subjects under the supervision of officers and even the governor himself. The *Omanhin* reiterated his knowledge of British government plans to grant self-governance to kings and chiefs of southern Ghana and lambasted the governor for the personal attacks. Aggery charged that he would no longer endure colonial tyranny, annoyances, and abuses, nor suffer the disunity that officers endeavored to create in his town.

With both combatants having reached tipping points, the governor decided that rather than allow the *Omanhin* to strike first, he would. Conran insisted that Aggery be made to answer questions relating to his unguarded reference to the Haitian revolution, fearing that the threat could mean an end to British hold over southern Ghana. The colonial administration discerned a criminal threat that needed to be nipped in the bud. Evidently, that perceived ultimatum was enough justification for the arrest of Aggery for failing to honor the summons of the governor and retorting that he scarcely knew the status of Conran, bluffing that the king of Cape Coast had nothing to do with a supposedly insufferable representative of the English Queen. The colonial administration consequently abolished the indigenous court system, deposed Aggery as king of Cape Coast, and dispatched him on a mail boat to Sierra Leone. Rationalizing his swift action in the deposition of the *Omanhin*, Conran indignantly explained that "from the moment King Aggery's Commissioners arrived from England, in September 1865, with the news of their being trained for self-government, I experienced from King Aggery much insubordinate and abusive language, indicating throughout his whole conduct the mad desire to govern, not only Cape Coast itself, but the whole Gold Coast, having lately adopted the title King of Cape Coast and its dependencies ... I received a production from him full of rebellious and insubordinate language, threatening me with the repetition of the Haitian scenes."[44] With *Omanhin* Aggery out of the picture, the colonial authorities, mindful of the incessant frustrations they had encountered, took additional preventive measures. The administration quickly declared the office and title of king abolished, replacing it with that of headman, who would swear an oath of allegiance to the Queen of England and obey the governor as her accredited representative.[45] When the *Asafo* and educated elite of Cape Coast rejected these conditions, the administration realized that the removal of Aggery might not suffice to end the seemingly interminable local contestations.

### OFFICIAL INTERESTS: RELOCATION OF THE COLONIAL CAPITAL

As early as 1874, the colonial administration was already planning to abandon the Cape Coast Castle as the seat of government. In a speech before the House of Lords in London, the fourth Earl of Carnarvon, Henry H. M. Herbert, referred to this proposal and identified three concrete considerations for the choice of a new capital city. The desire to move the capital included military motives, commercial concerns, and the sanitation situation. These factors, as well as their timing, made the decision to abandon the Cape Coast Castle quite curious. The town had served as the principal center of British operations since the Europeans had arrived in southern Ghana. After incessant altercations with the combined forces of Aggery, the *Asafo*, and the educated elite, the government considered either Accra or Elmina as an alternative location. The administration argued that regarding the military motive, Cape Coast had no additional advantages and that Accra, to the east, was a more desirable destination. Especially with the proposed consolidation of the Lagos and southern Ghana settlements, Accra became doubly attractive as a strategic locale. Elmina, to the west of Cape Coast, had a hilly district, a good water supply, and a port with convenient capacity to admit sizable craft ranging between forty and fifty tons. Although either Accra or Elmina could be possible capital, the Earl of Carnarvon opined that the real seat of government in time of war must serve as a strategic haven with adjoining hills to which the governor and his staff could retreat. Simple buildings such as stockades could be built along the way, with roads and other systems of communication connecting them to the seat of government on the coast. Accra happened to be about thirty miles from Aburi on the Akuapem Ridge. The latter had served as a quiet, luscious, cool base for many early European missionaries as well as their families. Considering the previous European settlements in that proximate neighborhood, most colonial officials preferred Accra, even though the town had a relatively poor coastal landing.

The major justification for the colonial government leaving Cape Coast high and dry increasingly centered on alleged sanitation problems. But the health and sanitation history of southern Ghana scarcely supported the clean bill of health that the administration accorded Accra and Elmina over Cape Coast.[46] The fourth Earl of Carnarvon, Henry H. M. Herbert, exaggerated the sanitation situation of the town as "perhaps one of the worst places that could have been selected. The soil was saturated through and through with sewage. There was decaying vegetable matter everywhere about, and the houses were crowded on one another. It deserved more than perhaps any other place the appellation of the White man's grave."[47] Although these observations drew shouts of "hear, hear," in the House of Lords in England, discerning public opinion in Cape Coast dismissed the concerns of Herbert as proverbial sour grapes, particularly since the town had served for many years as the center of the colonial administration and place of residence for numerous Europeans.

Sanitation in Cape Coast, indistinctly different from that of any major town or city in the country, became the major factor for stripping Cape Coast of its capital status; the colonial government's constant reference to the common practice of free-range animal rearing in the region became one of the major justifications for that denial. Additionally, European residents and visitors to the town left questionable accounts of disregard for proper spatial planning that impacted sanitation and health. Charles

Alexander Gordon, an army surgeon, said the following about Cape Coast:

> The part of the town occupied by the poorer classes consist of houses terribly huddled together, along the opposite faces of what is a deep valley, along which, in the rainy season, a considerable torrent runs, and where, during the dry [season], all kinds of filth the most abominable accumulate. From this ravine offshoots extend in various directions among the houses; myriads of frogs domesticate themselves ... In the parts of the town where European merchants or wealthy natives reside the houses are of a superior kind, being composed of brick, flat-roofed, and well white-washed ... The two principal streets are wide ... like boulevards. On an eminence at one end of the principal street, directly facing the Castle stands the Chapel of the Wesleyan Missionaries.[48]

Aspects of this description are equally present in the account of Brodie Cruickshank, who indicated that houses in Cape Coast appeared "huddled together in the most crowded manner ... without the slightest regard to light ... air, or the convenience of approach."[49] Responding to these denigrating and disparaging descriptions of their town, some of the educated elite asserted that the apparent lack of proper planning hardly had to do with any cultural imperative but was rather the direct result of the stalemate between colonial administration and indigenous political authority.[50] The situation was exacerbated by the increasing birth rate and influx of people bent on taking advantage of abundant commercial and educational opportunities in an increasingly urbanized Cape Coast. The educated elite averred that the administration interfered with and suppressed the power and authority of the kings and chiefs, who in turn strove against the expansion of colonial authority. This stalemate created an uncongenial atmosphere within which the institutions of these rival regimes rendered each other weak, dysfunctional, and ineffective.

The educated elite further stated that in precolonial times, the indigenous political regime had a system of municipal administration responsible for town planning, public works, sanitation, and other communal projects, effectively managed through the *Asafo* quarter or ward arrangement. The arrival of the Europeans and emergence of the colonial order, with its constant interference and attempts at regulating indigenous political organizations, had occasioned a near abandonment of most long-established environmental and public works planning systems. The *Asafo* could barely do any more than struggle for survival under the ever-increasing colonial pressure. Lamenting this situation, John Mensah Sarbah recounted how coastal Ghana had been treated as though it had an abject absence of meaningful indigenous institutions, language, national character, and ways of life.[51] In the same vein, Joseph Casely Hayford, a lawyer and nationalist, regretted that contact with the Europeans had resulted in a debilitating disorganization of time-honored municipal arrangements, forcibly substituted by the colonial government.[52] He alleged that as the administration failed to govern meaningfully, its constant interference in local affairs ended up preventing chiefs from effectively discharging their indigenous mandate and responsibilities regarding supervision of the built environment. Worsening this administrative stalemate, the expansion and growth of towns brought overcrowding and squalor, causing isolated disease outbreaks. For instance, individuals and groups quickly declared the town council system a failure when Accra recorded an outbreak of the bubonic plague, with the Legislative Council being largely censured for the filthy state of the town.[53] The press in its various publications took up the issue of bad drainage systems.[54]

The politics of sanitation, not uncommon in the history of colonial urban Africa, came up quite prominently in the case of Cape Coast. This scenario revealed that colonial medical actions amounted to expressions of the attitudes, objectives, and priorities of European rulers in Africa.[55] Colonial governments embarked on major projects of social engineering aimed at relocating people deemed undesirable away from select prestigious places. In the Cape Colony of early twentieth-century South Africa, powerful sanitation, disease, and epidemiological metaphors underpinned perceptions that went a long way to influence and even justify official action.[56] In most places, colonial authorities acted on the supposed medical menace the African presence posed. Consequently, a planned pattern emerged to set African and European urban communities physically apart. To ensure an air-tight system, colonial medical authorities in some cases created sanitary cordons of uninhabited space to forestall the spread of "African diseases" into European residential areas.[57] Sporadic outbreaks of epidemics provided justification for the suddenness with which the imposition of segregation and the concomitant relocation of supposedly unwanted people happened. Illustratively, the bubonic plague in Dakar, Senegal, justified the abrupt way in which a policy of residential segregation supplanted the earlier pattern of coexistence. On the advice of medical authorities, the colonial government started the Medina settlement as a separate African quarter.[58] Again, the bubonic plague, cholera, and smallpox in South Africa, particularly in the Transvaal and Natal provinces, provided justification for segregating Indians and Africans living in municipal locations. These arbitrary approaches, not peculiar to Africa, had precedents across Europe and therefore informed responses of the colonial authorities to various social problems.[59]

In Cape Coast, the sanitation situation proffered justification for a unique approach. Instead of the creation of a sanitary cordon to offset the threat of epidemics as pertained elsewhere in the continent, the colonial government elected to relocate the capital to a place where sanitation conditions differed insignificantly. This action lent indubitable credibility to lingering suspicions that the real motive for the move remained decidedly more political than supposed sanitation and security considerations. Yet in regular correspondences, colonial officers repeatedly referred to the congestion of the town as a sure source of sanitation problems.[60]

Colonial medical officers equally drew attention to the dangers of overcrowding, particularly caused by the reluctance of people to take advantage of newly created adjourning settlements. Conservative in their ideas, entrenched Cape Coast families showed no great desire to move into new suburbs. Others complained about distances between the town center and the new settlements. In yet another attempt at relieving the congestion, a site selected as a Hausa zongo, a secluded, predominantly Islamic community two miles along the Saltpond Road, was equally unappealing. Many people within the targeted group considered the settlement too distant for the convenience and economic expectations of an established trading community.

Increasing congestion brought in its wake the erection of structural accretions, such as wooden sheds and extensions to houses, without consultation with the colonial engineering authorities. Some unscrupulous sanitary inspectors worsened the situation with demands of bribes that further hampered the supervision of new buildings. To aggravate the situation, the increasing population far exceeded the capacities of available facilities such as public bathrooms and latrines. Since the authorities had not mandated that homeowners must provide those amenities, most people depended on the few places of convenience available to the public. As the population outgrew those facilities, people began to use portions of the beach as open latrines and dumping grounds for trash. The derelict state of many public latrines further exacerbated the problem as large drain outlets to the sea, including sections of the beach, became indiscriminately drafted for those purposes. The condition of drains into the lagoon mimicked those leading to the sea.

Scanty administrative and fiscal resources worsened the sanitation situation. Colonial administration correspondence constantly referred to staff shortages; the small number available was shifted around, leaving other places without medical officers or sanitary inspectors for an unreasonable long period of time.

Inadequate funds for hiring laborers to clear weeds, remove silt, and secure scavengers for other sanitation services hardly helped the situation. Fearing that an outbreak of a contagious disease in a place like Cape Coast would prove disastrous, the provincial engineer recommended that various proposed schemes to relieve overcrowding receive financial assistance from the colonial government. The engineer recommended a two-year budget of £10,000 that, in his expert estimation, would suffice to effect a great change in these pressing problems. The administration ignored the report and carried through its plan to relocate the colonial capital to Accra in the east.

Ironically, in the nineteenth century, *Omanhin* Aggery with his council decried Cape Coast hosting the seat of government as a pernicious presence that impeded the effective performance of his mandate—only for twentieth-century indigenous and opinion leaders to lament the stripping of the capital status.

### EXIGENCIES OF MODERNIZATION: EXCLUSION FROM RAILROAD INFRASTRUCTURE

The selection of Accra with its equally imperfect sanitation conditions strengthened the speculation that relocation of the capital had more to do with official interest in penalizing Cape Coast. As a result of the change, the town missed out on the benefits of much-needed economic infrastructural developments the colonial government had embarked on in the early twentieth century, especially during the boom in southern Ghana cocoa cultivation. As already intimated, the initial expansion and growth of Cape Coast had hinged primarily on its position as a commercial center that linked European commercial establishments with traders from the coast, inland territories, forest, savanna, and beyond, to the Niger and Sahel regions.[61] Long before trade with the Europeans, local trade existed between the *Fetu* Kingdom in the interior and Cape Coast, or *Oguaa*, on the coast. Traders from the former delivered corn, oil, and palm wine to the latter in exchange for fish and salt.[62] The arrival of the Europeans increased and diversified the volume of trade. In 1652, a Swedish company built a fortified lodge near the site of the present castle. In view of increasing European rivalry on this part of the coast, the Danes drove out the Swedes; the former, in turn, lost their position to the English in 1662.[63] The Company of Royal African Merchants, which took over the site from the Danes, expanded the fortifications and developed the structure into a larger edifice, making Cape Coast their main center of operations. Though the company soon went bankrupt, its successor, the Royal African Company, continued to use the town as the center of English trading operations on the coast.[64]

Until the eighteenth century, gold and other items, especially from the interior region of southern Ghana, remained the principal export through Cape Coast; however, the shipment of captives equally kept this port busy during the trans-Atlantic slave trade.[65] Most European imports such as textiles, metal products, cutlery, guns, weapons, and miscellaneous goods in the twentieth century entered southern Ghana through that same port.[66] Wealth derived from these shipments provided opportunities for a few individual traders and families to enhance their socioeconomic status at the expense of the king of *Fetu*. Edward William Barter, a mulatto who became quite influential in the commercial network of the town, remained the most notable of this group.[67]

European-chartered companies, with their powers of monopoly, restricted the number of merchants who could trade on the coast; however, that dominance began to wane after 1750, when the British Parliament revoked the charter of the Royal African Company.[68] From that point onward, a new commercial dispensation emerged that enabled all sorts of merchants to trade within the British jurisdiction on the coast on the payment of a small tax. Many among this new generation of traders, compared to the earlier group, settled for longer periods on the coast, lived with local women, and had families.[69] In 1828, when the British government contemplated abandoning the southern Ghana settlements, English merchants who traded in this area vehemently protested and eventually secured permission to take over its management. They received a rare grant from their government to help with the cost of administration. This group of merchants appointed Captain George Maclean in 1830 as president of the council in charge of local administration. He remained in office until the British government took full control of the area in 1843.[70] In the late 1840s, a new crop of mulatto merchants in Cape Coast replaced their European counterparts. Many members of this generation of traders, mainly Christian, received education at the various castle schools. Some inherited businesses from their European fathers, and others entered the trade on their own initiative. Many took advantage of their formal education and connections with the Europeans to become local agents for London firms, expanding their southern Ghana operations in the process.[71]

Hence, well into the late nineteenth century, Cape Coast had become one of the few prominent centers of trade that purveyed the wealth of both local trade and international commerce with Europe, making it a relatively prosperous town. In the absence of a technically constructed harbor, vessels anchored a considerable distance away from shore on the high seas as local men maneuvered canoes back and forth to load and unload trade items. This arrangement offered brisk business for fishermen as well as other individuals willing and able to help with the conveyance of goods to and from the foreign vessels. Furthermore, in the absence of a properly planned network of road and railroad infrastructure, ground transportation of export and import merchandise mainly occurred with people carrying goods on their heads or rolling them in casks through bush paths over long distances to the hinterland regions.[72] This tedious system of cargo transportation injected considerable money into the economy of Cape Coast as young men and women availed themselves of the opportunity, enduring the tedium of journeys into and out of the hinterland regions of southern Ghana. Well into the middle of the nineteenth century, particularly after the abolition of the trans-Atlantic slave trade, increasing trade in agricultural produce enhanced the enormous economic opportunities. The boom in cocoa cultivation during the first and second decades of the twentieth century facilitated the economic development of the coastal town. Considering the abounding economic opportunities, people from neighboring towns and interior districts eagerly sought employment, mainly as carriers and general laborers.

European commercial firms such as the Royal African Company, F. and A. Swanzy, and the Elder Dempster Shipping Lines experienced successful business operations, accentuating the relatively strong economic standing of Cape Coast, although other major towns of southern Ghana equally benefited from the emerging mercantile capitalist economy.[73] Many people availed themselves of the abounding opportunities, reifying the strong nascent commercial spirit among Africans, particularly women.[74] Women, who operated generally as wholesalers and retailers, constituted an essential and effective connection in the extensive network of distribution that supplied the bulk of goods throughout southern Ghana.[75] Wholesalers bought goods in bulk from the warehouses of importing European firms or from individual merchants and gave them out to retailing customers on credit. Some of these retailers sold items in regular markets; others purveyed theirs from neighborhood to neighborhood, door to door, or on the streets. This category of traders, over time, developed unique commercial-customer relations that in most cases allowed incentives such as bargaining and convenient terms of payment, in sharp contrast to the nonnegotiable price tags of European stores. Yet this burgeoning boom would burst amid the bad blood between Cape Coast and the colonial authorities.

## THE END OF AN ERA

The introduction of railroad transportation into southern Ghana in the closing stages of the nineteenth century paradoxically hurt rather than helped the burgeoning economic fortunes of Cape Coast. In 1894, the British Chamber of Commerce began strongly advocating for railroads and better roads. Enacted in 1898, the Railroad Ordinance empowered the colonial administration to acquire land for tracks and stations.[76] That same year, railroad construction began in earnest at Sekondi. Infrastructure was further expanded in the 1920s under Governor Frederick Gordon Guggisberg with the goal of providing transport and harbor facilities. The subsequent proposition of a Central Province Railroad from Huni Valley to Kade in 1927 stirred no mean degree of hope in Cape Coast. When the idea first came up in 1922, the chiefs, people, and the Aborigines' Rights Protection Society (ARPS) requested that the rail line be linked to Cape Coast as a major terminus. They expressed foreboding that if the government excluded their town, an ancient commercial center, from the network, its economy would wane. When the governor declined to consider those fears, *Omanhin* Mbra III, with the consent of his chiefs, headmen, and elders, presented a petition to the secretary of state for colonies in London on the issue, calling for a reconsideration of Guggisberg's decision not to construct a railroad with Cape Coast as an important base.

The governor countered that his rejection of the idea made sense considering larger administrative obligations to include the interests of up-country towns whose districts the proposed Central Province Railroad would traverse. He pointed out that the construction of a railroad based in Cape Coast would adversely affect towns such as Winneba and Saltpond. Guggisberg further indicated that the exclusion of Cape Coast from the railroad network, far from being a personal decision, was the judgment of a council of experts who felt that extensions and additions to the original Central Province Railroad scheme would not only increase cost upward of £30,000 per annum in maintenance but also require about 50 percent more locomotives and rolling stock. Mbra and his council responded that the inhabitants of Cape Coast also fell within the responsibility of the colonial government and should therefore be beneficiaries of the same official consideration in the matter of the proposed Central Province Railway project. Regarding the issue of maintenance costs, the *Omanhin* and his elders argued that the expected revenue from the Cape Coast line would cover all those expenses. To support this argument, they reminded Guggisberg of some of his own statements regarding the cost-benefit analysis of rail transport. In his address to the Legislative Council on March 1, 1923, the governor had commented on the cost effectiveness of railroads as a form of transportation because they possessed the comparative capacity to recover maintenance and capital cost. He had asserted further that sections of lines opened earlier in southern Ghana had brought increased revenue and that any other line that might be built would easily earn more than enough to cover expenditure on maintenance, capital outlay, and renewal. The *Omanhin* and other petitioners wondered how those optimistic observations would conversely apply in the case of a line based in Cape Coast. Moreover, they pointed out the incomprehensibility that of the three provinces into which the country had been divided, two should enjoy the benefit of the railroad to the neglect and disadvantage of the third.

Regarding the concern of the colonial government that the Cape Coast district might not have enough agricultural produce to run the railroad, the petitioners gave assurance that there would be an adequate supply of items because the railroad's completion would encourage many people to explore that farming opportunity. Again, this rebuttal hinged on the earlier expectations of Guggisberg regarding attendant prospects in one of his many official speeches. He had reiterated that farmers living far away from the railroads with loads of unsold cocoa would have no justifiable incentive to extend their farms until they knew about the government's commitment to provide the necessary infrastructure. An optimistic Governor Guggisberg had opined that once it became certain that a railroad would be constructed in a specific district, cocoa farms would increase in number. For instance, because of the rumor that a Central Province Railroad would be built in western Akim, farmers living around Nsuaem, Akim Swedru, and Akyease had boosted cocoa cultivation. Accordingly, the petitioners opined that the same trend would be replicated in the Cape Coast district to a greater degree. Imbued with this hope, Mbra and others denounced the preposterousness of the governor's defense, claiming that he was acting on expert counsel to exclude their town. After all, they recalled, two of his predecessors, J. P. Rodger and A. R. Slater, had made promises of a railroad for Cape Coast, and these governors had equally consulted experts who did due diligence in considering the proposal. Slater, for instance, had raised taxes on cocoa to help provide funds for establishing infrastructure that would impact a railroad for Cape Coast. He remained emphatic in his assurances that those needs had become urgent years ago and been exhaustively discussed but delayed for years.[77]

Touting these previous promises, the *Omanhin* and his council reiterated the economic reasons for requesting a railroad in their town. As in the past, they argued, the town remained the principal port in southern Ghana that traded with inland kingdoms such as Asante and Gyaman, where large quantities of gold dust originated for export to Europe and the United States. Monkey skins, guinea grains, maize, and other items, including rubber, were subsequent additions that even some Accra traders purchased to augment their exports.[78] In the early twentieth century, the volume of commodities hardly required railroads. To help the mining industry in the Tarkwa district with transportation, the colonial government had constructed a railroad from Sekondi to Tarkwa that hardly in any way interfered with the Cape Coast trade. Again, when the Ashanti Goldfields Corporation started its operation, all the machinery came through the port of this town and was carried in bits and pieces to the mines in the interior. With carriers supplied from the coast and its neighborhoods, Cape Coast was firmly connected to the interior, and its trade grew to an all-time high. Later, the Ashanti Goldfields Corporation and the government entered into an agreement that extended the railroad from Tarkwa to Kumasi. When cocoa cultivation to the east of the farther districts of the Accra port became vibrant, the government contemplated the construction of another railroad.

Rodger, governor at the time, bore in mind the benefits of infrastructural developments in other parts of the country and, in sympathy with Cape Coast, expressed concern about risks of trade depression and other complaints—for instance, because Kumasi had become an important trading center with a railroad connecting the Sekondi port. He expressed trepidation that Cape Coast would never again enjoy the practical monopoly over Asante trade as had been the situation in the past. Rodger nonetheless asserted that, with courage, resoluteness, and determination, the town would find the economic resilience to make up for its share of hinterland trade venturing into other economic opportunities. He suggested expansion of cocoa cultivation, augmented with the cultivation of cotton, sugarcane, maize, oil palm, and kola nut and increased trade in rubber as well as timber in the proximate fertile planting districts. Furthermore, the immediate neighborhood of Cape Coast had great prospects for animal husbandry as well as cultivation of fruits and vegetables. Rodger anticipated that, collectively, these crops could be traded as essential items for ships provisioning at its port and for the local markets. Alternatively, he observed that the town could establish a fruit trade with Europe, especially in bananas and pineapples, as it had with the West Indies. Turning his attention to the question of transportation, Rodger acknowledged the unsuitability of the few roads in the Central Province for motor traffic. As a temporary solution, he suggested the increased use of cask rolling, as in the Eastern Province, for transporting produce from the interior down to the coast. In the long term, he promised to improve and extend the road network with the hope that, given increased agricultural resources, a government railroad would eventually be constructed to connect the town to the planting districts of the interior—similar to the arrangement from which the Accra network had benefited. Provincial Commissioners W. C. F. Robertson, H. C. Grimshaw, and E. C. Eliot, all of whom extensively traveled the district at different times, had seconded those promises and given assurances to the chiefs and their people, according to Mbra.

With the steady growth of cocoa cultivation in southern Ghana, the people of Cape Coast found it necessary to remind the colonial government of those several promises regarding the railroad. Hugh Charles Clifford, who became governor after Rodger, pleaded that he had just assumed office and had much unfinished business to attend to. This business included harbor construction, water supply, and other infrastructural projects in Accra and Sekondi; therefore, Governor Clifford noted that it would be unwise for him to take on any additional projects. At the end of his tenure, a promissory bill on the issue of a railroad for Cape Coast passed as Ordinance No. 7 of 1919.[79] This move made the people happy because they felt that processes toward the realization of their long-awaited dream had started.

When Governor Guggisberg took over the reins of government after Clifford, he equally proffered indications of some action being taken on the proposed projects for Cape Coast. On his first visit to the town, he held a durbar at the castle where he announced his policy regarding the needs of the colony. On this occasion, he made his "Cape Coast will not be forgotten" statement.[80] Even though the governor scarcely specified what those words meant, the people assumed that the statement had to do with the realization of their desire for a railroad and water supply system. Guggisberg had occasion to repeat those vague words, greatly heightening hopes in the town.

Later, however, when Guggisberg announced his program for the improvement of the colony, the plan revealed a Central Province Railroad that excluded Cape Coast. The shock and disappointment of the people fueled general speculation that the entire program constituted a calculated attempt to ruin their town; therefore, the consequent protest were quite profound. Again, the chiefs and people argued that the exclusion of their town from the railroad project would take away produce that normally shipped through their port, particularly from the proximate districts where, on the strength of the Rodger promise, farmers had exerted enormous energy, time, and resources to increase cocoa cultivation. The protests came in the form of official letters and deputations to the office of the governor, but he remained unfazed, describing the eagerness to have a railroad network connected to Cape Coast as myopic because the view of Cape Coast as an ancient town overshadowed everything else. The *Omanhin* and his council without hesitation pointed out the inappropriateness of these comments and other disparaging remarks about the town, to no avail.

Chief W. Z. Coker, *Tufohin* of the Cape Coast *Asafo* companies, forced the issue at a meeting with the governor in 1922, reiterating the concern that if the town was effectively excluded from the proposed Central Province Railroad, the effects on trade would certainly cause a demographic decline. He observed that the principal supply of cocoa could get through Cape Coast from A-nyi-na-brim and Fo-su, but the considerable distance between Yan-ku-ma-si and Anyinabrim would discourage farmers from bringing their cocoa to the town; therefore, unless the line started and ended at Cape Coast, its trade and population would certainly be ruined. Chief Coker equally recalled that Rodger, while in office, had promised the town a railroad at an agricultural show in 1907.[81] However, Guggisberg stood his ground, reiterating that purely economic considerations underpinned the exclusion of Cape Coast.[82] With a dismissive air of finality, the governor posited that the proposed railroad scheme would pass so far north of the town that it would barely disrupt trade in any way.

In the end, Cape Coast suffered crippling consequences. When the construction of the line finished in 1927, all the cocoa supply from Nsu-aem and Ka-de went directly to Sekondi. Carriers who carted cocoa to Cape Coast, as well as canoe men who conveyed the produce to waiting vessels, lost their jobs. Since cocoa constituted one of the most profitable items shipped through its port, the dwindling economic fortunes of the town became palpable.[83] Many firms and businesses that specialized in export and import operations departed Cape Coast for the beckoning Accra and Sekondi ports. The regional headquarters of the Customs and Excise Department and the Elder Dempster Shipping Line Agency both moved to Sekondi in the west. Subsequently, some merchants joined the moving spree, and others stopped working due to loss of business. The previously easy money-making opportunities in Cape Coast whittled down, expelling artisans of all types, carriers, and educated young men and women. The deprivation of varied means of livelihood compelled yet more inhabitants to relocate to Tarkwa, Sekondi, and Kumasi in search of work. These waves of relocation had a telling effect on the population of Cape Coast, making it fall below that of Accra, Kumasi, Sekondi, and Takoradi.[84]

Undoubtedly, the neglect of Cape Coast during the modernization of economic infrastructure in southern Ghana hardly improved relations between the colonial government and the people. The exclusion of the town from the Railroad Ordinance became a point of contention, leading to all kinds of interpretation—including conspiracy theories. The *Asafo* and other indigenous organizations complained about unemployment among the young men, most of whom came from poor families. The unwillingness of Guggisberg to consider the numerous petitions on behalf of the town deepened ill feelings on the part of its people against the colonial government, especially among those who felt so strongly that the town had been betrayed. These resentments invariably found expression in the attitude toward the subsequent proposal of direct local taxation in 1929–1930. This tax proposition started as part of a comprehensive plan for the transformation of local administration pursued under the watch of Governors Slater and Jones, successively. The need to raise money came because of pressure from London to get the colonies to bear a larger share of the immense financial burden of sustaining the sprawling British Empire. Expenditure with respect to local development grew exponentially, particularly in education and sanitation management, leading to the pragmatic view that local populations should directly bear part of those costs. Even toward the end of the 1920s, southern Ghana was the only British colony in Africa without any form of direct taxation; introducing it, therefore, became crucial for the government yet completely unacceptable to the people.[85]

The Income Tax Ordinance sought to rope in all persons with earnings exceeding £40 a year to increase government revenue. To dissipate the anticipated popular resentment, it targeted just the few relatively well-to-do individuals first. This ordinance failed in the face of formidable protest as most of the people of southern Ghana acted collectively, decisively, and promptly.[86] The coastal educated elite, who in socioeconomic terms would have been the hardest hit group, led the campaign of dissension with slogans condemning taxation without representation as exploitation and oppression that caught on quite well with the ordinary people. The various provinces held violent protests, and in some coastal towns, the chiefs not only mobilized their people for demonstrations but also joined delegations to the local colonial officers and provincial commissioners. The protest campaigns gained momentum when members of the European mercantile community threw in their support. The climax came at the end of October 1931, when violent picketing occurred in Cape Coast and Sekondi. Governor T. S. W. Thomas, in his frustration, reiterated the official argument that for many years, the people of Cape Coast had gained notoriety among colonial political officers as the most difficult to work with in the whole of the colony because of their persistent opposition to government policies and measures.

## CONCLUSION

The persistent and resolute agency in coastal Ghana, especially in Cape Coast under *Amanhin* Amissah, Aggery, and Mbra III as well as their supporting cast of educated elite and *Asafo* between the nineteenth and twentieth centuries, underscores the notion that colonial officials did not always have their way. Colonial rule in southern Ghana showcased a diverse range of experiences. Coastal communities eventually understood the nature and manifestation of colonization, especially regarding its nature as essentially a project of control—not only in political and judicial matters but also economically and culturally. Accordingly, communities remained quite adamant in having their way and applied the most familiar indigenous modes to do so. This agency in Cape Coast produced particularly surprising and intriguing outcomes. The administration not only stripped the town of its original colonial capital city status but also made it suffer the denial of much-needed railroad infrastructure. That pointed agency compelled the administration, every now and then, to simultaneously seek conciliatory opportunities and apply measures that elicited all kinds of interpretation, including conspiracy theories. This perception hardly calmed matters down between the people and the administration, as the former explored other opportunities to refuse cooperation with the latter.

SEVEN

# "WE WON'T COOPERATE"

*Legislative Council Elections, 1932 Conflict, and Frustration of Colonial Authority*

COASTAL GHANA'S POLITICAL SITUATION BY the middle of the twentieth century had become complex—particularly in Cape Coast, where the culmination of local tensions and incessant contestations confounded officers of the administration. Accordingly, officials developed the perception that the inhabitants of the town were the most difficult constituency to work with in the entire colony. That official view described inhabitants as a people with varying critical and unhelpful attitudes toward government policies. Such descriptions made sense vis-à-vis the systematic pursuit of colonial interests. The *Omanhin* and his council had often been cited for refusing to cooperate with government officials, consistently offering both passive and active noncompliance.[1] The political undercurrents of the 1932 conflict unfolded against this intricate backdrop of mutual suspicion and mistrust.

## EXPANSION OF GOVERNANCE INSTITUTIONS

As part of the process of westernizing indigenous political institutions of southern Ghana, the administration implemented governance structures aimed at mitigating the dual difficulties of lack of officials and reticence of the British government to spend taxpayer money on colonies.[2] Among other considerations, new mechanisms, intended to achieve greater centralized control, sought a partial or complete tagging of the indigenous political establishment onto the overall machinery of government. Pursuant to these objectives, these political institutions functioned on the pivot of bills and ordinances. Accordingly, the introduction of the Native Jurisdiction Ordinance (NJO) came as an instrument of control that simultaneously enhanced indigenous powers of chiefs under the policy of indirect rule.[3] Within official circles, the main principle of indirect rule materialized: "For the purposes of local government, the institutions which native peoples have evolved for themselves, so that they may develop in a constitutional manner from their own past, guided and restrained by the traditions and sanctions which they have inherited (molded or modified as they may be on the advice of British Officers) and by general advice and control of those officers."[4] The NJO supposedly sought to make kings, chiefs, queen-mothers, and other identifiable indigenous leaders active agents in the machinery of government. Subjected to the guidance and advice of colonial political officers, the leaders of the indigenous political institutions would possess greater responsibility for implementing policies of the central government and initiating local development.[5] Significantly, the colonial establishment acknowledged the indispensability of indigenous political authorities to the notable disregard and exclusion of the educated elite as it attempted to introduce a new and all-inclusive system of governance.

In 1902, the administration formalized these new arrangements with the creation of a Secretariat for Native Affairs (SNA) and the appointment of a substantive secretary and small staff of traveling assistants for the unit. The new institution became the recognized arm of government for working with the indigenous states to settle succession challenges, chieftaincy disputes, and other matters relating to the proper ordering of indigenous authority. In 1904, the government appointed provincial commissioners for the three provinces into which the country had been divided. A provincial commissioner took up residence in Cape Coast, the administrative capital of the Central Province.[6] As part of the systematization of local government, it became mandatory for colonial officers to use requisite titles to address office holders within the indigenous political establishment.[7] During this early stage of the indirect rule policy, colonial officers sought to use the indigenous political establishment to maintain discipline among a category they described as unruly inhabitants in towns and villages across the country.[8] In 1916, the King of England further reinforced the colonial hierarchy with formal recognition of the governor as commander-in-chief of southern Ghana.[9] The King endorsed the establishment of a reconstituted Legislative Council to make all necessary laws for peace and order, with a bearing on good governance.

To achieve these objectives, the colonial government established the Municipal Corporations Ordinance of 1924 in Accra, Cape Coast, and Sekondi, the three major coastal cities, with provisions for the election of three representatives. To address doubts, disputes, or disagreements relating to elections, the Order-in-Council of 1925 allowed for presentation of petitions.[10] A petition of complaint regarding disputed elections of council members could be lodged with a division of the Supreme Court within a stipulated period of one month from the date of publication of election results.[11] The Order-in-Council equally made provision for the establishment of Provincial Councils, which had vested powers, among other responsibilities, to discharge all necessary functions assigned them.

### OBJECTION TO THE ORDER-IN-COUNCIL

The ordinance, published in the *Gold Coast Colony Gazette* at the end of 1925, met with a chorus of objections from Cape Coast as well as other major towns across the country. Most of the grievances revolved around the composition of the unofficial African representation and the method of its election. The proposed Legislative Council had a total membership of thirty, comprising sixteen officials (with the governor as president) and fourteen unofficial members, including five Europeans and nine elected Africans. The African representation consisted of three municipal members elected directly from each of the main coastal cities of Accra, Cape Coast, and Sekondi. Six provincial members would come from the three Provincial Councils of Chiefs, mainly made up of head chiefs or paramount chiefs who each had many chiefs under their authority. The Western Province had one representative; the Central Province had two, and the Eastern Province had three because of its linguistic diversity.[12]

Composition of the provincial membership became a source of concern for the intellectual and professional elite, causing them to raise objections to the entire Order-in-Council. They organized mass demonstrations at Cape Coast, Sekondi, and Elmina, arguing that participation of so-called natural rulers—kings, chiefs, queen-mothers, and headmen—in the Provincial Councils contravened long-standing cultural practices. Furthermore, since the ordinance insisted on proficiency in the English language as requisite for a greater degree of active participation in the proceedings of the council, the intellectuals opined that the number of natural rulers who qualified to perform proficiently in the Legislative Council as stipulated could almost be counted on the fingers of one hand.[13] They expressed foreboding that the natural rulers' lack of qualification would enable colonial officers to confound and overwhelm them during the sessions.

Additionally, the intellectuals opined that government description of natural rulers as "the true and accredited representatives of the illiterate masses," with formally educated people being marked out as a "foreign breed imported into the colony," could potentially foster discord and division.[14] Accordingly, the intellectuals insisted that they would cooperate with the government only if it allowed persons other than or in addition to the kings and chiefs to serve on the Legislative Council. They insisted that the administration allow the *Oman* or indigenous state councils to elect suitable, competent, and progressive people for that purpose. The educated elite and professionals maintained that they comprised an important and insightful group that should not be ignored. More compelling than anything else, they upheld the existence of a long history of cooperation between them and the kings, chiefs, queen-mothers, headmen, and other representatives of the indigenous political establishment in the interest of the larger populace. Besides boasting requisite higher education and legal training, the intellectuals and professionals argued that, in most cases, they possessed the financial wherewithal to better serve their people. Summing up their disapproval of the Order-in-Council, the intellectuals stated that "we and others have pointed out repeatedly that the root of objection to the present Provincial Councils lies in its being restricted to the Amanhin [plural of *Omanhin*] who have the right to vote for members to the Legislative Council from their ranks only. In other words, ... freedom of choice as to the persons to serve in the Legislative Council would remove all the difficulties."[15]

The government lost no time in responding to the concern about the educational qualification of the kings and chiefs as a "sweeping and unnatural accusation by Africans against their natural rulers."[16] Governor Guggisberg strongly defended the natural rulers:

> One cannot help being struck by the probability that the Natural Rulers of this country should not be allowed to take a greater right to unite in consultation on the welfare of the people they administer than the Head Chiefs and their Councilors. And what people have a greater right to form the majority of the African Members of this Council than the Head Chiefs who rule over the vast bulk of the people of this country? It is true that most of the Head

> Chiefs in this country are not educated; but on the other hand, there are a sufficient number with education enough to enable them take part in the proceedings of the Council. Naturally, if the Head Chiefs and their Councilors wish to retain the opportunities and the positions which the Government has given them, they will see to it that future generations of Chiefs and Councilors are educated.[17]

Further justifying the presence of natural rulers on the Legislative Council, the governor substantiated his argument by referring specifically to a chief he described as both formidable and well-informed, appreciably current on international issues and capable of drawing appropriate inferences.[18]

Guggisberg, in making that statement, undoubtedly had in mind Na-na Sir O-fo-ri A-tta, the *Omanhin* of Akyem Abuakwa in the Eastern Province. According to the governor, "the chief possessed a sound knowledge of the English Language, ability to express his thought in appropriate language, aptitude for debates, and a wide knowledge of the affairs of the world to the highest degree."[19] Guggisberg remonstrated that, considering his personal experience on the Legislative Council as governor, chiefs' contributions tended to be more perceptive and instructive than those of other African members. Whereas comments and contributions of other African members came across as mainly academic and therefore somewhat sterile, those of the chiefs were essentially pragmatic because of their nearness to the ordinary people. Regarding the accusation of the supposed inability of chiefs to perform in debates at the Legislative Council, Guggisberg maintained that although some value could be assigned to debating ability, it scarcely constituted a requisite qualification. Additionally, the governor averred that he hardly knew of any African member of the Legislative Council, chief or educated, who could hold his own in debates against senior colonial political officers, including the colonial secretary, attorney general, or secretary of native affairs.[20]

The intellectuals objected to the accusation that their intent hinged on scheming to replace the kings, chiefs, headmen, and others on the Legislative Council with their own members. They admitted that some of the chiefs had education but reiterated their insufficient number. Other senior colonial political officers retorted that the issue of inadequate count could equally be the case for intellectual and professional categories.[21] In light of the general lack of people, senior political officers contended that the pragmatic option inhered in drawing most elected African members of the council from a body closest to the everyday concerns and aspirations of the ordinary masses.

Relatedly, the government asserted that the Order-in-Council possessed the potential to unify the indigenous states, but the intellectuals and professionals hiding behind the Aborigines' Rights Protection Society (ARPS) fomented trouble and hindered those integrating initiatives. Touting the united front among the paramount chiefs and their subchiefs, the administration argued that from all indications, the indigenous leaders and their people welcomed the Provincial Council idea. The governor observed that bringing together the head chiefs and their advisers would help eliminate petty jealousies and misunderstandings, considering the need for cooperation and general goodwill among them.[22] He insisted that if any potential for division existed, it inhered in the intellectual and professional group's contradiction of the general recognition of chiefs as the natural rulers with the right to speak on behalf of the people.

H. S. Newlands, the acting secretary of native affairs, made further attempts to discredit the petition, charging that the document represented a minority view among intellectuals.[23] According to Newlands, the petition demonstrated mischievous tendencies among the executive committee of the Cape Coast branch of the ARPS. Dismissing the claim that the Order-in-Council violated customary practice, he argued that the ARPS was rather guilty of that charge given its posture toward the long-standing prerogative of the indigenous political establishment. Moreover, the acting secretary insisted that dwindling signatures on the documents and petitions of the ARPS constituted incontrovertible evidence of its lack of support. Marks and thumbprints had replaced elaborate signatures, suggesting to him that the ARPS appealed mainly to gullible kings, chiefs, queen-mothers, and headmen, who barely fathomed the meaning of what they appended their imprint to. He opined that the petition lacked the support of all who mattered within the indigenous political establishment. Concluding his remarks, Newlands observed that the document showed that neither the ARPS as a whole nor its diehard adherents upheld their own constitution, bylaws, rules, and regulations as strictly binding. The petition, he pointed out, contained contradictions and misrepresentations, as well as a debilitating lack of consistency in its submissions. The acting secretary cited a confusion of thought, policy, and practice on the part of the ARPS regarding the status of kings, chiefs, and headmen under the indigenous political constitution to reinforce his point. Quite significantly, the sole signatory of the petition, J. E. Casely Hayford, had himself in 1903 defended the constitutional position and powers of indigenous leaders in the following terms: "At the head of the native state stands pre-eminently the Ohin [king], who is chief magistrate and chief military leader of the state. He is first in the council of the country and the first executive officer. His influence is only measured by the strength of his character. He it is who represents the state in all its dealings with the outside world, he is supreme in his world, and, so long as he keeps within his own state."[24] Newlands, therefore, argued that the petition gave currency to a conception of customary law hardly in harmony with what the main signatory himself had once published as the "truth presented in the most authentic way."[25]

Evidently, Casely Hayford, who had championed the cause of the ARPS from the beginning, had entangled himself in some sort of contradiction. On February 24, 1924, he had intimated his approval of the Provincial Councils in these words: "In Your Excellency's message reference was made to the protection of Amanhin (Head Chiefs) by what is known as Provincial Councils. Sir, if they are to serve the purpose of enabling the Head Chiefs to select and elect from among themselves some of their numbers to represent them in the Legislative Council, I say, Sir, it would be an excellent scheme."[26] From all indications, Casely Hayford had in mind the words of John Mensah Sarbah, the greatest exponent of Fanti customary law and national constitution. Mensah Sarbah believed that should the policy of elective representation be introduced, "the most important rulers should possess the right to elect two or three representatives of their own order as members of the Legislative and Executive Councils."[27]

Therefore, some of the most important members of the ARPS had in various ways previously confirmed the power vested in the Provincial Councils to elect members to the Legislative Council from the ranks of chiefs only. To make matters worse for the group, most of the kings, chiefs, and headmen in other parts of southern Ghana lent their full support to the council proposition. For instance, on the issue of representation of the people, Nana Sir Ofori Atta reiterated the axiom that paramount chiefs unquestionably remained well placed among the people and thoroughly acquainted with the nature and extent of their everyday concerns. Ofori Atta remained convinced that chiefs qualified based on their strategic placement among the populace to serve on the Legislative Council; the intellectuals, he observed, lacked that privilege.[28] The latter scarcely traveled extensively but rather confined themselves to selected destinations on the railroads and roads where their professional duties took them. Ofori Atta warned that it would be criminal to leave the representation and articulation of the everyday aspirations of the people to a class of individuals who hardly took pains themselves to ascertain their nature.[29] In the raging debate on this issue, he remained one of the few leaders of the indigenous political establishment that invariably cooperated with the colonial administration.

## SPLIT SOCIETY

These remonstrations notwithstanding, the reconstituted Legislative Council had its first meeting in August 1926.[30] The ARPS not only failed to persuade the government to consider its petition but also hardly achieved its prime objective of preventing indigenous representatives from taking seats on the council. The eventual successful sitting of the new Legislative Council, along with the growing interest it engendered, dealt a severe blow to the ARPS, causing the emergence of divergent opinions that coalesced into two contending factions from within.

The diehards constituted the first group; they never backed down nor relented on the insistence that the colonial government respect their views on reforms regarding the Provincial and Legislative Councils. This group took the entrenched view that without these reforms, cooperation with the government would be impossible. Leading members of the group included personalities such as Kobina Sekyi, G. E. Moore, and *Omanhin* Kojo Mbra III.[31] The second group gradually came to terms with the reality that the general trend of affairs and thinking of the times called for a change of strategy—especially when, in their considered opinion, only centrist institutions such as the Legislative Council proffered any real hope of achieving requisite reformulation and reconceptualization of government policy. This view had among its prominent proponents intellectuals such as J. E. Casely Hayford, J. Glover-Addo, and Kobina Arku Korsah. This group, eventually referred to as the progressives, believed that although the constitution had fallen short of their expectations, the new electoral system should be recognized as a first step toward all-inclusive representation. Casely Hayford and his colleagues realized that the new Legislative and Provincial Councils had become permanent institutions of governance. The increasing number of individuals willing to seek election, according to them, meant that if members of the ARPS failed to act, the opportunity would be lost forever.[32] The progressives argued that the stance of the ARPS to boycott the Legislative Council, considering the prevailing circumstances, was defeatist and self-destructive.

The split had significant implications for Cape Coast as the nerve center of the opposition to government policies. The town served as the headquarters of the ARPS, the main political body that led organized and sustained noncooperation with government policy and action. Since its formation in 1897, the group had strengthened its hold and influence on Cape Coast, unreservedly identifying with the leaders of the indigenous political establishment. Besides winning the confidence of those leaders, it commanded respect among a considerable number of the populace. Consequently, polarization within the group developed into an open split in 1927, bringing in its wake serious repercussions for the town.

The nonchalant attitude of the government toward the petition infuriated the diehards, who became increasingly entrenched in the stance that the town should not cooperate with the colonial establishment. However, the views of Casely Hayford and his group gradually gained currency and garnered general support. According to them, the Legislative Council had come to stay and therefore was attractive despite relentless antagonism from Cape Coast.[33] Consequently, working for reform from within the Council seemed more reasonable than the alternative. Yet the diehards, as a matter of principle or of bitterness, refused to reconsider their position. This impasse notwithstanding, the administration proceeded with elections of municipal council members from Accra and Sekondi to the Legislative Council, holding them on separate dates in 1927; Glover-Addo and Casely Hayford won those elections, respectively. The *Gold Coast Leader* newspaper touted the elections as the "triumph of common sense."[34]

The elections in Accra and Sekondi produced a melodrama that pitted the progressives against the diehards in Cape Coast. Although the government remained determined to let the Legislative Council operate even in the face of persistent noncooperation, it sought to secure a complete house with the inclusion of a Cape Coast representative. In November 1927, Governor Sir Ransford Slater met with the *Omanhin*, chiefs, and people of the town to reason with them about the need to get their representative on the Legislative Council so that their views on important matters could be heard. To substantiate this necessity, the governor mentioned two crucial issues—namely, the water rate and the proposed closure of the local port—both of which could be effectively discussed in the sessions of the Council. Despite efforts on the part of the governor, the people took no practical steps to apply to the administration through the office of the *Omanhin* to conduct elections.

Subsequently, in July 1928, one section of the town, the Cape Coast Rate-Payers' Association, applied for elections to be held.[35] The *Omanhin* with his elders sought to obstruct the application process and advised the group at a town hall meeting to wait until the leaders of the indigenous political establishment decided on a position. Expectedly, much local resentment built up against the action of the association.[36]

As these developments unfolded, the Cape Coast Rate-Payers' Association emerged as the mouthpiece of the progressives, identifying with the changing times and attitudes of a section of the population toward the Legislative Council. The association believed that "self-injurious conservatism" had ruined Cape Coast and that the town needed to change with the times.[37] This group reiterated that developing the town, as well as making any desirable change to the constitution, could be accomplished effectively only from within the Legislative Council. The group made great efforts in explaining the clauses of the Order-in-Council and other regulations pertaining to the election of municipal members to the Legislative Council to those ready to listen and learn.[38] These explanations dispelled lingering shades of doubt and ignorance among many prospective uneducated voters concerning their legal rights under the provisions of the Order-in-Council. The association also managed to convince some well-educated people who only had casual knowledge of the provisions. Subsequently, membership of the group grew, especially among prominent members of the town who identified closely with its ideas and activities. Among this category included Kobina Arku Korsah, Henry Van Hien, Daniel Sackey, and William Ward Brew, vice president of the local chapter of the ARPS.[39] The president of the association at the time happened to be *Tufohin* Chief William Zacchaeus Coker, the supreme leader of the seven *Asafo* companies of Cape Coast and an ex-officio member of the *Oman* Council.[40]

W. Z. Coker became *Tufohin* of the *Asafo* system of Cape Coast in 1888. Prior to that, Coker served as chief registrar at the Supreme Court. Convicted in 1889 for embezzlement, he served a six-year jail term at the Elmina Castle.[41] On his release in 1894, Coker set out almost immediately to demonstrate to the local colonial officials that as *Tufohin* he remained, despite his tarnished image, indispensable in the affairs of the town.[42] He took advantage of the Asante War of 1895–1896 to regain favor with the administration, supplying the colonial military with local men as carriers. Afterward, he continued as a supplier of labor to both the government and private companies. Coker evidently made great grains from these ventures. He also remained an important personality associated with the indigenous judicial establishment. By the turn of the century, Coker had become one of the wealthiest and most well-informed people in Cape Coast.

Kobina Arku Korsah became another prominent member of the progressives and the Cape Coast Rate-Payers' Association.[43] He was educated at Mfantsipim School, Cape Coast, and Fourah Bay College, Freetown, Sierra Leone, where he graduated with a bachelor of arts degree in 1915. Korsah later entered Durham University in England and graduated with a bachelor of civil law degree in 1917.[44] In 1919, he received a bachelor of law degree from London University and had his call to the bar at Middle Temple. After 1917, when J. E. Casely Hayford initiated consultations to form the National Congress of British West Africa (NCBWA), Korsah, who had become moderately active in anticolonial politics as a student in England, entered Gold Coast politics and became assistant secretary to the Cape Coast branch of the NCBWA as well as an executive member of the ARPS later in 1922.

The diehard conservatives of the ARPS equally included prominent personalities, such as *Omanhin* Kojo Mbra III, William Essuman Gwira Sekyi, commonly called Kobina Sekyi, and G. E. Moore. Kojo Mbra became *Omanhin* in 1920 under somewhat challenging circumstances, contending with considerable disapproval from a section of the royal family. As a result of the division within the royal family, he gained little access to the royal stool and, therefore, was denied the performance of certain rites relevant to the dignity of a properly constituted indigenous political leader. Although he eventually had those rites performed for him, the rift hardly mended.[45] Like *Omanhin* Aggery before him, Kojo Mbra actively sought the advice of educated elite confidants, most prominently Kobina Sekyi. Colonial government official accounts stated that Kojo Mbra was, indubitably, a tool in the hands of Kobina Sekyi—the unquestionable gray eminence behind the ARPS whose attitude toward the colonial administration remained anything but helpful.[46] Be that as it may, Kojo Mbra's relationship with the colonial government amounted to a clear expression of his personal sentiments as much as those of the conservative section of the society.

Kobina Sekyi, one of the most remarkable nationalists of the second and third decades of twentieth-century southern Ghana, served as president of the ARPS from 1927 until its political demise in the 1950s. He had a distinguished career as a statesman, lawyer, philosopher, educator, and journalist. Sekyi received his education at the Cape Coast Wesleyan Primary and later at Mfantsipim School, where he became one of the celebrated "Faithful Eight."[47] In 1908, he graduated from Mfantsipim and taught in the same school until 1910, when he left for England to study at the University College of London. He graduated with a bachelor of arts in philosophy degree in 1914 and returned to Cape Coast the following year.[48] True to his training as a philosopher, Sekyi carefully considered the events that influenced the affairs of southern Ghana in general and his hometown in particular. In 1918, he went back to England and studied for a master of arts degree in philosophy, pursued legal studies at the Inner Temple, London, and received his call to the bar in 1919. Kobina Sekyi enrolled as a legal practitioner and mainly engaged in private practice. As a prolific writer and a social reformer, he became a member of the NCBWA and served as one of its several assistant secretaries. This diverse background undoubtedly informed his strong political stance, so much so that Governor Slater described him as a "very able but virulently anti-government lawyer."[49] In the words of Governor Shanton Thomas, Sekyi came across as "an extremist ... always in opposition to the government,"[50] while the lower echelon of the administration marked him out as both radical and conservative.[51] Sekyi remained a man eager to bring about progressive change, but only so long as indigenous cultures stood shielded from the derogatory ravages of Western civilization. He remained so formidable in this conviction that many of his own colleagues described him as a man who became more African the deeper he delved into Western philosophy.[52]

George E. Moore was yet another important personality in the drama that unfolded in Cape Coast. He also belonged to the conservative section of the ARPS. Born in Cape Coast, Moore attended the Government Boys' School from 1886 to 1895. He first worked as a treasury clerk at Cape Coast, later becoming a clerical officer in the West African Frontier Force in Jebba, northern

Nigeria.[53] Moore returned to Cape Coast in 1900 and secured a job as chief storekeeper in the service of the British expedition to Kumasi during the Yaa Asantewaa War, for which he received the Ashanti Medal. Moore later became a cocoa broker in the Eastern Province town of Akuapem in early 1920. He entered politics in 1924 as an uncompromising nationalist and served in the executive committee of the ARPS for many years. Moore and Kobina Sekyi became great friends, the former being instrumental in the latter securing a lucrative legal suit in which *Odikro* Kwame Kuma and Kwaku Amoa of Asamankese challenged the claim of Nana Sir Ofori Atta to the ownership of Asamankese and Akwatia lands.[54] Both Moore and Sekyi became quite influential within the antigovernment wing of the ARPS after the Guggisberg constitution of 1925 occasioned the split.

The scintillating situation of prominent men of Cape Coast finding themselves polarized between conservative and progressive camps hardly augured well for the town. When W. J. A. Jones became commissioner of the Central Province in January 1928, he and other colonial officers pursued special efforts to persuade Cape Coast municipal voters to elect a member to represent them on the Legislative Council.[55] In response, the Rate-Payers' Association sent a Van Hein–led delegation to seek audience with *Omanhin* Nana Mbra III and his counselors, including Kobina Sekyi, J. P. Brown, Chief Kwamina Ninfa V, Chief Kweku Arhin, and Chief J. H. Dadzie. After a difficult and testy meeting, the counselors refused to forward a formal application to the colonial government.

In June 1928, the acting governor on an official visit to Cape Coast appealed to the young men to be amenable to the changing times rather than "commit constitutional suicide."[56] After a promising meeting with the district commissioner, enthusiastic municipal voters, mobilized under the auspices of the Rate-Payers' Association, concluded that no legal obligation existed on their part to submit their application through the *Omanhin* or the *Oman* Council. They equally understood that indigenous political authorities had no legal right to control the actions of voters with respect to nomination of candidates, because that privilege lawfully belonged to the people. Any resident in the town could vote provided he or she satisfied the stipulations of the law. The district commissioner emphasized that any qualified resident could be nominated and elected to represent the town and its interests in the Legislative Council. In the end, the fact that the choice rested with the electorate became convincingly clear. Customary law hardly applied in the matter of nomination and election, as both processes were essentially foreign and therefore alien to local practice.

These interpretations of the electoral law empowered Coker and the progressive section of the ARPS, which loosely became synonymous with the Cape Coast Rate-Payers' Association, to formally request a proclamation of an election date from the government.[57] Subsequently, the acting governor fixed a date and published notification to that effect in the *Gold Coast Gazette*.[58] The association, with the support of Casely Hayford, nominated K. A. Korsah as its candidate, who was duly elected.

In the eyes of Kojo Mbra and his counselors, Coker as *Tufohin* of Cape Coast had gone beyond the bounds of indigenous propriety and needed to be disciplined. His actions, according to them, confirmed lingering suspicions of his collaboration with the colonial government. Coker received summons to appear before a high-level gathering of the *Asafo* companies at the instance of Kojo Mbra on July 31, 1928, to account for his apparent cooperation with the government, but he refused to attend.[59] The representatives of the *Anaafo, Ntsin, Nkum, Abrofonkoa, Akrampa*, and *Amanfur Asafo* companies present at the meeting passed a resolution deposing Coker as *Tufohin* because his refusal to appear before that powerful gathering amounted to an unpardonable breach of trust and a violation of the oath he had sworn on his installation. In his place, George Moore became the new *Tufohin* following popular acclamation—apparently with the approval of all the *Asafo* companies except *Bentsir*. This action against Coker aggravated tensions in the town.

### THE *TUFOHIN* INQUIRY

When *Bentsir Asafo*, to which Coker belonged, contested the elevation of Moore on the grounds that the office of *Tufohin* remained hereditary, the colonial government lost no time in instituting an inquiry into the issue of bona fide *Tufohin* of Cape Coast. According to the *Bentsir* company, customary practice stipulated that the *Tufohin* be chosen from among the descendants of a certain Kwamina Edu, and Moore did not belong to that lineage. The group further argued that the other *Asafo* groups should have formally approached them to follow customary practice in finding a successor to Coker, even if his deposition stood as right and proper. They concluded that Coker had not been given the benefit of a fair trial in accordance with customary company rites and accused the *Omanhin* of being behind the other companies causing the deposition.[60] The other companies rejected these claims and accusations, whereupon *Bentsir* unanimously rallied in support of Coker and resolutely refused to recognize his deposition or acknowledge the elevation of Moore. A bitter altercation ensued between the contending parties, which came to be known as the Coker Party and the *Omanhin* Party. These two groups formed along the political fault line between the progressives and the diehard conservatives in the town. Practically everybody in Cape Coast became involved on one side or the other. Charges and countercharges followed, including some against the *Omanhin* himself.

Deputy Secretary for Native Affairs H. W. Thomas, appointed to conduct the inquiry, concluded that the office of *Tufohin* remained the preserve of the Kwamina Edu family. Furthermore, although he declared Coker properly deposed, he denounced the elevation of Moore. Governor Slater accepted two of the Thomas Enquiry findings but rejected the one regarding the deposition of Coker for reasons rooted in customary law. Given this stance, speculations became rife that the governor favored the Coker Party; communication of these views to both disputing parties exacerbated the conflict. The *Omanhin* and his counselors insisted that neither the people of Cape Coast upheld the assumption regarding the hereditary nature of the office of *Tufohin* nor did the history of succession to that office. Moreover, they insisted, no permanent hereditary right to that public office inhered in any family or individual.

From the outset, colonial government officials seemed to side with Coker as *Tufohin*. W. J. A. Jones informed the *Omanhin* that under no circumstances would a permit for the parading of Moore in a *Tufohin* capacity be granted to the companies. The government informed the companies that its private investigations had revealed that Moore could hardly be the right candidate for consideration for the office because he had a West Indian father and a mother rumored to have descended from a background of bondage and servitude. The *Omanhin*, his counselors, and other supporters countered that Moore had been born in Cape Coast and made *Tufohin* by popular acclamation on account of his dedicated services to the town.

When Skene became provincial commissioner of the Central Province in 1929, he adopted the same stance. This consistent official slant led to furious complaints and protests from the *Omanhin* Party against local colonial officers, accused of bias and partiality. These complaints and protests produced some effect, as evident in excerpts of the report of Slater to the provincial commissioner at Cape Coast:

> I confess that the impression I get from every paper about Cape Coast Native Affairs that comes before me is that, however annoying it may be to the Provincial Commissioner whom the Omanhin so stubbornly opposed over the election and the Native Administration

Ordinance... the Omanhin has a substantial (and as far as I know influential) following at his back; in any case, it is very desirable that Government should avoid all semblances of taking sides in Cape Coast political affairs. Mbra III's opponents must work out their own salvation... Unless of course he commits any offense against the law, which he certainly hasn't done yet so far as I know.[61]

The governor's explicit concern for a show of impartiality in the dispute regarding the de jure *Tufohin* of Cape Coast reflected the seriousness of the situation.

The 1920s proved to be difficult years for the administration. The government ran short on funds because of the global economic slump, making it reel under incessant pressure from London for the colonies to bear a large share of financial burden. In view of this dire financial situation, direct taxation presented itself as the ready and pragmatic plan to provide financial relief for the government. Since the cooperation of indigenous political authorities would be crucial to the success of direct taxation plans, the governor and officers in Accra demanded absolute neutrality regarding the *Tufohin* matter.[62] In keeping with this stance, resident district and provincial commissioners in Cape Coast consistently refused the request for a permit to parade Moore anywhere. The pressure on local officials to issue a permit mounted when Coker died on March 3, 1932, leaving Moore as the only person with any claim whatsoever to the position of *Tufohin*.[63] To make the situation more complex, the Coker Party did not relented on its opposition to the overtures of Moore to the office; they insisted that the demise of Coker hardly justified a transfer or abrogation of their rightful claim to the office of *Tufohin*. This intransigence presented to the administration a difficult situation that worsened with sporadic *Asafo* company clashes elsewhere in the coastal parts of the Central Province. Apparently, the number of cases involving conflicts and clashes among the *Asafo* had increased in many other places in southern Ghana. The government had strong reasons to quash the increasing number of disturbances. Set against those in other places in the Central Province, the developing situation in Cape Coast portended a major incident that would cast the local officers in a bad light regarding their capacity to keep law and order.

## ASAFO CLASHES IN THE SALTPOND DISTRICT

Untoward political developments, particularly in the Central Province, became yet another source of concern for the administration. Elsewhere in the province, colonial officials and the police engaged in a flurry of maneuvers to deal with *Asafo* conflicts and clashes. Reports of these disturbances were communicated to the Colonial Office in London via confidential correspondences and dispatches. Consequently, the Colonial Office advocated complete caution and discretion in the handling of such situations. Reeling under pressure from London, the administration deflected in great measure onto its local officials and the police the need to control *Asafo* disturbances or, if possible, end them altogether.

Serious disturbances that resulted in fatalities between the *Asafo* companies of *Nar-kwa* and *Eku-mpu-ano* in the Saltpond district occurred in 1931 on the issue of fishing rights in a local lagoon.[64] On September 27, an innocuous misunderstanding arose between some *Narkwa* and *Ekumpuano* boys fishing in the *Narkwa* lagoon. The next day, a good number of boys from both villages went fishing again in the same spot; this time, the group from *Ekumpuano* turned out to be bigger boys apparently sent there for the express purpose of picking a quarrel. When one of these boys paddled his canoe over to where the *Narkwa* boys were fishing, orders for him to turn back came quickly. A quarrel ensued, during which a *Narkwa* boy insulted one of the *Asafo* company captains of *Ekumpuano*; without hesitation, the bigger boys from *Ekumpuano* tied and beat him up. Both parties subsequently left the lagoon to inform their respective elders about the incident.

Soon the men of *Ekumpuano*, armed with guns, cutlasses, and sticks, arrived and strategically put themselves in battle formation at a nearby village that offered a commanding view of any movement or approaches from *Narkwa*. As usual with *Asafo* companies, they started playing drums and singing war songs. The people of *Narkwa* came to the outskirts of their village to see this provocation for themselves. As a challenge, the men of *Ekumpuano* fired one shot into the lagoon and another into the sea. The people of *Narkwa*, who understood the meaning of the provocative *Ekumpuano* actions, armed themselves, reinforced their camp with many men, and charged on the group that had retreated as far as Assa-re-kwa. About a quarter of a mile from their village, the *Ekumpuano* men laid ambush in a coconut plantation on the seaward side at Assarekwa. When the armed men of *Narkwa* arrived at that location, they could not find their opponents; suspecting that some might be hiding in a nearby small hut, they set it ablaze. At that point, the men of *Ekumpuano* fired on them, and fighting ensued. Taken aback, the men of *Narkwa* ran helter-skelter. All told, three men lost their lives from the gunshots—two hailed from *Narkwa*, and the third from *Ekumpuano*. An old man from *Narkwa* succumbed to cutlass wounds when his side scattered, apparently unable to run fast enough.

Reports about the fight reached the office of the district commissioner late at night on September 28. He and other local officers, together with the assistant commissioner of police and a detachment from Saltpond, set out at about two thirty a.m. and arrived at *Narkwa* just before daybreak. The men of both villages went into hiding in bushes and neighboring settlements, leaving behind the women to make up their own stories, blaming either side on police inquiry. Eventually, after a thorough search, arrests, and investigation of principal witnesses, five men from *Narkwa* and six from *Ekumpuano* received various charges for fighting. The *Ekumpuano* village hired Kobina Sekyi, with his counterpart from Cape Coast, as legal counsel, paying a total of £100 for the cost of services rendered. The chief of *Narkwa* refused to hire a lawyer, insisting that his men acted in self-defense and under extreme provocation. He and his men also felt justified because Assarekwa fell within *Narkwa* jurisdiction.

When the case went before Assistant District Commissioner Henry Arthur Bonavia in Saltpond on October 17, 1931, the following points of law arose for the determination of the court: Did the accused persons of *Narkwa* act appropriately in physically responding to an unlawful fight? Would it not have been advisedly proper to report the incident to the police rather than take the law into their own hands? Did the men of *Ekumpuano* do right in perpetrating actions of extreme provocation as well as arming themselves and daring *Narkwa* to a fight? Discounting the history of previous fights between the groups, the court found all accused persons guilty of taking part in a disturbance that caused loss of lives and sentenced each to two months of imprisonment with hard labor and a fine of £20, in default of which two months and two weeks of hard labor would be added. Given these clashes in the Saltpond district and the developing situation in Cape Coast, the colonial authorities in the Central Province came under intense pressure.

### *OMANHIN* KOJO MBRA III AND INTERNAL OPPOSITION

The year 1931 turned out to be politically eventful in Cape Coast. Enormous tensions resulted from the dispute over whether the town should elect a representative to the Legislative Council. Additionally, the deposition of the late *Tufohin* Coker in 1928 left his supporters scouting for an opportunity for revenge; a precipitant occasion came in November 1931, when judgment in a land dispute at an indigenous tribunal went against a certain Cooke, an elder and supporter of the late Coker. The land dispute, hardly connected with the *Tufohin* case, went in favor of Chief Sakyiama, a member of the inner circle of *Omanhin* Kojo Mbra III.[65] Cooke and his supporters decided to contact the *Omanhin* for a discussion in the *Ahin-fie* (palace).[66] When Cooke and his entourage saw no one at the palace, they took a stool and other royal paraphernalia, such as drums and umbrellas. They justified their actions by insisting that the paraphernalia needed to be removed to a proper place of protection because on a lawful visit to the *Omanhin*, they had found no one in charge. Cooke placed around his house a guard made up of his supporters armed with axes, clubs, and cutlasses. This degree of vigilance gave indication of some readiness for defense in anticipation of an attack from the six *Asafo* companies that supported Kojo Mbra.

On receipt of intelligence about these events, Commissioner of the Central Province C. E. Skene, in the company of local officers such as Captain Lynch, Major Hamilton, Dawson, and Morris, rushed to the scene. After quieting the crowd, Skene and the district commissioner went to the palace on a tip-off about feverish preparations to retrieve the royal property. After heated and hectic discussions, they persuaded the *Omanhin* and his elders to leave the matter in the hands of the government with instructions to their followers not to take any hostile action against Cooke. This acquiescence only came after the *Omanhin* and his supporters had received avid assurance that local colonial officers would station a strong police cordon around the house to prevent the royal property from being removed to a different location. Skene and the district commissioner also managed to disperse the Cooke supporters. After further entreaties from the colonial authorities, Cooke agreed to hand over the matter, including the royal property, to the acting commissioner of Central Province for settlement—the only condition being that the handing over happen after further consultation with elders in the outlying villages. Cooke insisted that he could only conveniently consult them in the morning. By one o'clock in the afternoon, rumors of the paraphernalia being conveyed caused a great deal of disquiet. About five hundred armed young men in support of Cooke moved back to his house. On receiving news of this gathering, Kojo Mbra ordered the beating of *Asafo* company drums to summon those on his side to gather and confront the Cooke supporters. The police detachment in Cape Coast started mobilizing its forces to ensure a quiet night with reinforcements from Winneba and Sekondi. Following the swift intervention of the district commissioner, the *Omanhin* called off the *Asafo* mobilization while Cooke agreed to deliver the royal paraphernalia into the custody of Skene on the guarantee of a government inquiry into the matter. Skene supervised the hauling of the royal property into a waiting vehicle, transported it under a strong police escort, and placed it in a storeroom in the castle prison.

Even after persistent appeals from local colonial officials, Kojo Mbra refused to attend the inquiry into the matter. Suspecting collusion between Cooke and the authorities, the *Omanhin* insisted that the *Ahinfie* (palace) was the proper place to secure royal property—not the houses of individuals who insisted on being members of the royal family. The *Omanhin* promised cooperation with the inquiry only after the paraphernalia had been returned to him. The colonial officials replied that they had received the articles on the promise of an inquiry, which they would not violate. They further argued that in any event, the government could not be expected to act as bailiff for the *Omanhin*, simply retrieving the items (ownership of which had become a matter of dispute) and handing them back to him without offering the opposing party an opportunity to state its claim. After a detailed explanation of these positions, the *Omanhin* and his elders acquiesced to the administration retaining temporary possession of the royal paraphernalia. They rejected all alternative attempts at resolution offered in lieu of the inquiry, including the option of a judicial action against Cooke and his family, an indigenous state council mediation, and a coordinated compromise.

These alternative solutions came across to the *Omanhin* and his supporters as tricky, discerning that such offers could make the case drag on and become unbearably complex. For instance, a court case would not succeed because it would be difficult to determine the criminality of the action of Cooke and his line of the royal family. The *Ahinfie* belonged to the entire royal family, which possessed a claim to ownership of the paraphernalia. Furthermore, they had scarcely used violence in removing the items. The second solution could not be countenanced because of the impracticability of convening a properly constituted indigenous state council in Cape Coast given the tension, division, and abounding acrimony. The final alternative, a private reconciliation between the two parties, looked more promising, but on candid consideration it appeared as unproductive as the second option.

The inquiry established the propriety of the paraphernalia in contention, likewise all other royal property, being kept in the *Ahinfie*. In these deliberations, the governor, through Secretary for Native Affairs W. J. A. Jones, advised that under no circumstances should colonial political officers get involved in the internal affairs of Cape Coast; they must remain resolute and determined to preserve the peace. These local issues in the town hardly constituted the only concerns to engage the attention of the government. Overarching socioeconomic grievances equally lurked in the background.

## GLOBAL DEPRESSION, INCOME TAX PROPOSAL OPPOSITION, AND COASTAL GHANA DISTURBANCES

In 1931, the colonial government staggered under enormous economic discontentment from a large section of people, including intellectuals, common people from coastal Ghana, chiefs, and headmen, many of whom operated under the aegis of the ARPS. The onset of a global economic depression in the closing stages of 1929 led to a slump in the world market price for cocoa; this economic meltdown had serious implications because that commodity remained the mainstay of the economy. The economic depression had ripple effects on trade, with dwindling revenues accruing from custom duty.[67] Although fully aware of the history of violent resistance to direct taxation in the country, Governor Slater had no choice but to risk that controversial option as the immediate solution to the crippling economic situation.

Again not unaware of the volatile nature of this fiscal proposal, the governor conceded the likelihood of "insuperable obstacles to the eventual achievement of the policy," particularly in the coastal cities of Accra, Cape Coast, and Sekondi.[68] He observed that "education on European lines" had led to a "sophistic era" that had "aggrandized the commoner at the expense of the influence of local Chiefs."[69] Consequently, the situation had encouraged "both a democratic outlook, restiveness and the negation of native ideas of government."[70] Having received the green light from London to proceed, Slater declared his intention at a Legislative Council session for "an Ordinance to regulate the levying and collection of an income tax in the Colony."[71] According to him, "the necessity for direct taxation ... had been recognized by every government in British tropical Africa with the exception of the Gold Coast."[72] It remained long overdue, "when the Gold Coast Government also must in the interests of the people themselves fall in line with the other colonies."[73] As if to spite the people, the governor conclusively averred that income tax constituted the "common burden of civilization."[74]

The Legislative Council representatives for the coastal cities, particularly Accra, warned that the general economic depression, affecting everyday life, had cast an irritable and militant spirit over the people, making the new tax bill ill-timed and ill-advised. They argued that it would be unwise to discuss the idea of economically burdening ordinary men and women with the task of bailing out the government, especially when their own social responsibilities had been stretched to the seams.[75] Frederick Victor Nanka Bruce, the representative from Accra, pointed out that the general economic situation remained so bad for the people that even necessary projects seemed distasteful, suggesting that the colonial government would do well to balance its budget by cutting official salaries and using the government reserve fund in lieu of imposing a burdensome income tax.[76] In response to the view of the colonial government that citizens had an obligation to bear the cost of administration to the extent their means would allow, Nanka Bruce argued that the colonial administration remained largely alien and therefore an imposition—an institution the establishment of which the people hardly had a say in. Accordingly, he pointed out the overwhelming absence of popular goodwill on the part of ordinary men and women to endure sacrifices on behalf of the government. Since the administration proved unwilling to do much for the people, Nanka Bruce closed with the argument that "we remain where we are and try to balance our budget in some other way."[77]

As debates proceeded back and forth in the Legislative Council, the prolific southern Ghana press had a field day lambasting the government and called for a popular protest to the income tax measure. The newspapers that mounted a crusade against the proposal included the *Times of West Africa, Gold Coast Leader, Gold Coast Spectator,* and *Gold Coast Independent*. They castigated the government for its profligacy, diversion of untold revenue for the payment of official salaries as well as allowances, and insensitivity in failing to consider the dire circumstances of the people. These newspapers called for a withdrawal of the bill and warned that if the government persisted, the men and women of the colony would surely resist the implementation of the income tax policy.[78]

The colonial government barely budged in the face of the barrage of opposition, criticisms, warnings, and appeals. On October 27, 1931, a large gathering of youth, men, and women in Sekondi took matters into their own hands. Beating empty cans, singing, and dancing, the group displayed placards with inscriptions such as "Down! Down! Down! With Income Tax," "Income Tax Is Akin to Slavery," "If the Country Can't Pay, It Simply Can't Pay," "Away with Allowances," and "Practice Intensive Pruning."[79] The initially peaceful demonstration turned violent when the conduct of overly boisterous protesters spiraled out of control. Some protesters uprooted ornamental plants on government premises (offices and residences) and in businesses, including banks, while others hurled stones, randomly hurting people in the process.

In Shama, when the acting provincial commissioner of the Western Province, Sumner Wilson, arrived to explain the proposed bill, the *Omanhin* preempted him with the submission of a petition that rejected the "introduction of such an anomaly as the income tax."[80] The petition demanded instead a 10 percent cut in the remuneration of government officials. Here, as in Sekondi, women and children demonstrated in the town square, beating empty cans and other metallic objects while singing, dancing, and shouting insults and others hurled stones. The *Omanhin* escorted the acting provincial commissioner to his car through the noisy demonstrators, some of whom sought to manhandle him.[81] In the end, the government blamed the *Omanhin* of Shama for having covertly stirred up "ruffians" who had indulged in "a cheap display of impertinence."[82] The governor in his correspondence with the Colonial Office described Shama as "a notoriously ill-disciplined place."[83] He interjected this description and dismissal of Shama, essentially, to explain away the humiliating opposition to the Income Tax Bill. Official dispatches described the demonstrators as "roughs," "hooligans," and "cowboys."[84] Again, these correspondences referred to ignorant chiefs and incorrigible agent provocateurs perpetually misleading the hopeless lot.

In Cape Coast, where anticolonial government feelings remained strong, objections to the Income Tax Bill became a turbulent affair. Market women and their counterparts from the fishing community responded in large numbers to the gong-gong summons of *Omanhin* Kojo Mbra III early in the morning of October 28, 1931.[85] He forbade people from working and encouraged them to be on the streets to show their contempt for the proposed income tax measure. The usual noisy attitude that marked agitated groups appeared in full force as they hurled stones at the cars of European residents and destroyed public property such as lampposts and other fixtures. The men among the demonstrators, whom the government referred to as "riff raff" and "boat-boys," vented their anger on the police station and went on to clash with a detachment on security duty at the High Court. After nearly eight hours, the gong-gongs sounded again to end the violent demonstration. Some of the close associates of the *Omanhin*, namely Moore and Chief Sa-kyi-ama, persuaded the angry mob to return home.

Although no life-threatening injuries occurred, the open threat to law and order appeared quite concerning. Eventually, the situation became more troubling for the administration than anything else.[86] Swiftly, senior colonial officers condemned *Omanhin* Mbra III, referring to him as "the tool of W. E. G. Sekyi ... a notorious extremist."[87] The men and women who demonstrated came in for censure as hooligans who in no way represented the general populace of the town. No one in Sekondi and Shama faced prosecution; in Cape Coast, however, the police arrested and arraigned thirteen demonstrators before the courts. Two gained their freedom, while two others escaped from custody. Eight received sentences of three months in prison with hard labor, and one had a fine of £5, in default of which he faced imprisonment for a period of one month with hard labor.

Fear of the spread of violent opposition throughout the country compelled Governor Slater at an Executive Council meeting to authorize a postponement of the Income Tax Bill. At the same meeting, he agreed to consider the popular call for cuts in official salaries and allowances. These decisions caused discontentment among colonial officials, who variously referred to the government response as a "humiliating capitulation," "an awful example of weakness," and a "weak-willed surrender to the shouts of agitators."[88] The violent protests engendered the opinion among government officials that their response had been lamentably lenient. Although some saw forbearance on the part of the police as necessary for restoring order, others envisaged it as an ill-advised show of weakness that translated into an open invitation to likeminded people elsewhere in the colony to jump onto the band wagon.

### THE 1932 CAPE COAST CONFLICT

The eventful objections to the Income Tax Bill proposal in 1931 hardly mitigated the fault lines in Cape Coast after the death of Coker. On July 20, 1932, against the background of mounting tension, the *Supi* of *Ntsin Asafo* company applied formally to the district commissioner for a permit to hold a ceremony for the installation of company captains who had come into office in the previous ten years.[89] The *Supi* attached a program outlining principal events of the ceremony, including a public exhibition of the captains of *Ntsin Asafo* company in a procession with the *Tufohin* in the lead amid firing of musketry, drumming, singing, and dancing.[90] Known in local parlance as *Ati-ran*, this ceremony involved several activities and cost a pretty sum of money not only for the individual captains but also for the company as a whole.[91] However, the colonial officials denied the issuing of a permit to *Ntsin* for the ceremonial procession of *Asafo* captains. Captain Lynch maintained this attitude because *Ntsin* insisted on G. E. Moore parading with the group in his official capacity as *Tufohin*. Lynch kept the acting secretary of native affairs, Skene, informed about deliberations in connection with the *Ntsin* permit application. This briefing became doubly important because the latter would officially return to Cape Coast as provincial commissioner after being relieved of his interim duty in the secretariat.

The stance of the government occasioned a flurry of correspondence between *Omanhin* Mbra III and the officials. An infuriated Mbra ignored the acting commissioner of the Central Province and dealt directly with the acting secretary of native affairs and the acting colonial secretary. On September 12, 1932, Captain Lynch wrote to Mbra to remind him about the findings of the *Tufohin* inquiry. He drew attention to the fact that Moore did not belong to the descendants of Kwamina Edu and, therefore, was ineligible to occupy the office of *Tufohin*. Lynch further observed that the procedure adopted for his alleged elevation breached customary practice and expressed foreboding that his participation in the intended ceremony would cause serious offense to a large portion of the public.[92] The indeterminate nature of *Asafo* company boundaries, he feared, would equally make the situation potentially precarious.

In a reply to the commissioner of the Central Province, Mbra sought to assuage his fears while simultaneously rebuking him. He stated that five *Asafo* companies had unanimously agreed to give *Ntsin* free passage through their respective quarters. Mbra added that the commissioner of police, "*Tufohin*-elect" G. E. Moore, *Supis*, and captains of the companies had rehearsed their walk along the route to be traversed during the procession and that these arrangements had been settled to the mutual satisfaction of all parties concerned. In concluding his letter, Mbra interjected a stern rebuke for the commissioner:

> With the foregoing facts, especially the fact that the five companies, whose quarters will be traversed by the Ntsin Company, have given the latter permission to pass with the Tufohin G. E. Moore, I cannot imagine the grounds for your apprehension. And I should think that if you were dealing impartially in the matter, your duty should be to warn such person or persons who are bent on making mischief and to force him or them to enter a bond. People who threaten a breach

of peace are those who should be restrained and not those who like the Ntsin Company are peacefully disposed.

If on the face of the facts stated above, you insist upon refusing Ntsin Company that permit, we can only conclude that either certain people are working on your fears, or you are encouraging them in their attitude to frustrate the function of the company. I should be glad to have an immediate reply to this letter as the company has undergone considerable expense in their preparation for this ceremony and it would be difficult to cancel the function.[93]

The letter, which contained compelling arguments, put the government on edge. If pressure from the *Omanhin* Party did not appear aggravating enough, the adamance of the Coker Party pushed the situation to a precarious tipping point for the officials. Coker's sister, the spokesperson for the group with the *Supi* of the *Bentsir* company, barely budged in her refusal to recognize Moore and resolved to challenge the determination of Mbra to have him recognized as *Tufohin* via the *Atiran* ceremony of the *Ntsin Asafo*.[94] The Coker Party objected to the parading of Moore in the streets of Cape Coast and warned that, should the government fail to prevent it, a serious breach of the peace would occur. Acquiescing in the public parade of Moore leading a company to which he barely belonged would give tacit recognition to him as *Tufohin*. The group reiterated that, because the government had not recognized Moore as the occupant of the office, it would be unconstitutional for him to go in front of the *Ntsin* company. For his part, the *Supi* of *Bentsir* company insisted that any acquiescence on the part of the government to issue the permit would be tantamount to an act of great provocation to him and his members, as well as their allies in the outlying villages of Queen Anne's Point or Ekon, Amamoma, Apewosika, Kwesibra, and Kokwaado.[95]

The perplexing politics of coastal Ghana made things difficult for Skene, interim secretary of native affairs in Accra.[96] Under his watch, Cape Coast had already recorded a major violent demonstration following the Income Tax proposal of 1931. He wanted to avoid yet another disturbing occurrence; the interim secretary, therefore, decided to manage the troubling situation at a local level and, if possible, keep his superiors out of it (recurring disturbances during the tenure of officers hardly augured well for their political career). His previous experiences in the town made Skene understand the inevitability of a clash considering the issue at hand. As commissioner of the Central Province stationed in Cape Coast, he considered his temporary absence from the town on interim assignment in Accra as a godsend, loathing the idea of violence breaking out yet again under his supervision. The dilemma in which the interim secretary found himself manifested in contradictory statements issued to a couple of officers in the Central Province. When Captain Lynch went to Accra to attend a session of the Legislative Council, he took the original letter of *Omanhin* Mbra to seek the advice of his superior officer. Skene told him that he should issue a permit to *Ntsin Asafo* with the understanding that Moore would take no part in the procession. On a different occasion, he asked Bewes, the acting deputy provincial commissioner of the Central Province stationed in Cape Coast, to issue a permit for *Ntsin* to hold a ceremony and exhibit Moore in an official capacity in its own quarter but certainly not in territories belonging to the other companies. When Dawson, the acting district commissioner, received the communication on these instructions, he placed a phone call to Captain Lynch, still in Accra, for confirmation.[97] Lynch replied that he had not been consulted on that bit, but the order should be carried out if the acting secretary of native affairs so advised. Skene hoped that the worst would be over before he returned to Cape Coast.[98]

When the two factions learned of these separate instructions, tempers began to rise, and the impending trouble caused an "epidemic of agitation."[99] In the closing days of September 1932, the police dispatched a large reinforcement of detachments to the Central Province in preparation for the anticipated fight.

Quartered in Elmina, Saltpond, and Winneba, the detachments remained on alert to proceed to Cape Coast any time. Even though Skene had given instructions for the permit to be issued, Dawson, the acting district commissioner, tried to forestall any untoward action. He informed the *Supi* of *Ntsin* that the permit would be issued only on condition that the company either confine the performance of the ceremony to its quarter or proceed with Moore as an ordinary person (if the procession wished to pass through the wards of *Anaafo, Nkum, Abrofonkoa, Akrampa,* and *Amanfur Asafo* companies). Dawson added that since the parade practically embraced the whole town, the official display of any person whose position constituted a matter of dispute would pose a threat to public peace.[100] Conversely, *Omanhin* Mbra insisted that the indigenous Cape Coast constitution stipulated that the *Tufohin* remained responsible to him and the *Oman* for the conduct of the companies. Therefore, he would not keep Moore from his proper place in such an important ceremony.[101] It became clear that Mbra had spoken his mind and that any further discussion on the issue would be unproductive. The security imperatives set against the granting of a permit for a long overdue ceremonial customary practice presented an acute administrative problem for the local colonial officers.

On September 26, much to the cheer of the *Omanhin* Party and the chagrin of the Coker Party, the overly-delayed permit for the celebration of the week-long *Atiran* ceremony came through after the signing of the requisite bond.[102] The signature of Alfred Donald Dawson, acting district commissioner of Cape Coast, gave permission for *Ntsin* to exhibit *Asafo* flags as well as emblems and to fire guns on the occasion of the installation of their new *Asafohinfo* (captains) on Friday, September 30; Saturday, October 1; Monday, October 3; Tuesday, October 4; Thursday, October 6; Friday, October 7; and Saturday, October 8. The procession on October 1 would follow a rehearsed route from Aboom Wells, Kotokoraba Road, Jerusalem Street, Lighthouse

Road, Jackson Street via the Bread and Fruit Market to Papratem, *Ntsin* Street, Ashanti Road, Governor Rowe Road back to Kotokoraba and then to the headquarters of the company. The route designation in the permit remained completely confined to the quarter of the *Ntsin Asafo*.[103] On September 28, captains of the *Bentsir Asafo* went to see the district commissioner to review the flags that *Ntsin* proposed to exhibit; when informed about the prescribed route for the procession, they raised no objections.[104]

*Atiran*, as already intimated, was normally a week-long ceremony that involved great expenditure, on the part of both the company and the elected captains. Customary expectations required new captains to make profuse provision of alcoholic beverages for the rites and entertainment of the entire company.[105] On the night of September 30, the *Ntsin Asafo* kept vigil at the beach, much in keeping with aspects of their maritime culture, playing drums and singing songs. Those skilled in the intricate *Asafo* dance performed to the admiration of the gathering amid much drinking and camaraderie.

When the procession commenced under police supervision at nine o'clock the next morning, it barely included Moore.[106] But he subsequently joined the procession in his supposed capacity as *Tufohin*. Knowledge of the participation of Moore infiltrated the *Bentsir Asafo*, apparently through a few spies who scouted the procession. Their captains quickly warned local officers and police that they would have great difficulty restraining the overly turbulent members of their company from staging an attack if the intelligence was accurate and Moore headed the procession while it passed down Jackson Street. The captains of *Bentsir* explained that, although the permit mentioned that street, the street ran through territories that both companies claimed. A section of the Coker Party readied to fire on Moore should he remain at the head of the procession as it passed down Jerusalem Street. They enlisted the help of boisterous members of the fishing community in the *Bentsir Asafo*, who equally armed themselves and occupied strategic spots to attack the procession in defense of their quarter.

To avert the imminent danger, the commissioner of police tried to divert the procession away from Jackson Street through another lane. With only about seventy policemen, the commissioner failed to secure the consent of the *Asafo* members, whose conduct had become unmanageable with the excitement of company custom and intoxication from generous and liberal consumption of rum. Not even the threat of forfeiture of a £500 peace bond could persuade and dissuade the over three hundred fifty swaggering *Ntsin Asafo* company young men and their captains from their rehearsed route and the dawning danger. Other elements of the *Asafo* institution came into play as a sense of pride and bravery buoyed them on, responding with a sustained surge forward. Since meekness and weakness were scarcely part of their worldview, *Ntsin Asafo* hurled barbed insults at their enemies. The local officials and the police lost control over the situation. When the procession reached the intersection of Jackson and Lighthouse Hill Streets, Moore still headed the procession in his capacity as *Tufohin*.

The presence of certain women in the procession further exacerbated the situation. Their taunts, acerbic insults, and innuendos conveyed clear messages to *Bentsir*.[107] The aggrieved *Asafo* company could hardly contain the situation any longer, and so the first gun went off, signaling the beginning of an open assault that dispersed the procession as the men of *Ntsin* took cover and fired back. General gunfire erupted throughout the *Bentsir* quarter with great intensity for about thirty minutes, continuing sporadically for about two hours.[108] When persuasive attempts to disperse the men proved futile, the commissioner of police ordered his troops to clear the streets with force. Neither *Omanhin* Mbra nor his elders gave any assistance in suppressing the fight, and costly consequences ensued.

All told, five men lost their lives, with twenty-eight men and women sustaining different degrees of injury. Given the use of guns, the authorities of the administration declared a search for arms. The colonial authorities posted a battalion from the Royal West African Frontier Force at Cape Coast to cordon off areas that the police scoured for arms. They carried out a systematic house-by-house search and retrieved a considerable number of weapons. The force equally took into custody people known or suspected of being responsible for the confrontation and fight. Rumors were rife regarding reinforcement troop arrivals because of the determination of the government to arrest as many culprits as possible to deter further clashes, help curtail the incessant *Asafo* fights, and deal with opposition to its authority in Cape Coast. Nearly all the men and women involved in the clash had good reason to avoid police arrest. Several fled with the retreating companies to outlying villages situated some safe distances from the immediate reach of the law. A few braved the situation and remained in the town, but not without taking precautions, such as seeking refuge in houses other than their own; others, particularly the fishermen, fled to the beckoning sea in their canoes, sailing away from trouble with the law. The police nonetheless had quite a field day apprehending those who turned themselves in or whose hideouts some informants revealed. Overall, about 475 men and women went to jail.[109] In the ensuing trials, the chief justice posted additional magistrates to Cape Coast to assist with the disposal of cases. The most significant of these arrests remained that of George Moore, charged with disobeying the conditions the district commissioner had stipulated in the permit granted to the *Ntsin Asafo* company.

Correspondence among officials of the administration after the 1932 conflict repeatedly painted *Omanhin* Mbra and his counselors as security threats to be dealt with in much the same manner as his predecessor *Omanhin* Aggery.[110] The officials accused them of a consistent, willful misunderstanding of the instructions regarding the participation of Moore in the ceremony. Mbra, who would not countenance that official attitude toward him and his elders, in his report after the clash accused local officers of exhibiting double standards. Mbra recalled that Moore had exercised the functions of his office as *Tufohin* on several public occasions prior to the clash. He stated that Moore had, for instance, led the procession during the Empire Day celebrations that paraded about the town, including the quarter of *Bentsir Asafo* company. Furthermore, at the all-important funeral of J. P. Brown that same year, Moore as *Tufohin* had overseen six companies as the procession passed through Jackson Street, Chapel Square, and the *Bentsir* quarter to the cemetery. Mbra questioned the duplicity of the government in allowing him to appear on some occasions as *Tufohin* but forbidding it during the *Atiran* ceremony.

The local officers intimated that the attitude of Mbra toward the government, as reflected in his letters and bearing, ranged from passive insolence to open resistance. They accused him of failing to consult other persons who shared customary entitlement to make their opinions known in the ruling of the town; with a small cabal of counselors, Mbra had blatantly arrogated to himself the control of affairs. This small coterie, according to official speculation, consisted entirely of members of the ARPS, who resolutely resisted any measure that the government proposed, purportedly as a matter of mischief. Additionally, the officers alleged that this group suborned chiefs with threats, falsehoods, and half-truths as part of their strategy to usurp control of the affairs of the town. They accused Mbra of ignoring his responsibility as a natural ruler, accepting the subversive orders of the conservative executive committee of the ARPS and ill-advisedly throwing himself into that camp, which was largely suspected of being responsible for the writing of his official letters. *Omanhin* Mbra and his counselors objected to the picture painted of them within official circles. Collectively and resolutely, they prided themselves in being well within their rights as indigenous people to speak for and seek the interest of Cape Coast, with Mbra as the supreme leader and his counselors as accomplished and respected individuals who possessed the trust of the town. Even so, the officers retroactively blamed Mbra and his group of advisers for instigating the demonstrations against the Income Tax Bill in October 1931, which had resulted in a disgraceful and distasteful attack on the police station and individual Europeans in Cape Coast.

In view of these suspicions and accusations against Mbra, the government considered deposing him through the drafting of special legislation to deport him, along with his counselors, to any of those places where the British in the past had exiled kings and others from their various colonies. The only restraining element, the administration observed, was the lack of incriminating acts of subversion, especially as the group had always cleverly hidden behind the *Omanhin* and avoided detection. Alternatively, the officials hoped that the removal of *Omanhin* Mbra would create indigenous constitutional crises in Cape Coast that could play to the advantage of the administration. They convinced themselves that no other candidate the royal family presented would be acceptable to the counselors, creating an impasse that might occasion the automatic legal closing of the indigenous tribunal after an interregnum of one year, at which point the district commissioner would take over those duties. Neither of these proposed solutions could be implemented since both evinced the penchant of the government for harsh measures in view of the recurrent contestations it suffered in the town.

### CONCLUSION

That momentous clash in defiance of colonial authority in Cape Coast had been long in coming, except that its occurrence happened within the context of usual inter-*Asafo* disturbances, this time with an overlay of coastal Ghana politics. The situation built up from the testy relations between the administration asserting its power and the indigenous authorities and institutions contesting every move. In the 1920s and 1930s, these sour exchanges became irredeemable with the active participation of the educated elite in these institutions, particularly in the *Asafo*. Based on their extensive education, the elite envisaged unhindered access to political participation across all sectors; the colonial authorities, in suspicion, sought to prevent that and accused them of desiring to replace the indigenous authorities. Streamlining colonial governance machinery with the NJO, Provincial Councils, and the Municipal Corporations Ordinance of 1924 laid bare the intentions of the government—to disillusionment in Cape Coast, notably of educated elite who basked in the enduring trust of the indigenous institutions, with some of them in the inner circle of *Omanhin* Kojo Mbra III or operating under the ARPS and constantly contesting colonial policies. Against this setup and the municipal election-occasioned split within the ARPS, which division replicated itself in the entire town and complicated matters as *Asafo* rivalry, commingling with local politics, set the colonial government on edge. The *Tufohin* inquiry as well as the subsequent conduct of local officers became an albatross of suspected bias around the neck of the government. Then, with its officials scampering to prevent the looming *Asafo* clash amid a critical mass of preceding circumstances, such as similar clashes in the Saltpond district and determined opposition across southern Ghana to the income tax proposal, the worse fears of the colonial government materialized.

# CONCLUSION

ASPECTS OF EVERYDAY LIFE IN the nineteenth and twentieth centuries continually constituted matters of misunderstanding between coastal Ghana communities and the colonial government and, simultaneously, became modes of contestation for the former against the latter. Foremost in Cape Coast, indigenous social and political organizations ensured expedient responses to the government in its many attempts to regulate everyday life. Facets of the culture developed from living near and having a unique relationship with the sea. This book, among other considerations, upholds the historicization of the sea in accounting for the past of southern Ghana coastal communities. It emphasizes a clean break with overwhelming terrestrial perspectives that treat the sea as a border for landbound events, as though all cultural creations remain restricted to land. Hence, this emerging view reiterates that waterways do not represent empty, cultureless, historical voids, as societies that live near them carve aspects of their identities from interactions with those elements. Along these lines, inhabitants of Cape Coast particularly and coastal Ghana generally demonstrated remarkable agency in resolutely living their lives in preferred ways.

## CONCLUSION

In the late nineteenth century, the nascent British authority, desirous of expanding its power, disregarded the stipulations of bonds, treaties, and mutual agreements with the people of southern Ghana. Newly established British courts, originally limited to cases involving English men on the shoreline, expanded their jurisdiction over local men and women. These courts eventually hauled kings, chiefs, and other leaders of indigenous political institutions before them, to their bewilderment, as the government sought to restrict aspects of customary rites and practices.

Well into the early twentieth century, the British courts deepened their assault on the authority of kings and chiefs, relegating them to the background to ensure the entrenchment of colonial power. This process came at a rather high cost for the custodians of traditional law, who fought back fiercely, wrote official letters of protest, criticized government policies, and defied orders. In an effort to curtail these moves, the administration deployed military and police forces. Although administration was originally established incrementally on the part of English mercantile officials and the British government, the persistent use of military and police institutions occurred under both phases. The chiefs and people of coastal Ghana, especially *Omanhin* Aggery of Cape Coast, remained resolute, threatening to professionalize indigenous warrior organizations, particularly the *Asafo*, to meet the military machine squarely. Although the administration had its way in some instances, the story turned out differently in others, lending credence to the notion that colonialism, though a powerful force, constituted "a giddy variety of existential experiences."[1]

Colonialism established a bureaucratic regime that presented a new challenge. Although kings, chiefs, as well as ordinary men and women acted of their own accord, they equally found expediency in engaging with the bureaucracy through the expertise of their educated compatriots, giving the strong indication that formal education hardly amounted to a neglect of indigenous culture. Those elite beneficiaries participated in indigenous political institutions (particularly the *Asafo*) based on patrilineal associations and lineages in the various communities across the country, especially in Cape Coast, where that collaboration and participation remained notable.

The *Asafo*, one of the most visible facets of maritime culture, with its ideas of bravery, group pride, and militancy, constituted the main means of sociopolitical organization for ordinary men and women. The participation of *Asafo* groups in contesting government policies and actions, significantly in Cape Coast, went a long way to impact the transformation of old local conflicts into national politics, as the municipal election in the town demonstrated. The *Asafo* and *Ebusua* systems, important aspects of everyday life in coastal Ghana, were unique manifestations of the idea of gender complementarity among the coastal Akan societies. However, this complementarity hardly precluded tensions, as the two indigenous systems impinged on issues of identity, belongingness, inheritance, rights, and attendant responsibilities. Both systems often presented a point of convergence for social conflict imbued with paradoxical manifestations. Essentially, the *Asafo* united men and women with their fathers' brothers and sisters. This unity ironically created conflict between brothers and sisters and, curiously, between mothers and their children. In enforcing patrilineal group solidarities, the *Asafo* equally weakened family ties and fomented conflict among *Ebusua* kinsmen. Yet these two systems held society together, as both ensured leverage in the social well-being of the individual.

The protracted protest to the Crown Lands Bill reified the cultural and religious relevance of land beyond being an economic and political resource. Under the auspices of the Aborigines' Rights Protection Society (ARPS), based in Cape Coast with active branches scattered across the country, the people of southern Ghana retained their inalienable rights to land. The coastal communities optimized opportunities and processes of resistance available to them, eventually causing the colonial administration to abandon the Crown Lands Bill. In furtherance of that purpose, societies in southern Ghana drew inspiration from indigenous thoughts and philosophies on property ownership. These ideas upheld the sovereignty, dignity, pride, and audacity that underpinned group as well as individual acquisitions, expressions of which became intriguingly diversified, as simple artistic and symbolic usages occurred alongside contemporaneously with written words.

Accusations of government bias in local disputes appeared credible when officers, instead of taking swift, resolute decisions and actions, equivocated and exhibited confusion. Often, such reluctance or inaction cast a shadow of weakness as well as suspected complicity on the administration. For the people of Cape Coast, as with most of coastal Ghana, contesting colonial authority, its institutions, and everything it stood for reinforced the notion that modern governance constituted an establishment that ought to be held in great suspicion and sometimes contempt. The Fanti adage *A-ban wo twuw n'a-dze wo-nnsua no bi* encapsulates that perception; even Governor Slater confirmed that local attitude with the phrase "a democratic outlook, restiveness and the negation of ideas of Government."[2] The nature of colonial power and authority, as well as the creation of a professional standing army and police force, detracted from the expectations of the people. The processes and phases through which the administration entrenched itself evidently became clandestine and amounted to a betrayal of trust. The indigenous political system proffered considerable transparency, as aggrieved individuals had avenues to seek redress. When things became critical, individuals or groups could empower themselves and take control through the instrumentality of indigenous organizations. As these precolonial modes of rectification became inadmissible given the adamance of the administration, the people fought back using the same time-honored organizations the government sought to suppress. Consequently, the pivotal role of Cape Coast in the narrative of opposing the administration in coastal Ghana came at a heavy political and economic cost. The town lost its colonial capital status in the late nineteenth century and missed out on a necessary and crucial twentieth-century infrastructural development that would have facilitated its modernization. Suspicions of politically motivated intent on the part of the officials made the administration appear to be either placing its interests above those of the people and their ancient town or to be decidedly vindictive.

Furthermore, the administration endured constant contestation of its varied attempts at regulating everyday life, particularly in Cape Coast, where colonial political officers branded its people the most difficult to work with in the colony. The attitude of the people toward government measures and policies became increasingly critical and unhelpful, according to the official perception. Despite attempts of colonial officers to diffuse that attitude and regain the confidence of the people, the situation hardly improved. Accordingly, the 1932 *Asafo* clash proffered an occasion to conflate past conflicts and contemporary issues, including the municipal election, the split in the ARPS, and the *Tufohin* inquiry, to defy government authority. Belligerent *Asafo* companies, based on previous internal conflicts and antagonisms, denied the local officials requisite cooperation. The administration had forcibly had its way for so long that the *Asafo* groups considered the looming clash in 1932 an opportunity to raise the level of defiance. That action amounted to an exploitation of internal conflicts within the contest of challenge to colonial authority. Hence, set against an uneasy backdrop of *Asafo* clashes, recurrent resistance to the colonial government imposing a direct tax regime in southern Ghana, and devious divisions in Cape Coast over the Legislative Council elections, the national political underpinnings of the 1932 Cape Coast conflict became more evident than imagined.

CONCLUSION

The people of coastal Ghana cherished their values, views, culture, and expectations of everyday life. Insofar as the administration remained foreign, forceful, and nontransparent, the people held on and sought to control their own circumstances. These communities, with Cape Coast as the pivot, remained resolute in determining how to live even in the face of blatant official endeavors to regulate their preferred ways of life. In all these scenarios, mutual mistrust and suspicion abounded as aspects of everyday life became both a matter of conflict between coastal Ghana communities and the colonial government and a means of obstruction for the former against the latter. The aggregation of these occurrences reify the relevance of vicissitudes of everyday life to the appreciation of the historical narrative of southern Ghana—establishing its indigenous values, concepts, and expectations as crucial to why and how things happen.

The consistent colonial effort to control elements of everyday life caused the people of southern Ghana, especially those in Cape Coast, to fight back using the same targeted indigenous institutions, elevating the town into a notable place in the perplexing politics of the country even well after the twentieth century. This feat hinged on collaboration between indigenous political institutions—particularly the *Asafo*, a key factor in the maritime culture—the *Omanhin*, and the ever-engaged educated elite. More determined than ever, this cooperation fed off the mutual conviction of the participants of being well within their rights to speak for and seek the interest of the town, with the *Amanhin* as supreme rulers and their counselors, mostly the educated elite, as accomplished and respected residents. Although internal disagreement and division plagued these alliances, leading to a split especially in the twentieth century, the unmistakable characteristic Cape Coast mistrust of government manifested at all times; as the various groups continued that well-entrenched trend, reaffirming the notable place of the town in the politics of the country.

# NOTES

## INTRODUCTION

1. In a generic sense, "Akan" simultaneously refers to a variety of ethnic groups as well as their language. The Akan groups can be divided into various coastal and hinterland categories, originating from Pra and Ofin confluence. Constituting nearly 48 percent of the population, the Akan are the largest groups in southern Ghana. The major Akan groups include Asante, Fanti, Ahanta, Guan, Bono, Ahafo, Akyem, Akuapem, Akwamu, Kwahu, Sefwi, and Nzima. A thorough discussion of the various Akan groups is included in chapter 1.

2. G. G. Iggers and G. Edward Wang, *A Global History of Modern Historiography*, with contributions by Supriya Mukherjee (London: Pearson Longman, 2008), 275.

3. "Ghana" is used frequently in this work, sometimes interchangeably with "the Gold Coast" or its full version, "the British Gold Coast Colony," especially to reiterate the status of this West African nation as a historical entity cited in other scholarly works.

4. These Europeans, many of them of British and Dutch descent, documented the history of Ghana before, during, and after colonial rule. They wrote stories of the origins of various peoples and described ethnic groups and their interactions as well as trade with different Europeans groups. Some of these works include W. E. F. Ward, *A History of Ghana* (London: Allen and Unwin, 1967); John Fage, *Ghana: A Historical Interpretation* (Madison: University of Wisconsin Press, 1959); Brodie Cruickshank, *Eighteen Years on the Gold Coast of Africa* (London: Frank Cass, 1966); E. B.

Ellis, *A History of Gold Coast of West Africa* (New York: Greenwood, 1969); Dennis Austin, *Politics in Ghana 1946–1960* (London: Oxford University Press, 1964); E. L. R. Meyerowitz, *Akan Traditions of Origin* (London: Faber and Faber, 1952); David Kimble, *A Political History of Ghana: The Rise of Gold Coast Nationalism 1850–1928* (London: Oxford University Press, 1963).

5. New regions have been carved out of some of the old ones, bringing the total to sixteen. These include Ahafo, Ashanti, Bono, Bono East, Central, Eastern, Greater Accra, North East, Northern, Oti, Savannah, Upper East, Upper West, Volta, Western, and Western North.

6. These works include but are not limited to I. Wilks, *Asante in the Nineteenth Century: The Structure and Evolution of a Political Order* (London: Cambridge University Press, 1975); I. Wilks, *Forest of Gold: Essays on the Akan and the Kingdom of Asante* (Athens: Ohio University Press, 1993); I. Wilks, *Political Bi-polarity in Nineteenth Century Asante* (Edinburgh: Edinburgh University, 1970); L. W. Yarak, *Asante and the Dutch, 1744–1873* (Oxford: Clarendon Press, 1990); Jean Allman, *The Quills of the Porcupine: Asante Nationalism in an Emergent Ghana* (Madison: University of Wisconsin Press, 1993); Kwame Arhin, *Minutes of the Ashanti Farmers Association, 1934–1936* (Legon: University of Ghana, 1978); R. S. Rattray, *Akan-Ashanti Folktales* (Oxford: Clarendon Press, 1969); R. S. Rattray, *Ashanti Law and Constitution* (London: Oxford University Press, 1956); R. S. Rattray, *Religion and Art in Ashanti* (London: Oxford University Press, 1959).

7. Jean Allman, *"I Will Not Eat Stone": A Women's History of Colonial Asante* (Portsmouth, NH: Heinemann, 2000); Albert A. Boahen, *Yaa Asantewaa and the Asante-British War of 1900–1* (Oxford: James Currey, 2003); Asirifi Danquah, *Yaa Asantewaa: An African Queen Who Led an Army to Fight the British* (Kumasi: Asirifi Danquah, 2002).

8. See for instance, John Parker, *Making the Town: Ga State and Society in Early Colonial Accra* (Portsmouth, NH: Heinemann, 2000); Claire Robertson, *Sharing a Bowl: A Socio-economic History of Women and Class in Accra, Ghana* (Bloomington: Indiana University Press, 1984); D. Pellow, *Women in Accra: Options for Autonomy* (Algonac, MI: Reference, 1977).

9. Emmanuel K. Akyeampong, *Drink, Power, and Cultural Change: A Social History of Alcohol in Ghana, c. 1800 to Recent Times* (Oxford: James Currey, 1996), xv.

10. Emmanuel K. Akyeampong, *Between the Sea and the Lagoon: An Eco-social History of the Anlo of Southern Ghana c. 1850 to Recent Times* (Oxford: James Currey, 2001), 4.

11. Jeffrey W. Bolster, "Putting the Ocean in Atlantic History: Maritime Communities and Marine Ecology in the Northwest Atlantic, 1500–1800," *The American Historical Review* 113, no. 1 (Feb. 2008): 19–47. Bolster is discussed under the theoretical framework of this book.

12. Kobinah Minnah, interviewed by author, digital voice recording, Cape Coast, Central Region, Ghana, June 12, 2009; Nana Amba Ayiabah, interviewed by author, digital voice recording, Cape Coast, Central Region, Ghana, June 13, 2009; Ebo Johnson, interviewed by author, digital voice recording, Cape Coast, Ghana, June 5, 2009; Kweku Botse, interviewed by author, digital voice recording, Cape Coast, Ghana, June 22, 2009; Kobina Yallow, interviewed by author, digital voice recording, Cape Coast, Ghana, June 4, 2009.

13. Some of these references appear in the following: Robert Addo-Fenning, *Akyem Abuakwa 1700–1943: From Ofori Panin to Sir Ofori Atta* (Trondheim: Norwegian University of Science and Technology, 1997); J. A. Aggrey, *Asafo* (Tema: Ghana Publishing, 1978); Francis Agbodeka, "The Fante Confederation 1865–1869," *Transactions of the Historical Society of Ghana* 8 (1964): 82–123; Jean M. Allman, "The Youngmen and the Porcupine: Class, Nationalism, and Asante Struggle for Self-Determination, 1945–1957," *Journal of African History* 31, no. 2 (1990): 50–70; Kofi A. Busia, *The Position of the Chief in the Modern Political System of Ashanti* (London: Frank Cass, 1968); I. B. Chukwukere, "Perspectives on Asafo Institution of Southern Ghana," *Journal of African Studies* 7, no. 1 (1980): 50–75; I. B. Chukwukere, *Cultural Resilience: The Asafo Company System of the Fanti* (Cape Coast, Ghana: University of Cape Coast Press, 1970); A. K. Datta, "The Fanti Asafo: A Re-examination," *Africa* 42 (1972): 45–67; Harvey M. Feinberg, "African and Europeans in West Africa: Elminans and Dutchmen on the Gold Coast during the Eighteenth Century," *Transactions of the American Philosophical Society* 79, no. 7 (1989): 104–120. This article includes references to Elmina wards and the *Asafo* on pages 104–109. There is also a reference to ward conflicts on pages 118–120. M. J. Field, *Social Organization of the Ga People* (London: Crown Agents for the Colonies, 1940), 118–120; Dominic Fortescue, "The Accra Crowd, the Asafo, and Opposition to the Municipal Corporations Ordinance, 1924–25," *Canadian Journal of African Studies* 24, no. 3 (1990): 348–375; George P. Hagan, "An Analytical Study of Fanti Kinship," *Research Review* 4, no. 1 (1967): 35–57; J. E. Casely Hayford, *Gold Coast Native Institutions* (London: Frank Cass, 1970); Per Hernaes, *Slaves, Danes and African Coast Society* (Trondheim: Norwegian University of Science and Technology, 1995); J. C. DeGraft Johnson, "The Fanti Asafo," *Africa* 5, no. 3 (1932): 307–322; T. J. Johnson,

"Protest, Challenge, and Change: An Analysis of Southern Gold Coast Riots, 1890–1920," *Economy and Society* 1, no. 2 (1972): 164–193; Ray A. Kea, *Settlements, Trade, and Politics in Seventeenth-Century Gold Coast* (Baltimore: Johns Hopkins University Press, 1982); Li Anshan, "Asafo and Destoolment in Colonial Southern Ghana 1900–1953," *International Journal of African Historical Studies* 28, no. 2 (1995): 327–357; Mary McCarthy, *Social Change and the Growth of British Power in the Gold Coast: The Fante States, 1807–1874* (Lanham, MD: University Press of America, 1983), 105–106. This book has a short reference to the *Asafo* on pages 105–106, particularly with respect to the British governor's attempt to regulate the institution. I. Odotei, "The Ga and Their Neighbors" (PhD diss., University of Ghana, Legon, 1972). This dissertation has a short description of the *Asafo* among the Ga people. F. Ofori-Atta, "Amantoomiensa in the Political and Administrative Set-Up of Akyem Abuakwa" (BA thesis, University of Ghana, Legon, 1978); J. K. Osei-Tutu, *The Asafoi (Socio-military Groups) in the History and Politics of Accra (Ghana) from the Seventeenth to Mid Twentieth Century* (Trondheim: Norwegian University of Science and Technology, 2000); Maxwell Owusu, *Uses and Abuses of Political Power: A Case Study of Community and Change in the Politics of Ghana* (Legon, Ghana: University of Ghana Press, 2006); R. Porter, "The Cape Coast Conflict of 1803," *Transactions of the Historical Society of Ghana* 11 (1970): 30–45; John M. Sarbah, *Fanti National Constitution* (London: Frank Cass, 1968), 25–32; John M. Sarbah, *Fanti Customary Laws* (London: Frank Cass, 1968), 99–100; S. Shaloff, "The Income Tax, Indirect Rule and the Depression: The Gold Coast Riot of 1931," *Cahiers d'Etudes Africaines* 14, no. 54 (1974): 359–376; Jarle Simensen, "Commoners, Chiefs, and Colonial Government: British Policy and Local Politics in Akim Abuakwa, Ghana, under Colonial Rule" (PhD diss., University of Trondheim, Norway, 1975); Jarle Simensen, "Nationalism from Below: The Akyem Abuakwa Example," *Mitteillungen der Basler Afrika Bibliographien* 12 (1975): 31–57; Jarle Simensen, "Crisis in Akim Abuakwa: The Native Administrative Revenue Measure of 1932, Akyem Abuakwa and the Politics of Inter-war Period in Ghana," *Mitteillungen der Basler Afrika Bibliographein* 12 (1995): 110–125; Jarle Simensen, "Rural Mass Action in the Content of Anti-colonial Protest: The Asafo Movement of Akim Abuakwa, Ghana," *Canadian Journal of African Studies* 7 (1974): 25–41; A. K. Datta and R. Porter, "The Asafo System in Historical Perspective: An Inquiry into the Origin and Development of a Ghanaian Institution," *Journal of African History* 12, no. 2 (1971): 279–297; and John Argyle, "Kalela, Beni, Asafo, Ingoma, and the Rural-Urban Dichotomy," *African Studies* 50 (1991): 65–86.

14. Aggrey, *Asafo*.

15. J. B. Christaller, *Dictionary of the Asante and Fante Languages Called Twi* (Basel: Basel Evangelical Missionary Society, 1993), 100. See also F. Migeod, *Languages of West Africa* (London: Paul, Trench, Trubner, 1911), 13.

16. Chukwukere, *Cultural Resilience*.

17. DeGraft Johnson, "The Fanti Asafo," 307–322.

18. Ibid., 311.

19. DeGraft Johnson happened to be one of the few indigenes later admitted into the British colonial administration as a junior officer. His defensiveness, although surprising to many of his colleague officers, came across as understandable to a few of them.

20. Sarbah, *Fanti National Constitution*, 25–32; Sarbah, *Fanti Customary Laws*, 99–100.

21. Sarbah, *Fanti Customary Laws*, 100.

22. Sarbah, *Fanti National Constitution*, 25.

23. Datta and Porter, "The Asafo System in Historical Perspective," 279–297.

24. Ibid., 279.

25. Ibid.

26. Ibid., 281.

27. Datta, "The Fanti Asafo," 45–67.

28. Ibid., 58.

29. Argyle, "Kalela, Beni, Asafo, Ingoma, and the Rural-Urban Dichotomy," 65–86.

30. Ibid., 69.

31. Ibid., 70.

32. Roger Gocking, "The Historic Akoto: A Social History of Cape Coast, Ghana, 1848–1948" (PhD diss., Stanford University, California, 1981).

33. Ibid., 2–3.

34. Ibid., 5.

35. Ibid., 10.

36. Roger Gocking, *Facing Two Ways: Ghana's Coastal Communities under Colonial Rule* (Lanham, MD: University Press of America, 1999).

37. Ibid., 7.

38. S. Shaloff, "The Cape Coast Asafo Company Riot of 1932," *International Journal of African Historical Studies* 7, no. 4 (1974): 591–607.

39. Ibid., 591.

40. James C. Scott, *Weapons of the Weak: Everyday Forms of Peasant Resistance* (New Haven, CT: Yale University Press, 1985), xv–xxii.

41. Ibid., xvi.
42. Ibid.
43. Ibid.
44. Ibid.
45. Bolster, "Putting the Ocean in Atlantic History," 19–47.
46. Ibid., 20.
47. Ibid.
48. Ibid.
49. Ibid., 22.
50. Karin Amimoto Ingersoll, *Waves of Knowing: A Seascape Epistemology* (Durham, NC: Duke University Press, 2016), 6.
51. Kevin Dawson, *Undercurrents of Power: Aquatic Culture in the African Diaspora* (Philadelphia: University of Pennsylvania Press, 2018), 1.
52. Ibid., 2.
53. Ibid., 2–3.
54. Ibid., 4.
55. The Michigan State University Institutional Review Board–approved format.
56. Some of these methodological models are discussed in Nwando Achebe, *Farmers, Traders, and Warriors, and Kings: Female Power and Authority in Northern Igboland, 1900–1960* (Portsmouth, NH: Heinemann, 2006), 6.
57. Some in this category included Governor Maxwell; W. C. Wellman, secretary for native affairs; A. Duncan-Johnstone; and H. A. Blair.
58. The *Gold Coast Times*, established in 1874, had James Hutton Brew as editor. The *Gold Coast Aborigines*, 1897, belonged to the Aborigines' Rights Protection Society and had Attoh Ahuma and Reverend Egyir Sam as editors. With J. E. Casely Hayford Herbert Brown and Dr. Savage as editors, the *Gold Coast Leader* operated between 1902 and 1934. Reverend S. R. B. Solomon established the *Gold Coast Methodist Times*. Charles and Edmund Bannerman edited the *West African Herald*, while J. H. Hutton Brew with his nephew, J. E. Casely Hayford, edited the *Western Echo*, established in 1874.
59. Some of these personalities included *Supi* J. A. Hayfron of *Bentsir Asafo* company; *Supi* Kojo Nunoo, *Annafo Asafo* company; *Supi* Ebo Johnson, *Ntsin Asafo* company; *Supi* Insaidoo, *Nkum Asafo* company; *Supi* Kobina Minah, *Akrampa Asafo* company; Safohen Kweku Botse, *Abrofonkoa Asafo* company; *Supi* Yallow, *Amanfur Asafo* company; and Nana Amba Ayiaba, queen-mother of the *Oguaa* Traditional Area.

60. The spelling of Aggery in documents is a corruption or anglicization of the Fanti name *E-gyir* (with the initial "e" pronounced as a long "a"). Careful pronunciation of the anglicized Aggery will mimic the indigenous name Egyir. Unfortunately, Aggery in subsequent records and in contemporary times has been misspelled and pronounced as Aggrey (Ah-gray).

## 1. SETTLEMENT AND NASCENT SOCIETY

1. Albert A. Boahen, *Ghana: Evolution and Change in the Nineteenth and Twentieth Centuries* (London: Longman, 1975), 5.
2. Major Akan groups included the Twi-speaking hinterland groups—namely, Asante, Asante-Akyem, Kwahu, Akyem, Akwamu, Akuapem, Assin, Denkyira, Twifo, Sefwi, Bono, and Ahafo. The Fanti groups comprised Borbor, Nkusukum, Omanmu, Agona, Gomua, Enyan, Asebu, and Abora, all a few miles from the coast, and the coastal Oguaa, Edina, Akitakyi, Eguafo, Shama, Sekunde, Ahanta, Nzima, and so on.

> Scholars such as Shumway, *The Fante and the Slave Trade*, and Kiyaga-Mulindwa, "The Akan Problem," *Current Anthropology*, have sought to raise doubts about the nature, composition, beliefs, and practices of the Akan peoples. Privileging the interpretation of European sources, documents, and records over the interpretations of generations of Ghanaian scholars, which are significantly consistent with various credible Akan oral traditions, is quite troubling. Unity in diversity remains the hallmark of Akan uniqueness, as Akan peoples are one and the same with several mutually interrelated systems. The fact that the Asante and Fanti groups had a historical relationship of "fierce rivalry in the era of the slave trade" (Rebecca Shumway, *The Fante and the Transatlantic Slave Trade* [Rochester, NY: University of Rochester Press, 2011]) hardly contradicts the existence of cultural contiguities among various Akan groups. Generally, across world cultures, the unfortunate incidence of civil wars does not negate evidence of cultural contiguities and similarities in those societies. The different Akan groups exhibited a prototype federal system of sorts without an overarching central government,

especially among the rest of the Twi-speaking groups and Fanti-speaking peoples. Even with the Asante who, evidently, eventually created a semblance of overarching political structure, the position of *Asantehene* originally passed as that of a *primus inter pares* (first among equals).

Doubting and raising questions about the nature, composition, institutions, beliefs, and practices of the various Akan groups of people mimics the postmodernist radical pluralism philosophy that encourages reinterpretation of existing facts. Similarly, there have been intellectual discourses and debates about issues such as what Africa is, who bequeathed that name to the continent, who is African, and who constitutes the African diaspora.

3. Kobinah Minnah, interviewed by author, digital voice recording, Cape Coast, Central Region, Ghana, June 12, 2009; Nana Amba Ayiabah, interviewed by author, digital voice recording, Cape Coast, Central Region, Ghana, June 13, 2009; Ebo Johnson, interviewed by author, digital voice recording, Cape Coast, Ghana, June 5, 2009; Kweku Botse, interviewed by author, digital voice recording, Cape Coast, Ghana, June 22, 2009; and Kobina Yallow, interviewed by author, digital voice recording, Cape Coast, Ghana, June 4, 2009.

4. *Fetu* Kingdom developed in the interior, within the proximate northern reaches of Cape Coast. Formerly a great kingdom, it declined over the years and is now one of the thirty-six satellite towns and villages under the jurisdiction of Cape Coast. Minnah, interview; Ayiabah, interview; Johnson, interview; Botse, interview; and Yallow, interview.

5. Kwame Y. Daaku, *Trade and Politics on the Gold Coast 1600–1720* (London: Clarendon Press, 1970), 65.

6. W. T. Balmer, *History of the Akan Peoples* (New York: Greenwood, 1969), 46. See also E. L. R. Meyerowitz, *The Early History of the Akan States of Ghana* (London: Red Candle Press, 1970), 72. Also Minnah, interview; Ayiabah, interview; Johnson, interview; Botse, interview; and Yallow, interview.

7. J. J. Crooks, *Records Relating to the Gold Coast Settlements: From 1750 to 1974* (London: Frank Cass, 1973), 156.

8. William Bosman, *A New and Accurate Description of the Coast of Guinea: Divided into the Gold, the Slave, and the Ivory Coasts* (London: Frank Cass, 1967), 48.

9. Mary McCarthy, *Social Change and the Growth of British Power in the Gold Coast: The Fante States, 1807–1874* (Lanham, MD: University Press of America, 1983), ix.

10. Kwame Arhin, *The Cape Coast and Elmina Handbook: Past, Present and Future* (Legon: University of Ghana, 1995), 2.

11. A. D. C. Hyland, "Architectural History of Cape Coast," *Transactions of the Historical Society of Ghana* 16, no. 2 (1995): 164.

12. Ibid.

13. *Obrempong* (plural *Abrempong*) was mainly an indigenous title given to men of great and self-evident wealth, which in many cases translated into political power as well. People of this description became well known in their societies because of their economic and political standing. *Obrempong* in this context literally meant being prominent among the rich and famous.

14. Kwame Y. Daaku, "John Konny: The Last Prussian Negro Prince," *Tarikh* 1, no. 4 (1967): 55–64; David Henige, "John Kabes of Komenda: An Early Entrepreneur and State Builder," *Journal of African History* 17, no. 1 (1977): 1–19. On Eno Baisie Kurentsi, see Shumway, *The Fante and the Slave Trade*, 66.

15. Paul Erdmann Isert, *Letters on West Africa and the Slave Trade* (New York: Oxford University Press, 1992), 135.

16. Paul E. Lovejoy and Toyin Falola, eds., *Pawnship, Slavery, and Colonialism in Africa* (Trenton, NJ: Africa World Press, 2003). See also George Metcalfe, "Gold, Assortments and the Trade Ounce: Fante Merchants and the Problem of Supply and Demand in the 1770s," *Journal of African History* 28, no. 1 (1987): 27–41; Paul E. Lovejoy and David Richardson, "Trust, Pawnship and Atlantic History: The Institutional Foundations of the Old Calabar Slave Trade," *American Historical Review* 104, no. 2 (1999): 333–335; Peter Haenger, *Slaves and Slave Holders on the Gold Coast: Towards an Understanding of Social Bondage in West Africa* (Basel: Schleittwein, 2000).

17. PRAAD Adm. 1/2/417: Mill to Beard, Cape Coast Castle, September 17, 1775.

18. Daaku, *Trade and Politics on the Gold Coast 1600–1792*, 48. See also Gwendolyn Midlo Hall, *Slavery and African Ethnicities in the Americas: Restoring the Links* (Chapel Hill: The University of North Carolina Press, 2005), 102. Hall's account confirms Daaku's narration regarding the origins of the Europeans who erected the castles and forts; however, they disagree on the total number. The former puts it on the higher side than the latter—that is, thirty-two.

19. John W. Blake, *West Africa: Quest for God and Gold 1454–1578* (Totowa, NJ: Curzon, 1977), chapter 2; A. Van Dantzig, *Forts and Castles of Ghana* (Accra, Ghana: Sedco, 1980), 40–41; Per Hernaes, *Slaves, Danes, and African Coastal Society: The Danish Slave Trade from West Africa and*

*Afro-Danish Relations on the Eighteenth-Century Gold Coast* (Trondheim: Norwegian University of Science and Technology, 1995), section 2.

20. It is important to observe that scholars such as Larson and others have counseled against the ready and quick assumption that the African diaspora always exists outside of the continent. Larson for instance proffers convincing and compelling evidence to support his argument that the African continent ought not be thought of only as the dispensing center but also as a receiving one, as all the other known destinations for African peoples. See Pier M. Larson, "Horrid Journeying: Narratives of Enslavement and the Global African Diaspora," *Journal of World History* 19, no. 4 (December 2008): 431–464.

21. Hall, *Slavery and African Ethnicities in the Americas*, 59.

22. Ibid., 58–59.

23. Captives who embarked from the Elmina Castle became known as *Mina* in the Americas, and those from Fort Amsterdam at Kormantsi and Abandze went under the term *Koromantines*.

24. David Eltis, Paul E. Lovejoy, and David Richardson, "Slave Trading Ports: Towards an Atlantic-Wide Perspective 1676–1832," in *Ports of the Slave Trade (Bights of Biafra and Benin)*, ed. Robin Law and Silke Strickrodt (Stirling: University of Stirling, 1999), 19–20; Shumway, *The Fante and the Slave Trade*, 4.

25. Shumway, *The Fante and the Slave Trade*, 4.

26. Paul E. Lovejoy, *Transformations in Slavery: A History of Slavery in Africa* (New York: Cambridge University Press, 2000), chapter 3. The percentage breakdown includes Anomabo 36 percent, Cape Coast 26 percent, and Elmina 21 percent.

27. Michael A. Gomez, *Reversing Sail: A History of the African Diaspora* (Cambridge: Cambridge University Press, 2005), 65. See also Hall, *Slavery and African Ethnicities in the Americas*.

28. Kwaku Nti, "The Dynamics of Revenue and Relations: Contents and Discontents in Historic African Diaspora Experiences in Ghana," in *Contextualizing Africans and Globalization: Expressions in Sociopolitical and Religious Contents and Discontents*, ed. Ibigbolade S. Aderibigbe, Rotimi Williams Omotoye, and Lydia Bosede Akande (Lanham, MD: Lexington Books, 2016), 39–50. See also Kwaku Nti, "From Politics to Tourism: Pan-African Connections, Development, and Experiences of the Historic African Diaspora in Ghana," in *Ghana: Economic, Social, and Political Issues*, ed. Coleen Roscoe (New York: Nova Science, 2014), 1–14.

29. Daaku, *Trade and Politics on the Gold Coast 1600–1792*, xviii. See also James Anquandah, *Castles and Forts of Ghana* (Atlante: Ghana

Museums and Monuments Board, 1999), 15; Van Dantzig, *Forts and Castles of Ghana*, 20.

30. Crooks, *Records Relating to the Gold Coast*, 7.

31. Bosman, *A New and Accurate Description of the Coast of Guinea*, 14. Bosman was a chief factor of trade for the Dutch at the Castle of St. George d'Elmina. He kept records of activities in the region and later published a book that remains one of the often cited works on the history of Ghana. Of the twenty-one to thirty-two European forts and castles erected on the Gold Coast, fifteen still stand in Ghana. These include the Christiansborg Castle (Accra), Fort Good Hope (Senya Bereku), Fort Patience (Apam), Fort Amsterdam (Kromantsi and Abandze), Fort William (Anomabu), Cape Coast Castle (Cape Coast), St. Jorge (George) Castle (Elmina), Fort St. Sebastian (Shama), Fort Orange (Sekondi), Fort Batesstein (Butre), Fort Metal Cross (Discove), Gross Freiedrichsburg (Princesstown), Fort St. Anthony (Axim), and Fort Appolonia (Beyin). Forts and castles are listed here in the order of the towns in which they are located if one travels along the coast from Accra west to Beyin. See Anquandah, *Castles and Forts of Ghana*, 17.

32. PRO BT 6/10 Representation of Mr. John Whately, Birmingham, March 27, 1788, 354–357. See also PRO C 107/10 Joseph Grice to James Rogers & Co., Birmingham, June 27, 1792.

33. J. E. Inikori, "The Import of Firearms into West Africa, 1750–1807: A Quantitative Analysis," *Journal of African History* XVIII, no. 3 (1977): 339–368. See also R. A. Kea, "Firearms and Warfare on the Gold and Slave Coast from the Sixteenth to the Nineteenth Centuries," *Journal of African History* XII (1971): 200, n. 97; Bosman, *A New and Accurate Description of the Coast of Guinea*, 184–185.

34. Inikori, "The Import of Firearms into West Africa," 349.

35. Ibid., 354.

36. An analysis of 64,828 firearms imported into West Africa between 1757 and 1806 shows distribution among different types and regions. Inikori, "The Import of Firearms into West Africa," 356.

37. Early European records give vivid accounts of the expertise of fishermen and canoe men on the coast. Marees says that "the people that dwell within the land [referring to the hinterlands] can hardly brooke [sic] the seas . . . but their rowers and pilots that bring them aboard, are hardy enough, and are never sick, by reason of their daily using to the seas." Again, he refers to the skillful ability "to pass over the bars and carry their goods and provisions along the coast." He particularly mentions the canoe men of Cape Coast and Elmina as being "the fittest and most experienced

to manage and paddle the canoes over the bars and breakings." And of those of Axim and Winneba, Marees observes that they managed their canoes "over the worst and dreadful beatings of the seas." Pieter De Marees, *A Description and Historical Account of the Gold Kingdom of Guinea* (Oxford: Oxford University Press, 1987), 149–150, 157, 266.

38. "Legitimate trade" was the term used to describe the trade in palm oil, rubber, cocoa, palm kernel, animal skins, kola nuts, and other agricultural produce that gained commercial preeminence after the abolition of the slave trade. The nine main port towns on the Gold Coast included Half Assini, Axim, Sekondi, Cape Coast, Saltpond, Winneba, Accra, Ada, and Keta. See Gold Coast Gazette, Trade Supplement, 1922, 1923, 1924, and 1928, 102–129.

39. See Gold Coast Gazette, Trade Supplement, 1922, 1923, 1924, and 1928, 102–129. Other items imported into the Cape Coast port included lead, pipes, rum, iron and copper bars, soap, tallow, perfumery, and Manchester goods.

40. Trade Statistics—Principal articles exported from/imported into each port of the Gold Coast Colony, 1922, 1923, 1924, and 1928. Gold Coast Gazette, Trade Supplement 1922–1928, 112.

41. Gold Coast 1901 Census Report, 6.

42. Henry Swanzy, "A Trading Family in the Nineteenth Century Gold Coast," *Transactions of the Gold Coast and Togoland Historical Society* 2, no. 1 (1956): 87.

43. J. Hinderink and J. Sterkenburg, *Anatomy of an African Town: A Socio-economic Study of Cape Coast, Ghana* (Utrecht: State University of Utrecht, 1975), 16.

44. Gold Coast 1891 Census Report, 13.

45. M. Priestley, *West African Trade and Coast Society* (London: Oxford University Press, 1969), 15. This trade is discussed fully later in this chapter.

46. Priestley, *West African Trade*, 151–165; David Kimble, *A Political History of Ghana: The Rise of Gold Coast Nationalism, 1850–1928* (London: Oxford University Press, 1963), 6; H. J. Bevin, "The Gold Coast Economy About 1800," *Transactions of the Gold Coast and Togoland Historical Society* 2, no. 2 (1956): 68; G. E. Metcalfe, *Maclean of the Gold Coast* (London: Oxford University Press, 1962), 116.

47. F. L. Bartels, "Philip Quaque, 1741–1814," *Transactions of the Gold Coast and Togoland Historical Society* 1, no. 5 (1955): 153; F. L. Bartels, *The Roots of Ghana Methodism* (Cambridge: Cambridge University Press,

1965), 21. Quaque is an Anglicized version of the Akan name Kwaku or Kweku. It is now used as a last name or surname in various renditions such as Quacoe, Quaquo, and so on.

48. Bartels, *The Roots of Ghana Methodism*, 22.

49. Boahen, *Ghana: Evolution and Change*, 141.

50. John M. Sarbah, *Fanti National Constitution* (London: Frank Cass, 1968), xvi.

51. Albert A. Boahen, *Mfantsipim and the Making of Ghana* (Accra, Ghana: Sankofa, 1996), 119.

52. In 1901, there were 1,620 students in Cape Coast compared to 858 in Accra. See Gold Coast 1901 Census Report, 140.

53. Solomon Mensah, "Gold Coast Literacy," *Gold Coast Nation*, April 8, 1915.

54. J. B. Anaman, *The Gold Coast Guide* (London: Christian Herald, 1902), 165.

55. Attoh Ahuma, "The Gold Coast Youth," *Gold Coast Aborigines*, April 1899, 3. Newell, who provides a comprehensive study of literary culture in colonial Ghana, discusses other groups that developed in Cape Coast. These included William DeGraft's Society for Promoting Christian Knowledge, J. P. Brown's Private Literary Club, Party of Gentlemen's Literary Club, Gold Coast Union Association, *Mfantsi Amanbu Fekuw*, Three Wise Men Society, City Club, Gold Coast National Research Association, Gold Coast Young Men's Christian Association, and the Eureka Club. See Stephanie Newell, *Literary Culture in Colonial Ghana: How to Play the Game of Life* (Bloomington: Indiana University Press, 2002), 33–34.

56. Editorial, "Our Mission Statement," *Gold Coast Times*, March 28, 1874.

57. PRAAD Adm. 11/1/1473: Letter of *Omanhin* Codjoe Imbra to the District Commissioner, Cape Coast, December 31, 1904, 1–2. See chapter 2 for a detailed discussion of the *Asafo* and other indigenous Akan organizations in southern Ghana.

58. PRO CO 267/36: Letter of Maclean to the Committee of Merchants, dated March 4, 1844. See also G. E. Metcalfe, *Great Britain and Ghana: Documents of Ghana History 1807–1957* (London: Ipswich Book, 1964), 147.

59. Long before this time, the Asante had finished their many wars of expansion in the Gold Coast. Subsequently, they had to deal with the recalcitrant elements of the states, such as Denkyira, Akyem, and Assin, under their jurisdiction. Economically, they rallied against states whose

activities frustrated their direct access to the coastal trade with the Europeans. See Boahen, *Ghana: Evolution and Change*, 20–27.

60. PRO CO 267/36: Letter of Maclean to the Committee of Merchants, March 4, 1844. See also Metcalfe, *Great Britain and Ghana*, 147.

61. The alliance system pertained mainly to the domain of commercial relations, particularly where Fanti states had entrenched themselves in their role as middlemen in the trade between Europeans and the Gold Coast interior. Interior Gold Coast states—the Asante, for instance—wanted so much to have direct access to European trade that they would use any easy excuse to wage war on the Fanti peoples.

62. William H. Gillespie, *The Gold Coast Police 1844–1938* (Accra, Ghana: Government Printer, 1955), 129. See also PRO CO 96/4: Maclean to Stanley, Cape Coast Castle, February 5, 1844, 40; and Metcalfe, *Maclean of the Gold Coast*, 107–108.

63. Metcalfe, *Maclean of the Gold Coast*, 108.

64. British Parliamentary Papers, Report of the Select Committee 1842, 212–213. See also Metcalfe, *Great Britain and Ghana*, 180–181; and McCarthy, *Social Change and the Growth of British Power in the Gold Coast*, 145.

65. Metcalfe, *Great Britain and Ghana*, 180.

66. Ibid., 181.

67. Metcalfe reports that Maclean received a small special allowance of £120 in addition to the stipulated salary of his new position to forestall a loss of income from the change of status. See Metcalfe, *Great Britain and Ghana*, 182.

68. Ibid., 146. The Aggery spelling as it occurs in documents is a corruption or anglicization of the Fanti name *E-gyir* (with the initial "e" pronounced as a long "a"). A careful pronunciation of the anglicized Aggery will mimic the indigenous name Egyir. Unfortunately, Aggery in subsequent records and contemporary times has been misspelled and pronounced Aggrey (Ah-gray).

69. Swanzy's testimony before the Parliamentary Select Committee as in Metcalfe, *Great Britain and Ghana*, 146.

70. Brodie Cruickshank, *Eighteen Years on the Gold Coast of Africa: Including an Account of the Native Tribes and Their Intercourse with Europeans* (London: Frank Cass, 1966), 285.

71. Metcalfe, *Great Britain and Ghana*, 149.

72. Ibid.

73. PRO CO 96/22: Letter of James Bannerman to Earl Grey, Cape Coast Castle, January 14, 1851, 1.

74. Ibid., 5.

75. James Bannerman was one of the few prominent mulatto officials of the Gold Coast who became indispensable to the burgeoning British colonial administration. Earl Grey was the secretary of state in charge of colonies in the Colonial Office, London. See Metcalfe, *Great Britain and Ghana*, 179.

76. PRO CO 96/22: Letter of James Bannerman to Earl Grey, Cape Coast Castle, May 6, 1851, 3. See also Metcalfe, *Great Britain and Ghana*, 229.

77. Draft Report of the British Parliamentary Select Committee on Africa (Western Court) as cited in Metcalfe, *Great Britain and Ghana*, 247.

78. PRO CO 96/25: The Poll Tax Ordinance, April 19, 1852, signed by S. J. Hill and Chiefs of the Gold Coast. See also Metcalfe, *Great Britain and Ghana*, 181 and 330–332.

79. PRO CO 96/25: The Poll Tax Ordinance, April 19, 1852, signed by S. J. Hill and Chiefs of the Gold Coast. See also Metcalfe, *Great Britain and Ghana*, 230–232.

80. PRO CO 96/25: Letter of S. J. Hill to Grey, Cape Coast Castle, April 24, 1852. PRO CO 96/30: Letter of S. J. Hill to the Duke of Newcastle, May 31, 1854. See also Kimble, *A Political History of Ghana*, 176–177 and 187; and McCarthy, *Social Change and the Growth of British Power in the Gold Coast*, 161.

81. Metcalfe, *Great Britain and Ghana*, 232.

82. The clause stated that "the Chiefs be informed of the mode of application and be entitled to offer suggestions on this point as they may consider necessary."

83. PRO CO 96/52: Letter of the King, Chiefs and Other Residents of Cape Coast to Governor Andrew, Cape Coast, April 3, 1861, 3.

84. PRO CO 96/58: Letter of Chiefs of Cape Coast to Her Majesty's Secretary of State for the Colonies, Cape Coast, April 11, 1862, 4.

85. PRO CO 96/52: Letter of the King, Chiefs and Other Residents of Cape Coast, April 18, 1861, 5.

86. PRO CO 96/41: Letter of Benjamin Pine to Labouchere, Cape Coast Castle, August 31, 1857, 8. See also McCarthy, *Social Change and the Growth of British Power in the Gold Coast*, 148.

87. PRO CO 96/22: Letter of James Bannerman to Earl Grey, Cape Coast Castle, May 6, 1851, 4.

88. PRO CO 96/64: Letter of Hackett to Duke of Newcastle, Cape Coast Castle, May 12, 1864, 1–2.

89. PRO CO 96/43/11: Proclamation by Sir Benjamin Pine, Governor James Town Accra, March 22, 1858, 2.

90. Ibid.

91. PRO CO 96/58: Letter of the Chiefs of Cape Coast to Her Majesty's Secretary of State for Colonies, Cape Coast Castle, April 11, 1862, 4.

92. Ibid.

93. PRO CO 96/41: Letter of Benjamin Pine to Labouchere, Sierra Leone, August 31, 1857, 5.

94. PRO CO 96/54: Grievances of the Gold Coast Chiefs, Cape Coast, August 9, 1864, 7.

95. PRO CO 96/58: Petition of Chiefs of Cape Coast in Letter of Ross to Duke of Newcastle, Cape Coast, May 10, 1862, 1.

96. Albert A. Boahen, "Politics in Ghana," in *History of West Africa*, vol 1, ed. J. F. Ajayi and Michael Crowder (New York: Columbia University Press, 1972), 216.

97. Akin Mabogunje, "Overview of Research Priorities in Africa," *Urban Research in the Developing World* 2 (1994): 22.

## 2. EBUSUA AND ASAFO SYSTEMS

1. The *Asafo* and *Ebusua* systems have been integral to various Akan cultures and remain indispensable to the proper operation of the respective groups. The former, as an indigenous military system, provided protection in migrations from the Akan cradle to the different places of settlement with which they are currently identified. Over time, both have continued to evolve as entrenched institutions. The *Asafo* remains dynamic in its adaptations as Akan societies expand in population and territorial extent while borrowing other ideas and practices. Within the Cape Coast context, the *Akrampa, Abrofonkwa,* and *Amanfur Asafo* companies came into existence because of increasing contact with Europeans started the emergence of a new social unit of people who had European fathers on one hand and on the other hand captives brought into the country as artificers in the construction of fortifications. Correlatedly, the incidence of European influence, as in the choice of uniforms, flags, and even drums in these three *Asafo* companies, became more prevalent than in other groups that equally made changes to enhance their operations.

2. Other instructive works on this system among the Akan in general include R. S. Rattray, *Ashanti* (Oxford: Clarendon Press, 1923), 56–83; R. S. Rattray, *Ashanti Law and Constitution* (London: Oxford University Press, 1956), 34–51; R. S. Rattray, *Religion and Art in Ashanti* (London: Oxford University Press, 1959), 101–133; Melville J. Herskovits, "The Ashanti Ntoro: A Re-examination," *Journal of the Royal Anthropological Institute*

47 (1937): 102–137; M. Fortes, *Social Structure* (Oxford: Clarendon Press, 1949), 71–95; Meyer Fortes, "Kinship and Marriage among the Ashanti," in *African Systems of Marriage and Kinship*, ed. A. R. Radcliffe-Brown and Daryll Forde (London: International African Institute, 1950), 10–31; Eva L. Meyerowitz, "Concept of the Soul among the Akan of the Gold Coast," *Africa* 21, no. 1 (1950): 22–37; E. L. R. Meyerowitz, *The Sacred State of the Akan* (London: Faber and Faber, 1951), 20–48; J. B. Christensen, *Double Descent among the Fanti* (New Haven, CT: Human Relations Area Files, 1954), 3.

3. Kobinah Minnah, interviewed by author, digital voice recording, Cape Coast, Central Region, Ghana, June 12, 2009; Nana Amba Ayiabah, interviewed by author, digital voice recording, Cape Coast, Central Region, Ghana, June 13, 2009; Ebo Johnson, interviewed by author, digital voice recording, Cape Coast, Ghana, June 5, 2009; Kweku Botse, interviewed by author, digital voice recording, Cape Coast, Ghana, June 22, 2009; and Kobina Yallow, interviewed by author, digital voice recording, Cape Coast, Ghana, June 4, 2009.

4. *Akyeame* is the plural of the Akan word *Okyeame* or *Kyeame*; these words generally mean the official or recognized authoritative spokesperson of the group. For a detailed discussion of this position among the various Akan groups, see Kwesi Yankah, *Speaking for the Chief: Okyeame and the Politics of Akan Royal Oratory* (Bloomington: Indiana University Press, 1995).

5. Minnah, interview; Ayiabah, interview; Johnson, interview; Botse, interview; and Yallow, interview.

6. Other scholars who have also studied this system in part and in passing include Lystad, who refers to the local or town *Ebusua* as a lineage. See R. Lystad, *The Ashanti: A Proud People* (New Brunswick, NJ: Rutgers University Press, 1958), 55. Fortes, *Social Structure*, 71, refers to the *Ebusua* as a "localized matrilineage." See also E. L. R. Meyerowitz, *The Akan of Ghana* (London: Faber and Faber, 1958), 1; E. L. R. Meyerowitz, *Akan Traditions of Origin* (London: Faber and Faber, 1952), 5; E. L. R. Meyerowitz, *The Early History of the Akan States of Ghana* (London: Red Candle Press, 1970), 1; Kofi A. Busia, *The Position of a Chief in the Modern Political System of Ashanti* (London: Frank Cass, 1968), 20; Rattray, *Ashanti Law and Constitution*; Rattray, *Religion and Art in Ashanti*; and M. J. Field, *Akim-Kotoku: An Oman of the Gold Coast* (London: Crown Agents, 1948), 30. Field uses the term "clan." See also Christensen, *Double Descent*, 25.

7. The *Aberewatia*, given her longevity, was generally seen (and justifiably so) as the repository of knowledge regarding the genealogy of the family and, correlatedly, identity of all members of the *Ebusua*.

8. Minnah, interview; Ayiabah, interview; Johnson, interview; Botse, interview; and Yallow, interview.

9. Ibid.

10. Ibid.

11. Ibid. These constituted the core Akan *Ebusua* groups. However, scholars such as Christensen, *Double Descent*; John M. Sarbah, *Fanti Customary Laws* (London: Frank Cass, 1968), 10; J. B. Danquah, *Akan Society* (London: Bureau of Current Affairs, 1950), 1; and J. B. Danquah, *Gold Coast: Akan Laws and Customs* (London: Lutherworth Press, 1945), 9, all note that as a result of growth, expansion, and dispersal of the Akan to the various places where they are now found, there are at present a larger number of lineages. These use different names than the core groups and sometimes the same (or different) totems. Interestingly, aspects of these variations also appear in spellings, as in *Kwona, Kona, Konna*, and *Ekuona*; *Eburutu, Eburotu, Beretuo*, and *Bretuo*; *Yoko, Ayoko, Oyoko, Yokuo*, and *Yokoo*; and *Anona* and *Anana*. The totems for nearly all these variants remain the same.

12. According to Boahen, these enclaves included the Pra and Ofin confluence.

13. Minnah, interview; Ayiabah, interview; Johnson, interview; Botse, interview; and Yallow, interview.

14. *Amanhin* (plural) and *Omanhin* (singular) can refer to kings, chiefs, rulers, or leaders of the traditional state. *Aman* or *Oman* means the traditional state and *hin* refers to king, chief, ruler, or leader with subchiefs under his authority.

15. PRAAD Adm. 11/1/1634: Cape Coast Stool Enquiry, April 18, 1920. The military formation of the Akan remained similar. It consisted of scouts (*Akwansrafo*) and an advance guard (*Twafo/Tuafo*) with the main body (*Adontin*), the bodyguards of chiefs (*Gyase*), a rear guard (*Kyidom / Nkyidom*), the right (*Nifa*) and left (*Benkum*) wings following. In addition to political and military functions, these divisions had religious and judicial implications. In Cape Coast, for instance, the *Akomfodzi* took charge of religious rites (*Akomfo* were indigenous priests and priestesses). The *Akrampa*, who stood for peace (as the original Portuguese meaning indicates), had responsibility for judicial functions.

16. J. C. DeGraft Johnson, "The Fanti Asafu," *Africa* 5, no. 3 (1932): 308. See also Christensen, *Double Descent*, 118; and A. E. A. Asiamah, *The Mass Factor in Rural Politics: The Case of the Asafo Revolution in Kwahu Political History* (Accra, Ghana: Ghana Universities Press, 2000), 1.

17. Minnah, interview; Ayiabah, interview; Johnson, interview; Botse, interview; and Yallow, interview.

18. Ibid.

19. Ibid.

20. Jarle Simensen, "Rural Mass Action in the Context of Anti-colonial Protest: The Asafo Movement of Akim Abuakwa, Ghana," *Canadian Journal of African Studies* 7 (1974): 31.

21. Some indications of this view can be found in Akan proverbs such as *Ɛ-kaa nea o-nni nto-ma n-ko-aa nka yɛ gur Asafo a ye-nnwie da* (participation in *Asafo* activities or performing *Asafo* amounts to no excuse for the poor and irresponsible young man to fail to provide descent or full clothing for himself). Furthermore, *wɔ gur Asafo a wɔ kɔ fie* (when one performs *Asafo*, one must equally attend to the family at home) indicates that *Asafo* membership presents no excuse for negligence of domestic responsibilities.

22. PRAAD Adm. 11/1439. Case No. 43/1923: Petition from *Supi, Asafohinfo* and Elders of the *Bentsir* Company of Cape Coast to the Hon. Secretary of Native Affairs, January 23, 1928, 1.

23. Minnah, interview; Ayiabah, interview; Johnson, interview; Botse, interview; and Yallow, interview.

24. PRAAD Adm. 11/1/1473: A Guide to Cape Coast Company Emblems and Notes as to Meanings of Customs, 13–16.

25. PRAAD Adm. 11/1/1473: Petition of the *Supi, Asafohinfo* and Elders of the *Bentsir* Company to the Hon. Secretary of Native Affairs, January 23, 1928, 44–48.

26. Ibid.

27. PRAAD Adm. 11/1586: Gold Coast Telegraph from Hon. Commissioner of the Central Province to Hon. Colonial Secretary on the Subject, Fight at Cape Coast, February 27, 1915.

28. PRAAD Adm. 11/1/1473: A Guide to Cape Coast Company Emblems and Notes as to Meanings of Customs, 7–10.

29. Leaders of this company indicated that these emblems told all about their exploits in the past with other companies in Cape Coast as well as outside Cape Coast. They indicated fights won, as well as superiority resulting from the humiliation of other companies.

30. Minnah, interview; Ayiabah, interview; Johnson, interview; Botse, interview; and Yallow, interview.

31. PRAAD Adm. 11/1/1473: A Guide to Cape Coast Company Emblems and Notes as to Meanings of Customs, 8.

32. PRAAD SCT Vol. 5, Part 1: In the Matter of Land Acquired at Cape Coast for the Extension of African Hospital Grounds—Plan No. Z1649, 74–76.

33. PRAAD Adm. 11/1/1473: A Guide to Cape Coast Company Emblems and Notes as to Meanings of Customs, 9.

34. Their history compares to that of the occupants of the *A-la-ta* quarters of other coastal towns, such as Accra and Elmina. In southern Ghana, the word *A-la-ta-fo* referred to the people of Lagos, Nigeria, indicating a preponderance of men and women from Lagos among the workmen of the castle. The word *Alata* was a local corruption of the Yoruba expression *A-ra ne A-ta*, literally, "I buy and sell." The occurrence of the word *Alata* in southern Ghana speaks to the time-honored issue of migration across West Africa. With Nigeria quite close to Ghana, there was a trend of people from the former migrating to the latter—particularly the Yoruba, many of whom engaged in a great deal of petty trading or buying and selling. When their customers in southern Ghana complained about items being overly expensive, the Yoruba traders would retort in their language, *Ara ne Ata*. The people in southern Ghana corrupted that expression into *Alata* as a term of reference for them, which eventually came to be applied to Nigerians in general in Ghanaian parlance.

> According to E. J. P. Brown, the castle started as a Portuguese lodge in the early part of the seventeenth century, named Carbo Corso. The Dutch rebuilt it in about 1630, abandoned it, and in 1658, the Swedes rebuilt, fortified, and renamed it Carolusburg (Charles Town). It suffered a Dutch recapture in 1659, but the *Fetu* Kingdom besieged it and took over in 1660. The Swedes regained possession until 1663, when the king of *Fetu* surrendered the castle to the Dutch. In 1664, Admiral Sir Robert Holmes attacked Cape Coast and took it from the Dutch. See E. J. P. Brown, *Gold Coast and Ashanti Reader* (London: Frank Cass, 1929), 122–123.

35. Minnah, interview; Ayiabah, interview; Johnson, interview; Botse, interview; and Yallow, interview.

36. Ray A. Kea, *Settlements, Trade, and Politics in the Seventeenth-Century Gold Coast* (Baltimore: Johns Hopkins University Press, 1982), 41.

37. The name *Amanfur* derives from the Fanti expression *Aman fufur*: *Aman* (state or town) and *Fufur* (new). Therefore, *Amanfur* implies a new town, new community, or emerging social unit in the new part of town.

38. The crocodile is deemed sacred to most Ga-speaking people.

39. PRAAD Adm. 11/1/1634: Cape Coast Stool Enquiry, April 14, 1914, 14.

40. Minnah, interview; Ayiabah, interview; Johnson, interview; Botse, interview; and Yallow, interview.

41. In local parlance, these outlying towns and villages had other descriptions or references, such as *n-koa-dom*, "servile group of followers," or *ha-ban-asi-dom*, "rural or village groups/followers," equally emphasizing the farming occupation of these ones as a hinterland people. Minnah, interview; Ayiabah, interview; Johnson, interview; Botse, interview; and Yallow, interview.

42. *Tufohin* broken into its various Fanti word component becomes *Tu* (gun), *Fo* (people), and *hin* (king or chief). Significantly, every member of an *Asafo* company had the obligation to own a gun.

43. *Supifo* is the plural form while *Supi* is singular.

44. Minnah, interview; Ayiabah, interview; Johnson, interview; Botse, interview; and Yallow, interview.

45. The deep knowledge of the *Kyirema* in these matters made it possible for him to discern the precise times when spirits could be invoked. Minnah, interview; Ayiabah, interview; Johnson, interview; Botse, interview; and Yallow, interview.

46. George P. Hagan, "An Analytical Study of Fanti Kinship," *Research Review* 4, no. 1 (1967): 35–57.

47. George P. Hagan, "Aspects of Social Change among the Effutu" (PhD diss., Oxford University, Oxford, 1974), 15. See also George P. Hagan, *Divided We Stand: A Study of Social Change among the Effutu of Coastal Ghana* (Trondheim: Norwegian University of Science and Technology, 2000), 130.

48. Tensions and conflicts with respect to inheritance abated somewhat in the twenty-first century due to a variety of factors, including acquisition of formal education, internal family factors (especially the conduct and behavior of individuals), and government regulations put into place because indigenous arrangements had adversely affected generations of women in marriage situations. The PNDC intestate succession law is a typical instance of these kinds of interventions.

## 3. COASTAL COMMUNITIES, INTERGROUP WRANGLING, AND ASPECTS OF THE COLONIAL EXPERIENCE

1. M. N. Pearson, "Littoral Societies: The Concept and the Problems," *Journal of World History* 17, no. 4 (2006): 353. See also F. Braudel, *The Mediterranean and the Mediterranean World: The Age of Philip II* (New York: Harper Collins, 1992), 111.

2. Alfred W. Crosby, *The Columbian Exchange: Biological and Cultural Consequences of 1492* (Westport: Greenwood Press, 1972); William Beinart, "African History and Environmental History," *African Affairs* 99, no. 395 (2000): 269.

3. L. Febvre, *A Geographical Introduction to History* (London: Paul, Trench, Trubner, 1925), 137.

4. Emmanuel K. Akyeampong, *Between the Sea and the Lagoon: An Eco-social History of the Anlo of Southern Ghana, c. 1850 to Recent Times* (Oxford: James Currey, 2001), 12. Akyeampong, however, cites a couple of exceptions: see 12, fn. 26.

5. B. Klein and G. Mackenthun, "Sea Changes: Historicizing the Ocean," *Journal of World History* 16 (2005): 102. See also David W. Cohen and E. S. Atieno Odhiambo, *Siaya: The Historical Anthropology of an African Landscape* (London: James Currey, 1989), 114–115.

6. Nana Afarfohin, interviewed by author, digital voice recording, Cape Coast, Central Region, Ghana, July 4, 2009.

7. Ibid.

8. The Anlo of Keta and its immediate environs, including Kedzi and Vodza, might cringe at the claim of the sea's beneficence in this context given the experience of persistent coastal erosion. Akyeampong's book, *Between the Sea and the Lagoon*, 15, reveals how on two fronts—flooding on the lagoon side and coastal erosion on the seaside—the Anlo were threatened. Many thoughtful Anlo wondered whether their intrusive inscriptions on the natural world had resulted in this ecological imbalance.

9. Ibid.

10. With the growth and expansion of the town, this center of operation would eventually include Ola.

11. William Bosman, *A New and Accurate Description of the Coast of Guinea: Divided into the Gold, the Slave, and the Ivory Coasts* (London: Frank Cass, 1967), 47.

12. Ibid.

13. Akyeampong, *Between the Sea and the Lagoon*, 8.

14. Local salt harvesting, which is still done in most fishing communities along coastal Ghana, involves the making of several shallow, square dams in an area of land close to the shore. During high tides, these dams flood with seawater; on recession of the tide, when the trapped seawater evaporates with time, the people harvest the salt crystals in baskets and bags.

15. E. L. R. Meyerowitz, *The Early History of the Akan States of Ghana* (London: Red Candle Press, 1970), 71–72.

16. Adam Jones, *German Sources for West African History 1599–1669* (Wiesbaden: Franz Steiner Verlag, 1983), 231–232. See also Bosman, *A New and Accurate Description of the Coast of Guinea*, 38, 48.

17. A. P. Brown, *The Fishes and Fisheries of the Gold Coast* (London: Crown Agents for the Colonies, 1930), 23. The Ga settled east of the Fanti enclaves, which had settlements in the western section of the southern Gold Coast.

18. J. M. Grove and A. M. Johansen, "The Historical Geography of the Volta Delta, Ghana, During the Period of Danish Influence," *Bulletin de l'Institut Fondamental d'Afrique Noire* 30, no. 4 (1968): 1388.

19. Ibid.

20. J. Barbot, *A Description of the Coasts of North and South Guinea* (London: Frank Cass, 1723), 149–150, 256, 266. See also Christian C. Reindorf, *History of Gold Coast and Asante: Based on Traditions and Historical Facts Comprising More Than Three Centuries from about 1500 to 1860* (Basel: Basel Mission Book Depot, 1951), 37.

21. Rebecca Shumway, *The Fante and the Slave Trade* (Rochester, NY: University of Rochester Press, 2011), 34.

22. The *wawa* tree, botanically referred to as Triplochiton Scleroxylon of the Malaceae family, is largely found in West Africa.

23. Kevin Dawson, *Undercurrents of Power: Aquatic Culture in the African Diaspora* (Philadelphia: University of Pennsylvania Press, 2018), 102.

24. Great Britain Hydrographic Office, *Africa Pilots* (London: 1893), Vol. 2, 35, 42, 142, 181, 208, notably 36 and 37. See also W. E. F. Ward, *My Africa* (Accra, Ghana: Ghana Universities Press, 1991), 112.

25. Pieter De Marees, *Description and Historical Account of the Gold Kingdom of Guinea* (Oxford: Oxford University Press, 1987), 119.

26. Afarfohin, interview.

27. Ibid.

28. In early attempts at writing or documenting their knowledge about Africa, European travelers, sailors, correspondents under the auspices of learned societies, trading companies, missionary societies, colonial officials, colonial government anthropologists, wives of colonial officials, and biographers of early European explorers gave interesting and amateurish accounts of the different genres of music and song across the continent. A typical example is the account of Clapperton, which Lander describes in his work, *Records of Captain Clapperton's Last Expedition to Africa* (London: 1830), 292–296.

Clapperton said the following:

On the morning of Thursday, the 12th, we left Chiadoo, followed by the Chief and an immense crowd of both sexes, among whom were hundreds of children, the ladies enlivening us with songs at intervals, and the men blowing on horns and beating gongs and drums, without any regard to time, forming altogether a most barbarous concert of vocal and instrumental music, which continued to our great inconvenience and annoyance till we arrived at Matone, when they took leave of us and returned ... Yet even on these instruments they perform most vilely, and produce a horribly discordant noise, which may, perhaps, be delightful to their own ears; but to the strangers, if they have the misfortune to be too near the performers, no sounds can be harsher and more disagreeable than such a concert.

29. Although *nkoba* under normal circumstances refers to a fishing hook in the Fanti dialect, its heavy repetition in the context of this song is for onomatopoeic effect, especially in conjunction with other sounds that combine the long "o," "e," and "i," as in *oooo* as well as *eeiii*.

30. Emile Vercruijsse, "Fishmongers, Big Dealers, and Fishermen: Cooperation and Conflict between the Sexes in Ghanaian Canoe Fishing," in *Female and Male in West Africa*, ed. Christine Oppong (London: George Allen and Unwin, 1983), 188.

31. Ibid.

32. Jones, *German Sources for West African History*, 231–232. See also Bosman, *A New and Accurate Description of the Coast of Guinea*, 38, and 48.

33. P. E. Perez-Mallaina, *Spain's Men of the Sea: Daily Life on the Indies Fleets in the Sixteenth Century* (Baltimore: Johns Hopkins University Press, 1998), 224.

34. Ibid.

35. Marcus Rediker, *Between the Devil and the Deep Blue Sea: Merchant Seamen, Pirates, and the Anglo-American Maritime World, 1700–1750* (Cambridge: Cambridge University Press, 1987), 2.

36. Knut Weibust, *Deep Sea Sailors: A Study in Maritime Ethnology* (Stockholm, Sweden: V. Petterson, 1969), 453. Indeed, Perez-Mallaina, quoting Rediker, explains that this propensity toward conflict and resistance has an interesting proof in the English language. The word "strike," which now means a cessation of work, has maritime origins: it once meant to take down a sail. Its meaning to designate cessation of work gained currency from 1768 onward, when English sailors frequently immobilized

merchant ships by taking down the sails. See Perez-Mallaina, *Spain's Men of the Sea*, 453–454.

37. Gold Coast 1926A: The Gold Coast: A Review of the Events of 1924–1926 and the Prospects of 1926–1927, 111. See also Dominic Fortescue, "The Accra Crowd, the Asafo, and Opposition to the Municipal Corporations Ordinance, 1924–1925," *Canadian Journal of African Studies* 24, no. 3 (1990): 357.

38. Gold Coast 1926A: The Gold Coast: A Review of the Events of 1924–1926 and the Prospects of 1926–1927, 112.

39. Gold Coast 1926B: Report on the Objection Lodged with the Colonial Secretary against the Application of the Municipal Corporations Ordinance, 1924, to the Town of Accra, with Enclosures Including Minutes of Evidence, Session Papers, No. 1, 1925–1926, 17.

40. Gold Coast 1926B: Report on the Objection Lodged with the Colonial Secretary against the Application of Municipal Corporations Ordinance, March 1924, 12–14.

41. Great Britain: Command Paper 1103–9, 1921. Gold Coast Report for 1919, 60–63.

42. Gold Coast 1926B: Report on the Objection Lodged with the Colonial Secretary against the Application of Municipal Corporations Ordinance, 1924.

43. Gold Coast 1922: Municipal Annual Reports for the Year 1921, 25–26.

44. Gold Coast 1926C: Report on the Enquiry held by the Honorable C. W. Welman, Secretary for Native Affairs on a Commission by His Excellency the Governor issued under the Commissions of Enquiry Ordinance and dated February 26, 1925, Session Paper, No. 10, 1925–1926, 41–42.

45. Ga *Mantsɛ* in a sense means landlord or landowner, the equivalent of *Omanhin* of the Ga people of Accra.

46. See also PRO CO 96/665/10: Petition to King George V from the *Asafoi* of Accra, May 9, 1925, 14.

47. Gold Coast 1926B: Report on the Objection Lodged with the Colonial Secretary against the Application of the Municipal Corporations Ordinance, 1924, 15.

48. Gold Coast 1923C: Report by the Town Councils' Committee on the Constitution and Working of Existing Town Councils of the Colony, Session Paper, No. 17, 1922–1923, 20.

49. Ibid., 21.

50. Ibid., 23.

51. PRO CO 96/665/10: Petition to King George from the *Asafoi* of Accra, April 30, 1926.

52. Gold Coast 1926B: Report on the Objection Lodged with the Colonial Secretary against the Application of the Municipal Corporations Ordinance, 1924, 34.

53. Ibid., 35.

54. PRO CO 96/654/18836: Memorandum by the Secretary of Native Affairs (SNA), April 4, 1925.

55. PRO CO 96/655/32858: Inspector General of Police versus *Asafoatse* Djator and Others. Record of Proceedings in the Supreme Court of the Gold Coast Colony, Eastern Province, June 27, 1925, 5.

56. PRO CO 96/654/18836: Memorandum by the Secretary for Native Affairs (SNA), April 4, 1925, 10.

57. Gold Coast 1926B: Report on the Objection lodged with the Colonial Secretary against the Application of the Municipal Corporations Ordinance, 1924.

58. For Guggisberg, being compelled to shelve one of his most important schemes was "the only real disappointment" of his tenure as governor. R. E. Wraith, *Guggisberg* (London: Oxford University Press, 1967), 212.

59. See chapter 2 for a detailed discussion of the Cape Coast *Asafo* system.

60. PRAAD Adm. 11/1/1473: The Voluntary Surrender of Objectionable Flags and Emblems by Cape Coast Companies: Opening Address by Hon. Commissioner of the Central Province, 1–9.

61. Ibid., 1.

62. E. B. Ellis, *The Tshi-Speaking People of the Gold Coast of West Africa: Their Religion, Manners, Customs, Laws, Language, Etc.* (Oosterhout, The Netherlands: Anthropological, 1966), 275.

63. PRAAD Adm. 11/1/1473: The Voluntary Surrender of Objectionable Flags and Emblems by Cape Coast Companies: Opening Address by Hon. Commissioner of the Central Province, 9.

64. Ibid., 5.

65. PRAAD Adm. 11/1/1473: A Guide to Cape Coast Company Emblems and Notes as to Meanings of Customs, 12.

66. Esi Sutherland-Addy, "Discourse and Asafo: The Place of Oral Literature," *Transactions of the Historical Society of Ghana* 2 (1998): 87.

67. PRAAD Adm. 11/1/1473: A Guide to Cape Coast Company Emblems and Notes as to Meanings of Customs, 13.

68. PRAAD Adm. 11/1/1473: The Voluntary Surrender of Objectionable Flags and Emblems by Cape Coast Companies: Opening Address by Hon. Commissioner of the Central Province, 5.

69. PRAAD Adm. 11/1439 Case No. 11/1931: Letter of Acting Secretary of Native Affairs to Hon. Colonial Secretary, January 17, 1931, 20.

70. PRAAD Adm. 11/1/1473: Letter of Sub-assistant Commissioner of Police, Police Office, Cape Coast, to the District Commissioner, Cape Coast, October 4, 1904, 5.

71. Ibid., 9.

72. Ibid., 12.

73. Ibid., 14.

74. PRAAD Adm. 11/1/1473: Letter of Aborigines Rights Protection Society, Cape Coast, to the Hon. Colonial, Accra, October 1904, 5.

75. PRAAD Adm. 11/1/1473: Letter of Sub-assistant Commissioner of Police, Police Office, Cape Coast, to the District Commissioner, Cape Coast, October 4, 1904.

76. Emmanuel K. Akyeampong, *Drink, Power, and Cultural Change: A Social History of Alcohol in Ghana, c. 1800 to Recent Times* (Oxford: James Currey, 1996), xxi, and 8.

77. Reindorf, *History of Gold Coast and Asante*, 122.

78. PRAAD Adm. 11/1/1473: Confidential Letter from District Commissioner, Cape Coast Castle, to Hon. Commissioner of the Central Province, Cape Coast, December 12, 1905, 4–5. See also Kwaku Nti, "The Role of Alcohol in the 1905 Conflict between the Anaafo and Ntsin Companies of Cape Coast," *Transactions of the Historical Society of Ghana* 2 (1998): 53.

79. PRAAD Adm. 11/1/1473: Opening Address by the Hon. Commissioner of the Central Province, March 6, 1909, 5.

80. PRAAD Adm. 11/1/1473: Confidential Letter from District Commissioner, Cape Coast Castle, to Hon. Commissioner of the Central Province, Cape Coast, December 12, 1905, 2.

81. Ibid., 9.

82. Ibid., 10.

83. PRAAD Adm. 11/1/1473: Confidential Letter from District Commissioner, Cape Coast, to Hon. Commissioner of the Central Province, August 4, 1908, 3.

84. PRAAD Adm. 11/1/1473: Opening Address by the Hon. Commissioner of the Central Province, March 6, 1909, 5.

85. Ibid., 6.

86. See Sutherland-Addy, "Speaking War and Peace," paper presented at the Asafo History Program Workshop 1997 at the Institute of African Studies, University of Ghana, Legon, December 17–18, 1997. See also David Kimble, *A Political History of Ghana: The Rise of Gold Coast Nationalism*

*1850–1928* (London: Oxford University Press, 1963), 228. He writes, for instance, that "while the siege of Elmina was quietly proceeding, some of the beleaguered townsmen counter-attacked an outlying Cape Coast village, killed and captured several inhabitants. This was a signal for the men of Cape Coast, led by their Headman, Quassie Attah, to take up arms despite the strict instructions and threats they received. Horton tells how they 'flew to arms and marched into the field, amidst the hurrahs of their women and children.'

> Ussher described them as 'incited by their women,
> ever the instigators of mischief here'" (CO 96/76:
> Confidential Dispatch No. 32 of April 6, 1868, 9.
> Kimble, *A Political History of Ghana*, 228).

87. PRAAD Adm. 11/1/1473: Letter of District Commissioner, Cape Coast, to the Hon. Commissioner of the Central Province, October 3, 1904, 2.

88. PRAAD Adm. 11/1/1473: Letter of District Commissioner, Cape Coast, to the Hon. Commissioner of the Central Province, December 11, 1905, 1.

89. Akyeampong, *Drink, Power, and Cultural Change*, 24.

90. Ibid. See also Adam Jones, "'My Arse for Akou': A Wartime Ritual of Women in the Nineteenth Century Gold Coast," *Cahiers d'Etudes Africaines* 132 (1992): 545; Ellis, *The Tshi-Speaking People of the Gold Coast of West Africa*, 226; E. E. Obeng, *Ancient Ashanti Chieftaincy* (Tema: Ghana Publishing, 1986), 20.

91. Sutherland-Addy, "Speaking War and Peace," 21–22.

## 4. ART, SYMBOL, AND THE WRITTEN WORD

1. These statements normally come up in discussions of the "it takes a village" concept. The second statement is popularly attributed to societies in South Africa, which locally say *U-mun-tu N-gu- mun-tu N-ga-ban-tu*.

2. Kobinah Minnah, interviewed by author, digital voice recording, Cape Coast, Central Region, Ghana, June 12, 2009; Nana Amba Ayiabah, interviewed by author, digital voice recording, Cape Coast, Central Region, Ghana, June 13, 2009; Ebo Johnson, interviewed by author, digital voice recording, Cape Coast, Ghana, June 5, 2009; Kweku Botse, interviewed by author, digital voice recording, Cape Coast, Ghana, June 22, 2009; and Kobina Yallow, interviewed by author, digital voice recording, Cape Coast, Ghana, June 4, 2009.

3. Ibid.

4. The *Adinkra* symbols that originated among various Akan groups expressed indigenous philosophical thoughts and concepts. Although the symbols were mainly used within the Akan textile industry, with time they gained general use in areas from architecture to jewelry designs to property decorations and identification.

5. Nana Afarfohin, interviewed by author, digital voice recording, Cape Coast, Central Region, Ghana, July 4, 2009.

6. F. L. Bartels, "Education in the Gold Coast," *African Affairs* 48, no. 193 (October 1949): 304. The Portuguese builders named it Castelo de Sao Jorge da Mina.

7. These included *Elemente des Akuapim Dialects de Odshi Sprache* (1853) and *Grammatical Outline and Vocabulary of Oji Language with Special Reference to the Akuapem Dialect, Together with a Collection of Proverbs by the Natives* (1854).

8. Christaller argued that *Akuapem* as an Akan dialect reflected an inherent similitude with Fanti and steered the middle course between other Akan dialects in phonetics, structure, and expression. It easily reflected the peculiarities of both strands insofar as they rarely conflicted with each other "and therefore [was] the best capable of being enriched from both sides" (Ofosu Appiah in *Dictionary of African Christian Biographies*, or DACB). David Asante concurred with this assertion and observed that *Akuapem* easily admitted enrichment and admixture. Fanti was equally capable of that feat, but *Akyem* did not work well with that kind of interface.

9. According to Ofosu Appiah, Christaller did not think much of the Mfantsi grammar that D. L. Carr and J. P. Brown put together and published in Cape Coast. He was critical of the authors for making the Fanti they wrote mimic the principles of English orthography, which he vehemently rejected as being unsuitable for the Akan dialects. Based on this criticism, J. P. Brown produced another, much better edition.

10. Between 1859 and 1866, Christaller translated the following books into Twi: The Acts of the Apostles, the four Gospels, and the Epistles, such as Romans, Peter I and II, James, Jude, John I, II, and III, Corinthians I and II, Galatians, Ephesians, Philippians, Colossians, Thessalonians I and II, Timothy I and II, Titus, Philemon, Hebrews, and Revelations.

11. In the late 1870s, the Basel Mission had a book and tract depository at Christiansborg Middle School. They equally established a printing press in Akropong and a book and Bible depot in Accra that sold literature in

Twi, Ga, and English. Similarly, the Wesleyan Methodist Mission in 1882 opened a bookstore and printing press, with their first Fanti publication appearing in 1885.

12. Stephanie Newell, *Literary Culture in Colonial Ghana: How to Play the Game* (Bloomington: Indiana University Press, 2002), 206.

13. It is imperative to note the element or dynamic of continuity and change in these discussions. Ethnographic statements about material objects predate the contemporary era, as do Christianity and Islam in these parts of the country. These ethnographic expressions, time-honored assertions about property ownership evoking faith in traditional religions, Christianity, and Islam, still pertain in the contemporary times—albeit more fanciful, catchy, and increasingly featuring popular global words, phrases, and statements than in the past, when the practice of etching inscriptions on property started.

14. Afarfohin, interview.

15. Pidgin English, in other contexts referred to as broken English, became the kind of English used in West Africa, largely in British colonies, among people who did not possess a strong command of standard English, or the Queen's English. It had its own grammar, sentence structure, and local infusions, as with the Creole language that developed elsewhere. The popularity of pidgin English grew with the incidence of its being spoken among students, even including well-educated people quite proficient in the English language.

16. Albert A. Boahen, *Topics in West African History* (London: Longman, 1966), 11. See also Nehemia Levtzion, *Islam in West Africa: Religion, Society, and Politics to 1800* (New York: Routledge, 1994).

17. The Fanti rendition of *ɛsramufuɔ* is *ɛ-sar-mu-fo*.

18. The most intriguing history of the infiltration of Islam into the Asante Kingdom hinges on one of its kings or *Asantehene*, Kwame Karikari, who became a practicing Muslim and suffered destoolment (or removal) from that high office. In the estimation of the kingmakers as well as elders, Islam remained so foreign that a practicing golden stool occupant was not only opprobrious but also antithetical to the upholding of the traditional religion, indispensable to the sanctity of the throne and veneration of the ancestors. However, the Asante still found it expedient to seek and use the services of Islamic religious medicine men, or marabouts, whose skill in the making of magical talismans, charms, and amulets for protection in warfare became indispensable to the *Nsu-man-kwa* division of the kingdom.

## 5. "HƐN-ARA HƐN A-SAA-SE NYI"

1. *Hɛnara Hɛn Asaase Nyi* (Fanti), alternatively, *Yɛn Ara Yɛn Asaase Ni* (Twi), was a loaded Akan expression that accentuated right of land ownership based on several factors, including historical and cultural underpinnings. See Robert Addo-Fenning, *Akyem Abuakwa 1700–1943: From Ofori Panin to Sir Ofori Atta* (Trondheim: Norwegian University of Science and Technology, 1997), 143. Queen-mother, also in Akan parlance *Ohe-maa*, and *Oman Baa-tan*, was a female ultimate high position, as can be deduced from the term, within the indigenous political systems of various Akan groups. The term implies that queens served as mother figures for their respective societies. In these cultures, queens were not wives of kings and chiefs. They could variously be grandmothers, biological mothers, aunts, sisters, or cousins of the kings and chiefs given the matrilineal system of inheritance (one of the major, definitive practices of all the Akan groups).

2. Catherine Coquery-Vidrovitch, "The Process of Urbanization," *African Studies Review* 34 (1991): 1. See also Sara Berry, *Chiefs Know Their Boundaries: Essays on Property, Power, and the Past in Asante, 1896–1996* (Oxford: James Currey, 2001); Sara Berry, *No Condition Is Permanent: The Social Dynamics of Agrarian Change in Sub-Saharan Africa* (Madison: University of Wisconsin Press, 1993).

3. S. Hymer, *The Political Economy of the Gold Coast and Ghana* (New Haven, CT: Yale University, 1969), 4.

4. PRO CO 96/12/3: Statement by Joseph Chamberlain, Secretary of State for the Colonies, at the House of Commons, August 22, 1895, 1.

5. Hymer, *The Political Economy of the Gold Coast and Ghana*, 4.

6. Kwame Arhin, *The Cape Coast and Elmina Handbook: Past, Present and Future* (Legon: University of Ghana, 1995), 1.

7. Hymer, *The Political Economy of the Gold Coast and Ghana*, 4.

8. Eric Berg, "Backward-Sloping Labor Supply Functions in Dual Economies: The African Case," *Quarterly Journal of Economics* 15, no. 4 (1961): 468. But it could be argued that it barely, in fact, took strong measures to increase the labor supply in southern Ghana, as was the case in other African colonies.

9. PRAAD Adm. 12/2/59: Precise of Information Concerning the Colony of the Gold Coast and Ashanti, 1904, 1–2.

10. PRAAD Adm. 12/3/57: Report of the Transport Department, 1901, 20.

11. Hymer, *The Political Economy of the Gold Coast and Ghana*, 10.

12. PRO CO 96/121: Letter of Governor Freeling to Lord Carnarvon, May 29, 1877, 2.

13. Hymer, *The Political Economy of the Gold Coast and Ghana*, 10.

14. David Kimble, *A Political History of Ghana: The Rise of Gold Coast Nationalism, 1850–1928* (London: Oxford University Press, 1963), 342.

15. Hymer, *The Political Economy of the Gold Coast and Ghana*, 11.

16. PRO CO 96/121: Letter of Lord Carnarvon to Governor S. Freeling, April 21, 1877, 3.

17. PRO CO 96/121: Letter of Governor Freeling to Lord Carnarvon, May 29, 1877, 9.

18. Ibid.

19. PRO CO 96/267: Letter of J. H. Brew to the Marquis of Ripon, London, March 22, 1895, 3.

20. Ibid., 4.

21. Ibid., 5.

22. Editorial, "Gold Coast Lands and the Crown Lands Ordinance," *Gold Coast Methodist Times*, February 1895.

23. Editorial, "This Is Our Land," *Gold Coast Chronicle*, March 1895; Editorial, "Gold Coast Lands and the Crown Lands Ordinance."

24. PRO CO 96/257: Petition from the King, Chiefs, Headmen, and Counselors of Abura to Governor Maxwell, February 23, 1895, enclosed in Dispatch No. 196, from Governor Maxwell to Ripon, May 11, 1895, 5.

25. PRO CO 96/257: Letter of Governor Maxwell to Ripon, May 9, 1895, 2.

26. Ibid., 4.

27. PRO CO 96/54/12: Gold Coast Government Gazette (Extraordinary), March 10, 1897, no. 4, 45.

28. Editorial, "This Is Our Land"; Editorial, "Gold Coast Lands and the Crown Lands Ordinance."

29. C. J. Bannerman, Legislative Council Debates, Accra, June 29, 1897, 498.

30. Governor Maxwell, Legislative Council Debates, Accra, June 29, 1897, 500.

31. Ibid., 501.

32. Editorial, "ARPS Mission Statement," *Gold Coast Express*, April 22, 1897; Editorial, "It Has Come to Stay," *Gold Coast Independent*, May 1, 1897.

33. Palavers in this context constituted formal meetings arranged between kings, queens, chiefs, headmen, and other representatives of the

indigenous political order and the colonial government to discuss matters of governance, government policy, etcetera. At some of these meetings, treaties, agreements, disagreements, conflicts, and other issues of mutual interest formed part of the discussions. The term "palaver" eventually came to refer to individual items or issues for discussion, as in a matter or case to be dealt with.

34. Editorial, "ARPS Mission Statement"; Editorial, "It Has Come to Stay."

35. PRO CO 96/294: Letter of Governor Conran to the Secretary of State for Colonies, August 15, 1867, 1. Governor Edward Conran, concerned about the growing influence of the intellectuals, referred to them as "so-called scholars (those 'natives' who can read and write) and petty 'native' lawyers who cling like leeches to the skirts of their ignorant Kings and Chiefs."

36. PRO CO 96/296: Letter of Sir William Blackhall to the Secretary of State for Colonies, October 20, 1897, 4.

37. See also Roger Gocking, "The Historic Akoto: A Social History of Cape Coast, Ghana, 1848–1948" (PhD diss., Stanford University, California, 1981), 102.

38. At least in Accra and Akim Abuakwa, there were instances where the two groups had mutual suspicions and pursued different agendas.

39. Kimble, *A Political History of Ghana*, 345.

40. Ibid., 346.

41. PRO CO 96/295: Dispatch from Governor Maxwell to Lord Chamberlain, July 1, 1897, 3.

42. PRO CO 96/292: Dispatch No. 169 from Governor Maxwell to Chamberlain, May 4, 1897, 5.

43. Kimble, *A Political History of Ghana*, 347.

44. Strayer indicates that European racism affected the educated elite, whose aspirations most clearly threatened the racial divide. Europeans remained exceedingly reluctant to allow even the most highly educated Asian and Africans to enter the higher ranks of colonial service. See Robert W. Strayer, *Ways of the World: A Brief Global History with Sources*, vol. 2, *Since 1500* (New York: Bedford/St. Martin's, 2011), 931.

45. Editorial, "We Won't Cooperate," *Gold Coast Methodist Times*, July 31, 1897.

46. Ibid.

47. Ibid.

48. John M. Sarbah, *Fanti Customary Laws* (London: Frank Cass, 1968), 120.

49. "Mulatto" as a term generally referred to people of mixed parentage, mainly African and European parents from all kinds of relationships.

50. Sarbah, *Fanti Customary Laws*, 123.

51. Editorial, "The Land Question," *Gold Coast Methodist Times*, July 20, 1897.

52. Kimble, *A Political History of Ghana*, 344. Mensah Sarbah wanted every individual in southern Ghana to be educated in the "correct and true knowledge of the constitutional history of his dear native land." He was one of the few in the first generation of scholars to make efforts in that direction. Eventually, he wrote two books dealing with the history, custom, practice, and usage of the Fanti and Akan peoples of the Gold Coast.

53. PRO CO 96/306: Telegram from Fanti Kings, Chiefs, Etc., to Queen Victoria and the Colonial Office, December 13, 1897, 1.

54. Ibid.

55. PRO CO 96/310: Report of the Proceedings of the Deputation, 1898, 115.

56. Ibid.

57. Ibid.

## 6. THE POLITICS OF MODERNIZATION AND CLASH OF OFFICIAL AND INDIGENOUS INTERESTS

1. Informal colonialism started discreetly with the Europeans, especially the British, establishing themselves on the southern Ghana coast (previously referred to as the Gold Coast). It became more or less formalized with the dubious Bond of 1844 that parties variously interpreted, the British on the one hand and local chiefs on the other. Formal colonialism took effect from the period of European scramble and partition of Africa sanctioned by the Berlin Act of 1885 at the Berlin Conference of November 15, 1884–January 30, 1885.

2. PRO CO 96/3/1: Dispatch No. 94, Letters of Connor to Sir G. Grey, December 8, 1864, 1. *Omanhin* literally means "king of the land." *Amanhin* is the plural form of *Omanhin*.

3. PRO CO 96/28/1: Dispatch No. 72, Cruickshank to Newcastle, September 7, 1853, 8.

4. Ibid., 9.

5. PRO CO 96/31: Letter of Connor to George Grey, Cape Coast Castle, February 2, 1856, 10.

6. PRO CO 96/94: Preamble to the Fanti Confederation Scheme of 1872, 5–8. See also Cardwell, Parliamentary Debates, House of Commons, May 20, 1864, 121; J. A. B. Horton, *Letters on the Political Condition of the Gold Coast* (London: Frank Cass, 1970), 20.

7. PRO CO 96/94: Report of the Select Committee on Africa (Western Coast): Evidence of Ord in Reply to Question 932, 112.

8. Editorial, "The Governor and the Chiefs," *African Times*, December 23, 1864. See also PRO CO 96/95: Petition of October 25, 1864, from Chiefs, Headmen and Other Inhabitants of Cape Coast to the Governor.

9. PRO CO 96/94: Report of the Select Committee on Africa (Western Coast): Evidence of Ord in Reply to Question 932, 113.

10. Though referred to in colonial records as "John Aggery," his indigenous name was Nana Egyir. Apparently, the Aggery spelling is a corruption or anglicization of Egyir. A careful pronunciation of the anglicized Aggery will still sound as the indigenous name Egyir. Unfortunately, Aggery in subsequent records and in contemporary times has been misspelled and pronounced Aggrey (Ah-gray).

11. As a young man, *Omanhin* Aggery took pride in the achievements of his ancestors. Throughout his tenure as king and in all situations, Aggery proved himself committed to the protection and independence of Cape Coast. His resolve firmed up after swearing an oath that, among other things, enjoined him to do everything—even to his peril—to maintain ancestral standards, add to them, and protect his people.

12. S. J. S. Cookey, *King Jaja of the Niger Delta: His Life and Times, 1821–1891* (New York: Nok Publishers, 1974). See also David Kimble, *A Political History of Ghana: The Rise of Gold Coast Nationalism, 1850–1928* (London: Oxford University Press, 1963), particularly chapter 5, 192.

13. PRO CO 96/74: Unsigned Petition from Aggery to Carnarvon, Enclosed in Dispatch No. 66, January 23, 1867, to Blackhall, 6.

14. G. E. Metcalfe, *Great Britain and Ghana: Documents of Ghana History 1807–1957* (London: Ipswich Book, 1964), 305.

15. Ibid.

16. Ibid., 307.

17. PRO CO 96/72: Petition of King Aggery, Cape Coast, to Governor Colonel Conran, September 1866, 5.

18. PRO CO 96/70: Letter of Colonel Conran to Cardwell, Cape Coast, January 11, 1866.

19. PRO CO 96/72: Petition of King Aggery, Cape Coast, September 1866, Enclosed in Blackall to Carnarvon, Sierra Leone, October 17, 1866, 4.

20. Metcalfe, *Great Britain and Ghana*, 308.

21. PRO CO 96/67: Letter of W. C. Finlason, Cape Coast, to Acting Colonial Secretary, March 11, 1865, 6.

22. PRO CO 96/67: Letter of R. Pine, Cape Coast, to *Omanhin* Aggery, March 14, 1865, 1.

23. PRO CO 96/67: Letter of *Omanhin* Aggery, Cape Coast, to Governor R. Pine, March 13, 1865, 1. In his words, "the compact, understanding, spirit, and usages spoken of, are left still so undefined and in the dark, that I'm no wiser today than I was yesterday... I trust Your Excellency is not unprepared to set bounds to my jurisdiction as King and point out where I should go and where I should not go."

24. Ibid., 6.

25. William H. Gillespie, *The Gold Coast Police 1844–1938* (Accra, Ghana: Government Printer, 1955), 2.

26. PRO CO 96/41: Letter of Freeman to R. Pine, Cape Coast, June 25, 1857, 4.

27. Gillespie, *The Gold Coast Police*, 9.

28. Ibid., 13.

29. Ibid., 14.

30. PRO CO 96/67: Letter of *Omanhin* Aggery, Cape Coast, to Governor R. Pine, March 13, 1865.

31. PRO CO 96/67: *Executive Council Minutes* of March 15, 1865, 212.

32. Ibid., 216.

33. PRO CO 96/68: Letter of *Omanhin* Aggery, Cape Coast, to Governor Colonel Conran, Enclosed in Dispatch No. 123, October 23, 1865, to Cardwell, 2.

34. PRO CO 96/67: *Executive Council Minutes* of October 16, 1865, 221.

35. PRO CO 96/41: Letter of Freeman to R. Pine, Cape Coast, June 25, 1857, 2.

36. PRO CO 96/71: Dispatch No. 1, from Blackall to Cardwell, April 19, 1866, 5.

37. PRO CO 96/68: Letter of *Omanhin* Aggery, Cape Coast, to Governor Colonel Conran, Enclosed in Dispatch No. 123, October 23, 1865, 6.

38. PRO CO 96/71: Dispatch No. 1, from Blackall to Cardwell, April 19, 1866, 5.

39. Ibid.

40. PRO CO 96/72: Letter of Chiefs Cudjoe Ayee, Cofie Atta, and Others, Cape Coast, August 8, 1866, 1.

41. PRO CO 96/72: Letter of *Omanhin* Aggery, Cape Coast, to Hamilton, August 9, 1866, 3.

42. PRO CO 96/74: Letter from Colonial Secretary to *Omanhin* Aggery, Enclosed in Dispatch No. 2, from Blackall to Carnarvon, January 15, 1866, 4.

43. PRO CO 96/72: Letter of *Omanhin* Aggery, Cape Coast, to Governor Colonel Conran, Enclosed in Dispatch No. 109, to Blackall, December 7, 1866, 2.

44. PRO CO 96/74: Address by Governor Colonel Conran, Cape Coast, December 10, 1866, enclosed in Dispatch No. 112, to Blackall, December 31, 1866, 1.

45. Metcalfe, *Great Britain and Ghana*, 365.

46. PRO CO 96/202: Petition of Principal Inhabitants of Cape Coast to the Secretary of State, June 5, 1889, enclosed in Dispatch No. 180, from Brandford Griffith to Knutsford, June 18, 1889, 2.

47. Ibid.

48. C. A. Gordon, *Life on the Gold Coast* (London: Bailliere, Tindall, and Cox, 1874), 4.

49. Brodie Cruickshank, *Eighteen Years on the Gold Coast of Africa: Including an Account of the Native Tribes and their Intercourse with Europeans* (London: Frank Cass, 1966), 23.

50. J. E. Casely Hayford, *Gold Coast Native Institutions* (London: Frank Cass, 1970), 109.

51. PRO CO 96/202: Petition of Principal Inhabitants of Cape Coast to the Secretary of State, June 5, 1889, Enclosed in Dispatch No. 180, from Brandford Griffith to Knutsford, June 18, 1889, 8.

52. Casely Hayford, *Gold Coast Native Institutions*, 111.

53. W. J. Simpson, *Sanitary Matters in Various West African Colonies and the Outbreak of Plagues in the Gold Coast* (London: Crown Agents, 1909), 10. See also *Legislative Council Debates*, statement by W. H. Grey, November 6, 1911, 343.

54. Editorial, "Gold Coast Drainage and Sanitation," *Gold Coast Independent*, July 20, 1918.

55. K. D. Patterson, "Disease and Medicine in African History: A Bibliographical Essay," *History in Africa* 1 (1974): 142.

56. M. W. Swanson, "The Sanitation Syndrome: Bubonic Plague and Urban Native Policy in Cape Colony, 1900–1909," *Journal of African History* 18, no. 3 (1977): 388.

57. J. S. Lafontaine, *City Politics: A Study of Leopoldville, 1962–1963* (Cambridge: Cambridge University Press, 1970), 19.

58. Raymond F. Betts, "The Problem of the Medina in the Urban Planning of Dakar, Senegal, 1914," *Urban African Notes* 4, no. 3 (1969): 5.

See also Raymond F. Betts, "The Establishment of the Medina in Dakar, Senegal, 1914," *Africa* 41, no. 1 (1971): 143.

59. Swanson, "The Sanitation Syndrome," 390.

60. PRAAD Adm. 23/1/435: Letter from Acting Deputy Director of Health, Accra, to the Hon. A. F. E. Fieldgate, Esq., Commissioner, Central Province, Cape Coast, September 27, 1943, 9.

61. Kwame Arhin, *The Cape Coast and Elmina Handbook: Past, Present and Future* (Legon: University of Ghana, 1995), 2. The local name for Cape Coast, *Oguaa* or *Ooegwa* (as in European records), confirms this account. The name *Oguaa* was derived from the Akan words *gua* or *dwa* (market). The name came about because the settlement started as a small but important market and developed into a major trading center.

62. William Bosman, *A New and Accurate Description of the Coast of Guinea: Divided into the Gold, the Slave, and the Ivory Coasts* (London: Frank Cass, 1967), 48.

63. W. E. F. Ward, *A History of Ghana* (London: Allen and Unwin, 1967), 81.

64. Roger Gocking, "The Historic Akoto: A Social History of Cape Coast, Ghana, 1848–1948" (PhD diss., Stanford University, California, 1981), 44.

65. Ray A. Kea, *Settlements, Trade, and Politics in the Seventeenth-Century Gold Coast* (Baltimore: Johns Hopkins University Press, 1982), 207.

66. These imports included textiles (thin silk cloths or taffetas, nap or pile cloths, linen, woolen cloths of different kinds, carpets, etc.); metal and metalwork (iron bars, axes and hatchets, spades, copper basins of different forms and sizes, copper pots and buckets, tin ware, pots, pans, etc.); cutlery and weapons (matchlock and firelock, muskets, gunpowder, knives of different sorts, cutlasses); and miscellaneous items (beads and corals, earthenware, mirrors, hats, shirts, leather bags, etc.). See Kea, *Settlements, Trade, and Politics*, 207.

67. Bosman, *A New and Accurate Description of the Coast of Guinea*, 51. His career proved quite like that of his counterparts John Kabes and John Konny of Komenda, eighteen miles to the west of Cape Coast. For a fuller account, see Kwame Y. Daaku, *Trade and Politics on the Gold Coast, 1600–1720* (London: Clarendon Press, 1970), 115. See also David Henige, "John Kabes of Kommenda: An Early African Entrepreneur and Early State Builder," *Journal of African History* 17, no. 1 (1977): 1.

68. Ward, *A History of Ghana*, 144.

69. The best known of these coastal families with European fathers or relations included the Brews, originally from Anomabu; see M. Priestley,

*West African Trade and Coast Society* (London: Oxford University Press, 1969); and the Swanzy family, also in Henry Swanzy, "A Trading Family in the Nineteenth Century Gold Coast," *Transactions of the Gold Coast and Togoland Historical Society* 2, no. 1 (1956): 87.

70. J. J. Crooks, *Records Relating to the Gold Coast Settlements from 1750 to 1874* (London: Frank Cass, 1973), 251.

71. Edward Reynolds, *Trade and Economic Change on the Gold Coast, 1807–1874* (London: Longmans, 1974), 80.

72. Gold Coast 1901 Population Census Report, 6.

73. J. Hinderink and J. Sterkenburg, *Anatomy of an African Town: A Socio-economic Study of Cape Coast, Ghana* (Utrecht: State University of Utrecht, 1975), 16.

74. Cruickshank, *Eighteen Years on the Gold Coast of Africa*, 28.

75. Ione Acquah, *Accra Survey: A Social Survey of the Capital of Ghana, Formerly Called the Gold Coast* (London: University of London, 1958), 69.

76. PRAAD Adm. 14/12/52: Report of the Central Province Trade Routes Committee, Vol. 6, 1928–1929, 30.

77. Governor A. R. Slater, *Legislative Council Debates*, No. 7, 1918–1919, July 4, 1919, 240.

78. PRAAD Adm. 14/12/52: Report of the Central Province Trade Routes Committee, Vol. 6, 1928–1929, 12.

79. Ibid., 17.

80. Ibid.

81. PRO CO 96/54/12: Extraordinary Gazette 40, June 29, 1907, 64.

82. PRAAD Adm. 14/12/52: Report of the Central Province Trade Routes Committee, Vol. 6, 1928–1929, 35.

83. Hinderink and Sterkenburg, *Anatomy of an African Town*, 38.

84. Ibid., 39.

85. Kimble, *A Political History of Ghana*, 356.

86. PRAAD Adm. 12/3/59: Confidential Dispatches to the Secretary of State, July 5, 1933, to December 29, 1933, 12.

## 7. "WE WON'T COOPERATE"

1. PRAAD Adm. 12/3/59: The Hon Justice J. Aitken, Report by . . . into Certain Charges of Official Misconduct Preferred against Mr. C. E. Skene, Provincial Commissioner, Gold Coast, Enclosure 1 in Gold Coast Confidential of November 30, 1933, 10.

2. Jarle Simensen, "Crisis in Akyem Abuakwa: The Native Administration Revenue Measure of 1932: Akyem Abuakwa and the Politics of the Inter-war Period in Ghana," *Mitteilungen der Basler Afrika Bibliographien* 12 (1995): 110.

3. The Native Jurisdiction Ordinance has been described as a "double purpose" instrument of control, which, on the one hand, bolstered the indigenous authority of docile, "protected" chiefs and, on the other hand, hamstrung chiefs deemed intractable and independent minded. See Robert Addo-Fening, Akyem *Abuakwa 1700–1943: From Ofori Panin to Sir Ofori Atta* (Trondheim: Norwegian University of Science and Technology, 1997), 157.

4. H. F. Morris and J. S. Read, *Indirect Rule and the Search for Justice: Essays in East Africa Legal History* (Oxford: Oxford Clarendon Press, 1972), 3.

5. R. L. Stone, "Rural Politics in Ghana in the Inter-War Period: Some Comparisons between Akyem Abuakwa and the States of the Central Province," *Mitteilungen der Basler Afrika* Bibliographien 12 (1975): 120.

6. The others were the Eastern and Western Provinces, with administrative capitals in Koforidua and Sekondi, respectively.

7. Roger Gocking, "The Historic Akoto: A Social History of Cape Coast, Ghana, 1848–1948" (PhD diss., Stanford University, California, 1981), 184.

8. Stone describes indirect rule as having two stages. He argues that in the noninterventionist stage, government officials become concerned with regulating the native states, whereas during the interventionist stage, they implement colonial policy through the chiefs "to make the native order a living part of the machinery of government." See R. L. Stone, "Colonial Administration and Rural Politics in South Central Ghana, 1919–1951" (PhD diss., Cambridge University, Cambridge, 1974), 67–90. Indeed, Governor Slater used that same description for the new policy in 1930. See A. R. Slater, *Native Administration in the Gold Coast and Its Dependencies: Confidential Minutes* (Accra, Ghana: Government Printing Office, 1930), 150.

9. The Gold Coast Colony (Legislative Council) Order-in-Council, 1925, 19.

10. Ibid., Clause XXXII, 35.

11. The relevance of this clause to the 1932 conflict will be discussed later in this chapter.

12. The Eastern Province has three different major ethnic groups: Ga-Adangbe, Ewe, and Akan.

13. PRAAD Adm. 12/3/45: Summary of Notes on the Petition of the Gold Coast Aborigines' Rights Protection Society, September 28, 1926, 5.

See also The Gold Coast Colony (Legislative Council) Order-in-Council, 1925, 19.

14. PRAAD Adm. 12/3/45: Summary of Notes on the Petition of the Gold Coast Aborigines' Rights Protection Society, September 28, 1926, 5.

15. Editorial, "Petition of the G.C.A.R.P.S.," *Gold Coast Leader*, March 26, 1927.

16. PRAAD Adm. 12/3/45: Summary of Notes on the Petition of the Gold Coast Aborigines' Rights Protection Society, September 28, 1926, 3.

17. Governor Guggisberg, *Legislative Council Debates*, February 22, 1926, 455.

18. PRAAD Adm. 12/3/45: Summary of Notes on the Petition of the Gold Coast Aborigines' Rights Protection Society, September 28, 1926, 4.

19. PRAAD Adm. 12/3/45: Letters of Governor Guggisberg to the Right Honorable L. S. Amery, MP, Secretary of State for Colonies, November 9, 1926–July 14, 1927, 2.

20. Ibid.

21. PRAAD Adm. 12/3/45: Letter of H. S. Newlands, Acting Secretary of Native Affairs to the Rt. Hon. L. S. Amery, MP, Secretary of State for Colonies, 3.

22. PRAAD Adm. 12/3/45: Letter of Governor Guggisberg to the Rt. Hon. L. S. Amery, MP, Secretary of State for Colonies, April 21, 1927, 3.

23. PRAAD Adm. 12/3/45: Letter of H. S. Newlands, Acting Secretary of Native Affairs to the Rt. Hon. L. S. Amery, MP, Secretary of State for Colonies, 1.

24. J. E. Casely Hayford, *Gold Coast Native Institutions* (London: Frank Cass, 1970), 50.

25. PRAAD Adm. 12/3/45: Letter of H. S. Newlands, Acting Secretary of Native Affairs to the Rt. Hon. L. S. Amery, MP, Secretary of State for Colonies, 1–2.

26. PRAAD Adm. 12/3/45: *Gold Coast Hansard*, 1925–1926, 282.

27. John M. Sarbah, *Fanti Customary Laws* (London: Frank Cass, 1968), 101.

28. *Legislative Council Debates*, February 22, 1926, 344.

29. Ibid., 346.

30. David Kimble, *A Political History of Ghana: The Rise of Gold Coast Nationalism, 1850–1928* (London: Oxford University Press, 1963), 447.

31. Ibid., 448.

32. Editorial, "The Legislative Council Elections and the New Order," *Gold Coast Leader*, June 18, 1927.

33. Ibid.

34. Editorial, "The Triumph of Common Sense," *Gold Coast Leader*, September 1927.

35. The Cape Coast Rate-Payers' Association was a typical example of the African construction of fresh voluntary groups in response to the exigencies of colonial urbanization and market economy.

36. Judgment Book, SCT 5/6/3, July 28, 1926–January 17, 1934: Decision of Woolhouse Bannerman—Re: Election of a Municipal Member, November 28, 1928, 213.

37. Ibid.

38. Ibid., 215.

39. All these men happened to be part of the educated elite; most of them had become lawyers and, therefore, were quite important in their respective communities.

40. PRAAD Adm. 11/1/1109: Minute Paper No. 3478/88 from Chief Justice to His Excellency, the Governor, July 10, 1888, 10.

41. PRAAD Adm. 11/1/1109: Letter of District Commissioner, Cape Coast, to the Hon. Colonial Secretary, September 10, 1902.

42. PRAAD Adm. 11/1/1109: The Coker File, 1931, 2.

43. He became known as Sir K. A. Korsah after being knighted. Sir Korsah eventually became the first indigenous chief justice of the Gold Coast and of independent Ghana.

44. L. H. Ofosu-Appiah, ed., *Encyclopedia Africana: Dictionary of African Biography, Ethiopia–Ghana* (New York: Reference, 1977), 26.

45. PRAAD Adm. 1/2/172: J. L. Atterbury, Acting Commissioner of the Central Province, Cape Coast Stool Affairs Enquiry, November 25, 1920, 2.

46. PRAAD Adm. 1/2/172: Letter from Governor Slater to Cunliffe-Lister, April 22, 1932, 1.

47. The Faithful Eight is a term of endearment used in the history of Mfantsipim School to refer to the group of students who, against all odds, continued their education at a difficult phase during which the new institution struggled for survival. Essentially, the eight students made a decision that kept hope alive for the school to continue and become what it has become known for throughout the years.

48. Isaac S. Ephson, *Gallery of Gold Coast Celebrities 1632–1968* (Accra, Ghana: Ilen, 1969), 123. See also Ofosu-Appiah, *Encyclopedia Africana*, 315.

49. PRAAD Adm. 1/2/172: Letter from Governor Slater to Cunliffe-Lister, April 22, 1932, 1.

50. PRO CO 96/717/21750: Letter from Shanton Thomas to Cunliffe-Lister, June 23, 1934, 3.

51. K. A. B. Jones-Quartey, "Kobina Sekyi: A Fragment of Biography," *Research Review* 4, no. 1 (1967): 78.

52. J. A. Langley, "Modernization and Its Malcontents: Kobina Sekyi of Ghana and the Re-statement of African Political Theory, 1892–1956," *Research Review* 6, no. 3 (1970): 89.

53. Ofosu-Appiah, *Encyclopedia Africana*, 269.

54. PRAAD Adm. 1/2/99: Letter from Northcote to Cunliffe-Lister, October 14, 1932.

55. PRAAD Adm. 12/3/59: Confidential Dispatches to Secretary of State for Colonies, July 5, 1933, to December 29, 1933, Enclosure 1, 10, in Gold Coast Confidential of 30.11.33. Report by the Hon. Mr. Justice J. Aitken into Certain Charges of Official Misconduct Preferred against Mr. C. E. Skene, Provincial Commissioner, Gold Coast.

56. Ibid.

57. "The Truth about the Cape Coast Municipal Election," *Gold Coast Leader*, September 1928.

58. PRO CO 96/67/3: *Gold Coast Gazette*, 64 (1928), 30.

59. PRAAD Adm. 12/3/59: Confidential Dispatches to Secretary of State for Colonies, July 5, 1933, to December 29, 1933, Enclosure 1 in Gold Coast Confidential of 30.11.33. Report by the Hon. Mr. Justice J. Aitken into Certain Charges of Official Misconduct Preferred against Mr. C. E. Skene, Provincial Commissioner, Gold Coast.

60. PRAAD Adm. 12/3/59: Confidential Dispatches to Secretary of State for Colonies, July 5, 1933, to December 29, 1933, Enclosure 1, 11, in Gold Coast Confidential of 30.11.33. Report by the Hon. Mr. Justice J. Aitken into Certain Charges of Official Misconduct Preferred against Mr. C. E. Skene, Provincial Commissioner, Gold Coast, 11.

61. PRAAD Adm. 12/3/59: Minute Paper, No. 10, 2.

62. Kimble, *A Political History of Ghana*, 446.

63. PRAAD Adm. 12/3/59: Confidential Dispatches to Secretary of State for Colonies, July 5, 1933, to December 29, 1933, Enclosure 1 in Gold Coast Confidential of 30.11.33. Report by the Hon. Mr. Justice J. Aitken into Certain Charges of Official Misconduct Preferred against Mr. C. E. Skene, Provincial Commissioner, Gold Coast, 16.

64. SNA File No. 322/31: Sub File No. 1 CSO 21/21/48: Narkwa-Ekumpuano Riot, September 28, 1931, 1.

65. SNA File No. 1414/31/11 S. 1 and 1414/31/18: Stool Disturbances in Cape Coast, Enquiry Dated November–December 1931, 36.

66. Broken into its component parts, the word *Ahinfie* is made up of *Ahin*, meaning "kings or chiefs," and *fie*, meaning "home or residence."

67. PRAAD Adm. 12/3/54: Letter from Governor Sir Ransford Slater to Lord Passfield, August 16, 1931, 4–5.

68. PRO CO 96/693/6599: Confidential Letter from Governor Sir Ransford Slater to Lord Passfield, February 18, 1930, 1.

69. Ibid.

70. Ibid.

71. Ibid.

72. Ibid., 2.

73. Ibid.

74. Governor Slater, *Legislative Council Debates*, September 24, 1931, 275.

75. S. Shaloff, "The Income Tax, Indirect Rule, and the Depression: The Gold Coast Riots of 1931," *Cahiers d'Etudes Africaines* 14, no. 54 (1974): 362.

76. *Legislative Council Debates*, September 24, 1931, 379.

77. Ibid.

78. Editorial, "This Is Not the Time," *Times of West Africa*, April 1930; Editorial, "No Taxation Here," *Gold Coast Leader*, April 1930; Editorial, "Government Must Save Itself," *Gold Coast Times*, April 1930; Editorial, "Down with Income Tax," *Gold Coast Spectator*, April 1930; and Editorial, "Already Burdened," *Gold Coast Independent*, April 1930.

79. PRAAD Adm. 12/3/55: Dispatch from H. J. O'Connor, Commissioner of Police, to the Inspector General of Police, Accra, October 27, 1931, 1–2.

80. PRAAD Adm. 12/3/55: Petition from the Office of the *Omanhin*, Shama, to the Acting Provincial Commission of the Western Province, October 29, 1931, enclosed in Northcote to J. H. Thomas, November 3, 1931, 1.

81. PRAAD Adm. 12/3/55: Letter from Sumner Wilson, Acting Provincial Commissioner of the Western Province, Sekondi, to the Colonial Secretary, October 30, 1931, 1.

82. Ibid.

83. PRAAD Adm. 12/5/171: Confidential Dispatch from Northcote to Fiddian, November 2, 1931, 1.

84. Ibid.

85. PRAAD Adm. 12/3/55: Dispatch from H. Pilgrim Morris, Assistant Commissioner of Police, Cape Coast, to the Colonial Secretary, November 2, 1931, enclosed in Slater to Cunliffe-Lister, December 7, 1931, 3.

86. Shaloff, "The Income Tax, Indirect Rule, and the Depression," 368.

87. PRAAD Adm. 12/3/55: Dispatch from H. Pilgrim Morris, Assistant Commissioner of Police, Cape Coast, to the Colonial Secretary, November 2, 1931, enclosed in Slater to Cunliffe-Lister, December 7, 1931, 5.

88. Ibid.

89. PRAAD Adm. 12/3/59 Confidential Dispatches to the Secretary of State, July 7, 1933, to December 19, 1933; Enclosure 3 Schedule of Documents No. 1. Letter of A. B. Josiah, *Supi*, No. 3 Company to the District Commissioner, Cape Coast, through Nana Mbra III, July 20, 1932, 6.

90. PRAAD Adm. 12/3/59: Confidential Dispatches to the Secretary of State, July 5, 1933, to December 19, 1933; Enclosure 3 Schedule of Documents No. 2 Amended Program of the Installation of *Asafohin* of No. 3 Company, Cape Coast on the 16, 17, 19, and 24 of September 1932, Signed by A. B. Josiah. Letter of A. B. Josiah, *Supi*, No. 3 Company to the District Commissioner, Cape Coast, through Nana Mbra III, July 20, 1932, 9.

91. PRAAD Adm. 12/3/59: Schedule of Documents No. 16: Mr. J. C. DeGraft Johnson's Minute to Mr. Skene, August 1932.

92. PRAAD Adm. 12/3/59: Schedule of Documents No. 7: Confidential Letter of Acting Commissioner of the Central Province to Nana Mbra III, September 12, 1932, 38.

93. Ibid.

94. PRAAD Adm. 12/3/59: Schedule of Documents No. 6: Affidavit of Nancy Coker, September 1932, 2.

95. PRAAD Adm. 12/3/59: Schedule of Documents No. 13: Grounds of Protest; Enclosed in No. 12, Letter of Kwesi Sekyi, Acting for the Supi of the *Bentsir* (No. 1) *Asafo* Company, to Secretary of Native Affairs, September 13, 1932, 1.

96. PRAAD Adm. 12/3/59: Schedule of Documents No. 20: Extracts from Confidential Diary on Cape Coast District for the Month of September 1932, 15.

97. PRAAD Adm. 12/3/59: Schedule of Documents No. 21: Mr. Bewes's Note to Mr. Dawson Recording the Instructions Received from Mr. C. E. Skene, 15.

98. PRAAD Adm. 12/3/59: Confidential Dispatches to Secretary of State for Colonies, July 5, 1933, to December 29, 1933, Enclosure 1 in Gold Coast Confidential of 30.11.33. Report by the Hon. Mr. Justice J. Aitken into Certain Charges of Official Misconduct Preferred against Mr. C. E. Skene, Provincial Commissioner, Gold Coast.

99. PRAAD Adm. 12/3/59: Schedule of Documents No. 21: Mr. Bewes's Note to Mr. Dawson recording the instructions received from Mr. C. E. Skene, 16.

100. PRAAD Adm. 12/3/59: Schedule of Documents No. 27: Letter from Acting District Commissioner, Cape Coast, to Nana Mbra III, *Omanhin* of *Oguaa*, September 20, 1932, 16.

101. PRAAD Adm. 12/3/59: Schedule of Documents No. 7: Letter of *Omanhin* Mbra III to Acting Commissioner of the Central Province, September 12, 1932, 14.

102. PRAAD Adm. 12/3/59: Schedule of Documents No. 28: Form 3, Bond by . . . Application for Permission to Celebrate Native Custom or Exhibit Company Flags, Section 13, 10.

103. PRAAD Adm. 12/3/59: Schedule of Documents No. 42: Letter from Lynch and Dawson, District Commissioner and Assistant District Commissioner, Respectively, to the Hon. Commissioner of the Central Province, Cape Coast, November 19, 1932.

104. PRAAD Adm. 12/3/59: Schedule of Documents No. 33: Letter from Acting Commissioner of the Central Province, Cape Coast, to the Hon. Secretary of Native Affairs, Victoriaborg, Accra, October 2, 1932, 14.

105. J. C. DeGraft Johnson, "The Fanti Asafu," *Africa* 5, no. 3 (1932): 322.

106. PRAAD Adm. 11/1/243: Letter from G. A. S. Northcote, Acting Governor to Right Honorable Sir Philip Cunliffe-Lister, October 14, 1932. See also Letter from Acting Commissioner of the Central Province to the Hon. Secretary of Native Affairs, Victoriaborg, Accra, October 2, 1932, 10.

107. PRAAD Adm. 11/1/234: Schedule of Documents No. 43: Letter from Hon. Commissioner of the Central Province, Cape Coast, to Hon. Colonial Secretary, Victoriaborg, Accra, November 19, 1932, 18.

108. PRAAD Adm. 11/1/222: Letter from Acting Commissioner of the Central Province to the Hon. Secretary of Native Affairs, Victoriaborg, Accra, October 2, 1932, 1.

109. Ibid. See also PRAAD Adm. 11/1/435: Letter from Acting Commissioner of the Central Province to the Hon. Secretary of Native Affairs, Victoriaborg, Accra, October 2, 1932, 2.

110. SNA File No. 5: Sub. File No. 470 CSO 21/21/56 Relations between *Oguaa* State and Government, Central Province Confidential, from Mr. C. E. Skene, Provincial Commissioner of the Central Province, Cape Coast to the Governor, Accra, October 22, 1932, 5.

## CONCLUSION

1. Terence O. Ranger, *Dance and Society in Eastern and Central Africa, 1890–1970: The Beni Ngoma* (London: Heinemann, 1975), 2.

2. *Aban wo twuw n'adze wonnsua no bi* literally means "the institution of government represents a burdensome baggage to be dragged and not comfortably carried on the head."

>PRAAD Adm. 12/3/59: Schedule of Documents No. 33: Letter from Acting Commissioner of the Central Province, Cape Coast, to the Hon. Secretary of Native Affairs, Victoriaborg, Accra, October 2, 1932. See also PRAAD Adm. 12/3/54: Letter from Governor Sir Ransford Slater to Lord Passfield, August 16, 1931.

# BIBLIOGRAPHY

PRIMARY SOURCES

*Archival Materials/Documents*

**The National Archives, United Kingdom of Great Britain**

British Parliamentary Papers: Report of the Select Committee 1842, 212–213.
PRO CO 267/36: Letter of Maclean to the Committee of Merchants.
PRO CO 96/22: Letter of James Bannerman to Earl Grey, Cape Coast Castle, January 14, 1851.
PRO CO 96/665/10: Petition to King George V from the *Asafoi* of Accra, May 9, 1925.
PRO CO 96/654/18836: Memorandum by the Secretary of Native Affairs (SNA), April 4, 1925.
PRO CO 96/655/32858: Inspector General of Police versus *Asafoatse* Djator and Others. Record of Proceedings in the Supreme Court of the Gold Coast Colony, Eastern Province, June 27, 1925.
PRO CO 96/94: Preamble to the Fanti Confederation Scheme of 1872.
PRO CO 96/72: Petition of King Aggery, Cape Coast, September 1866, enclosed in Blackall to Carnarvon, Sierra Leone, October 17, 1866.
PRO CO 96/54/12: Gold Coast Government Gazette (Extraordinary), March 10, 1897.
PRO CO 96/310: Report of the Proceedings of the Deputation, 1898.
PRO CO 96/67/3: Gold Coast Gazette, 1928.

Great Britain: Command Paper 1103–1109, 1921. Gold Coast Report for 1919. London: Her Majesty's Stationery Office (HMSO), 60–63.

Great Britain Hydrographic Office. *Africa Pilots*. 3 Volumes. London: 1893.

## Public Record Administration and Archives Department (PRAAD), Accra

PRAAD Adm. 12/3/59: Confidential Dispatches to the Secretary of State, July 5, 1932–December 1933.

PRAAD Adm. 11/1/1473: A Guide to Cape Coast Company Emblems and Notes as to Meanings of Customs.

PRAAD Adm. 11/1/1473: Letter of *Omanhin* Codjoe Imbra to the District Commissioner, Cape Coast, December 31, 1904.

PRAAD Adm. 11/1/1634: Cape Coast Stool Enquiry.

PRAAD Adm. 12/3/45: Gold Coast Hansard, 1925–1926.

PRAAD Adm. 12/3/58: Tufohin Enquiry, 1929.

Gold Coast 1923C: Report by the Town Council Committee on the Constitution and Working of Existing Town Councils of the Colony. Session Paper, No. 17, 1922–1923. Accra, Ghana: Government Printer, 1924.

Gold Coast 1926A: The Gold Coast: A Review of the Events of 1925–1926 and the Prospects of 1926–1927. Accra, Ghana: Government Printer, 1928.

Gold Coast 1926B: Report on the Objection Lodged with the Colonial Secretary against the Application of the Municipal Corporations Ordinance, 1924, to the Town of Accra, with Enclosures Including Minutes of Evidence. Session Paper, No. 1, 1925–1926. Accra, Ghana: Government Printer, 1927.

Gold Coast 1926C: Report on the Enquiry Held by the Honorable C. W. Welman, Secretary for Native Affairs, on a Commission by His Excellency the Governor Issued under the Commissions of Enquiry Ordinance, February 26, 1925. Session Paper, No. 10, 1925–1926. Accra, Ghana: Government Printer, 1926.

Gold Coast 1922: Municipal Assembly Reports for the Year 1921. Accra, Ghana: Government Printer, 1922.

Gold Coast 1891 Census Report. Accra, Ghana: Government Printer, 1891.

Gold Coast 1901 Census Report. Accra, Ghana: Government Printer, 1901.

Gold Coast Gazette: Trade Supplement, 1922, 1923, 1924, and 1928. Accra, Ghana: Government Printer, 1928.

Gold Coast Population Census Report 1891–1911. Accra, Ghana: Government Printer.

Legislative Council Debates, No. 7, 1918–1919. Accra, Ghana: Government Printer.

The Gold Coast Colony (Legislative Council) Order-in-Council, 1925. Accra, Ghana: Government Printer, 1925.

PRAAD Adm. 23/1/435: Letter from Acting Deputy Director of Health, Accra to the Hon. A. F. E. Fieldgate, Esq., Commissioner, Central Province, Cape Coast, September 27, 1943.

PRAAD Adm. 12/3/59: Confidential Dispatches to the Secretary of State, July 5, 1933–December 29, 1933.

PRAAD Adm. 12/3/59: The Hon Justice J. Aitken, Report by... into Certain Charges of Official Misconduct Preferred against Mr. C. E. Skene, Provincial Commissioner, Gold Coast. Enclosure 1 in Gold Coast Confidential of November 30, 1933.

PRAAD Adm. 12/3/45: Summary of Notes on the Petition of the Gold Coast Aborigines' Rights Protection Society, September 28, 1926.

PRAAD Adm. 12/3/45: Letters of Governor Guggisberg to the Right Honorable L. S. Amery, MP, Secretary of State for Colonies, November 9, 1926–July 14, 1927; April 21, 1927.

PRAAD Adm. 12/3/45: Letter of H. S. Newlands, Acting Secretary of Native Affairs to the Rt. Hon. L. S. Amery, MP, Secretary of State for Colonies.

PRAAD Adm. 12/3/59: Confidential Dispatches to Secretary of State for Colonies, July 5, 1933–December 29, 1933. Enclosure 1 in Gold Coast Confidential of 30.11.33. Report by the Hon. Mr. Justice J. Aitken into Certain Charges of Official Misconduct Preferred against Mr. C. E. Skene, Provincial Commissioner, Gold Coast.

SNA File No. 322/31: Sub File No. 1 CSO 21/21/48 Narkwa-Ekumpuano Riot, September 28, 1931.

SNA File No. 1414/31/11 S. 1 and 1414/31/18: Stool Disturbances in Cape Coast, Enquiry Dated November–December 1931.

PRAAD Adm. 12/3/54: Letter from Governor Sir Ransford Slater to Lord Passfield, August 16, 1931.

PRAAD Adm. 12/3/59 Confidential Dispatches to the Secretary of State, July 5, 1933–December 19, 1933. Enclosure 3 Schedule of Documents No. 2 Amended Program of the Installation of *Asafohin* of No. 3 Company, Cape Coast on September 16, 17, 19, and 24, 1932, Signed by A. B. Josiah. Letter of A. B. Josiah, *Supi*, No. 3 Company to the District Commissioner, Cape Coast, through Nana Mbra III, July 20, 1932.

Judgment Book, SCT 5/6/3, July 28, 1926–January 17, 1934: Decision of Woolhouse Bannerman—Re: Election of a Municipal Member, November 28, 1928.

PRAAD Adm. 12/3/59: Schedule of Documents No. 33: Letter from Acting Commissioner of the Central Province, Cape Coast, to the Hon. Secretary of Native Affairs, Victoriaborg, Accra, October 2, 1932.

SNA File No. 5: Sub. File No. 470 CSO 21/21/56 Relations between *Oguaa* State and Government, Central Province Confidential, from Mr. C. E. Skene, Provincial Commissioner of the Central Province, Cape Coast to the Governor, Accra, October 22, 1932.

## Newspapers

Ahuma, Attoh. "The Gold Coast Youth." *Gold Coast Aborigines*, April 3, 1899.

Coker, W. Z. "The Truth about the Cape Coast Municipal Election." *Gold Coast Leader*, September 1928.

Editorial. "Already Burdened." *Gold Coast Independent*, April 1930.

Editorial. "ARPS Mission Statement." *Gold Coast Express*, April 22, 1897.

Editorial. "Down with Income Tax." *Gold Coast Spectator*, April 1930.

Editorial. "Gold Coast Drainage and Sanitation." *Gold Coast Independent*, July 20, 1918.

Editorial. "Gold Coast Lands and the Crown Lands Ordinance." *Gold Coast Methodist Times*, February 1895.

Editorial. "Government Must Save Itself." *Gold Coast Times*, April 1930.

Editorial. "The Governor and the Chiefs." *African Times*, December 23, 1864.

Editorial. "It Has Come to Stay." *Gold Coast Independent*, May 1, 1897.

Editorial. "The Land Question." *Gold Coast Methodist Times*, July 20, 1897.

Editorial. "The Legislative Council Elections and the New Order." *Gold Coast Leader*, June 18, 1927.

Editorial. "No Taxation Here." *Gold Coast Leader*, April 1930.

Editorial. "Our Mission Statement." *Gold Coast Times*, March 28, 1874.

Editorial. "Petition of the G.C.A.R.P.S." *Gold Coast Leader*, March 26, 1927.

Editorial. "This Is Not the Time." *Times of West Africa*, April 1930.

Editorial. "This Is Our Land." *Gold Coast Chronicle*, March 1895.

Editorial. "The Triumph of Common Sense." *Gold Coast Leader*, September 3, 1927.

Editorial. "We Won't Cooperate." *Gold Coast Methodist Times*, July 31, 1897.

Mensah, Solomon. "Gold Coast Literacy." *Gold Coast Nation*, April 8, 1915.

## Oral Interviews

Ababio, Kwesi. Senior spokesman for the *Omanhin* of Cape Coast. Interviewed by author. Digital voice recording. Cape Coast, Central Region, Ghana, June 10, 2009.

Abeiku, Kweku. Retired teacher. Interviewed by author. Digital voice recording. Cape Coast, Central Region, Ghana, September 6, 2009.

Adjoa, Maame. Petty trader. Interviewed by author. Digital voice recording. Cape Coast, Central Region, Ghana, August 13, 2009.

Adu, Kweku. Retired civil servant and community leader. Interviewed by author. Digital voice recording. Cape Coast, Central Region, Ghana, July 6, 2009.

Afarfohin, Nana. Elder and chief fisherman. Interviewed by author. Digital voice recording. Cape Coast, Central Region, Ghana, July 4, 2009.

Aidoo, Nana. Petty trader and fisherman. Interviewed by author. Digital voice recording. Cape Coast, Central Region, Ghana, September 10, 2009.

Akyere, Esi Mina. Trader and *Asafoakyere*. Interviewed by author. Digital voice recording. Cape Coast, Central Region, Ghana, July 2, 2009.

Arhin, Nana Kobina. Retired headmaster and opinion leader. Interviewed by author. Digital voice recording. Cape Coast, Central Region, Ghana, June 4, 2009.

Arhinful, Nana Kofi. Canoe owner and fisherman. Interviewed by author. Digital voice recording. Cape Coast, Central Region, Ghana, August 15, 2009.

Arthur, Kweku. Retired civil servant. Interviewed by author. Digital voice recording. Cape Coast, Central Region, Ghana, September 15, 2009.

Atta, Adjoa. Market woman and *Asafoakyere*. Interviewed by author. Digital voice recording. Cape Coast, Central Region, Ghana, July 20, 2009.

Atta, Kofi. Canoe owner and retired civil servant. Interviewed by author. Digital voice recording. Cape Coast, Central Region, Ghana, July 5, 2009.

Atta, Nana. Fish seller. Interviewed by author. Digital voice recording. Cape Coast, Central Region, Ghana, September 4, 2009.

Atta, Nana Kwesi. *Omanhin* of *Oguaa*. Interviewed by author. Digital voice recording. Cape Coast, Central Region, Ghana, June 1, 2009.

Botse, Kweku. *Safohin* of *Abrofonkoa Asafo* (No. 5) company. Interviewed by author. Digital voice recording. Cape Coast, Central Region, Ghana, June 22, 2009.

Dadzie, Egya Payin. Fisherman and *Asafo* elder. Interviewed by author. Digital voice recording. Cape Coast, Central Region, Ghana, August 3, 2009.

Essuon, Akua. *Obaapayin* and market woman. Interviewed by author. Digital voice recording. Cape Coast, Central Region, Ghana, October 6, 2009.

Ewusi, Kofi. Elder and opinion leader. Interviewed by author. Digital voice recording. Cape Coast, Central Region, Ghana, July 22, 2009.

Eyiaba, Nana Amba. Queen-mother of Effutu. Interviewed by author. Digital voice recording. Cape Coast, Central Region, Ghana, June 13, 2009.

Fynn, Ebo Kobina. Headmaster and community leader. Interviewed by author. Digital voice recording. Cape Coast, Central Region, Ghana, July 29, 2009.

Hayfron, J. A. *Supi* of *Bentsir Asafo* (No. 1) company. Interviewed by author. Digital voice recording. Cape Coast, Central Region, Ghana, June 13, 2009.

Hweaseambo, Adwoa. Trader and wife of a fisherman. Interviewed by author. Digital voice recording. Cape Coast, Central Region, Ghana, July 3, 2009.

Idun, Kojo. Retired headteacher. Interviewed by author. Digital voice recording. Cape Coast, Central Region, Ghana, August 1, 2009.

Insaidoo, Kojo. *Supi* of *Nkum Asafo* (No. 4) company. Interviewed by author. Digital voice recording. Cape Coast, Central Region, Ghana, June 5, 2009.

Johnson, Ebo. *Supi* of *Ntsin Asafo* (No. 3) company. Interviewed by author. Digital voice recording. Cape Coast, Central Region, Ghana, June 5, 2009.

Kwahin, Nana. *Asafoakyere* of *Bentsir Asafo* (No. 1) company. Interviewed by author. Digital voice recording. Cape Coast, Central Region, Ghana, June 16, 2009.

Mansa, Esi. *Asafokyere*. Interviewed by author. Digital voice recording. Cape Coast, Central Region, Ghana, October 10, 2009.

Minnah, Kobina. *Supi* of *Akrampa Asafo* (No. 6) company. Interviewed by author. Digital voice recording. Cape Coast, Central Region, Ghana, June 12, 2009.

Nunoo, Kojo. *Supi* of *Anaafo Asafo* (No. 2) company. Interviewed by author. Digital voice recording. Cape Coast, Central Region, Ghana, June 17, 2009.

Nyaneba, Esi. Fish seller and *Asafoakyere*. Interviewed by author. Digital voice recording. Cape Coast, Central Region, Ghana, October 5, 2009.

Nyanyanoa, Aba. Fish seller and wife of a fisherman. Interviewed by author. Digital voice recording. Cape Coast, Central Region, Ghana, August 11, 2009.

Nyimfa, Nana Kwamina. Chief and *Nimfahin* of *Oguaa*. Interviewed by author. Digital voice recording. Cape Coast, Central Region, Ghana, September 7, 2009.

Osam, Ato. Fisherman. Interviewed by author. Digital voice recording. Cape Coast, Central Region, Ghana, September 17, 2009.

Otu, Kwesi. Retired fisherman. Interviewed by author. Digital voice recording. Cape Coast, Central Region, Ghana, June 30, 2009.

Oyemam, Afua. Market queen-mother. Interviewed by author. Digital voice recording. Cape Coast, Central Region, Ghana, October 12, 2009.

Panyin, Ato Kwamina. Canoe owner and fisherman. Interviewed by author. Digital voice recording. Cape Coast, Central Region, Ghana, August 5, 2009.

Panyin, Nana Adjoa. Fish seller. Interviewed by author. Digital voice recording. Cape Coast, Central Region, Ghana, September 20, 2009.

Prah, Kwamina. *Odomankoma Kyerema* (master divine drummer). Interviewed by author. Digital voice recording. Cape Coast, Central Region, Ghana, May 19, 2009.

Quansah, Nana Esi. Retired nurse. Interviewed by author. Digital voice recording. Cape Coast, Central Regional, Ghana, August 9, 2009.

Sukwei, Araba. Fish seller. Interviewed by author. Digital voice recording. Cape Coast, Central Region, Ghana, June 11, 2009.

Yallow, Kobina. *Supi* of *Amanfur Asafo* (No. 7) company. Interviewed by author. Digital voice recording. Cape Coast, Central Region, Ghana, June 4, 2009.

## SECONDARY SOURCES

### *Theses, Dissertations, and Other Unpublished Works*

Adu Poku, B. "History and Constitution of the Oguaa State." BA thesis, University of Ghana, Legon, 1979.

Anshan, Li. "Social Protest in the Gold Coast: A Study of the Eastern Province in the Colonial Period." PhD diss., University of Toronto, Canada, 1993.

Baku, D. E. K. "An Intellectual in National Politics: The Contribution of Kobinah Sekyi to the Evolution of Ghanaian National Consciousness." PhD diss., University of Sussex, UK, 1987.

Barnes, F. D. "The Fetu Afahye of the People of Oguaa State." BA thesis, University of Ghana, Legon, 1971.

Cawson, A. "Local Politics and Indirect Rule in Cape Coast, Ghana, 1928–1957." PhD diss., Oxford University, Oxford, 1975.

Gocking, Roger. "The Historic Akoto: A Social History of Cape Coast, Ghana, 1848–1948." PhD diss., Stanford University, California, 1981.

Hagan, George P. "Aspects of Social Change among the Effutu of Winneba." PhD diss., Oxford University, Oxford, 1974.

Nti, Kwaku. "The Clash of Traditional Military Organizations: A Study of Inter-Asafo Relations in the Cape Coast Municipality 1900–1932." MPhil thesis, University of Ghana, Legon, 1998.

Odotei, I. "The Ga and Their Neighbors." PhD diss., University of Ghana, Legon, 1972.

Ofori-Atta, F. "Amantoomiensa in the Political and Administrative Set-Up of Akyem Abuakwa." BA thesis, University of Ghana, Legon, 1978.

Osei-Tutu, J. K. "Local Protest under Colonial Rule c. 1900–1950: The Asafo Movement of Kwahu." MPhil thesis, University of Trondheim, Norway, 1994.

Quansah, A. K. E. "The History of Cape Coast before the Transfer of the Capital to Accra." BA thesis, University of Ghana, Legon, 1980.

Sanders, J. "The Political Development of the Fante in the Eighteenth and Nineteenth Centuries: A Study of a West African Merchant Society." PhD diss., Northwestern University, Chicago, 1980.

Simensen, Jarle. "Commoners, Chiefs, and Colonial Government: British Policy and Local Politics in Akim Abuakwa, Ghana, under Colonial Rule." PhD diss., University of Trondheim, Norway, 1975.

Stone, R. L. "Colonial Administration and Rural Politics in South Central Ghana, 1919–1951." PhD diss., Cambridge University, Cambridge, 1974.

Sutherland-Addy, Esi. "Speaking War and Peace." Paper presented at the Asafo History Program Workshop 1997 at the Institute of African Studies, University of Ghana, Legon, December 17–18, 1997.

Tachie Mensah, J. A. "A History of Cape Coast." BA thesis, University of Ghana, Legon, 1972.

Tetteh Addy, J. "The History of Cape Coast from the Earliest Times to the Nineteenth Century." BA thesis, University of Ghana, Legon, 1975.

## Journal Articles and Book Chapters

Achebe, Nwando. "Nwando Achebe—Daughter, Wife, and Guest—A Researcher at Crossroads." *Journal of Women's History* 14, no. 3 (2002): 9–31.

Agbodeka, Francis. "The Fanti Confederation, 1865–1969." *Transactions of the Historical Society of Ghana* 8 (1964): 82–123.

Allman, Jean M. "The Youngmen and the Porcupine: Class Nationalism and Asante Struggle for Self-Determination, 1954–1957." *Journal of African History* 31, no. 2 (1990): 50–70.

Anshan, Li. "Asafo and Destoolment in Colonial Southern Ghana, 1900–1953." *International Journal of African Historical Studies* 28, no. 2 (1995): 327–357.

Argyle, John. "Kalela, Beni, Asafo, Ingoma and the Rural: Urban Dichotomy." *African Studies* 50 (1991): 65–86.

Arhin, Kwame. "Diffuse Authority among the Coastal Fanti." *Ghana Notes and Queries* 9 (1966): 20–35.

Bartels, F. L. "Education in the Gold Coast." *African Affairs* 48, no. 193 (October 1949): 300–311.

———. "Philip Quaque, 1741–1816." *Transactions of the Gold Coast and Togoland Historical Society* 1, no. 5 (1955): 153–177.

Beinart, William. "African History and Environmental History." *African Affairs* 99, no. 395 (2000): 269–302.

Berg, Eric. "Backward-Sloping Labor Supply Functions in Dual Economies: The African Case." *Quarterly Journal of Economics* 15, no. 4 (1961): 468–492.

Betts, Raymond F. "The Establishment of the Medina in Dakar, Senegal, 1914." *Africa* 41, no. 1 (1971): 143–152.

———. "The Problem of the Medina in the Urban Planning of Dakar, Senegal, 1914." *Urban African Notes* 4, no. 3 (1969): 5–15.

Bevin, H. J. "The Gold Coast Economy About 1800." *Transactions of the Gold Coast and Togoland Historical Society* 2, no. 2 (1956): 68–80.

Birmingham, David. "A Note on the Kingdom of Fetu." *Ghana Notes and Queries* 9, no. 1 (1966): 102–125.

Boahen, Albert A. "The Origins of the Akan." *Ghana Notes and Queries* 9, no. 1 (1966): 15–35.

———. "Politics in Ghana." In *History of West Africa, Vol. 1*, edited by J. F. Ajayi and Michael Crowder. New York: Columbia University Press, 1972.

Bolster, Jeffrey W. "Putting the Ocean in Atlantic History: Maritime Communities and Marine Ecology in the Northwest Atlantic, 1500–1800." *The American Historical Review* 113, no. 1 (Feb. 2008): 19–47.

Christensen, J. B. "The Role of Proverbs in Fante Culture." *Journal of the International African Institute* 28, no. 6 (1958): 232–243.

Chukwukere, I. B. "Perspectives on the Asafo Institution in Southern Ghana." *Journal of African Studies* 7, no. 1 (1980): 50–75.

Collier, J. F., and Michelle Z. Rosaldo. "Politics and Gender in Simple Societies." In *Sexual Meanings*, edited by Sherry Ortner and Harriet Whitehead, 229–275. Cambridge: Cambridge University Press, 1981.

Coquery-Vidrovitch, Catherine. "The Process of Urbanization." *African Studies Review* 34 (1991): 1–98.

Daaku, Kwame Y. "John Konny: The Last Prussian Negro Prince." *Tarikh* 1, no. 4 (1967): 55–64.

Datta, A. K. "The Fante Asafo: A Re-examination." *Africa* 42 (1972): 45–67.

Datta, A. K., and R. Porter. "The Asafo System in Historical Perspective: An Inquiry into the Origin and Development of a Ghanaian Institution." *Journal of African History* 12, no. 2 (1971): 279–297.

Davis, Dona L., and Jane Nadel-Klein. "Gender, Culture and the Sea: Contemporary Theoretical Approaches." *Society and Natural Resources* 5 (1992): 135–145.

DeGraft Johnson, J. C. "The Fanti Asafu." *Africa* 5, no. 3 (1932): 307–322.

Fage, John D. "The Administration of George Maclean on the Gold Coast, 1830–1844." *Transactions of the Gold Coast and Togoland Historical Society* 1, no. 4 (1955): 54–71.

Feinberg, Harvey M. "Africans and Europeans in West Africa: Elminans and Dutchmen on the Gold Coast during the Eighteenth Century." *Transactions of the American Philosophical Society* 79, no. 7 (1989): 104–120.

Ffoulkes, Arthur. "The Company System in the Cape Coast Castle." *Journal of African Society* 7, no. 25 (1907): 36–51.

Fortes, Meyer. "Kinship and Marriage among the Ashanti." In *African Systems of Marriage and Kinship*, edited by A. R. Radcliffe-Brown and Daryll Forde, 10–31. London: International African Institute, 1950.

Fortescue, Dominic. "The Accra Crowd, the Asafo, and the Opposition to the Municipal Corporations Ordinance, 1924–25." *Canadian Journal of African Studies* 24, no. 3 (1990): 348–375.

Gocking, Roger. "Indirect Rule in the Gold Coast: Competition for Office and the Invention of Tradition." *Canadian Journal of African Studies* 28, no. 3 (1994): 421–447.

Grove, J. M., and A. M. Johansen. "The Historical Geography of the Volta Delta, Ghana, during the Period of Danish Influence." *Bulletin de l'Institut Fondamental d'Afrique Noire* 30, no. 4 (1968): 1374–1421.

Gutking, Peter C. W. "The Canoemen of the Gold Coast (Ghana): A Survey and an Exploration in Pre-colonial African Labor History." *Cahiers d'Etudes Africaines* 29, no. 3 (1989): 339–376.

———. "Trade and Labor in Early Precolonial African History: The Canoemen of Southern Ghana." In *The Workers of African Trade*, edited by Cathrine Coquery-Vidrovitch and Paul E. Lovejoy. Beverly Hills, CA: Sage, 1985.

Hagan, George P. "An Analytical Study of Fanti Kinship." *Research Review* 4, no. 1 (1967): 35–57.

Henige, David. "Abrem Stool: A Contribution to the History and Historiography of Southern Ghana." *International Journal of African Historical Studies* 6 (1973): 1–18.

———. "Akan Stool Succession under Colonial Rule: Continuity or Change?" *Journal of African History* 14, no. 2 (1977): 203–226.

———. "John Kabes of Kommenda: An Early African Entrepreneur and Early State Builder." *Journal of African History* 17, no. 1 (1977): 1–19.

———. "Kingship in Elmina before 1869: A Study in Feedback and the Traditional Idealization of the Past." *Cahiers d'Etudes Africaines* 55, no. 3 (1974): 499–520.

———. "Packaging Scholarship." In *Africanizing Knowledge: African Studies across the Disciplines*, edited by Toyin Falola and Christian Jennings, 400–415. New Brunswick, NJ: Transactions, 2002.

———. "The Problem of Feedback in Oral Traditions: Four Examples from the Fante Coastlands." *Journal of African History* 14, no. 21 (1978): 223–235.

Herskovits, Meville J. "The Ashanti Ntoro: A Re-examination." *Journal of the Royal Anthropological Institute* 47 (1937): 102–137.

Hyland, A. D. C. "Architectural History of Cape Coast." *Transactions of the Historical Society of Ghana* 16, no. 2 (1995): 135–169.

Inikori, J. E. "The Import of Firearms into West Africa, 1750–1807: A Quantitative Analysis." *Journal of African History* XVIII, no. 3 (1977): 339–368.

Johnson, T. J. "Protest, Challenge, and Change: An Analysis of Southern Gold Coast Riots, 1890–1920." *Economy and Society* 1, no. 2 (1972): 164–193.

Jones, Adam. "'My Arse for Akou': A Wartime Ritual of Women in the Nineteenth Century Gold Coast." *Cahiers d'Etudes Africaines* 132 (1992): 545–566.

Jones-Quartey, K. A. B. "Kobinah Sekyi: A Fragment of Biography." *Research Review* 4, no. 1 (1967): 89–102.

Kea, R. A. "Firearms and Warfare on the Gold and Slave Coast from the Sixteenth to the Nineteenth Centuries." *Journal of African History* XII (1971): 185–213.

Kiyaga-Mulindwa, D. "The Akan Problem." *Current Anthropology* 21, no. 4 (1980): 503–506.

Klein B., and G. Mackenthun. "Sea Changes: Historicizing the Ocean." *Journal of World History* 16 (2005): 102–107.

Lalu, Premesh. "The Grammar of Domination and the Subjection of Agency: Colonial Texts and Modes of Evidence." *History and Theory* 39, no. 4 (2000): 45–68.

Langley, J. A. "Modernization and Its Malcontents: Kobina Sekyi of Ghana and the Restatement of African Political Theory, 1892–1956." *Research Review* 6, no. 3 (1970): 76–102.

Larson, Pier M. "Horrid Journeying: Narratives of Enslavement and the Global African Diaspora." *Journal of World History* 19, no. 4 (December 2008): 431–464.

Lovejoy, Paul E., and David Richardson. "Trust, Pawnship, and Atlantic History: The Institutional Foundations of the Old Calabar Slave Trade." *American Historical Review* 104, no. 2 (1999): 333–355.

Mabogunje, Akin. "Overview of Research Priorities in Africa." *Urban Research in the Developing World* 2 (1994): 22–43.

Maylam, Paul. "Dead Horses, the Baby and the Bathwater: 'Post-Theory' and the Historian's Practice." *South African Historical Journal* 42 (2000): 121–135.

Metcalf, George. "Gold, Assortments and the Trade Ounce: Fante Merchants and the Problem of Supply and Demand in the 1770s." *Journal of African History* 28, no. 1 (1987): 27–41.

Meyerowitz, Eva L. "Concept of the Soul among the Akan of the Gold Coast." *Africa* 21, no. 1 (1950): 22–37.

Miller, Joseph C. "History and Africa/Africa and History." *American Historical Review* 104, no. 1 (1999): 1–32.

Ninson, Kwame. "Economic Modernization and Social Change: Evidence from Mumford, a Ghanaian Fishing Village." *Africa* 61, no. 1 (1991): 98–116.

Nti, Kwaku. "Action and Reaction: An Overview of the Ding-Dong Relationships between the Colonial Government and the People of Cape Coast." *Nordic Journal of African Studies* 11, no. 1 (2002): 1–37.

———. "The Dynamics of Revenue and Relations: Contents and Discontents in Historic African Diaspora Experiences in Ghana." In *Contextualizing Africans and Globalization: Expressions in Sociopolitical and Religious Contents and Discontents*, edited by Ibigbolade S. Aderibigbe, Rotimi Williams Omotoye, and Lydia Bosede Akande, 39–50. Lanham, MD: Lexington Books, 2016.

———. "From Politics to Tourism: Pan-African Connections, Development, and Experiences of the Historic African Diaspora in Ghana." In *Ghana: Economic, Social, and Political Issues*, edited by Coleen Roscoe, 1–14. New York: Nova Science, 2014.

———. "King Aggery's Loud Voice: Whose Voice?" *Transactions of the Historical Society of Ghana* 7 (2003): 253–270.

———. "The Role of Alcohol in the 1905 Conflict between the Anaafo and Ntsin Asafo Companies of Cape Coast." *Transactions of the Historical Society of Ghana* 2 (1998): 49–55.

Okonjo, Kamene. "The Dual Sex Political System in Operation: Igbo Women and Community Politics in Midwestern Nigeria." In *Women in Africa*, edited by Nancy J. Hafkin and Edna Bay, 45–58. Stanford, CA: Stanford University Press, 1976.

Patterson, K. D. "Disease and Medicine in African History: A Bibliographical Essay." *History in Africa* 1 (1974): 141–148.

Pearson, M. N. "Littoral Society: The Concept and the Problems." *Journal of World History* 17, no. 4 (2006): 353–374.

Peterson, B. "Culture, Resistance and Representation." *SADET: The Road to Democracy in South Africa* 2 (2006): 161–185.

Porter, R. "The Cape Coast Riot of 1803." *Transactions of the Historical Society of Ghana* 11 (1970): 30–45.

Price, Roy. "Caribbean Fishing and Fishermen: A Historical Sketch." *American Anthropologist* 86, no. 6 (1989): 104–125.

Ranger, T. O. "Connexions Between 'Primary Resistance' Movements and Modern Mass Nationalism in East and Central Africa." *Journal of African History* 9, no. 3 (1968): 437–453.

Shaloff, S. "The Cape Coast Asafo Company Riot of 1932." *International Journal of African Historical Studies* 7, no. 4 (1974): 591–607.

———. "The Income Tax, Indirect Rule and the Depression: The Cape Coast Riots of 1931." *Cahiers d'Etudes Africaines* 14, no. 54 (1974): 359–376.

Simensen, Jarle. "The Asafo of Kwahu, Ghana: A Mass Movement for Local Reform under Colonial Rule." *International Journal of African Historical Studies* 8 (1975): 383–406.

———. "Crisis in Akyem Abuakwa: The Native Administration Revenue Measure of 1932, Akyem Abuakwa and the Politics of Inter-war Period in Ghana." *Mitteilungen der Basler Afrika Bibliographien* 12 (1995): 110–125.

———. "Nationalism from Below: The Akyem Abuakwa Example." *Mitteilugen der Basler Afrika Bibliographien* 12 (1975): 31–57.

———. "Rural Mass Action in the Context of Anti-colonial Protest: The Asafo Movement of Akim Abuakwa, Ghana." *Canadian Journal of African Studies* 7 (1974): 25–41.

Smith, R. "The Canoe in West Africa." *Journal of African History* 11, no. 4 (1970): 515–533.

Stoeltje, Beverly J. "Asante Queen Mothers: A Study in Female Authority." *Annals of the New York Academy of Sciences* 1 (2000): 44–71.

Stone, R. L. "Rural Politics in the Inter-war Period: Some Comparisons between Akyem Abuakwa and the States of the Central Province." *Mitteilungen der Basler Afrika Bibliographien* 12 (1975): 91–115.

Sudarkasa, Niara. "The Status of Women in Indigenous African Societies." In *Women in Africa and the Diaspora*, edited by Rosalyn Terborg-Penn, 25–41. Washington, DC: Howard University Press, 1987.

Sutherland-Addy, Esi. "Discourse and Asafo: The Place of Oral Literature." *Transactions of the Historical Society of Ghana* 2 (1998): 87–100.

Swanson, M. W. "The Sanitation Syndrome: Bubonic Plague and Urban Native Policy in the Cape Colony, 1900–1909." *Journal of African History* 18, no. 3 (1977): 387–410.

———. "Urban Origins of Separate Development." *Race* 10 (1968): 31–40.

Swanzy, Henry. "A Trading Family in the Nineteenth Century Gold Coast." *Transactions of the Gold Coast and Togoland Historical Society* 2, no. 1 (1956): 87–120.

Vercruijsse, Emile. "Fishmongers, Big Dealers, and Fishermen: Co-operation and Conflict between the Sexes in Ghanaian Canoe Fishing." In *Female and Male in West Africa*, edited by Christine Oppong, 188–201. London: George Allen and Unwin, 1983.

## Books

Achebe, Nwando. *Farmers, Traders, Warriors, and Kings: Female Power and Authority in Northern Igboland, 1900–1960*. Portsmouth, NH: Heinemann, 2006.

Acquaah, Gaddiel R. *Oguaa Aban*. London: Longmans, 1968.
Acquah, Ione. *Accra Survey: A Social Survey of the Capital of Ghana, Formerly Called the Gold Coast*. London: University of London, 1958.
Addo-Fenning, Robert. *Akyem Abuakwa 1700–1943: From Ofori Panin to Sir Ofori Atta*. Trondheim: Norwegian University of Science and Technology, 1997.
Adler, P., and N. Barnard. *ASAFO: African Flags of the Fante*. London: Thames and Hudson, 1993.
Agbodeka, Francis. *African Politics and British Policy in the Gold Coast*. Evanston, IL: Northwestern University Press, 1971.
Aggrey, J. A. *Asafo*. Tema: Ghana Publishing, 1978.
Akyeampong, Emmanuel K. *Between the Sea and the Lagoon: An Eco-social History of the Anlo of Southeastern Ghana, c. 1850 to Recent Times*. Oxford: James Currey, 2001.
———. *Drink, Power, and Cultural Change: A Social History of Alcohol in Ghana, c. 1800 to Recent Times*. Oxford: James Currey, 1996.
———, ed. *Themes in West Africa's History*. Oxford: James Currey, 2006.
Allman, Jean. *"I Will Not Eat Stone": A Women's History of Colonial Asante*. Portsmouth, NH: Heinemann, 2000.
———. *The Quills of the Porcupine: Asante Nationalism in an Emergent Ghana*. Madison: University of Wisconsin Press, 1993.
Amadiume, Ifi. *Male Daughters, Female Husbands: Gender and Sex in an African Society*. London: Zed Books, 1987.
Anaman, J. B. *The Gold Coast Guide*. London: Christian Herald, 1902.
Andersen, D. *Histories of the Hanged: The Dirty War in Kenya and the End of Empire*. New York: Norton, 2005.
Anquandah, James. *Castles and Forts of Ghana*. Atlante: Ghana Museums and Monuments Board, 1999.
Apter, David. *The Gold Coast in Transition*. Princeton, NJ: Princeton University Press, 1955.
Arhin, Kwame. *The Cape Coast and Elmina Handbook: Past, Present and Future*. Legon: University of Ghana, 1995.
———. *Minutes of the Ashanti Farmers Association, 1934–1936*. Legon: University of Ghana, 1978.
———. *Papers on the Symposium on the City of Kumasi: The Historical Background*. Legon: University of Ghana, 1990.
———. *Traditional Rule in Ghana: Past and Present*. Accra, Ghana: Sedco, 1985.
Asiamah, A. E. A. *The Mass Factor in Rural Politics: The Case of the Asafo Revolution in Kwahu Political History*. Accra, Ghana: Ghana Universities Press, 2000.

Atkins, John. *A Voyage to Guinea, Brazil, and the West Indies in His Majesty's Ships the "Swallow" and "Weymouth" 1735*. London: Cass, 1970.

Austin, Dennis. *Politics in Ghana 1946–1960*. London: Oxford University Press, 1964.

Ayittey, George B. N. *Indigenous African Institutions*. New York: Transnational, 2006.

Balmer, W. T. *A History of the Akan Peoples of the Gold Coast*. New York: Greenwood, 1969.

Barbot, J. *A Description of the Coasts of North and South Guinea*. London: Frank Cass, 1723.

Bartels, F. L. *The Roots of Ghana Methodism*. Cambridge: Cambridge University Press, 1965.

Berry, Sara. *Chiefs Know Their Boundaries: Essays on Property, Power, and the Past in Asante, 1896–1996*. Oxford: James Currey, 2001.

———. *No Condition Is Permanent: The Social Dynamics of Agrarian Change in Sub-Saharan Africa*. Madison: University of Wisconsin Press, 1993.

Blake, John W. *West Africa: Quest for God and Gold 1454–1578*. Totowa, NJ: Curzon, 1977.

Blalock, H. M. *Power and Conflict: Toward a General Theory*. Newbury Park, CA: Sage, 1989.

Blankson, S. *Fetu Afahye*. Cape Coast, Ghana: University of Cape Coast Press, 1973.

Bledsoe, C. *Women and Marriage in Kpelle Society*. Stanford, CA: Stanford University Press, 1980.

Boahen, Albert A. *African Perspectives on Colonialism*. Baltimore: Johns Hopkins University Press, 1987.

———. *Ghana: Evolution and Change in the Nineteenth and Twentieth Centuries*. London: Longman, 1975.

———. *Mfantsipim and the Making of Ghana*. Accra, Ghana: Sankofa, 1996.

———. *Topics in West African History*. London: Longman, 1966.

———. *Yaa Asantewaa and the Asante-British War of 1900–1*. Oxford: James Currey, 2003.

Bohannan, Paul. *Africa and Africans*. New York: Natural History Press, 1964.

Bosman, William. *A New and Accurate Description of the Coast of Guinea: Divided into the Gold, the Slave, and the Ivory Coasts*. London: Frank Cass, 1967.

Boulding, Kenneth E. *Conflict and Defense: A General Theory*. New York: Harper and Brothers, 1962.
Bowdich, E. T. *Mission from Cape Coast Castle to Ashantee*. London: Frank Cass, 1966.
Bozzoli, Belinda, ed. *Labor, Township and Protest*. Johannesburg, South Africa: Ravan, 1979.
Braudel, F. *The Mediterranean and the Mediterranean World: The Age of Philip II*. New York: Harper Collins, 1992.
———. *The Structures of Everyday Life: The Limits of the Possible*. New York: Harper and Row, 1981.
Brokensha, D., D. M. Warren, and O. Werner, eds. *Indigenous Knowledge Systems and Development*. Washington, DC: University Press of America, 1970.
Brown, A. P. *The Fishes and Fisheries of the Gold Coast*. London: Crown Agents for the Colonies, 1930.
Brown, E. J. P. *Gold Coast and Ashanti Reader*. London: Frank Cass, 1929.
Brown, Ras Michael. *African-Atlantic Cultures and South Carolina Lowcountry*. Cambridge: Cambridge University Press, 2012.
Busia, Kofi A. *The Position of the Chief in the Modern Political System of Ashanti*. London: Frank Cass, 1968.
———. *Report on Social Survey of Sekondi-Takoradi on Behalf of the Government of the Gold Coast*. London: Crown Agents for the Colonies, 1950.
Cardinall, A. W. *The Gold Coast*. Accra, Ghana: Government Printer, 1931.
Carlston, K. S. *Social Theory and African Tribal Organization*. Urbana: University of Illinois Press, 1968.
Casely Hayford, J. E. *Gold Coast Native Institutions*. London: Frank Cass, 1970.
Christaller, J. B. *Dictionary of the Asante and Fante Languages Called Twi*. Basel: Basel Evangelical Missionary Society, 1993.
Christensen, J. B. *Double Descent among the Fanti*. New Haven, CT: Human Relations Area Files, 1954.
Chukwukere, I. B. *Cultural Resilience: The Asafo Company System of the Fante*. Cape Coast, Ghana: University of Cape Coast Press, 1970.
Claridge, W. W. *History of Gold Coast and Ashanti*. London: Frank Cass, 1964.
Cohen, David W., and E. S. Atieno Odhiambo. *Siaya: The Historical Anthropology of An African Landscape*. London: James Currey, 1989.
Collier, J. F., and S. J. Yanagisako, eds. *Gender and Kinship: Essays toward a Unified Analysis*. Stanford, CA: Stanford University Press, 1987.

Collins, Robert O., ed. *Historical Problems of Imperial Africa*. Princeton, NJ: Markus Wiener, 2000.

Cookey, S. J. S. *King Jaja of the Niger Delta: His Life and Times, 1821–1891*. New York: Nok Publishers, 1974.

Crooks, J. J. *Records Relating to the Gold Coast Settlements from 1750 to 1874*. London: Frank Cass, 1973.

Crosby, Alfred W. *The Columbian Exchange: Biological and Cultural Consequences of 1492*. Westport: Greenwood Press, 1972.

Crowder, M., ed. *West African Resistance: The Military Response to Colonial Occupation*. London: Hutchinson, 1971.

———. *West Africa under Colonial Rule*. Evanston, IL: Northwestern University Press, 1968.

Crowder, M., and I. Obaro, eds. *West African Chiefs*. New York: African, 1970.

Cruickshank, Brodie. *Eighteen Years on the Gold Coast of Africa: Including an Account of the Native Tribes and Their Intercourse with Europeans*. London: Frank Cass, 1966.

Curtin, Philip, Steven Feierman, Leonard Thompson, and Jan Vansina. *African History: From Earliest Times to Independence*. London: Longman, 1995.

Daaku, Kwame Y. *Trade and Politics on the Gold Coast, 1600–1720*. London: Clarendon Press, 1970.

Daniel, Ebo. *A Tale of Cape Coast*. Accra, Ghana: Woeli, 2006.

Danquah, Asirifi. *Yaa Asantewaa: An African Queen Who Led an Army to Fight the British*. Kumasi: Asirifi Danquah, 2002.

Danquah, J. B. *Akan Society*. London: Bureau of Current Affairs, 1950.

———. *The Gold Coast: Akan Laws and Customs*. London: Lutherworth Press, 1945.

Dawson, Kevin. *Undercurrents of Power: Aquatic Culture in the African Diaspora*. Philadelphia: University of Pennsylvania Press, 2018.

Dickson, Kwamina B. *Historical Geography of Ghana*. Oxford: Oxford University Press, 1969.

Dirks, N. B., ed. *Colonialism and Culture*. Ann Arbor: University of Michigan Press, 1992.

Edsman, B. M. *Lawyers in Gold Coast Politics c. 1900–1945: From Mensah Sarbah to J. B. Danquah*. Uppsala, Sweden: Uppsala University, 1979.

Ellis, E. B. *A History of the Gold Coast of West Africa*. New York: Greenwood, 1969.

———. *The Tshi-Speaking People of the Gold Coast of West Africa: Their Religion, Manners, Customs, Laws, Language, Etc.* Oosterhout, The Netherlands: Anthropological, 1966.

Ephson, Isaac S. *Gallery of Gold Coast Celebrities, 1632–1968.* Accra, Ghana: Ilen, 1969.

Epstein, A. L. *The Administration of Justice and the Urban African.* London: Her Majesty's Stationery Office, 1953.

Fage, John. *Ghana: A Historical Interpretation.* Madison: University of Wisconsin Press, 1959.

Fair, Laura. *Pastimes and Politics: Culture, Community, and Identity in Post-abolition Urban Zanzibar, 1890–1945.* Athens: Ohio University Press, 2001.

Falola, Toyin, and Christian Jennings, eds. *Africanizing Knowledge: African Studies across the Disciplines.* New Brunswick, NJ: Transaction, 2002.

———. *Sources and Methods in African History: Spoken, Written, Unearthed.* Rochester, NY: University of Rochester Press, 2003.

Fanon, Franz. *The Wretched of the Earth.* New York: Grove Press, 1963.

Farias, P. F. de Moraes, and Karin Barber, eds. *Self-Assertion and Brokerage: Early Cultural Nationalism in West Africa.* Birmingham, UK: University of Birmingham, 1990.

Febvre, L. *A Geographical Introduction to History.* London: Paul, Trench, Trubner, 1925.

Feinberg, Harvey M. *Africans and Europeans in West Africa: Elminas and Dutchmen on the Gold Coast during the Eighteenth Century.* Philadelphia: American Philosophical Society, 1989.

Ferguson, James. *Expectations of Modernity: Myths and Meanings of Urban Life on the Zambian Copperbelt.* Berkeley: University of California Press, 1999.

Field, M. J. *Akim-Kotoku: An Oman of the Gold Coast.* London: Crown Agents, 1948.

———. *Religion and Medicine of the Ga People.* London: Oxford University Press, 1937.

———. *Social Organization of the Ga People.* London: Crown Agents for the Colonies, 1940.

Fink, H. *Religion, Disease and Healing in Ghana: A Case Study of Traditional Dormaa Medicine.* Munich: Trickster Verlag, 1990.

Fisher, R. *Dealing with Conflict.* Cambridge, MA: Harvard Business Review Press, 1983.

Forde, C. D., ed. *African Worlds: Studies in the Cosmological Ideas and Social Values of African Peoples*. London: Oxford University Press, 1954.

Fortes, M. *Social Structure*. Oxford: Clarendon Press, 1949.

———. *The Web of Kinship among the Tallensi*. London: Oxford University Press, 1946.

Fortes, M., and E. E. Evans-Pritchard, eds. *African Political Systems*. London: Oxford University Press, 1940.

Freund, Bill. *The Making of Contemporary Africa: The Development of African Society since 1800*. Bloomington: Indiana University Press, 1984.

Fynn, John K. *Oral Tradition of the Fante States Abeadze*. Legon: University of Ghana, 1975.

———. *Oral Tradition of the Fante States Abrem*. Legon: University of Ghana, 1974.

———. *Oral Tradition of the Fante States Edina/Elmina*. Legon: University of Ghana, 1974.

———. *Oral Tradition of the Fante States Eguafo*. Legon: University of Ghana, 1974.

———. *Oral Tradition of the Fante States Kommenda*. Legon: University of Ghana, 1974.

Gillespie, William H. *The Gold Coast Police 1844–1938*. Accra, Ghana: Government Printer, 1955.

Glazier, J. *Land and the Uses of Tradition among the Mbere of Kenya*. Lanham, MD: University Press of America, 1985.

Gluckman, Max. *Custom and Conflict in Africa*. Oxford: Basil Blackwell, 1959.

Gocking, Roger. *Facing Two Ways: Ghana's Coastal Communities under Colonial Rule*. Lanham, MD: University Press of America, 1999.

Gomez, Michael A. *Reversing Sail: A History of the African Diaspora*. Cambridge: Cambridge University Press, 2005.

Gordon, C. A. *Life on the Gold Coast*. London: Bailliere, Tindall, and Cox, 1874.

Haenger, Peter. *Slaves and Slave Holders on the Gold Coast: Towards and Understanding of Social Bondage in West Africa*. Basel: Schleittwein, 2000.

Hafkin, N. J., and E. G. Bay, eds. *Women in Africa: Studies in Social and Economic Change*. Stanford, CA: Stanford University Press, 1976.

Hagan, George P. *Divided We Stand: A Study of Social Change among the Effutu of Coastal Ghana*. Trondheim: Norwegian University of Science and Technology, 2000.

Hair, Paul Edward Hedley, Adam Jones, and Robin Law. *Barbot on Guinea: The Writings of Jean Barbot on West Africa 1678–1712*. 2 Vols. London: Hakluyt Society, 1992.
Hall, Gwendolyn Midlo. *Slavery and African Ethnicities in the Americas: Restoring the Links* Chapel Hill: The University of North Carolina Press, 2005.
Hawthorne, N. *Journal of an African Cruiser*. New York: Wiley and Putman, 1845.
Henige, David P. *The Chronology of Oral Tradition: Quest for a Chimera*. Oxford: Clarendon Press, 1974.
Hernaes, Per. *Slaves, Danes and African Coast Society*. Trondheim: Norwegian University of Science and Technology, 1995.
Hinderink, J., and J. Sterkenburg. *Anatomy of an African Town: A Socio-economic Study of Cape Coast, Ghana*. Utrecht: State University of Utrecht, 1975.
Hopkins, A. G. *An Economic History of West Africa*. London: Longman, 1973.
Horton, J. A. B. *Letters on the Political Condition of the Gold Coast*. London: Frank Cass, 1970.
Hymer, S. *The Political Economy of the Gold Coast and Ghana*. New Haven, CT: Yale University, 1969.
Iggers, G. G., and Q. Edward Wang. *A Global History of Modern Historiography*. With contributions by Supriya Mukherjee. London: Pearson Longman, 2008.
Ingersoll, Karin Amimoto. *Waves of Knowing: A Seascape Epistemology*. Durham, NC: Duke University Press, 2016.
Irvine, F. R. *The Fishes and Fisheries of the Gold Coast*. London: Crown Agents for the Colonies, 1947.
Isert, Paul Erdmann. *Letters on West Africa and the Slave Trade*. New York: Oxford University Press, 1992.
Jones, Adam. *German Sources for West African History 1599–1669*. Wiesbaden: Franz Steiner Verlag, 1983.
Jones-Quartey, K. A. B. *A Summary History of the Ghana Press, 1822–1960*. Accra, Ghana: Ghana Information Services Department, 1974.
Kea, Ray A. *Settlements, Trade, and Politics in Seventeenth-Century Gold Coast*. Baltimore: Johns Hopkins University Press, 1982.
Kimble, David. *A Political History of Ghana: The Rise of Gold Coast Nationalism, 1850–1928*. London: Oxford University Press, 1963.
Konadu, Kwasi. *Our Own Way in This Part of the World: Biography of an African Community, Culture and Nation*. Durham, NC: Duke University Press, 2019.

Lafontaine, J. S. *City Politics: A Study of Leopoldville 1962–1963*. Cambridge: Cambridge University Press, 1970.

Law, Robin, and Silke Strickrodt. *Ports of the Slave Trade: Bights of Biafra and Benin*. Stirling: University of Stirling, 1999.

Levtzion, Nehemia. *Islam in West Africa: Religion, Society, and Politics to 1800*. New York: Routledge, 1994.

Linnekin, Jocelyn. *Sacred Queens and Women of Consequence*. Ann Arbor: University of Michigan Press, 1990.

Little, K. *West African Urbanization*. Cambridge: Cambridge University Press, 1965.

Lloyd, C. *The British Seamen, 1200–1860: A Social Survey*. London: Collins, 1968.

Lovejoy, Paul E. *Transformations of Slavery: A History of Slavery in Africa*. New York: Cambridge University Press, 2000.

Lovejoy, Paul E., and Toyin Falola, eds. *Pawnship, Slavery, and Colonialism in Africa*. Trenton, NJ: Africa World Press, 2003.

Lystad, R. *The Ashanti: A Proud People*. New Brunswick, NJ: Rutgers University Press, 1958.

MacDonald, G. *The Gold Coast*. New York: Negro Universities Press, 1969.

Manoukian, M. *Akan and Ga-Adangme Peoples of the Gold Coast*. London: Oxford Press, 1950.

Marees, Pieter De. *Description and Historical Account of the Gold Kingdom of Guinea*. Oxford: Oxford University Press, 1987.

Maxwell, J. *The Gold Coast Handbook*. London: Government of the Gold Coast, 1928.

McCarthy, Mary. *Social Change and the Growth of British Power in the Gold Coast: The Fante States, 1807–1874*. Lanham, MD: University Press of America, 1983.

McPhee, A. *The Economic Revolution in British West Africa*. London: Frank Cass, 1926.

Merton, R. *Social Theory and Social Structure*. Glencoe, IL: Free Press, 1957.

Metcalfe, G. E. *Great Britain and Ghana: Documents of Ghana History 1807–1957*. London: Ipswich Book, 1964.

———. *Maclean of the Gold Coast*. London: Oxford University Press, 1962.

Meyerowitz, E. L. R. *The Akan of Ghana*. London: Faber and Faber, 1958.

———. *Akan Traditions of Origin*. London: Faber and Faber, 1952.

———. *The Early History of the Akan States of Ghana*. London: Red Candle Press, 1970.

———. *The Sacred State of the Akan*. London: Faber and Faber, 1951.

Migeod, F. *Languages of West Africa*. London: Paul, Trench, Trubner, 1911.
Morris, H. F., and J. S. Read. *Indirect Rule and the Search for Justice: Essays in East Africa Legal History*. Oxford: Oxford Clarendon Press, 1972.
Newell, Stephanie. *Literary Culture in Colonial Ghana: How to Play the Game of Life*. Bloomington: Indiana University Press, 2002.
Ninson, Kwame A. *Politics, Local Administration, and Community Development in Ghana, 1951–1966: A Case Study of Community Power and Its Impact on Socio-economic Development at Cape Coast*. Boston: Boston University Press, 1977.
Nkansah-Kyeremateng, K. *Akan Heritage*. Accra, Ghana: Sebewie, 1999.
Obeng, E. E. *Ancient Ashanti Chieftaincy*. Tema: Ghana Publishing, 1986.
Odotei, Irene K. *Chieftaincy in Ghana: Culture, Governance and Development*. Legon: Sub-Saharan, 2006.
———. *"Man-Woman," Gender and Management: A Case Study of Women Canoe Owners at the Tema Fishing Harbor*. Legon: Institute of African Studies, University of Ghana, 2003.
———. *Sea Power, Money Power: Ghanaian Migrant Fishermen and Women in the Republic of Benin*. Legon: University of Ghana, 2002.
———. *There Is Money in the Sea: Ghanaian Migrant Fishermen and Women in the Ivory Coast*. Legon: University of Ghana, 2002.
Ofosu-Appiah, L. H., ed. *The Encyclopedia Africana: Dictionary of African Biography Ethiopia-Ghana*. New York: Reference, 1977.
Opoku-Agyeman, K. *Cape Coast Castle: A Collection of Poems*. Accra, Ghana: Afram, 1996.
Oppong, Christine. *Female and Male in West Africa*. London: George Allen and Unwin, 1983.
Ortner, S., and H. Whitehead, eds. *Sexual Meanings*. Cambridge: Cambridge University Press, 1981.
Osei-Tutu, J. K. *The Asafoi (Socio-military Groups) in the History and Politics of Accra (Ghana) from the Seventeenth to Mid Twentieth Century*. Trondheim: Norwegian University of Science and Technology, 2000.
Ottenberg, Simon. *Double Descent in an African Society: The Afipko Village-Group*. Seattle: University of Washington Press, 1968.
Owusu, Maxwell. *Uses and Abuses of Political Power: A Case Study of Community and Change in the Politics of Ghana*. Legon, Ghana: University of Ghana Press, 2006.
Parker, John. *Making the Town: Ga State and Society in Early Colonial Accra*. Portsmouth, NH: Heinemann, 2000.

Peil, M. *Cities and Suburbs: Urban Life in West Africa.* New York: African, 1981.

Pellow, D. *Women in Accra: Options for Autonomy.* Algonac, MI: Reference, 1977.

Perez-Mallaina, P. E. *Spain's Men of the Sea: Daily Life on the Indies Fleets in the Sixteenth Century.* Baltimore: Johns Hopkins University Press, 1998.

Philips, J. E. *Writing African History.* Rochester, NY: University of Rochester Press, 2005.

Phillips, A., ed. *Survey of African Marriage and Family Life.* London: Oxford University Press, 1953.

Poewe, K. *Matrilineal Ideology.* New York: Academic Press, 1981.

Priestley, M. *West African Trade and Coast Society.* London: Oxford University Press, 1969.

Prins, A. H. J. *Sailing from Lamu: A Study of Maritime Culture in Islamic East Africa.* Assen, The Netherlands: Van Gorcum, 1965.

Radcliffe-Brown, A. R., and D. Forde, eds. *African Systems of Marriage and Kinship.* London: International African Institute, 1950.

Ranger, Terence O. *Dance and Society in Eastern and Central Africa, 1890–1970: The Beni Ngoma.* London: Heinemann, 1975.

Rattray, R. S. *Akan-Ashanti Folktales.* Oxford: Clarendon Press, 1969.

———. *Ashanti.* Oxford: Clarendon Press, 1923.

———. *Ashanti Law and Constitution.* London: Oxford University Press, 1956.

———. *Religion and Art in Ashanti.* London: Oxford University Press, 1959.

Rediker, Marcus. *Between the Devil and the Deep Blue Sea: Merchant Seamen, Pirates, and the Anglo-American Maritime World, 1700–1750.* Cambridge: Cambridge University Press, 1987.

Reindorf, Christian C. *The History of Gold Coast and Asante: Based on Traditions and Historical Facts Comprising More Than Three Centuries from about 1500 to 1860.* Basel: Basel Mission Book Depot, 1951.

Reynolds, Edward. *Trade and Economic Change on the Gold Coast 1807–1874.* London: Longmans, 1974.

Robertson, Claire. *Sharing the Same Bowl: A Socio-economic History of Women and Class in Accra, Ghana.* Bloomington: Indiana University Press, 1984.

Robinson, David. *Paths of Accommodation: Muslim Societies and French Colonial Authorities in Senegal and Mauritania, 1880–1920.* Athens: Ohio University Press, 2000.

Rude, G. *The Crowd in History*. London: Wiley, 1964.
Sampson, M. J. *Gold Coast Men of Affairs*. London: Dawson, 1937.
Sarbah, John M. *Fanti Customary Laws*. London: Frank Cass, 1968.
———. *Fanti National Constitution*. London: Frank Cass, 1968.
Scott, James C. *Weapons of the Weak: Everyday Forms of Peasant Resistance*. New Haven, CT: Yale University Press, 1985.
Shumway, Rebecca. *The Fante and the Transatlantic Slave Trade*. Rochester, NY: University of Rochester Press, 2011.
Silverblatt, Irene. *Moon, Sun, and Witches: Gender Ideologies and Class in Inca and Colonial Peru*. Princeton, NJ: Princeton University Press, 1987.
Simmel, Georg. *Conflict and Group Affiliations*. Translated by Kurt H. Wolff and Reinhard Bendix. New York: Free Press, 1966.
Simpson, W. J. *Sanitary Matters in Various West African Colonies and the Outbreak of Plagues in the Gold Coast*. London: Crown Agents, 1909.
Skinner, E. P. *Peoples and Cultures of Africa*. New York: Natural History Press, 1961.
Slater, A. R. *Native Administration in the Gold Coast and Its Dependencies: Confidential Minutes*. Accra, Ghana: Government Printing Office, 1930.
Smith, M. E. *Those Who Live from the Sea: A Study in Maritime Anthropology*. New York: West, 1977.
Stone, J. C. *Africa and the Sea: Proceedings of a Colloquium at the University of Aberdeen*. Aberdeen, Scotland: Aberdeen University, 1985.
Strathern, Marilyn. *The Gender of the Gift*. Berkeley: University of California Press, 1988.
Strayer, Robert W. *Ways of the World: A Brief Global History with Sources*. Vol. 7, *Since 1500*. New York: Bedford/St. Martin's, 2011.
Switzer, Les. *Power and Resistance in an Africa Society: The Ciskei Xhosa and the Making of South Africa*. Madison: University of Wisconsin Press, 1993.
Szereszewski, R. *Structural Changes in the Economy of Ghana, 1891–1911*. London: Weidenfeld & Nicolson, 1965.
Tropp, J. A. *Natures of Colonial Change: Environmental Relations in the Making of the Transkei*. Athens: Ohio University Press, 2006.
Van Dantzig, A. *Forts and Castles of Ghana*. Accra, Ghana: Sedco, 1980.
Van-Onselen, Charles. *New Babylon, New Nineveh: Everyday Life on the Witwatersrand, 1886–1914*. Johannesburg, South Africa: Jonathan Ball, 2001.
Vansina, Jan. *Oral Tradition: A Study in Historical Methodology*. Chicago: Aldine, 1965.

Vansina, Jan, and Carolyn Keyes Adenaike. *In Pursuit of History: Fieldwork in Africa*. Portsmouth, NH: Heinemann, 1996.

Vercruijsse, Emile. *The Dynamics of Fanti Domestic Organization: A Comparison with Fortes' Ashanti Survey*. Cape Coast, Ghana: University of Cape Coast, 1972.

Vercruijsse, E. V. W., Lydi M. Vercruijsse-Dopheide, and Kwasi J. A. Boakye. *Composition of Households in Fante Communities: A Study of the Framework of Social Integration*. Cape Coast, Ghana: University of Cape Coast, 1972.

Ward, W. E. F. *A History of Ghana*. London: Allen and Unwin, 1967.

———. *My Africa*. Accra, Ghana: Ghana Universities Press, 1991.

Warren, D. M. *The Akan of Ghana: An Overview of Ethnographic Literature*. Accra, Ghana: Pointer, 1973.

Weibust, Knut. *Deep Sea Sailors: A Study in Maritime Ethnology*. Stockholm, Sweden: V. Petterson, 1969.

Weiner, A. B. *Women of Value, Men of Renown: New Perspectives in Trobriand Exchange*. Austin: University of Texas Press, 1976.

White, L. Stephan, F. Meischer, and David W. Cohen, eds. *African Words, African Voices: Critical Practices in Oral History*. Bloomington: Indiana University Press, 2001.

Wilks, I. *Asante in the Nineteenth Century: The Structure and Evolution of a Political Order*. London: Cambridge University Press, 1975.

———. *Forest of Gold: Essays on the Akan and the Kingdom of Asante*. Athens: Ohio University Press, 1993.

———. *Political Bi-polarity in Nineteenth Century Asante*. Edinburgh: Edinburgh University, 1970.

Wilson, G. *The Analysis of Social Change*. Cambridge: Cambridge University Press, 1945.

Wraith, R. E. *Guggisberg*. London: Oxford University Press, 1967.

Yankah, Kwesi. *Speaking for the Chief: Okyeame and the Politics of Akan Royal Oratory*. Bloomington: Indiana University Press, 1995.

Yarak, L. W. *Asante and the Dutch, 1744–1873*. Oxford: Clarendon Press, 1990.

# INDEX

Abandze, 37
Abiding cooperation, 4
Aborigines' Rights Protection Society (ARPS), 25, 47, 147, 188, 203, 240
Abraham, J. D., 147
*Abrempong Asafo*, literally, "company of the rich and famous," 74
Aburi on the Akuapem Ridge, 179
Accra, 9, 10, 23, 37, 43, 91, 92, 102–106, 142, 164, 178, 179, 181, 184, 190–199, 200, 207, 208, 216, 223, 224, 229, 230, 246, 248, 250, 254, 257, 258, 260–266, 269, 270, 273, 274, 278, 277, 281, 282–287, 291–299, 303, 306, 315–320, 322–329, 330–334
achievement of community interests, 4
acquisition of fishing skills, the, 26
acquisition of formal European education, the, 4
acquisition of maritime acquaintanceship, the, 89
active agents contesting and influencing the sociopolitical transformations, 30
activism, 4
*Adinkra* motifs, 121
Adu Boahen, 31
advantage of the momentary confusion, 2
affiliations to indigenous institutions, 16
Africa, 10, 15, 16, 37–38, 39, 54, 62, 122–123, 131, 136–137, 141, 161, 162, 181, 182, 195, 223, 245, 248, 249, 252–258, 260–269, 276–279, 281–285, 294, 295, 296, 305–306, 310, 311, 313, 317, 320–328, 330–334
African brokers, The, 151
African brokers hardly gained, 151
African cultural practices and institutions, 134
African societies, The, 21, 117
*Afro-Danish Relations on the Eighteenth-Century Gold Coast*, 256
Aggrey, J. A., 13
agricultural produce, 139, 187, 189
*Ahin-fie* (palace), 220
Akan bassinet, 31
Akan culture, 13
Akan dialects, 34, 123, 273
Akan groups, 7, 13, 31, 62, 63, 65, 68, 83, 85, 131, 134, 139, 245, 253, 252, 261, 273, 276

Akan indigenous political and military organizations, 6
Akan peoples and their respective societies, 62
Akan societies, 6, 32, 240, 262
Akuapem, 32, 34, 123, 179, 212, 245, 253, 273
Akyem Abuakwa, 34, 123, 202, 248, 250, 276, 285, 303, 313, 315
Akyeampong, Emmanuel, 11, 87
alienable entitlements, 146
anthropological interpretation of the nature and function of the *Asafo* in some Fanti communities, 13
analysis of the eastern and southern Africa case studies, 16
anatomy of the system, 13
ancient empire of Ghana, 31
Andreas Riis, 123
Anglicization, 16, 17
Anlo, 11, 12, 247, 267, 315; and Fanti peoples, 11
Anomabo Fort, 37, 38
Anomabo Fort (also known as Fort Charles) in 1674, 38
Anomabu, 53, 57, 164, 258, 283
archival documents, 24
arrival of Colonial Office personnel, 54
arrival of the Europeans, 32, 181, 185
Art, Symbol, and the Written Word, 117
Artistic Signs and Symbols, 118
*Asafo* (patrilineal), 4–8, 5, 11–19, 23–29, 26, 28, 48, 59, 61, 62, 63, 68–69, 70–79, 80–85, 98, 101–109, 110–116, 121, 125, 163, 164, 173, 174, 175, 178, 181, 193, 194, 196, 209, 213, 214, 216, 217, 218, 220, 221, 227, 228, 229, 230–239, 240–249, 251, 257, 262–265, 269, 271, 273, 293, 300–306, 311–318; and the *Ebusua* (matrilineal) systems, 5
*Asafo* Alliance Systems, 77
*Asafo* companies, 7, 14, 23, 24, 48, 73, 77, 79, 83, 107, 110, 112, 114, 115, 164, 175, 209, 213, 214, 217, 218, 220, 228, 231, 242, 262
*Asafo* company members with their elders, 69
*Asafo* conflicts, 6, 14, 102
*Asafo* development, 14
*Asafo* dynamic, 7, 83
*Asafo* groups, 6, 8, 70, 73, 74, 81, 98, 102, 107, 214, 240, 242
*Asafo* Hierarchy, 78
*Asafo* institution, 25, 27, 101, 233
*Asafo* membership, 4, 27, 265
*Asafo* ranks highly in coastal Ghana along social, political, and economic lines, 7
*Asafo* system, 6, 13, 14, 15, 16, 17, 25, 27, 78, 79, 209
*Asafo* system as an essential component of Fanti and Akan culture, especially political and military aspects, 13
*Asafo* units, 5
*Asafo, Ebusua*, and Crucial Social Expectations, 82
Asante invaded the coast in 1863, 160
Asante Kingdom, 34
Ashanti, 10, 33, 151, 191, 212, 232, 246, 248, 261–262, 266, 272, 276, 306, 308, 315, 318, 326, 328, 330, 334
aspects of coastal Ghana culture, 24
aspects of daily life, 2, 7
Atlantic coast, 12
Atlantic coast of West Africa, 12
Atlantic Ocean, 39
Atlantic to the Americas, 36
Attoh Ahuma, 47, 142, 251, 257
audacity, dignity, and sovereignty in property acquisition, 118
avenues existed for the strong expression of patrilineal influences, 6

Bannerman brothers (Charles and Edmund), 47
Basel Mission, 123, 269, 273, 330

Beach Groups and Activities, The, 92
beliefs, 11–13, 64, 87, 112, 121; about origins of the system, 11–13; among the Fanti peoples, 13
beneficiaries of European established schools in Cape Coast, 16
*Bentsir* and *Ntsin* companies in 1859, 108
*Bentsir* and *Ntsin*, 27, 107, 108, 111, 115; the principal belligerents of the 1932 conflict that engulfed all other groups, 27
bid to live, 21
Blankson Wood, 165, 171, 172
blatant use of military power, 162
blood constitutes the essence of *Ebusua* membership, 64
Bolster, W. Jeffrey, 12, 19
bondage and servitude in the police force, 169
books of Psalms, John, and Revelations, 128
Bourret, F. M., 10
breaching of bonds, 23
Brenya Lagoon, 90
brisk port city, the, 29
British administration, 2, 52, 162
British built Fort William in 1753, 38
British colonial commissioners, 24
British colonial enterprise, 167
British Company of Merchants Trading to Africa, 38
British Crown, 138, 141, 142
British Empire, 18, 195
British experience in the Malay Peninsula, 144
British Gold Coast, 11
British government, 51, 138, 140, 141, 162, 176, 186, 198, 239
British judicial officers, 52
British judiciary in Cape Coast, 57
British land regulation standards in Ghana, 8
British law, 57, 176

British maritime cases, 57
British mercantile officials, 158
British policy of indirect rule, 16, 150
British political discourses, 163
British protection, 144, 160
British public opinion, 163
British territory, 139
British troops in Cape Coast, 162
British West Indies, 38
British-oriented educational system, 123
Brodie Cruickshank, 10, 180, 245, 258, 281
Brown, J. P., 46, 114, 147, 150, 212, 235, 257, 266, 273
burgeoning colonial administration, 166

canoe with a biblical inscription reflecting influences of Christianity, A, 129
canoe with a misspelled Islamic inscription, A, 132
Canoe with English inscription evoking a Christian theme, 129
Canoe with inscription *Nyame Nye Me Boafo*, 127
capacity of ordinary people, 18
capacity to float, 4
Cape Coast, 4–9, 10–19, 20–29, 21, 29, 30, 32, 32–38, 40–49, 52–59, 60, 61, 68, 72–79, 83, 84, 88, 89, 90, 91, 94, 98, 102, 107, 122, 123, 142–149, 150, 154, 157–159, 161–169, 171–179, 180–189, 190–199, 200–209, 210–219, 221–229, 230–239, 240–249, 252–259, 260–267, 271–279, 280–289, 290–299, 300–308, 311–318, 320, 324, 328, 334; similarly referred to as *Oguaa* or *Iguae*, 32
Cape Coast Castle, 37, 38, 40, 75, 164, 168, 174, 178, 254, 258–262, 273, 278, 306, 318, 328
Cape Coast clash of 1932, 23
Cape Coast petition, 143

Cape Coast settlement, 23, 25, 32; comprised an admixture of *Etsii* and Fanti, 32
Cape Coast town council, 23
Cape Coast, and indigenous institutions, 25
Cape Coast's fortunes, 29
Cape Coast 1932 Conflict, The, 227
Captain George Maclean, 49, 167
Captain Lynch, 24, 220, 227, 228, 230
Caribbean, 38, 311
case of coastal Ghana societies, 21
category of documents that came up in the Cape Coast, 24
Casely Hayford, J. E., 47, 206, 210, 249, 251, 281, 285
causal factors of inter-*Asafo* conflict in Cape Coast between 1860 and 1909, 27
central argument of this book, 2
central government machinery, 9
Central Province Railway, 23, 189
chagrin of local colonial officers, 6
chagrin of the chiefs, 54
chagrin of the Coker Party, 231
chagrin of the governor, 146
character, 5
characteristic of the *Asafo* system, 17
characteristics and belief systems of the respective property owners, 121
chief divine drummer, 5
Chief J. H. Dadzie, 212
Chief Kwamina Ninfa V, 212
Chief Kweku Arhin, 212
chief of Cape Coast, 23
Chief W. Z. Coker, 193
chiefs, 2, 3, 23, 39, 49, 50, 51, 52, 53, 54, 55, 56, 57, 58, 59, 60, 61, 70, 71, 75, 79, 104, 105, 134, 137, 138, 139, 142, 143, 144, 145, 146, 147, 148, 149, 150, 151, 152, 154, 155, 156, 159, 160, 161, 163, 167, 169, 174, 175, 176, 180, 181, 188, 192, 193, 195, 198, 200, 201, 202, 203, 204, 205, 208, 222, 225, 235, 239, 263, 276, 279, 278, 285, 290
chiefs in coastal Ghana, 3
Chiefs of the Protectorate, 148
Christian missionary effort, 122
Christianity, 122, 126, 131, 133, 275
Christiansborg Castle, 37, 106, 258
Chukwukere, I. B., 13, 248
civil record books, 23
Civil Service Ordinance (CSO), 23
Claridge, W. W., 10
Clash of Courts, The, 165
coast of Ghana, 41
coastal belt, 4, 99, 130, 131, 132
coastal communities, 2, 3, 5, 9, 13, 20, 21, 41, 86, 87, 88, 92, 93, 94, 98, 99, 158, 160
Coastal Community *Asafo* and Conflict in Accra, 102
Coastal Community *Asafo* and Conflict in Cape Coast, 107
coastal Fanti towns, 35
coastal Ghana, 2
coastal Ghana communities, 116, 117, 238
Coastal Ghana communities, 86
coastal Ghana politics, 25, 236
coastal Ghanaians, 16
coastal town, 4, 11, 14, 33, 37, 187
coastal town with remarkable agency in the history of the country, 4
coastline of Ghana, 41
cocoa farming, 10
Coker Party and the *Omanhin* Party, 214
Coker, W. Z., 209
collective well-being, 41, 68
colonial administration, The, 2, 6, 9, 10, 27, 28, 29, 124, 138–139, 140, 143–144, 147, 149, 150, 154, 161, 165, 166, 171–174, 177–180, 206, 224, 240, 249, 260
colonial authorities, 2, 5, 8, 9, 12, 18, 26, 28, 57, 70, 81, 122, 135, 142, 160, 170, 175, 177, 182, 187, 219, 220, 234, 237

Colonial Capital, The, 178
colonial experience, 2, 62
colonial government, 2, 6, 12, 24, 28, 70, 85, 86, 99, 101–107, 133, 136, 139, 140–147, 148, 150–153, 160, 168, 169, 175, 179, 181–182, 189, 190, 192, 194, 195, 199, 210, 212, 214, 215, 222, 224, 237, 242, 243, 269, 277
colonial government actions, 2
colonial impositions, 19
Colonial Militarism, 167
Colonial Office, 54, 56, 138, 141, 154–155, 157, 159, 217, 225, 260, 278
Colonial Office in London, 138, 159, 217
colonial officers, 2, 6, 9, 11, 23, 24, 30, 114, 138, 157, 161, 175, 182, 199, 200, 212, 215, 220, 226, 231
colonial regime, 2
colonial rule, 6, 11, 13, 14, 21, 26, 158, 162, 163, 245
colonial urbanization, 8, 29, 287
colonization, 10, 48, 196
Commissioner Eliot, 114
common property of the village, 152
Common statements within African societies, 117
communal property, 134
communities in coastal Ghana, 9, 19
community survival, 41, 115
compatriot recipients of European education, 2
component of the coastal Ghana commerce with Europe, 44
concession-granting process, 137
conflict, 9, 11–17, 25, 27, 29, 49, 58, 74, 78, 82, 83, 85, 107, 108, 109, 110–116, 127, 135, 165–166, 197, 215, 234, 240–243, 271, 285
conflict between *Omanhin* Aggery and the colonial administration, The, 165
confluence of the Pra and Ofin rivers, The, 31
constant struggle between the peasantry and those who seek to extract labor, The, 18
constituency, 11, 30, 197
contact with Europeans, 10, 262
contemporary era, 10, 275
continent of Africa, 136
conventional geographies, 19
conventional indigenous religious thought, 99
core aspects of the coastal Ghana chieftaincy institution, 3
corn, 33, 68, 185
counsel for the kings, 152
crab designation, 5
Crabs of Cape Coast, 4
creeping imperialism, 11
Crown Land Ordinance, 142
Crown Lands Bill, 8, 28, 137–138, 141, 143, 145, 152–155, 157, 240–241
Crown Lands Bill of 1894, 138, 152
Crown Lands Bill of 1897 and "Public Lands, The, 145
cultural interaction, 16
cultural milieu, 2, 6, 21
cultural milieu, indispensable for understanding the social experience in coastal Ghana, 2
*Culture*, 2, 6, 8, 10, 16, 18, 26, 30, 251, 257, 269, 275, 306, 311, 320, 322, 325, 328, 330
cultures developed around maritime locations, 3
curiosity of the colonial authorities, 5

Danish challenges, 33
Danish governor's Agricultural and Trade Report, 91
Danquah, J. B., 31, 263, 320
David Kimble, 10, 246, 260, 274, 278, 279, 285
DeGraft Johnson, J. C., 13, 23, 24, 249, 263, 293, 295
DeGraft Johnson, J. W., 147

delegations, 2, 195
demand for gold, 136
Denkyira and Assin, 34
Dennis Austin, 10, 246
Deputy Secretary for Native Affairs H. W. Thomas, 214
descendants of Kwamina Edu, 228
determination of *Omanhin* Aggery to obstruct British efforts, 29
development of canoe, 89
development of maritime culture, 26
development of the modern monetary or contemporary economy, 135
direct symbolic confrontation with authority, 18
disciplinary boundaries, 19, 20
discipline, 41, 79
division of older Swahili towns, 15
duality of *Ebusua* and *Asafo* structures, 62
Durham University in England, 210
Dutch West Indian Company School, 122
dynamic relationship between the Anlo and the geographic space in which they lived, 11
dynamic relationship between the fishing or coastal community of the town and the sea, 12
dynamics of cultural practices, 3
dynamics of indigenous values, 6

early colonial Gold Coast, 11
East Africa, 141
*Ebusua,* Women, Blood, and Lineage, 63
*Ebusua* (matrilineal), 5
*Ebusua Akyeame,* 65
*Ebusua* and *Asafo* systems, 62
*Ebusua* groups, 84, 263
*Ebusua* membership, 64
*Ebusua* system, 63, 64, 65, 67, 68, 83, 84

economic and political trappings of power, 28
economy, 9, 11, 12, 38, 42, 87, 102, 135, 136, 186, 187, 188, 223, 287
ecosystems, 19
editorials, 2, 25, 142, 146
educated class in Cape Coast, 17
educated indigenous representatives, 146
*Effutu* people, 32
element of competition in inter-*Asafo* relations, 15
element of rivalry among the Cape Coast *Asafo* groups, 8
Ellis, E. B., 10, 271
Elmina Castle, 37, 209, 256
emergence of conspiracy theories, 9, 29
emergence of plantation economies in the Americas, 35
emerging colonial rule, 26
emerging development, 2
emerging European educational system from the mid-eighteenth century, 122
empowerment of the values, 21
enacted against Cape Coast, 5
encroachment, 3, 29, 52, 162
Encroachment Everyday Life and Customary Rite Performances, 52
encroachment of colonial administration, 3
English as a lingua franca in coastal Ghana, 28
English as a lingua franca in coastal Ghana through the initial facilitation of missionary and colonial authorities, 28
English courts, 3, 52, 53, 54, 59, 60
Eno Baisie Kurentsi, 35, 254
enslaved people, 35, 75
entrenched ideas of indigenous property, 2
entrenching growing power, 29

INDEX 325

environmental history, 11, 87
environmental history of the Anlo, 11
era after—that generation of academic historians, 10
era of literacy in both indigenous and English languages, 125
established hegemony, 32
Establishment of Formal Education, 44
estuarial environment, 5
ethnic groups, 10, 31, 32, 62, 156, 170, 245, 285
Euro-African environments, 16
European education, 2, 4, 16, 23, 24, 29, 48, 122
European education in coastal Ghana, 122
European gold prospectors, 137
European magistrates under the British judicial officers, 52
European mining concerns, 137
European mining prospectors, 144
European trading nations, 36
Europeanization, 16, 17
Eva L. R. Meyerowitz, 10, 31
Everyday life, 21, 26, 52, 134, 318, 333; also extends to political relations (within communities and with neighboring societies), 21; including arrangements and mechanisms available when dealing with consequent complications, 21
excessive powers, 146
exchange of linen cloth, 33
Expansion and improvement of the railroad infrastructure in southern Ghana, 9
Expansion of Governance Institutions, 197
export-import sector, 9
expressions of dignity, 27

external origins of the Akan people, 31

F. and A. Swanzy, 32, 35, 59, 72, 187; and the Elder Dempster Shipping Lines, 187
family, the, 11, 32, 35, 59, 63–67, 72, 79, 84, 95, 114, 117, 120, 134, 139, 143, 152, 153, 156, 170, 210, 214, 215, 221–222, 236, 240, 262, 265, 269, 284
Fanti, 7, 11–15, 24–26, 26, 32, 32–35, 33, 34, 41, 46, 48, 52, 57, 62–63, 68, 83, 85, 90–92, 98, 109, 117, 118, 124, 132, 140, 154, 160, 205, 241, 245, 248, 249, 250–258, 261–269, 271, 273, 275, 276, 277, 278, 279, 285, 295, 299, 305, 306, 308, 318, 332, 334
Fanti and Akan culture, The, 13
Fanti component in the historiography of the country, The, 11
Fanti customary law, The, 7, 205
Fanti dialect, The, 33, 34, 13, 271
Fanti National Political Society, 48
Fanti peoples, 7, 11, 13, 34, 62, 68, 90, 91, 92, 109, 258
Fanti states, 7, 13, 34, 258
Fanti strand of Akan identity and culture, 32
feminist methodologies, 22
*Fetu* fishing settlement, 60
*Fetu* hunter story, 32
*Fetu* king, 32
*Fetu* Kingdom, 32, 33, 184, 252, 266
fifteenth-century Portuguese influence, 33
Finlason, W. C., 165, 281
first generation of Ghanaian academic historians, 10
fishing communities, 27, 92, 97, 98, 99, 117, 267
fishing community in Cape Coast, 4
fishing expertise among the people of Cape Coast, 89

fledgling British administration, The, 162
folk praise poem of Cape Coast, 4
forms of class struggle, The, 18
forms of peasant resistance, The, 18
Fort Amsterdam, 37, 256, 258; in the twin towns of Kromantsi and Abandze, The, 37
Fort Charles, 38
Frederick Victor Nanka Bruce, 224
Freeman, J. B., 47
From Earliest Times to the Nineteenth Century, 26, 31
fundamental element of *Asafo* membership, 4
fundamental feature, 15

Ga, 10, 34, 77, 91, 104, 105, 106, 246, 248, 250, 267, 269, 275, 285, 303, 322, 326, 329
gender complementarity, 6, 85
general situation of coastal Ghana communities, 88
generational lines, 2
geological reports, 136
George E. Moore, 211
*Ghana Evolution and Change in the Nineteenth and Twentieth Centuries*, 253
gold deposits, 33, 36, 37, 42, 76, 77, 135, 136, 137, 138, 139, 140, 143, 185, 190
*Global History of Modern Historiography, A*, 245, 324
Glover-Addo, J., 206
*Gold Coast Aborigines* newspaper, 47
Gold Coast Aborigines' Rights Protection Society (GCARPS), 47, 147, 286, 285, 296
*Gold Coast Chronicle*, 142, 146, 278, 298
Gold Coast Corp, 167
*Gold Coast Methodist Times*, 47, 142, 146, 151, 251, 278, 277, 278, 298, 299
Gold Coast Militia and Police, 168

Gold Coast, 10, 11, 14, 16, 17, 36, 37, 46, 47, 49, 93, 136, 141, 142, 146, 147, 148, 150, 151, 167, 168, 170, 174, 177, 199, 207, 210, 213, 223, 224, 245, 246, 248, 249, 250–258, 260–269, 271–279, 281–289, 291–299, 302–308, 310, 313, 315–320, 322–324, 326, 330, 332; as a nominal reference—along with other names such as Ivory Coast, 36, 328; Grain Coast, 36, 93; and Slave Coast, 36
Gold mining, 136
gold mining sector, 136
government forces, 168
government intervention, 12
government revenue, 161, 195
Governor Andrew, 57, 260
Governor George Maclean, 171
Governor Guggisberg, 106, 190, 192, 201, 285, 296
Governor Hill, 55, 56
Governor Hodgson, 154
Governor Maxwell, 143, 144, 150, 154, 251, 278, 277
Governor Richard Pine, 161
Governor Stanford Freeling, 138
Governor T. S. W. Thomas, 196
Governor William Bradford Griffith, 141
Grain Coast, The, 36, 93
great millennial movements, 19
Greater Accra, 10
grievances known to the colonial administration through picketing, delegations, protest letters, newspaper articles, and editorials, 2
Growth of British Power and Response of Chiefs, The, 48
growth of coastal societies of Ghana, 16
Guggisberg constitution of 1925, 212
guns (specifically muskets), 33

Hans Nicolaus Riis, 123
heavy losses for the Fanti societies, 160

INDEX 327

Henry H. M. Herbert, 178, 179
Herbert Brown, 47, 251
heritable right of occupancy, 145
High-Sea Experiences, 99
Hint of Islamic Inclination, The, 130
hinterland Akan Twi-speaking neighbors, 20
historian of feudalism, 19
historical constituency, 11
historical occurrences in coastal Ghana, 27
Historical Undercurrents, 26, 86
historical writing on Ghana, 10
historicizations of oceans and seas, 19
historiography of Ghana, 10, 12
history, 2, 3, 4, 5, 9, 10, 11, 12, 13, 18, 19, 20, 21, 22, 24, 25, 26, 34, 35, 36, 37, 41, 46, 60, 66, 74, 75, 77, 86, 87, 102, 107, 108, 109, 116, 162, 179, 181, 201, 215, 219, 223, 245, 258, 266, 275, 278, 287, 335
history of Ghana, 9, 10, 245, 258
hopes for (colonial) government intervention in the battle with erosion, The, 12
House of Lords in London, 178
human history, 34

idea of collective ownership, 27
Ideas from the cultural repertoire, 2
Ideas from the cultural repertoire of coastal communities, 2
ideas within *Asafo* units, 5
image of two crocodiles, The, 121
Immediate political developments in coastal Ghana preceding the 1932 clash, 29
impact of the sea, 18
imperialism, 11
implementation of colonial policies, 29
implementation of the Municipal Corporations Ordinance 1924, 105
implicit power of the British Empire, 18

implicit understandings and informal networks, 18
importance of social settings and structures for the comprehension of subtle variations in the history of Ghana, 3
inalienable natural rights of absolute ownership, 152
incessant labor, 35
Income Tax Bill proposal in 1931, 227
Income Tax Ordinance, 195
incongruous legal institutions, 165
indecision of colonial officers, 2
indictment of the militaristic nature of the colonial administration, 173
indigenous and English courts, 3
indigenous court, 159, 160, 165, 166, 177
indigenous court sentenced Blankson Wood, 165
indigenous cultivation practices, 144
indigenous establishment, 26
indigenous ideas about ownership, 116
indigenous ideas of resistance, 18
indigenous institutions, 2, 3, 4, 6, 7, 11, 16, 17, 22, 23, 24, 25, 30, 116, 237
indigenous languages, 28, 123, 124, 129, 133
indigenous leaders in southern Ghana, 174
indigenous leaders of Cape Coast, 143
Indigenous Militancy, 167
indigenous organizations, 2, 3, 5, 6, 12, 27, 41, 195, 241
indigenous political authorities, 140, 150, 154, 198, 213, 216
Indigenous political authorities in the central and western parts of southern Ghana, 142
indigenous political institutions, 16, 239, 243
indigenous political leadership, 139
indigenous political order, 16, 59, 161, 174, 277

indigenous political, economic, and cultural wisdom, 134
indigenous royal parlance, 118
indigenous sociopolitical institutions, 3
infrastructural development, 2, 3, 8, 29
infrastructural development in southern Ghana, 29
inhabitants in the new bill, 146
initial facilitation of missionary, 28
initial relations between the people of Cape Coast, 41
innovative histories, 19
inscriptions of books, 128
institution among the Fanti, 13
interest of southern Ghana, 12
intergenerational and gender-based conflict, 11
intriguing issue of colonial urbanization and infrastructural development, 29
invocation of Marc Bloch, 19
invoking concomitant spiritual elements, 5
iron-working technology, 32
Islam and Christianity, 131
issues of everyday life, 86
Issues of gender, 27
Ivory Coast, 36, 328

Jamaica, 38
James C. Scott, 18, 250
James Coleman Fitzpatrick, 159
James Crowther, 24
James Hutton Brew launched the *Gold Coast Times*, 47
James Robert Thompson, 159
James Swanzy, 55
James Town, 105, 261
John Argyle, 15, 251
John D. Fage, 10
John Kabes, 35, 254, 282, 308
John Konny, 35, 254, 282, 306

Jones W. J. A., 212, 215, 222; became commissioner of the Central Province in January 1928, 212
Joseph E. Casely Hayford, 155
Judiciary, Military, and Urbanization, 158

Kanaka Maoli (native Hawaiians), 20
Karin Amimoto Ingersoll, 20, 251
Keta, 11, 12, 90, 92, 260, 267
Keta and Cape Coast, 11
kinds of resistance, 19
king of Abura, 142
king of Asante, 160
King of Cape Coast, 177
kingdom, 10, 34, 252, 275
Kings and Chiefs of the Protectorate, 148
kinship, 10, 43, 63, 74, 83, 84
Kobina Arku Korsah, 206, 209
Kobina Sekyi, 45, 206, 210, 211, 212, 219, 289, 310
Kromantsi, 37, 258
Kumasi, 123, 191, 194, 212, 246, 315, 320
Kumasi, the Asante capital, 123
Kwaku Amoa of Asamankese, 212
Kwamina Edu, 79, 214, 228
Kwamina Edu family, 79
Kwamina Nimfa claim, 32

labor market, The, 137
lack of respect, 4
Lagoons, 41, 89; and smaller inland water bodies served as long-lasting laboratories for experimentation, 89
Land, 26, 87, 134, 139, 142, 147, 150, 151, 152, 266, 278, 298, 323; remained the property of the ancestors, 139, 152; and the people, 139
land tenure, 152
landownership nonnegotiable issues pivotal to everyday life, 28
Lands Bill, 138, 143, 145, 146, 150–155

INDEX

lands of the southern Ghana colony, 141
legal role of the *Asafo* in the indigenous tribunal system, 7
legends of origination from the ocean, 20
Legislative Council, 8, 16, 17, 25, 26, 29, 140, 144, 145, 146, 147, 151, 154, 155, 169, 181, 189, 197, 199–209, 212, 213, 219, 223, 230, 278, 281, 284, 285, 286, 291, 296, 298
Legislative Council Debate collection from 1925 to 1933, 25
Legislative Council elections, 17
Legislative Council Elections, 1932 Conflict, and Frustration of Colonial Authority, 26, 197
Letters and comments from British colonial commissioners, 24
life in coastal Ghana, 6, 19, 101, 240
light-emitting celestial bodies, 121
Lighthouse Hill Streets, 233
lineages, 63, 240, 263
linkages from precedent conflicts, 17
lived experiences of colonial southern Ghana, 335
Livelihood, 41, 47, 58; and socioeconomic developments, 41; on the coast of Ghana hinged on the manifold resources acquired from streams, ponds, 41; rivers, 21, 31, 41, 153, 155, 157; lagoons, 41, 89; and, ultimately, the sea, 41
loads of unsold cocoa, 190
local beneficiaries of European-established schools, 4
local colonial officers, 9, 30
local histories of various ethnic groups, 10
locals and the colonial administration, 27
long history of vibrant maritime culture, 41
loss of capital city status, 9

mail boat to Sierra Leone, 177
major social institutions, 5, 13, 25, 46; the *Asafo* (patrilineal) and the *Ebusua* (matrilineal) systems, 6, 13, 14, 15, 16, 17, 25, 27, 78, 79, 209; remained pivotal to coastal communities, 5, 82
marginalization in the late colonial and postcolonial political economy, 12
*Maritime*, 2, 6, 8, 10, 16, 18, 26, 30, 271, 306, 330, 332, 334
maritime culture, 13, 20, 26, 41, 62, 92, 116, 232, 240, 243
*Maritime Culture and Everyday Life*, 2, 6, 8, 10, 16, 18, 26
*Maritime Culture and Everyday Life* explores social setting; operational dynamics; indigenous institutions and assaults on their power and authority; entrenched ideas of indigenous property, 2
Marquis of Ripon, 141, 278
marriage, 11, 67, 76, 265
master-divine drummer, 79
matrilineal Akan societies, 6
matrilineal societies, 6
matters of misunderstanding, 2, 238
means of livelihood, 27, 164, 194
mechanical and industrial gold mining, 138
Mensah Sarbah, 14, 24, 45, 46, 147, 151–154, 181, 205, 278, 320
methodological model, 22
*Mfantsi Amanbu Fekuw*, 48, 257
*Mfantsi* National Educational Fund, 46
Mfantsipim School, 46
Michigan State University Summer Support Fellowship, 22
Middlebelt and a larger part of the coastal stretch, 31
miles of cultural backdrop, 21

militant colonial administration, 172
military traditions, 32
militia and police in the early nineteenth century, 167
missionary education and training, 44
Moore, G. E., 206, 210, 227–228
modern Ghana, 31
modernity, 11
momentary confusion, 2
Municipal Council election, 16
municipal elections for representation on the new Legislative Council, 29
mushrooming of indigenous and English courts, 3
mutually dependent issues, 3

Nana Sir Ofori Atta, 205, 212
national boundaries, 19
national leaders to everyday people, 3
Native Administrative Measure, 29
Native Jurisdiction Ordinance (NJO), 198
"native" states, 16
natural resources, 41, 87, 135
natural rights to property, 143
nature of the people of Cape Coast, 5
neighboring societies, 21, 42
new historical constituency, 30
new Lands Bill of 1897, 145, 146
New Zealand, 141
newspaper articles, 2
*Nkum* company, 75
non-British citizens, 161
northern faith, the, 131
north-south religious dichotomy across Africa, 131
nuances of society, culture, and history of coastal Ghana, 3

oath, the, 5, 78, 162, 177, 213, 279
Objection to the Order-in-Council, The, 199
*Obrempong* Kojo, 35, 74, 75

*Odikro* Kwame Kuma, 212
official acts of commission and omission, 162
official protest to the Land Bill of 1897, 147
officials of the British administration, The, 2
Ofin river, The, 31, 245, 263
*Oguaa*, 4, 32, 43, 184, 252, 253, 282, 294, 295, 298, 300, 302, 303, 315
old British residents, 54
old port city, 8
*Omanhin* Aggery, 29, 160, 162, 164, 165, 177, 184, 210, 234, 239, 279, 281
*Omanhin* Aggery and the Entrenchment of Colonial Administration, 160
*Omanhin* Kojo Mbra III and Internal Opposition, 219
*Omanhin* Kojo Mbra III, 206, 210, 226, 237
*Omanhin* of Cape Coast, 161
Onshore or drag net fishing, 96
operational dynamics, 2
Order-in-Council of 1925, 17, 29, 199
ordinary weapons of relatively power, 18
organized groups of men and women, 2
originality of *Maritime Culture*, 18
origins of colonial establishment, 20
origins and power of indigenous institutions, the, 23
Osu castle, The, 105, 122
ownership expressed in the emphatic Fanti statement, 118

*Panyarring*, 35; meaning "seize or capture," 35
participation in common activities and affiliations to indigenous institutions, 16
parts of Africa, 9, 76
patrilineal associations, 4
patrilineal connections, 17
patrilineal systems, 6

INDEX 331

*pawnship*, 35
penchant for conflict, 14, 27
people of Cape Coast, 12, 19, 55, 90, 143, 161, 196
people of coastal Ghana, 20, 21, 28, 41, 239, 243
people of Keta, 12
period of decline for Cape Coast, 8
pervasive influence of indigenous organizations, 27
Philip Quaque, 44, 260, 305
political and military responsibilities, 15
political motivations, 5, 9
political order, 16, 162
political problems for the town, 8
political relations, 21
politics of Cape Coast, 25
politics of colonial urbanization, 3, 29
Poll Tax Ordinance, 56, 60, 260
popular indigenous organizations, 2
ports of Cape Coast, 23
postcolonial political economy, 12
power, 2, 3, 11, 18, 23, 28–29, 34–35, 43, 48–52, 55, 58, 59, 60, 61, 66, 71, 73, 87, 101, 105, 110–117, 120, 121, 125, 128, 134, 135, 141–149, 156, 159–168, 171, 174, 180, 205, 237, 239, 241, 254; and authority, 2, 3, 29, 49, 51, 59, 60, 101, 134, 146, 163, 167, 168, 180, 241
Pra river, The, 31, 245, 263
precolonial era, 11, 180
present peoples of Ghana, 31
principle of indirect rule, 198
proceedings of the indigenous court, 166
process of urban social formations, 11
proliferation of English courts, 60
property of the ancestors, 139
protest letters, 2
protest to colonial rule, 16
proximity of coastal Ghana to the Atlantic Ocean, 19

public land, 145
Public Record and Archives Administration Department (PRAAD) in Accra, 23

Queen of England, 143, 166, 172, 177
queen-mothers, 134, 138–139, 142–149, 151, 152, 155, 156, 198, 200, 201, 204

railroad transportation into southern Ghana, 188
rampant scuffles and disturbances in the nineteenth century, 13
Rattray, R. S., 10, 246, 262
recognition of Amissah as *Omanhin*, 160
reign of *Omanhin*, 29
reports on acting district commissioner, 23
rest of the world, 31, 100
retail price of wines and spirits, 161
Reverend Egyir Asaam, 47
Reverend H. Wharton, 47
*Reversing Sail, 256; A History of the African Diaspora*, 256
right of the people to ownership of land, 145
rightful custodians of the land, 137
rigid disciplinary boundaries, 20
rival military formations, 17
rivers, 21, 31, 41, 153, 155, 157
Roger Gocking, 16, 249, 277, 282, 285
Royal African Company, 43, 185, 187
royal stool, 79, 210
rural communities, 19

*Safohin* O. Cromwell, 114
*Safohin* Thomas Aggrey, 114
Scanty infrastructure, 136
Scripted Forms: English and Complex Combinations, 128
sculpture in wood, 118
Secretariat for Native Affairs (SNA), 198

Secretary of Native Affairs C. W. Wellman, 106
Secretary of State George Frederick Robinson, 141
Secretary of State Henry Howard Herbert, 138
secular beliefs, 21
seminal cultural resource, 143
Settlement and Nascent Society, 31
seventy that fought a thousand, The, 5
Sey, J. W., 150
share of emerging development dispensation under the colonial regime, 2
significance of land endured at multiple levels, 134
Skene, G. E., 23
Slave Coast, 36, 37, 258, 310
small basins, 33
smaller inland water bodies, 89
snub of local culture, 4
social and cultural space, 21
Social and kinship, 84
social and political institutions, 27
social change, 11
social cohesiveness, 41
social conflict, 240
social differentiation, 11
social engagement, 19
social experience, 2
social history, 11, 25; of alcohol in Ghana, 11
social institutions, 5, 13, 25, 46
social setting, 2, 116
social structures, 11, 12, 21, 87
Society for the Propagation of the Gospel (SPG), 44
sociocultural practices of various Akan groups, 25
sociocultural settings, 27
socioeconomic developments, 41
sociopolitical fabric of the indigenous state, 13

sociopolitical transformations, 11, 15, 17, 30
South Africa, 9, 141, 182, 272, 311, 318, 332, 333
southern Ghana, 4, 7, 8, 9, 12, 25, 29, 33, 37, 38, 40–45, 65, 77, 87, 90, 101, 103, 115, 123, 130–138, 140, 141, 142, 143, 144, 145, 146, 147, 148, 150, 151, 152, 156, 157, 158, 162, 163, 167, 169–178, 184–199, 205, 210–211, 216, 224, 237, 238, 240–245, 257, 266, 276, 278, 335
southern Ghana press, 151, 224
sovereignty, 27, 51, 118, 139, 162, 241
Sovereignty of Private Property Ownership, 26, 117
spread and entrenchment of Christianity, 126
spread of Islam from the north to the Sahara and Sahel regions, 131
St. George Castle, Elmina, 122
Stanley Shaloff, 17
state and kingdom formation, 10
statement of ownership and the contentment, 28
strategies of local peoples in response to colonial government actions, 2
struggle for independence, 10
struggle for political control, 26
Superintendent Webb, 114
Supreme Court in Cape Coast, 57
survey, 136; and geological reports of the administration, 136
sustainable development, 11
Swahili towns, 15

taboos, 99
Takoradi harbor, The, 23
temperance movements, The, 11
Terrence Ranger, 15
Thomas Edward Bowdich, 10
Three popular traditions of origin, 32
Times of West Africa, 224

INDEX
333

Trade, 33, 91, 250, 253, 252, 254, 255, 256, 260, 266, 269, 282, 284, 294, 308, 310, 320, 324, 326, 330, 332; initially consisted of the exchange of linen cloth, 33; small basins, 33; brass pans, 33; rum, assorted spirits, 33; ammunition, 33, 42; and guns (specifically muskets) for gold, 33, 36, 37, 42, 76, 77, 135, 136, 137, 138, 139, 140, 143, 185, 190; corn, fish, and other similar supplies, 33
traditional and westernized boundaries, 16
traditional violence, 17
trans-Atlantic slave trade, 35, 36, 37, 38, 39, 42, 70, 185, 187
transportation in the twentieth century, 137
trans-Saharan caravan trade, 131, 136
treatment of the ports of Cape Coast and Saltpond on the opening of the Takoradi harbor, 23
Troops of soldiers, 169
Try Company, 46
Tuesday: A Day of Rest, Recuperation, and Revitalization, 98
*Tufohin* of Cape Coast, 216
*Tufohin* Inquiry, The, 214
turbulent precincts of Cape Coast, 17
twentieth centuries, 7, 11, 41, 43, 46, 70, 122, 125, 137, 196, 238
Twi and English dictionary, 123
Twi language, 31, 123
types of land ownership, 134

unbending idea of property ownership, 28
understanding the social experience, 2
"undesirable people" from certain locations in Cape Coast, 9
uneasy relations between the people of Cape Coast, 29
unexplored historical narrative, 30

unity in diversity, 121
University of Cape Coast, 22, 29, 248, 317–318, 334
University of Ghana, Legon, 29, 22, 273, 302, 303, 304
use of simple artistic features and symbols to hybrid forms, 27

Vernacular and the Heavy Influence of Christianity, 124
Victoria Park, 114
vitality of everyday life, 21
Volta, 10, 91, 246, 269, 308

walls of the European fortifications, 143
War Office in London, 169
Ward, W. E. F., 10, 245, 269, 282
warrior organization, 13
weapons of the weak, 18, 19
Wesleyan Collegiate School under the new name Mfantsipim School, 46
West Africa, 12, 16, 31, 34, 36, 37, 38, 41, 90, 131, 136, 162, 163, 170, 210, 224, 246, 248, 249, 254, 258, 262, 266, 269, 271, 272, 275, 291, 298, 305, 306, 308, 313, 315, 317, 320, 322, 323, 324, 326, 328, 330
*West African Herald*, 47, 251
West Indian Regiment, 49, 168
western Gold Coast, 14
westernized boundaries, 16
widespread denunciation of the bill, 142
Wilhelm Johann Muller, 91, 98
wine and spirit traders, 161
Winneba, 188, 221, 231, 260, 303
work and leisure time, 21
work ethic among coastal fishing communities, 98
world market, 136, 223

Yaa Asantewaa War, 212
*Yabiw* version, 32

KWAKU NTI is Associate Professor of History at Georgia Southern University. His research interests include lived experiences of colonial southern Ghana, the African diaspora (historic and contemporary), and the processes and pathways of globalization in world history.

For Indiana University Press

Tony Brewer, Artist and Book Designer
Brian Carroll, Rights Manager
Gary Dunham, Acquisitions Editor and Director
Anna Francis, Assistant Acquisitions Editor
Brenna Hosman, Production Coordinator
Katie Huggins, Production Manager
Darja Malcolm-Clarke, Project Manager/Editor
Dan Pyle, Online Publishing Manager
Stephen Williams, Marketing and Publicity Manager
Jennifer Witzke, Senior Artist and Book Designer